Moses in Biblical and Extra-Biblical Traditions

Beihefte zur Zeitschrift für die alttestamentliche Wissenschaft

Herausgegeben von
John Barton · Reinhard G. Kratz
Choon-Leong Seow · Markus Witte

Band 372

Walter de Gruyter · Berlin · New York

Moses in Biblical and Extra-Biblical Traditions

Edited by
Axel Graupner and Michael Wolter

W
DE
G

Walter de Gruyter · Berlin · New York

∞ Printed on acid-free paper which falls within the guidelines of the ANSI
to ensure permanence and durability.

ISBN 978-3-11-019460-9
ISSN 0934-2575

Library of Congress Cataloging-in-Publication Data

A CIP catalogue record for this book is available from the Library of Congress.

Bibliographic information published by the Deutsche Nationalbibliothek

Die Deutsche Nationalbibliothek lists this publication in the Deutsche Nationalbibliografie;
detailed bibliographic data are available in the Internet at http://dnb.d-nb.de.

Vorwort

Der vorliegende Band basiert auf einem Seminar über das Thema „Moses in Biblical and Extrabiblical Traditions", das vom 5. bis 7. Januar 2006 an der Universität Bonn stattfand und an dem Bibelwissenschaftler aus den Theologischen Fakultäten der Universitäten Leiden, Oxford und Bonn teilnahmen. Als institutioneller Rahmen der Tagung fungierte das EUROPAEUM, ein Netzwerk von acht europäischen Universitäten, zu dessen Gründungsmitgliedern die Universitäten dieser drei Städte gehören.

Das Erscheinen des Bandes gibt uns die Möglichkeit, vielfachen Dank abzustatten: Wir danken dem EUROPAEUM und seinem Generalsekretär, Dr. Paul Flather (Oxford), für die Unterstützung der Tagung.

Darüber hinaus gilt unser Dank den Herausgebern der „Beihefte zur Zeitschrift für die Wissenschaft vom Alten Testament" (BZAW) für die Aufnahme dieses Bandes in ihre Reihe.

Ohne die Hilfe von Bonner wissenschaftlichen und studentischen Mitarbeitern hätte dieser Sammelband nicht publiziert werden können: Die Register wurden erarbeitet von Maren Bohlen, Jochen Flebbe, Gerd Maeggi, Leonie Stein und Nikolai Tischler, der zudem mit großer Akribie die einzelnen Beiträge nach den Vorgaben des Verlages formatiert hat. Sie alle haben sich mit großem Engagement auch an den Korrekturen bei der Erstellung der Druckvorlage beteiligt. Für ihren Einsatz und ihre Sorgfalt möchten wir uns darum an dieser Stelle bei ihnen allen herzlich bedanken.

Last but not least bedanken wir uns bei Sabina Dabrowski, die den vorliegenden Band im Verlag Walter de Gruyter nicht nur in der gewohnt sachkundigen und zuverlässigen Weise, sondern auch mit großer Freundlichkeit betreut hat.

Bonn, am 15. Mai 2007   *Axel Graupner und Michael Wolter*

Inhaltsverzeichnis

Zur Einführung

von Axel Graupner und Michael Wolter

Die in diesem Band versammelten Beiträge widmen sich einem komplexen Thema, indem sie jeweils Ausschnitte beleuchten, und dabei einen weiten Bogen vom Alten Testament über die Septuaginta, Qumran und antik-jüdische Literatur zum Neuen Testament und weiter zur Gnosis und zu Eusebius von Caesarea schlagen.

Mark J. Harris gibt einen kritischen Überblick über naturwissenschaftliche Erklärungsversuche des Meerwunders Ex 14 und sucht den Unterschied zwischen ihnen und exegetischen Zugängen zum Text zu bestimmen – mit der Absicht „to close the gap between them" (S. 5). Sein Vorschlag lautet, die Vielfalt der Zugangsweisen als Reichtum zu betrachten und „in creative tension" (S. 30) zu halten.

Axel Graupner plädiert dafür, Ex 19,3b–8 als Proömium der Sinaiperikope zu lesen, das Israels Sonderstellung unter den Völkern durch ein hierokratisches Verfassungsprogramm konkretisiert und in mehrfacher Hinsicht interpretatorische Funktion erfüllt, dabei weitgespannte Beziehungen herstellt, um divergente Konzeptionen der Gründungsgeschichte Israels zu integrieren.

Udo Rüterswörden widmet sich hermeneutischen und exegetischen Grundfragen des Deuteronomium. Er erinnert daran: „Deuteronomy is not the final address of Moses, but it contains it" (S. 51) und gibt einen Überblick über das Überschriftensystem des Buches, das gleichsam sein narratives Gerüst bildet. Außerdem bestimmt er ausgehend von Dtn 1,5 den Inhalt des Deuteronomiums und stellt die Frage: „Does Torah only exist in the mode of its explanation and application and is Moses its first hermeneutic?" (S. 57) Den Schluss bildet eine kritische Auseinandersetzung mit dem Versuch Ansgar Moenikes, eine „Tora ohne Mose" aus hiskijanischer Zeit zu rekonstruieren.

Sebastian Grätz geht der Rezeption der Mosegestalt in prophetischer Literatur nach. Nimmt der Berufungsbericht Jeremias ein vorgeprägtes Mosebild auf und – wenn ja – mit welchen theologischen Intentionen? Seine Antwort lautet: Jer 1,4–10 greift bereits auf das dtr redigierte Prophetengesetz Dtn 18,9ff (bes. V. 15.18) und Moses Berufung Ex 3 (bes. V. 9–12) zurück, um Jeremia als legitimen Nachfolger Moses zu charakterisieren. Dabei steigern die Verfasser – auch darin an das Prophetengesetz des Deuteronomium anknüpfend – die Bedeutung des prophetischen Amtes, in dem sie es mit königlichen Zügen ausstatten (Jer 1,5.10). Als Buch-Ouvertüre konzipiert, möchte der Berufungsbericht den Leser dazu anleiten, das literarisch fixierte Prophetenwort als in Kontinuität zur Tora stehend zu lesen. Dass in dieser Perspektive Jer 1,4–10 als ein später, nachexilischer Text erscheint, versteht sich von selbst.

Johannes Schnocks durchmustert die Aufnahmen der Mose-Gestalt im Psalter (77,21; 90,1a; 99,6; 103,7; 105,26; 106,16.23.32f) und stößt dabei auf unterschiedliche theologische Konzepte, in denen sich das Wachstum des vierten Psalmenbuchs spiegelt. Die älteste Schicht bilden Ps 90 – 92; 102; 103*. Sie antworten auf den in Ps 89 beklagten Untergang der Davidsdynastie, indem sie David durch Mose als paradigmatischen Beter ersetzen. Zugleich lenken sie vor dem Hintergrund der Erfahrung des Gerichts den Blick auf Mose als *den* Fürbitter Israels. Ps 93 – 100; 103,19–22 bilden eine erste Ergänzungsschicht, die eine „andere Bewältigungsstrategie für das untergegangene Königtum" verfolgt: „das Konzept des Königtums JHWHs, erfahrbar in der Schöpfung und in der Theologie des Tempels" (S. 87). Beide Konzepte werden in Ps 99 sekundär zusammengeführt. Die jüngste Schicht bilden Ps 104 – 106. In ihnen wird „die prophetisch-interzessorische Bedeutung des Mose von der richtenden Funktion der Priesterschaft genauso abgelöst, wie die universale Offenheit gegenüber den Völkern von eher engen Sammlungsbestrebungen" (S. 88).

Warum gibt die Septuaginta die Wendung משנה התורה הזאת Dtn 17,18 mit τὸ δευτερονόμιον τοῦτο wieder, so dass das Deuteronomium als „a law over against the first law" (S. 96) erscheint? Folgt man *Arie van der Kooij*, verbirgt sich in der Unterscheidung zwischen erstem und zweitem Gesetz der Versuch, Sinaiperikope und Deuteronomium zusammenzudenken: „Roughly speaking, one can say that the laws in Exodus – Numbers are mainly dealing with the priesthood, the cult and related matters, whereas those of Deut are particularly concerned with the life of the people, both in religious and in moral affairs" (S. 96). In dieser Zuordnung spiegele sich die Verfassung Judas in hellenistischer Zeit wider, wie sie in 19,6 et al. greifbar wird: „the first law in Exodus – Numbers" enthält „the laws of the priests, and the second law in Deut … the law of (the representatives of) the people" (S. 97). Da beide Gesetze durch Mose vermittelt werden, erscheint der Gesetzgeber auch als Verfassungsgeber.

Die folgenden drei Beiträge sind dem Mose-Bild der Qumrantexte gewidmet. Im Mittelpunkt steht dabei das Fragment 4Q377, das aus unterschiedlichen Perspektiven in den Blick genommen wird. *Wido van*

Peursen gibt eine kurze Einführung in dieses Fragment und konzentriert sich dann auf die in der zweiten Hälfte von 4Q377 2 II vorgenommene Relecture der Sinai- und Horebüberlieferungen der Bücher Exodus und Deuteronomium. Er zeigt, dass die Darstellung aus einer Vielzahl von biblischen Texten und Traditionen zusammengesetzt ist und nicht lediglich auf einem einzigen Text basiert. Wichtig ist ihm, dass Mose in dem untersuchten Text zu keinem Zeitpunkt als ein engel- oder gottgleiches Wesen dargestellt wird.

Zu einem vergleichbaren Ergebnis kommt *Phoebe Makiello*, die die Mosedarstellungen in 4Q374 und 4Q377 einer detaillierten Analyse unterzieht: Sie arbeitet heraus, dass die angelomorphen und sogar theomorphen Kategorien, auf die die Mose-Darstellungen in beiden Texten zurückgreifen, ihn an keiner einzigen Stelle zu einer engelhaften Mittlergestalt werden lassen. Mose bleibt vielmehr stets ein menschliches Wesen.

Einem anderen Aspekt des Mosebildes der Qumrantexte widmet der Beitrag von *Heinz-Josef Fabry* seine Aufmerksamkeit: auf die Darstellung Moses als Gesalbten in 4Q377. Er zeigt, dass dieses Attribut Mose weder eine königliche noch eine priesterliche Funktion zuschreiben will, sondern von der Absicht bestimmt ist, ihn als geistbegabten Propheten zu kennzeichnen und dabei gewissermaßen „zum Urbild des eschatologisch-messianischen Vorläufer-Propheten" (S. 152) werden zu lassen.

Pierluigi Lanfranchi's Beitrag beschäftigt sich mit einem Ausschnitt aus der Überlieferungsgeschichte des Mose-Bildes im hellenistischen Judentum: Mit Hilfe des Aufweises von lexikalischen und darstellerischen Entsprechungen meint er, wahrscheinlich machen zu können, dass Philo von Alexandrien die *Exagoge* des Ezechiel nicht nur gekannt, sondern auch für seine eigene Mose-Darstellung herangezogen hat.

Im Anschluss daran geht *Hywel Clifford*'s Untersuchung der Charakterisierung Moses als idealen Philosophen und Weisen bei Philo nach. Er stellt sie in den Kontext des kulturellen Milieus, in dem sich das hellenistische Judentum Philos vorfand, und sieht die diesbezügliche Mosedarstellung des alexandrinischen Philosophen von apologetischen Intentionen geleitet, denen sich auch die Aufmerksamkeit verdankt, die Philo der Tugend als Zentralbegriff jüdischer Weisheit und griechischer Philosophie zukommen lässt.

Dem Verhältnis von Assumptio Mosis und Judasbrief ist der Beitrag von *John Muddiman* gewidmet. In Auseinandersetzung mit Richard Bauckham wird in ihm die alte These bekräftigt und mit neuen Argumenten versehen, dass Jud 9 auf den verlorenen Schluss der Mai-länder Handschrift der AssMos Bezug nimmt, der eine Art Entrückungserzählung sowie die in Jud 9 erwähnte Auseinandersetzung zwischen dem Erzengel Michael und dem Teufel enthalten haben müsse.

Die abschließenden drei Beiträge stellen christliche Mose-Bilder in den Mittelpunkt: *Stefan Schapdick* gibt einen ausführlichen Überblick über das Mose-Bild des Johannesevangeliums und betont, dass sein Verfasser weder die Autorität Moses in Zweifel zieht noch die Tora abrogiert. Moses Autorität werde vielmehr in die alles bestimmende christologische Perspektive integriert. In diesem Rahmen fungiere er als Zeuge für die Berechtigung von Jesu Anspruch, der authentische Offenbarer Gottes zu sein.

Den Überlieferungen von Jannes und Jambres und ihrer Geschichte ist der Beitrag von *Johannes Tromp* gewidmet. Er kommt zu dem Ergebnis, dass Jannes und Jambres in 2.Tim 3,1–9 nicht als ägyptische Zauberer, sondern als hebräische Apostaten im Dienst Belials dargestellt werden, die sich dem Exodus-Auftrag Moses widersetzt hätten. Im Hintergrund des neutestamentlichen Textes stehe eine Überlieferung, wie sie in CD 5,17–19 erkennbar wird, und nicht im Apokryphon von Jannes und Jambres. Letzteres basiere vielmehr seinerseits auf 2.Tim 3,8–9.

Christopher M. Tuckett macht in seinem Beitrag darauf aufmerksam, dass die Gestalt des Mose in zahlreichen gnostischen Texten keine oder nur eine sehr geringe Rolle spielt und Mose in ihnen darum als so etwas wie ein „absent friend" (S. 237) angesehen werden könne. Die wenigen Texte, in denen er tatsächlich Erwähnung findet, thematisieren Mose dabei gerade nicht als Empfänger und Übermittler der Tora. Sie verfolgen darüber hinaus die Intention, ihn herabzusetzen, und zwar vor allem als Autor der biblischen Schöpfungsberichte, die durchweg als unzutreffend dargestellt werden. Aus diesem Sachverhalt zieht Tuckett die vorsichtige Schlussfolgerung, dass die Wurzeln des Gnostizismus weniger im Judentum als in bestimmten Formen des Platonismus zu suchen seien.

Sabrina Inowlocki untersucht in ihrem Beitrag die Mose-Darstellungen in der Praeparatio Evangelica und der Demonstratio Evangelica des Eusebius von Caesarea. Sie zeigt, dass Mose von Eusebius als Scharnier innerhalb des christlich-jüdisch-paganen Diskurses benutzt wird. In der antipaganen Apologetik der Praeparatio mache Eusebius ihn zu einem Vertreter des Christentums, während er in der antijüdischen Apologetik der Demonstratio sehr viel ambivalenter dargestellt werde.

How did Moses part the Red Sea?
Science as salvation in the Exodus tradition

by Mark J. Harris

1. Introduction

This article will survey interpretation of the Sea Event in Exod 14, focussing especially on scientific 'explanations' of the movement of the water, the most essentially 'miraculous' part of the narrative. It will discuss the difference in approach between natural scientists and biblical scholars, and will present an approach which draws on both historical and theological categories, in an attempt to close the gap between them.

Those who are perceptive may notice that the title which I have chosen for this article narrows-down my interpretative options prematurely. First, I appear to have glossed over the fact that two independent explanations are often seen for the movement of the waters in the Sea Event. On the one hand there is a naturalistic drying-up due to a 'strong east wind' (Exod 14,21), usually attributed to the Yahwist, and on the other there is a spectacular and miraculous 'parting' of the sea into two walls of water as Moses holds his staff aloft (14,22), attributed to the Priestly source. Second, I appear to have neglected the long-standing debate on whether יַם־סוּף should be rendered 'Sea of reeds' or 'Red Sea'. In each case, my title suggests that I have chosen one possible option, without any discussion of the matters in hand. It will become clear later on that it is not my intention to narrow down the options, but rather to *expand* on them. Instead, my choice of title reflects the overwhelming significance of this particular miracle in the popular and religious imagination, which includes many natural scientists. This miracle, it is believed, is the key to understanding Israel's divine election, through God's direct work in history. As Noth put it: 'all the previous acts of God against the Egyptians seem like a prelude which culminates in the decisive event at the sea.'[1] In short, the Sea Event

---

1   M. Noth, Exodus, London 1962, 104.

defines the idea of the salvation offered by the Judaeo-Christian God like no other. Indeed, for the Christian specifically, the Sea Event has a miraculous significance matched only by the resurrection of Jesus.[2] As a result, for today's ordinary believer, the picture of the Sea Event is defined much more effectively by, for instance, Charlton Heston as Moses standing before a parted and towering Red Sea in Cecil B De-Mille's 1956 film *The Ten Commandments*, than the image of a soggy marshscape with the Israelites hopping from one dry patch to another. And it is no surprise that, many centuries before Cecil B. DeMille, rab-binic interpretations of Exod 14 had already scaled new imaginative heights.

In contrast, scholarly interpretations of the Sea Event have sought to downplay the miraculous elements and to discern a naturalistic, his-torical, or mythological kernel in their place. Like the resurrection of Jesus, this most normative of miracles has not escaped yearnings to know 'what really happened'[3], but to know it only insofar as it is expli-cable within the modernist categories of history and science. As J. Max-well Miller put it: 'One of the standard tenets of modern historiography is that natural explanation for a given phenomenon or event is prefer-able to an explanation that involves overt divine intervention. When speculating about "actual historical events" behind the biblical account of Israel's past, therefore, what historians often do, in effect, is to bring the biblical story in line with reality as we moderns perceive it.'[4]

Science therefore, as the paradigmatic enterprise of modernity, is the interpretative hermeneutic which undergirds historical-critical scholarship. It is because of science that much of contemporary biblical scholarship considers the question '*What* really happened at the Sea Event?' to be of more ultimate significance than '*Why* did it really hap-pen?' Indeed, the latter question would be seen by many biblical schol-ars to verge on the naïve, as suggesting that the historical claims of the narrative were being taken too much at face value. The same would be true for any ostensibly-historical biblical narrative: the question of '*Why*?' ought to be answerable only after the first vital stage of analysis has been exhausted – namely the determination of the veracity of those historical claims, the '*What*?' question.

It is ironic then, that natural scientists who write on the Bible, and who attempt to answer the '*What*?' question using modern science,

---

2   J. Rogerson, The Supernatural in the Old Testament, Guildford/London 1976, 46.
3   Adapting von Leopold v. Ranke's famous phrase, '*wie es eigentlich gewesen*'.
4   J.M. Miller, Reading the Bible Historically: The Historian's Approach, in: To Each Its Own Meaning: An Introduction to Biblical Criticisms and Their Application, eds. S.L. McKenzie / S.R. Haynes, London, 12.

almost invariably do so in such a way that makes it clear they are really more interested in the '*Why*?' question. Most scientists appear to take the claims of the narrative at face value, and use it to put forward astonishing and imaginative (but still naturalistic) 'explanations'. This will become clear shortly, in the review of interpretations of the Sea Event. To reiterate, biblical scholars tend to look to mundane and naturalistic explanations, while natural scientists – *who by definition are concerned with the mundane and naturalistic* – often look to the miraculous and spectacular. The fact that they do so sheds interesting light both on the innate doubt (scepticism?) of the biblical scholar, and the innate faith (gullibility?) of the scientist, while both are seeking ostensibly to answer the same question: "*What* really happened?"

In effect, the scientists pass straight on to the second stage of interpretation: they treat the historical claims of the narrative in terms of scientific phenomena which are so unlikely that they are effectively themselves an answer to '*Why* did it really happen?'. And, in moving straight to the question of '*Why* did it really happen?', the scientists effectively bypass the hermeneutical rules of modernity (although they use its language). Instead, they stretch back to what the original authors and editors were seeking to say, namely: 'This happened because of YHWH.' Since many of the scientists write from an apparent position of faith, they see their work at least partly in terms of apologetics, rather than 'disinterested' historical investigation.

Let us now turn to the narrative itself, treating it as a unity for the moment and only mentioning source analysis in passing. There are a number of features which interpreters who seek a naturalistic explanation find particularly enticing:

1. The epiphany of YHWH in the pillar of fire/cloud (13,21.22; 14,19.24) – usually assigned to the J source.
2. The 'strong east wind', which 'drives the sea back' and 'turns it into dry land' (14,21) – usually assigned to the J source.
3. The dividing of the waters, forming a wall to the right and to the left (14,21–22,29) – usually assigned to the P source.
4. The return of the waters, drowning the Egyptians (14,26–28) – in both sources.

Features 1. and 3. are rarely touched upon explicitly in scientific or 'rational' explanations of the Sea Event. On the other hand, as Hyatt has pointed out[5], feature 2., the 'strong east wind' (14,21), has formed the keystone to many of the modern explanations, especially those that favour a particularly mundane approach. This is easy to see: a strong

---

5   J.Ph. Hyatt, Commentary on Exodus, London 1971, 154.

east wind is neither inherently miraculous in itself, nor especially unusual – it is a natural phenomenon which all can appreciate from everyday experience. But, we must first highlight two hazards which are rife
to this approach. The first is that the 'strong east wind' is read as a literal and physical wind; mythological or symbolic alternatives are not
taken into account, even though they may contain a great deal of cre-
dence; we will consider these later. But the second and more serious
danger is that an explanation which focuses on the mundane and everyday may satisfy the modern desire to understand 'What really happened' in terms of everyday experience, but it certainly misses the main
point of the narrative. As the text makes clear, this was not an everyday
event: the 'strong east wind' was sent by YHWH (14,21). In other
words, however familiar the biblical author may have been with strong
east winds in everyday life, this one at least was of divine, not natural,
origin. Hence, to highlight the *mundanity* of the narrative at the expense
of its remarkability is straightaway to begin to misinterpret it, as surely
as does an approach which highlights the *remarkable* aspects over the
mundane. We will come back to this later, but for the moment, we will
look in more detail at the interpretations which make principal use of
the strong east wind.[6]

2. Naturalistic explanations for the Sea Event

(a) *The 'strong east wind' over inland lakes or marshes*

The most everyday explanations – which also turn out to be those favoured chiefly by biblical scholars – have the strong east wind blowing
over marshland, or perhaps a shallow lagoon, somewhere in the eastern
part of the Nile Delta region. As with all of the other possible explanations, geography is important here. The Exodus narrative does not explain exactly what type of body of water the Sea of the Event was, but
it does try to locate it fairly precisely – 'Tell the Israelites to turn back
and camp in front of Pi-hahiroth, between Migdol and the sea (ם‌י), in
front of Baal-zephon; you shall camp opposite it, by the sea (ם‌י)'

---

6   Perhaps the most mundane explanation of all is that the Sea Event was in reality a
     military encounter, and that any role played by the natural world was secondary at best.
     Hay makes this suggestion, as does Hyatt to some extent (L.S. Hay, What really hap-
     pened at the Sea of Reeds?, JBL 83 [1964] 397–403, here 401–402; Hyatt, Commentary
     on Exodus, 157).

(14,2).[7] The exact location of these places is fraught with uncertainty, especially that of the Sea. In most places in the narrative, it is referred to simply as הַיָּם, 'the sea' (14,2.9.16.21.23; 15,1–4), but significantly, in a few places it is יַם־סוּף (13,18; 15,4.22). The traditional rendering of יַם־סוּף as 'Red Sea' follows the lead of the Septuagint and Vulgate. However, in recent years, those who advocate the idea that the Sea was a shallow lake or marsh argue that יַם־סוּף should be translated more literally as 'Sea of Reeds'. In which case, there is a highly attractive location at the eastern end of the Delta – a line of lakes running north-south from the Mediterranean to the Gulf of Suez, which included the Ballah lakes, Lake Timsah, and the Bitter lakes. Significantly, these lakes are met from the west by a roughly east-west-running geographical feature, the Wadi Tumilat, which formed an important highway in ancient Egypt, and is often assumed to have provided the escape route for the Israelites fleeing from Goshen.

In his 2003 book, *On the Reliability of the Old Testament*, Kenneth Kitchen provides an excellent example of this approach. This book was written to promote the credibility of the Old Testament, but ironically, Kitchen highlights the mundanity of the Sea Event so strongly as to verge on dismissing it altogether as a remarkable event.[8] As Kitchen says, 'the ability of Delta winds to move water ("a strong east wind", Exod.14,21) is independently attested down to modern times.'[9] It is not clear exactly what these attestations are, because Kitchen only cites one piece of evidence. This is the work of Aly Bey Shafei, published in 1946, who, in the course of investigating ancient Egyptian irrigation, reconstructed a possible route for the Exodus, and described how the water level in lakes in the Delta region may be affected by the wind.[10] Shafei demonstrates this with the example of the road from Baltim to Borg el Borollos[11], which becomes covered in water when a strong west wind blows, but dry when the wind blows from the east. Unfortunately, Shafei does not explain just how deep is the water covering the road. However, as far as one can tell from the accompanying photographs, it

---

7   A number of interpreters assign this verse to P, and argue that it was written too late after the event to represent an authentic geographical memory; others disagree.
8   K.A. Kitchen, On the Reliability of the Old Testament, Grand Rapids, MI / Cambridge 2003, 261–263; but see especially note 46 on p. 556.
9   Kitchen, ibid., 556.
10 A.B. Shafei, Historical Notes on the Pelusiac Branch, the Red Sea Canal and the Route of the Exodus, Bull. de la Société Royale de Géographie d'Égypte 21 (1946) 231–287.
11 Baltim is some 5 km south of the northernmost tip of the Nile Delta, and thus very close to the Mediterranean coast, while Borg is actually on the coast, about 10 km to the west-northwest of Baltim. The road between them runs along the eastern edge of Lake Borollos.

is only ankle-deep, just a matter of 10 cm or so. But it seems that this example is sufficient to solve the question of what happened at the Sea Event for Kitchen, who, largely following the work of Hoffmeier[12], places the Sea in question at the north of Lake Timsah or the south of the southernmost Ballah lake.[13]

In a much earlier study, Har-El also highlights the Wadi Tumilat as a strong contender for the escape route[14], but places the Sea further south along the north-south chain of lakes, at the Bitter Lakes, which are 20–40 km north of the Gulf of Suez. The Bitter Lakes are particularly attractive to Har-El because, he says, there is a narrow underwater ridge between the Large and Small Bitter Lake, where the depth of water is only four feet, so that, if a strong wind blew all night, perhaps a narrow ford might become exposed at this location.[15] Like Shafei, Har-El cites an anecdotal example from his own experience in support. He mentions how the Sea of Galilee can be affected by winds; for example when a strong westerly wind blows over it, the water is driven eastwards and the east coast is subjected to waves of two to three metres in height. Unfortunately Har-El's example from Galilee does not provide much illumination, because he does not explain whether there is an actual drop in the water level on the west coast, and if so, how significant it might be. Likewise, he does not make it clear whether this example can be transferred over to the Bitter lakes – whether such a shallow body of water would be able to sustain waves of this height, nor whether they might assist crossing on foot.

Hyatt looks further north than either of these authors, placing the crossing at the southern end of Lake Manzaleh, or in the marshy lagoon just south of it, near modern-day Qantara.[16] He has also provided the most literal conjecture so far which makes use of the wind, providing naturalistic explanations for several more features of the narrative. According to Hyatt, if a strong, hot wind blew for some days from the east or north-east, it could dry up such a marshy lagoon, or at least reduce its water level considerably. He provides no empirical or anecdotal evidence to support this suggestion. But, he believes that such a wind may also bring sand and dust, which might explain the darkness mentioned in the text (14,20). The Israelites were able to cross over because they were only lightly armed, while the Egyptian chariots became bogged

---

12   J.K. Hoffmeier, Israel in Egypt: The Evidence for the Authenticity of the Exodus Tradition, New York / Oxford 1996.

13   Kitchen, Reliability, 261.

14   M. Har-El, The Sinai Journeys: The Route of the Exodus, Ridgefield 1983, 314.

15   Har-El, ibid., 351–353.

16   Hyatt, Commentary on Exodus, 154–160.

down. The appearance of a sudden violent storm with rain, thunder and lightning caused the Egyptians to panic, which the text describes as YHWH looking down upon the Egyptians host in a pillar of fire and cloud (14,24).[17] Hyatt admits that this reconstruction is quite speculative, but his approach offers a valuable example of just how much of the narrative can be explained using relatively everyday natural phenomena, if one is so inclined.

It is interesting at this point to look at the recent work of Hoffmeier, who puts forward a very similar geographical route for the Exodus to these scholars, but takes a completely different approach to the Sea Event itself.[18] Indeed, Hoffmeier's work is by far the most detailed and comprehensive study of the geographical situation thus far attempted, and he claims to have located most of the toponyms of the Exodus account with a high degree of confidence. The Wadi Tumilat is again crucial as providing the key escape route, and in his most recent book, he argues that three of the place names used by the text itself (14,2) to locate the Sea – Baal-Zephon, Pi-hahiroth, and יַם־סוּף – are bodies of water which are also indicated in a contemporary Egyptian text.[19] The fourth toponym in 14,2, Migdol, he also identifies, this time as a frontier fort close to Tell el-Borg, at the northern end of the Ballah lakes. A further key part of Hoffmeier's work is the geological discovery that the Mediterranean coastline came further south than it does today, and that just north of the Ballah lakes (which no longer exist) there was a tidal lagoon (also no longer existent). Therefore, argues Hoffmeier, the toponyms of 14,2 locate the Israelites precisely on a small strip of land between the Ballah lakes and this ancient lagoon. The Sea of the Event probably then corresponds to the northern edge of the Ballah lakes, and the biblical author quite deliberately pointed to this specific location using Egyptian toponyms of the thirteenth century which had been lost by the time of the Priestly source.[20] Indeed, for Hoffmeier, the narrative has such a precise specificity as to suggest that it is unlikely that it was fabricated, or a historicised version of a myth, strong evidence that the Sea Event took place at a specific geographical location, and at a particular time in history.

It is interesting then, that, given the high confidence in which he holds the geographical and historical authenticity of the narrative, Hoffmeier is reluctant to attempt to describe what actually might have

---

17 Th.W. Mann, The Pillar of Cloud in the Reed Sea Narrative, JBL 90 (1971) 15–30.
18 Hoffmeier, Israel in Egypt; idem, Ancient Israel in Sinai: The Evidence for the Authenticity of the Wilderness Tradition, Oxford 2005.
19 Hoffmeier, ibid., 107.
20 Hoffmeier, ibid., 108–109.

happened in the Sea Event itself. Like the authors we mentioned previously, who posited a similar geographical interpretation to Hoffmeier, but without his detailed archaeological and geological work to support it, he could have gone on quite naturally to invoke the strong wind as the mechanism of the miracle. However, this is where he definitely will not go. In his 1996 book he concludes: 'The scope of this book does not permit me to delve into the phenomenon of the miracle at the sea, but I am sympathetic with Bright who observed, "If Israel saw in this the hand of God, the historian certainly has no evidence to contradict it!"'[21] And in his 2005 book he is similarly cautious: 'the theophany of the sea crossing occurred in a specific geographical location and at a particular time in history. Neither the phenomenologist of religion, nor anyone else for that matter, is equipped to explain how the event happened or what might be the source behind it.'[22]

It is highly relevant to the purpose of this article to ask why Hoffmeier felt able to proceed with such confidence in interpreting the narrative historically, only to hesitate at the final hurdle: description of the Sea Event itself. Why did he do so? Is it out of respect for the religious significance of the Event, or is it because he felt that, by its nature, a purported miracle such as this lies beyond the realm of historical enquiry? At this point we begin to touch on the nature and meaning of miracles, and it may be appropriate to recall some wise words of H. H. Rowley:

> Many modern minds are disturbed by the miraculous element in the story of the deliverance from Egypt and elsewhere in the Old Testament. On the other hand it is sometimes alleged that critical scholarship is based on the denial of the possibility of miracle. Let me say with clarity and candour that I am a critical scholar and that I neither begin nor end with any such denial...The miracle stories [of the Old Testament] can neither be uncritically accepted as historical, nor uncritically rejected as fancy. Each example must be examined for itself, in the light of the character of the narrative in which it stands and the purpose for which it appears to have been written. But that there is a truly miraculous element in the story, I am fully persuaded.[23]

It is clear therefore, that critical evaluation of an ostensibly historical narrative such as that of Exod 14 cannot be complete without a critical evaluation of its centrepiece, the Sea Event itself. One cannot realistically treat part of the narrative historically and uphold its authenticity, whilst refusing even to countenance comment on another part. After all, any alleged event which occurs in historical time and space must be

---

21   Hoffmeier, Israel in Egypt, 215.
22   Hoffmeier, Ancient Israel in Sinai, 108.
23   H.H. Rowley, The Faith of Israel, London 1956, 57–58.

open to historical and scientific enquiry; Hume's infamous definition of miracle as a rupture in the laws of nature clearly will not do, and the fact that the Sea Event can be described effectively using any number of scientific models illustrates this. So Hoffmeier's approach must be judged as lacking in its interpretative force: he upholds the narrator's assertion that the Sea Event was a real event which occurred in an authentic historical context, but effectively denies the narrator's equally forceful assertion that it involved historical and material reality: wind, water, hosts of people.

With this in mind, and having investigated the relatively mundane explanations which place the miracle at an inland body of shallow water or marshland, it is time to turn to more spectacular explanations which bring the nature of miracle into sharper focus.

(b) The 'strong east wind' over the Gulfs of Suez and Aqaba

It is notable that none of the above models for the Sea Event have cited any hard scientific or geographical arguments which make it plausible, or even conceivable, that a wind might be able to shift or dry-up a body of water. We must turn therefore to the work of natural scientists, the oceanographers Nof and Paldor, primarily.[24] What is particularly striking about their work is that they consider, not a shallow lake or marsh, but the Red Sea itself. This is because, they state, 'the lakes [between the Gulf of Suez and the Mediterranean Sea] are too small to allow a significant drop in the water level due to wind.'[25] Indeed, the observations of Aly Bey Shafei of water covering a road in the Delta region do not contradict this point, since the water he observed was only ankle-deep. If Nof and Paldor are right, they would appear to be making an important point: any explanation which makes use of an inland lake is unlikely to be able to provide a full and sufficient explanation of the central point of the narrative – that it was *the Sea itself* which provided the final and decisive deliverance from the Egyptians. An inland lake may have provided enough of an impedance to the Egyptians that their chariot wheels became 'clogged' (14,25), which would then allow for the Israelites to turn and overcome their pursuers by force of arms (as suggested by Hay). But it hardly seems possible that the Egyptians

24 D. Nof / N. Paldor, Are There Oceanographic Explanations for the Israelites' Crossing of the Red Sea?, Bull. of the American Meteorological Society 73 (1992) 305–314; D. Nof / N. Paldor, Statistics of Wind over the Red Sea with Application to the Exodus Question, Journal of Applied Meteorology 33 (1994) 1017–1025.

25 Nof/Paldor, Statistics, 1024.

could have all been overwhelmed and drowned by ankle-deep water itself.

There is one circumstance in which it might be possible still to hold onto the idea that the Sea of the Event was an inland lake, and that is if the lake was connected to the Mediterranean or Red Sea. This is just what Davies suggests – that the Bitter Lakes may well have been continuous with the Red Sea in ancient times[26], and Hoffmeier makes a detailed historical, geographical and geological argument in support.[27] Hence, if Nof and Paldor are right about the inability of an *isolated* inland lake to change its water level sufficiently, then an interpretation which is faithful to the spirit of the narrative (and of the Song of the Sea, Exod 15) should also take into account the action of a major sea such as the Red Sea or the Mediterranean. This is just what Nof and Paldor do.

Nof and Paldor present the results of calculations for two possible oceanographic processes which may have caused the waters of the Gulf of Suez to recede, at its most northerly and shallowest present-day point. One of the possible models is a tsunami (i.e. a tidal wave resulting from an underwater earthquake) arriving at the northern head of the Gulf from the main body of the Red Sea. However, Nof and Paldor consider that this model is less satisfactory because it does not match the biblical narrative so closely. On the other hand, their presentation of a 'wind setdown' model relates quite closely to certain aspects of the narrative.[28] This model invokes a strong wind that blows along the Gulf and pushes the water away from the shoreline overnight, as in 14,21. Nof and Paldor calculate that, even for moderate storm winds with a wind speed of about 20 ms^{-1}, the sea could recede by as much as 1 km, and the level drop by 2.5 m at the coast.[29] This is a result of the unusual geometry of the Gulf, and they note that related effects have been seen during storms in lakes with a similar shape e.g. Lake Erie.[30] Upon an abrupt dropping of the wind, the sea would return rapidly to its original position. Nof and Paldor point out that their model may even explain

---

26 G.I. Davies, The Way of the Wilderness: A Geographical Study of the Wilderness Itineraries in the Old Testament, Cambridge et al. 1979, 72–73.
27 Hoffmeier, Israel in Egypt, 207–210.
28 'Wind setdown' is the blowing of water away from a shore, and 'wind setup' onto the shore.
29 But note that, because of the geometry of the Gulf of Suez, their storm wind has to blow from the north-northwest (Nof/Paldor, Are There Oceanographic Explanations, 307), and not the east as indicated by the text (14,21). Given Nof and Paldor's insistence on explaining the text as fully as possible, this is a curious oversight which they do not comment upon.
30 Nof/Paldor, ibid., 313.

how the Israelites could be said by the text to cross on dry ground with the waters to their right and left, if the topography of the sea bed in ancient times was different from today and contained a natural ridge. A related explanation has been given by Ben-Menahem, who has pointed out that the spring tide can reach a peak of 2 m in the Gulf, which may thereby have facilitated the crossing.[31] However, this seems less likely to provide a mechanism which might catch the Egyptians off-guard sufficiently that they were swept away.

A particularly interesting feature of Nof and Paldor's study is that they attempt to determine the likelihood of such a storm wind in the Gulf of Suez. This is a very imprecise and difficult calculation, but they estimate that the likelihood is of the order of once every 1,000 to 3,000 years. Nof and Paldor suggest that 'the Red Sea crossing has been termed a "miracle" simply because the above likelihood period is greater than the human life span, so that even if it occurred at a given time prior to the legendary crossing, it was not remembered by later generations.'[32] This is partly why they dismiss a similar explanation made by Dayan which combines both wind and tide in the Gulf of Suez. According to Nof and Paldor's calculations, Dayan's model has a much lower likelihood than theirs, resulting in a likelihood of no more than once in 30,000 to 60,000 years. In other words, Nof and Paldor believe that their explanation is at least ten times more likely, and so is to be favoured.

Of course, if the Sea Event was truly a miracle, then comparing likelihoods of different explanations is not a good way of assessing their suitability as interpretative models. On the other hand, if one does not believe that the Sea Event was literally a miracle ('the great work which YHWH had done', 14,31), then likelihoods and probabilities are as good a criterion as any other. Nof and Paldor do not comment on their belief as to what or who ultimately lies behind the Sea Event, but a particularly prominent scientist who does, and who uses their model, is Colin Humphreys.[33] Humphreys is a full advocate of the miraculous nature of the Sea Event, but since he interprets it as a perfectly natural phenomenon at the same time, he therefore argues that the miracle is wholly in the timing – that the Israelites were at the right point at the right time, while the Egyptians were not. Indeed, Humphreys states

31 A. Ben-Menahem, Cross-dating of Biblical History via Singular Astronomical and Geophysical Events Over the Ancient Near East, Quarterly Journal of the Royal Astronomical Society 33 (1992) 175–190.

32 Nof/Paldor, Statistics, 1024.

33 C.J. Humphreys, The Miracles of Exodus: A Scientist's Discovery of the Extraordinary Natural Causes of the Biblical Stories, London / New York 2003.

clearly what many scientists believe, that it is not the nature of an event which makes it miraculous (since a natural cause can practically always be found for any purported miracle), but the timing. A good example is the tradition found in Joshua 3, where the River Jordan stops flowing just when the Israelites need to cross. The fact that a ready natural explanation can be found for this moves Humphreys to comment, 'I believe this natural explanation makes the miracle more, not less, believable.'[34]

Humphreys offers a particularly honest and revealing case of how a scientist may interpret biblical texts. In that sense, his book is more personal confession than exegesis. Part of the interest lies in Humphreys' style, which shows up very clearly the difference in approach between biblical scholars and natural scientists. Indeed, Humphreys' book has not been well received by biblical scholarship. And he himself displays what can only be described as hostility in turn towards biblical scholarship, coupled with a high degree of confidence in his own intellectual powers. The result is almost a caricature of the self-assured natural scientist who believes that he can shed real objective light on every question he turns to. As Johnstone put it in a review of Humphreys' book: 'Humphreys' predominant ignoring of scholarly tradition is matched by a breath-taking self-belief and self-reliance on his own personal experience.'[35]

The book is composed partly of a number of vignettes where Humphreys describes his holiday trips to Egypt and Sinai, in the course of which, again and again, he stumbles over evidence which proves that the events of Exodus took place literally there. He also provides naturalistic explanations for practically every miraculous event in the Exodus narrative, even down to the small details. So certain is he of his main point, that Mount Sinai is one of the active volcanoes of northwest Saudi Arabia, that he says: 'I ask you, the readers, to come to this book with an open mind on where Mount Sinai might be and a willingness to believe in the possibility that the leading biblical scholars in the world might be wrong on this issue[36] … Most biblical scholars are not scientists and so are unaware of the powerful arguments I have presented in this chapter that Mount Sinai was a volcano.'[37]

Humphreys' insistence that Mount Sinai was an active volcano is an important part of his explanation of the Sea Event. He argues that

---

34   Humphreys, ibid., 5.
35   W. Johnstone, Review of Humphrey's The Miracles of Exodus, JSSt 50 (2005) 373–379.
36   Humphreys, Miracles, 67.
37   Humphreys, ibid., 93.

the volcano in eruption provided the pillar of fire and cloud mentioned by the biblical text, and that it appeared to go before the Israelites precisely because they headed straight for it.[38] This led them to the head of the Gulf of Aqaba, not the inland lakes, and probably not the Gulf of Suez either. Humphreys therefore transfers Nof and Paldor's wind set-down model from the Gulf of Suez to the Gulf of Aqaba. This enables him to utilise a hurricane-strength northeast wind (rather closer to the text's 'east wind' than Nof and Paldor's north-northwest wind) to suggest that 'for a hurricane in the Gulf of Aqaba that pushes the water back about 800 yards, I've calculated that the height of the wall of water is approximately four feet. This height could easily be doubled to about eight feet by changes in atmospheric pressure.'[39] Humphreys even explains how he visited Eilat on one of his holidays in order to identify the ridge of land which must have provided the Israelites' path through the sea, with water to their right and left.[40] And true to the spirit of his very detailed and literalistic interpretations, Humphreys also accounts for the drowning of the Egyptians, by calculating the size of returning bore wave which would result if his strong northeast wind suddenly stopped blowing. He estimates that a wall of water travelling at eleven miles per hour would travel back up the Gulf of Aqaba, and 'would knock over a horse and its rider and hurl them into the sea'.[41]

We will return to Humphreys again, when we discuss the general approach which scientists seem to take towards the Sea Event. But for now we leave the explanations which revolve on the strong east wind, and turn to a family of more spectacular – but still fully scientific – explanations.

(c) The eruption of Thera

In the last 30 years, numerous scientific models of the Sea Event have been put forward which utilise a catastrophic volcanic eruption known to have occurred on the Aegean island of Thera around the mid-second millennium BCE. It was first suggested that the eruption had played a central role in bringing Minoan civilisation to an end on Crete at around

---

38 Humphreys, ibid., 165–169.
39 Humphreys, ibid., 253.
40 Underwater ridges in the Gulf of Aqaba have been suggested as providing a possible escape route for the Israelites by H. Blum, The Gold of Exodus: The Discovery of the Most Sacred Place on Earth, London 1998.
41 Humphreys, Miracles, 256.

1450 BCE.[42] This proposal was taken up by many geologists and archaeologists, and by the 1970's it seemed clear that the Theran eruption had been an unparalleled catastrophe in world history. It was estimated that the eruption was three times more energetic than that of Krakatoa in 1883, which had ejected a vast cloud of ash to a height of 80 km into the atmosphere. Java and Sumatra were in complete darkness for two days, and when the volcanic crater collapsed, a tsunami was created which reached a height of 36 m at their coasts, drowning nearly the entire coastal population.[43] By contrast, the tsunami resulting from the collapse of the Thera crater was estimated to have been 210 m high at its point of origin, and to have produced unrivalled devastation around the Aegean coast. It must even have reached the coasts of Egypt and Palestine: the height of the tsunami at Jaffa was calculated to have been 7 m.[44] A further factor contributing to the devastation was the fallout of volcanic ash, which was proposed to have formed a layer more than 10 cm in thickness in central Crete and thereby to have made agriculture impossible.[45] The Minoans that survived are thought to have migrated to mainland Greece, Palestine and Egypt, as part of the phenomenon known as the 'Sea People'.[46]

A number of authors have looked for traces of the Theran eruption in ancient literature. One intriguing suggestion that received a substantial amount of attention in the 1960/70's was that the destruction of Minoan civilisation may have formed the basis of Plato's Atlantis legend.[47] But more importantly for our purposes, it has been argued that the eruption also played a decisive role in the Exodus.[48] The first nine of the ten plagues of Egypt were explained as the sequence of natural events that might be expected from the storms, earthquakes and fallout

42   D. Ninkovich / B.C. Heezen, Santorini Tephra, in: Submarine Geology and Geophysics eds. W.F. Whittard / R. Bradshaw, London 1965, 413–452, here 440–441; B. Downey / D. Tarling, The end of the Minoan civilisation, New Scientist 13 September, 103 (1421) (1984) 48–52.
43   Ninkovich/Heezen, Santorini Tephra, 435–436; A.G. Galanopoulos / E. Bacon, Atlantis: The Truth Behind the Legend, London 1969, 114–115; P. McL. D. Duff (ed.), Holmes' Principles of Physical Geology, London 1992, 253–254.
44   Galanopoulos/Bacon, Atlantis, 111.
45   Ninkovich/Heezen, Santorini Tephra, 443.
46   Ninkovich/Heezen, ibid., 447; J.V. Luce, The End of Atlantis: New Light on an Old Legend, Frogmore (UK) 1970, 131–134.
47   J.G. Bennett, Geo-physics and human history: New light on Plato's Atlantis and the Exodus, Systematics 1 (1963) 127–156; Ninkovich/Heezen, Santorini Tephra, 440–450; Galanopoulos/Bacon, Atlantis; Luce, The End of Atlantis.
48   Bennett, Geophysics, 149–152; Galanopoulos/Bacon, Atlantis, 192–193.

of volcanic ash that would accompany such a tremendous eruption, even as far away as Egypt.[49]

The Theran eruption was also implicated in the Sea Event. As always, the location of the Sea is crucial. Following the by-now widespread rendering of יַם־סוּף as 'Sea of Reeds', Galanopoulos and Bacon believed that the Israelites must have crossed over a shallow lake or lagoon containing reeds, of which there is any number of candidates between Egypt and Sinai.[50] The most likely, they believed, is Lake Bardawil (known by classical authors as Lake Sirbonis), a shallow lagoon on the Mediterranean coast of Sinai. Galanopoulos and Bacon place the Israelites on the shore of Lake Bardawil at the final moment of the eruption of Thera, just as the now-empty volcanic cone collapsed due to the weight of seawater covering it. An enormous volume of water rushed into the collapsed cone, and water ebbed away from the entire eastern Mediterranean coast. A tsunami would have soon followed, striking the Egyptian coast 15 to 30 minutes later. This may have given the Israelites enough time to cross the Lake before the tsunami swept in and covered the pursuing Egyptians.

However, in the 1980's a major controversy developed over the precise dating of the Theran eruption and its effects on Minoan civilisation. Doubts began to creep in when it was reported that layers of Theran ash had been found in Crete which *predated* the Minoan destruction. It was also discovered that the previous estimates of ash fallout over Crete had been vastly overestimated, and had probably not caused agricultural problems after all.[51] After this, a rapid sequence of papers appeared proposing new dates for the eruption and new archaeological interpretations. The dates began to cluster in the range 1650–1600 BCE, almost 200 years *before* the end of Minoan civilisation.[52]

The current consensus is that the 1960/70's estimates of the date and magnitude of the eruption were completely wrong. The eruption actually occurred in the seventeenth-century BCE, and was of a relatively moderate size, comparable with several eruptions of the past 200

---

49 Bennett, Geophysics, 138–141; Galanopoulos/Bacon, Atlantis, 197–198.
50 Galanopoulos/Bacon, ibid., 193–197.
51 N. Herz / C.J. Vitaliano, Archaeological geology in the eastern Mediterranean, Geology 11 (1983) 49–53, here 51.
52 A.C. Renfrew, Introductory Remarks, in: Thera and the Aegean World III, ed. by D. Hardy / A.C. London 1990, 11–12; S. Manning, The Eruption of Thera: Date and Implications. in: ibid., 29–40. – Work is still ongoing on the problem, and the most recent estimate for the date of the eruption is 1639 – 1616 BCE (S.W. Manning et al., Chronology for the Aegean Late Bronge Age 1700–1400 B.C., Science 312 [2006] 565–569) or 1627 – 1600 BCE (W.L. Friedrich et al., Santorini Eruption Radiocarbon Dated to 1627–1600 B.C., Science 312 [2006] 548).

years.[53] The eruption had rather little effect on Crete; Minoan civilisation was brought to an end by some other means. The tsunami produced
by the eruption was also considerably smaller and less damaging than
previous estimates.[54]

This clearly presents major problems for the hypothesised link between the Exodus and the eruption of Thera. Although the eruption was
much less violent than was previously thought, it is still possible that it
produced a tsunami and a cloud of ash that threw Egypt into darkness
for some time.[55] But the date of the eruption is now known to be several
hundred years earlier than that assumed by the catastrophe theorists,
and some 400 years before the most likely date of the Exodus, in the
thirteenth century BCE. The second problem concerns the route of the
Exodus. The suggestion that a tsunami facilitated the Sea Event neces-
sitates the Israelites taking the Mediterranean coastal route out of Egypt
and crossing Lake Bardawil. And indeed, Bardawil had been a favour-
ite of biblical scholars looking for a location for the Sea of the Event
for a number of years, as shown, for instance, by the suggestions of
Hermann[56], and of Noth.[57] The narrow sandbar which forms a barrier
separating the lake from the open sea was well-known by classical authors such as Strabo as a useful trade route, but one which occasionally
presented natural hazards not dissimilar to those which the Egyptians
experienced at the Sea Event.[58] However, this route is now much less
favoured as a possible escape path for the Israelites, for two reasons.[59]
First, archaeological work has shown that there was most likely a heavy
military presence in this area. And second, it is now thought that the all-
important sandbar had probably not grown far enough to connect with
the mainland until Persian or Greek times. This all makes it highly im-
plausible as an escape route for the fleeing Israelites in the second millennium. In any case, the text appears to rule out this route (13,17).[60]

---

53 D.M. Pyle, The global impact of the Minoan eruption of Santorini, Greece, Environ-
    mental Geology 30 (1997) 59–61.
54 K. Minoura et al., Discovery of Minoan tsunami deposits, Geology 28 (2000) 59–62.
55 The Tempest Stele of Ahmose (ca.1530 BCE) has been cited as literary evidence of the
    effects of the eruption on Egypt (K.P. Foster / R.K. Ritner, Texts, Storms, and the Thera
    Eruption, JNES 55 [1996] 1–14), although this too has been disputed (M.H. Wiener /
    J.P. Allen, Separate Lives: The Ahmose Tempest Stela and the Theran Eruption, JNES
    57 [1998] 1–28).
56 S. Hermann, Israel in Egypt (SBT 2/27), London 1973, 60–63.
57 Noth, Exodus, 110.
58 G.I. Davies, The Wilderness Itineraries and Recent Archaeological Research, VT.S 40
    (1990) 161–175.
59 Hoffmeier, Israel in Egypt,183–184.
60 Hoffmeier, ibid., 183.

In spite of these seemingly-insurmountable problems with the Thera hypothesis for the Exodus, interpreters continue to put it forward, albeit often at a rather popular level. Ian Wilson is a good example: in 1985 he cited the Theran eruption as the probable cause of both the Plagues of Egypt and the Sea Event, occurring around 1450 BCE.[61] And then in 1999 he published substantially the same explanation but now with a revised date of around 1550 – 1500 BCE (although this is still nowhere near the widely-accepted scholarly dates for either the Theran eruption or the Exodus).[62] Likewise, Lamoreaux in 1995[63], Salzman in 2005[64], and most recently Trevisanato in 2005 and 2006[65] – all have published accounts of the Exodus explained by the Theran eruption, in spite of considerable scholarship, both scientific and biblical, which indicates that this model cannot reasonably be sustained.

It is clear that the reason Thera continues to attract interpreters is the fascination with global catastrophe, which extends to the wider public. For instance, a BBC documentary shown on primetime British television in 2002 (*Moses*, presented by Jeremy Bowen) revelled in the disasterist elements of the Thera hypothesis, presenting it as something new, and a major advance in understanding of the historical roots of the Exodus. It seems that catastrophe theorists, like conspiracy theorists, are rarely dissuaded from their viewpoints, even by the inconvenient weight of contrary scholarly opinion. For many, such spectacular inter-pretations bring an excitement and novelty which lends extra weight to their credibility, despite the fact that they inevitably involve a string of highly remarkable and exceptional circumstances. Indeed, the excite-ment and novelty of scientific explanations like the Thera hypothesis match that of cinematic portrayals of the Event, such as Cecil B De-Mille's *The Ten Commandments*, mentioned in the Introduction. And the persistence of those who purvey such incredible explanations sug-gests something of the air of religious faith, an important point of this article.

---

61 I. Wilson, The Exodus Enigma. London 1985; idem, Exodus: The True Story: Behind the Biblical Account. San Francisco et al. 1985.
62 I. Wilson, The Bible is History, London 1999.
63 P.E. LaMoreaux, Worldwide environmental impacts from the eruption of Thera, Environmental Geology 26 (1995) 172–181.
64 R.S. Salzman, The True Story of the Hebrew Exodus from Egypt, New York / Shanghai 2005.
65 S.I. Trevisanato, Ancient Egyptian doctors and the nature of the biblical plagues, Medi-cal Hypotheses 65 (2005) 811–813; idem, Treatments for the burns in the London Medical Papyrus show the first seven biblical plagues of Egypt are coherent with Santorini's volcanic fallout, Medical Hypotheses 66 (2006) 193–196; idem, Six medical papyri describe the effects of Santorini's volcanic ash, and provide Egyptian parallels to the so-called biblical plagues, Medical Hypotheses 67 (2006) 187–190.

(d) Cosmic catastrophe

Immanuel Velikovsky was the catastrophe theorist to end them all.
Particularly in his best-selling book *Worlds in Collision*[66], Velikovsky
put forward the idea that cosmic disturbances have more than once
profoundly influenced the course of civilisation on Earth in historical
times – once in the second millennium BCE and again in the eighth
century BCE. Important in his approach was a synthesis of ancient
texts, traditions and folklore from around the globe. From this evidence,
Velikovsky suggested that a gigantic comet must have passed in near
proximity to the earth, causing a number of catastrophes: among them a
huge earthquake, a global tidal wave, mountains changing shape, and
the earth slowing down in its rotation. The Sea Event was one such
outcome of this gigantic comet – seas worldwide were drawn upwards
miles high because of the gravitational attraction of the nearby comet,
the earth was covered in darkness, the seabed was exposed, and after
the comet had passed by, the Mediterranean came crashing into the Red
Sea as a gigantic tsunami. The Israelites, safely on the opposite shore,
thus found their salvation from the Egyptians in this terrifying moment
of annihilation.[67]

   Velikovsky offers a simultaneously terrifying and fascinating
apocalypse, but his work is more a testimony to faith in a hypothesis
rather than the well-tried scientific process of suggestion, peer review,
counter-suggestion and refinement. For, shortly after its original publication in 1950, and ever since, many scientists have condemned the
book as fantasy, contradicting the basic laws of physics.[68] This did not
appear to affect the book's popularity substantially though, because it is
still in print more than fifty years later, and the subject of many internet
pages where the subject of cosmic catastrophes is enthusiastically discussed.

(e) Mythological explanations

Although they do not invoke natural science, there is a further class of
rational explanations of the Sea Event which must be mentioned. These
are best grouped together as 'mythological', since they consider the
influence of Ancient Near Eastern myth as crucial to the origin and

---

66   I. Velikovsky, Worlds in Collision, London 1972.
67   Velikovsky, ibid., 78–82.
68   See, for example R. Huggett, Cataclysms and Earth History: The Development of
     Diluvialism, Oxford 1989, 165.

development of the Sea Event tradition. In particular, these interpretations tend to see the Event as in part or whole a kind of historicisation
of the recurring myth of conflict between the creator god and the great
primeval sea (יָם), his enemy. Thus, for instance, Eakin points to a naturalistic and historical kernel of the story where the Israelites crossed a
dried-out portion of the seashore and the Egyptians became mired in the
sand or mud.[69] Over time this kernel became embellished with the motif
of the waters dividing, which ultimately derives from the Canaanite
myth of conflict where Baal splits Yam in two. And Brevard Childs
adds to this the further possibility that perhaps the story was also coloured by elements of the story of the Jordan crossing, and by the poetic
Song of the Sea, with the upshot that the tradition eventually received
by the Priestly author was rather different from the much earlier Yah-
wistic account.[70]

Likewise, mythological explanations have been made for the puzzle
of the location of יַם־סוּף, principally by Snaith[71], and by Batto[72]. They
suggest that יַם־סוּף literally means 'Sea of End/Extinction', and should
be understood geographically as the Red Sea, the limitless sea at the
end of the land and therefore the realisation of the mythological sea of
primeval chaos. The P author localised the Sea Event here in order to
make the miraculous delivery appear even more effective.

So these mythological explanations, while not utilising the ideas of
modern science, and perhaps even being rather agnostic about the historical roots of the tradition, still offer a rational explanation. And if the
sceptical rationalist already doubts the miraculous and spectacular elements of the account of the Sea Event, then mythological interpretations give added support to his scepticism, for now a clear developmen-
tal logic of embellishment may be traced through the tradition. The
effect is, of course, to cement doubt on the historicity of much, if not
all, of the account of the Sea Event given in Exod 14. The biblical
scholar William Johnstone provides a good example of such a rational
sceptic:

It is again as futile, therefore, to attempt to locate this theological
affirmation [the exodus] in geographical detail as it is to date the exodus to a precise historical moment. There is no reason to deny that by
'Sea' the biblical writer has in mind the Red Sea ... Rationalistically to
replace the 'Red Sea' by the 'reed sea' is entirely beside the point and

---

69   F.E. Eakin, The Reed Sea and Baalism, JBL 86 (1967) 378–384.
70   B.S. Childs, A Traditio-Historical Study of the Reed Sea Tradition, VT 20 (1970)
      406–418.
71   N.H. Snaith, יַם־סוּף: The Sea of Reeds: The Red Sea, VT 15 (1965) 395–398.
72   B.F. Batto, The Reed Sea: Requiescat in pace, JBL 102 (1983) 27–35.

one hopes that it may be dropped from scholarly discussion. Much more relevant are those interpretations which find in the motif of the Sea a reflection of Israelite polemical appropriation of the ancient Near Eastern cosmic myths of the battle between the creator god and the great deep.[73]

Johnstone's point is made even more clearly in his review of Humphreys' book, discussed in section 2.(b) of this article:

Humphrey's explanation of the biblical material is moving in the wrong direction: it is scaling down the paranormal into the normal. The biblical accounts, on the contrary, move in the opposite direction: they use the language of ordinary experience to extrapolate beyond the confines of that ordinary experience and beyond the limits of ordinary speech. The language of theological discourse is inescapably metaphorical. The Bible uses natural language, and the phenomena of the natural world to which it refers (what other resources of human speech are available?), not simply to be examined on its own terms but to point beyond itself. The metaphor and the whole cluster of all possible metaphors have only an allusive function in the attempt to articulate something about God who is beyond speech. Miracle is, so to speak, a metaphor in physical terms: it is similarly an attempt to portray and to express the presence and action of the inexpressible transcendent in and through the contingent actions of the world.[74]

While there is much good sense in Johnstone's approach, it runs the risk of taking rationalism to its logical extreme and uncritically denying the possibility of objective salvation due to YHWH altogether, the key point of the Sea Event. The rational approach will often tend to 'demythologise' miracles, and treat them as parables or ciphers of a deeper reality, a more sufficient truth. But taking the point of H.H. Rowley mentioned earlier, a truly historical and critical interpretation must respect the integrity and purpose of the original author(s), and acknowledge that the miracles are seen themselves as the truth, because they are the concrete acts of salvation of God in the world. After all, the theological function of Scripture is to bear witness (as evidence) to the fundamental truth of those acts of salvation, and to the fundamental truth of the one who made them possible. For this reason, it is necessary now to look in detail at the question of rationalism, objectivity, and faith in the process of interpretation.

---

73   W. Johnstone, Exodus, Sheffield 1990, 35.
74   Johnstone, Review, 374.

3. Rationalism and faith in interpretations of the Sea Event

The above review of explanations for the Sea Event has not been exhaustive; rather, it has attempted to provide a broad overview of the different *types* of interpretation, and particularly, of the types of *interpreters*. For it is clear that, although every interpretation has been made in the name of history or of science, there is a very broad spectrum of opinions as to what constitutes a plausible explanation. Linked with this is the idea of rational against un-rational (faith-based) explanation. The most mundane (and ostensibly the most rational) natural explanations are those which involve a strong wind over a shallow inland lake or marsh. These are perhaps the easiest to accept in our modern world. And they are the types of explanation most favoured by professional biblical scholars, but by and large not by interpreters with a background in the natural sciences. Instead, natural scientists seem to prefer explanations which invoke more spectacular, or at least ostensibly more unlikely, elements. Indeed, it is the coming together of multiple unlikelihoods which can be so delightful to the natural scientist, at least in Humphreys' case. His belief is that science not only explains the miracles of the Exodus fully, but heightens the sense of the miraculous. As he puts it: 'The insights provided by modern science suggest that the Exodus text has often been misinterpreted by scholars. The real meaning of the text, suggested in this book, is frequently more dramatic than the traditional interpretation. The Exodus story revealed in this book is truly astonishing, amazing, and inspirational.'[75]

Biblical scholars though, exhibit the opposite tendency, to downplay – or at least to try to see through – the 'astonishing, amazing, and inspirational' elements of the narrative. Their background in textual analysis and criticism means that they are often ready to highlight one particular strand of the text over another, and to seek to explain that strand alone as the most historically-authentic key to the whole text. This is why the 'strong east wind' is often the focus of biblical scholars in particular, since it is seen as being a more naturalistic motif than the motif of the parting of the waters into a wall on the right and left. These two motifs are often separated into two constituent strands of the narrative: the wind is usually associated with the older J source, while the parting of the waters is associated with the considerably later P source.[76]

---

75 Humphreys, Miracles, 339.
76 See, for example, B.S. Childs, The Book of Exodus: A Critical, Theological Commentary, Louisville, KY 1974, 218–222.

This approach can be criticised on a number of fronts. First, there is the observation of Hay, oft-repeated, that, although the literary critics agree that the narrative of the Sea Event is not a unity, but rather a composite of several traditions, yet no critic has been able to provide a compelling reconstruction of the constituent strands.[77] Second, it is clear that even at the key point where the reconstruction is most often agreed upon – namely at the description of the miracle, where the wind is said to come from J, and the parting of the waters from P – this has been made largely on the basis that the more naturalistic motif of the wind must be earlier than the more supernatural motif of the walls of water. However, as Noth points out, even the J account is fundamentally supernatural in its conception; ignoring or deleting elements in the story will not obtain a more historical or rational report.[78] This leads to an important conclusion: when biblical scholars downplay the more remarkable (P) elements of the story in favour of the ostensibly more naturalistic (J) elements, they are performing more of an act of accommodation than they are of critical interpretation. In this instance, modernist scruples are blunting (or even diverting) the critical scalpel. Brevard Childs puts it well:

For the modern critical reader the hermeneutical problem is posed by the earlier J account which stresses the effect of 'natural causes' (strong east wind, dry sea bed, panic among Egyptians), and the later P account which is 'supernaturally' oriented (splitting of the sea, wall of water, etc.). On the basis of this critical evidence the usual hermeneutical move is to suggest that the original crossing was viewed as resulting from a series of natural events, and that the later writer sought to articulate the theological *meaning* of the event by extending the imagery into the supernatural. This allowed the modern biblical theologian to speak of the great act of God at the exodus in delivering his people while at the same time to regard the event historically as little more than the accidental escape of some slaves across a treacherous marsh.[79]

Natural scientists on the other hand, who may or may not be aware of such niceties as source criticism, are more inclined to approach the text as a *unity*, and to try to explain every strand of the narrative together, including those labelled as mythological. This is perhaps down to the nature of scientific enquiry, which tends to see an explanation which accounts for *more* of the data as inherently superior to one which accounts for *less* of them. The upshot is that, from the perspective of

---

77 Hay, What really happened ...?, 399.
78 Noth, Exodus, 119–120.
79 B.S. Childs, The Book of Exodus: A Critical, Theological Commentary, Louisville, KY 1974, 228.

biblical scholarship, natural scientists who write on the Bible have a rather quaint, literalistic, and trusting way of reading texts. They appear to take what is said at face-value, on trust, and there is a sense in which they are performing an act of faith. If the modernist approach is usually said to be one of intrinsic scepticism towards supernatural claims, it is clearly not the case here, because natural scientists who write on the Bible appear to approach it with anything but scepticism.[80]

As a consequence, the explanations favoured by natural scientists have a clear tendency to be more spectacular – or at least less mundane – than those of many biblical scholars. But at the same time, the explanations favoured by scientists are at heart *rational* explanations, since they stem from well-authenticated and well-established natural processes. We have a paradox then: the scientists' explanations are as rational as those of biblical scholars, but they are also more incredible (less believable) and therefore require a greater degree of faith.[81]

Equally paradoxical is the fact that biblical scholars are not immune from employing essentially faith-based arguments in the name of rationalism. For one criticism in particular which can be levelled at the more mundane explanations favoured by biblical scholars is that they have the tendency to lose the sense of a truly remarkable event. And these more mundane explanations face the serious drawback of being less capable of explaining how the Egyptians could all have been so signally destroyed by the Sea. As Hay says of this type of explanation, 'the process of rationalising has been carelessly pursued; for whereas the water must be assumed to have been *shallow* enough to account in a credible way for the wind's removal of it, it must then be assumed to have been *deep* enough upon its return to sweep away the entire Egyptian force.'[82] And until firm geographical and scientific evidence is presented that a strong wind is actually capable of changing the level of

---

80 In fact, it is a caricature to label the ancients as basically gullible compared to moderns. Josephus, for instance, gives a clearly 'rationalised' description of the Sea Event, and acknowledges the place of scepticism ('on these matters, everyone is welcome to his own opinion', Ant. II.xvi.3). Likewise, Artapanus gives a possible naturalistic explanation of the Event (Moses took advantage of a low tide), although Artapanus himself prefers a more miraculous understanding (in Eusebius Praep. Evang. IX.27).

81 A similar point can be made about the many millions in the modern world who believe in phenomena such as crop circles and UFO's – they call upon science not to discredit or qualify these beliefs, but to support them. As has been pointed out by Corner, science is a double-edged sword – it can be used both to debunk superstitious belief and to support it (M. Corner, Signs of God: Miracles and their Interpretation Aldershot/Burlington 2005, 188).

82 Hay, What really happened ...?, 398. But note that Hay holds the eccentric opinion that the Sea Event probably had rather little, if anything, to do with the water, which is only a secondary motif in the story.

one of the inland lakes of the Delta by more than a matter of centime-
tres, this type of explanation will remain a completely groundless
speculation anyway. The biblical scholars who rely on it are therefore
putting their trust in an untested hypothesis; they are performing an act
of faith, but naming it rational and historical enquiry. Noth, for one,
wisely urges caution.[83] So it is clear that scientists and biblical scholars
alike have their blind spots: both employ faith in the course of their
interpretations, while insisting on the importance of rational enquiry.

My point is that critical interpretation of the Sea Event is not a
question of applying critical rationality against un-rational assumption,
neither is it a matter of distinguishing an historical core from mythological or imaginative accretions, and neither is it the application of
science against faith. Interpretation cannot be as neatly-divided as opposing these categories to each other might suggest, and neither can it
occupy the spectrum between them. Instead, interpretation will always
involve an interpenetrating complex of rationality and assumption, science and faith, history and mythology: each category relies and builds
upon the other, and this is inescapable. In effect it is the postmodern-
ist's point, that – in this particular case of a purported miracle of the
significance and complexity of the Sea Event – it is not possible to interpret it in a disinterested and truly objective way. In any case, there
most likely never was a single, truly objective description of the Sea
Event. It is as well for the critical interpreter to be aware of this.

4. 'Critical' interpretation of the Sea Event

We turn now to considering whether there is a way forward, a fully
critical method of interpretation along the lines suggested by H. H.
Rowley; it must utilise the strengths both of literary analysis, and of
historical and scientific explanations, incredible or otherwise. What is
more, it must be pluralistic. The harmonistic analysis of each scientist
we have looked at, and the reductive analysis of each biblical scholar
we have looked at, are both going in the wrong direction. They are both
narrowing-down the interpretative options, rather than, in this crucial
instance, *expanding* upon them. Johnstone, again in his review of Humphrey's book, makes an excellent point:

It seems to me, following in the wake of generations of critics, a
harmonistic reading is the product of a radical misunderstanding; the
biblical material is composite and full justice is done to it not in silenc-

---

83   Noth, *Exodus*, 116.

ing one of the voices or in smoothing over the competition between the voices but in allowing each its full play in dialogue. For this is yet another feature of theological language: by definition, the inexpressible cannot be exhausted by explicit statements; it is also conveyed by gaps in, between, and beyond the unharmonized testimonies of the witnesses. Truth is not so much a once-for-all given as the production of meaning through the unending competition of voices in dialogue. The recognition of this compositeness is not an impoverishment but an enrichment of the appreciation of the biblical account.[84]

Johnstone is absolutely right: even when considering the Sea Event alone, the Bible's fundamentally pluriform witness to it should be affirmed, not squashed into another, more uniform, pattern *which it almost certainly never possessed*. The pluriform witness is the key, and also shows how to deal critically with the many scientific explanations. Scientific explanations, even those which are highly spectacular and unlikely, can be critically useful and enriching, as long as each is not taken to be the sole answer. Each must be sifted and judged as part of the whole, but not rejected out-of-hand on rational grounds alone, since they are all based on rationalism. There should be a sense in which the plausible scientific explanations contribute to a wider statement of what happened in the Sea Event which also impinges on *why* it happened. In the same way, all of the textual strands must be held together, albeit in a difficult tension.

A good example of the solution which I have in mind comes with the resurrection narratives in the four gospels. Each is an attempt, by means of narrative, to explain in the medium of words and human concepts, what is ultimately inexplicable, even though, *crucially but paradoxically, it involves material reality* (a human body). And each is notably different. The evangelists grasp at the truth using human concepts which are on the verge of their and our understanding. My point is that both literary and scientific models of the Sea Event can be seen to operate in the same way – they complement each other, since each offers a different but incomplete view. Of course, some models are altogether less suitable than others, and we might think particularly of Velikovsky, or the Theran eruption, which fail some of the basic criteria. But nevertheless, they offer perhaps a useful critical boundary to the portfolio of appropriate interpretations. And in any case, we must also judge some of the comparatively mundane interpretations offered by some biblical scholars in a not too dissimilar light, as being little more than unfounded speculations not based on empirical reasoning. The point is

---

84 Johnstone, Review, 378.

that, while each has been founded on rational analysis, each also has a substantial component of un-rational assumption, or faith.

To summarise, I have discussed a number of scientific, literary and mythological explanations for the Sea Event of Exod 14. Some have been of a more everyday and commonsense character than others, some have verged on fantasy, and others have been entirely straightforward (especially the mythological explanations). Each interpretation has been grounded ultimately on rational analysis, but each explanation has been shown to contain various crucial (almost faith-based) assumptions which are revealing of the author's own approach. Each explanation can and should be critiqued and judged on various levels, including rationalism, geographical and historical likelihood, and theological significance. But the point which I have tried to make is that a fully critical interpretation cannot be achieved by selecting one explanation over another on the grounds of rationalism, but rather by holding a plurality of explanations in creative tension. There is much more that will be said later about interpretations of the Sea Event, and especially about literary interpretations, and there is much more which must be said theologically too, but I regard this as the essential methodological starting point.

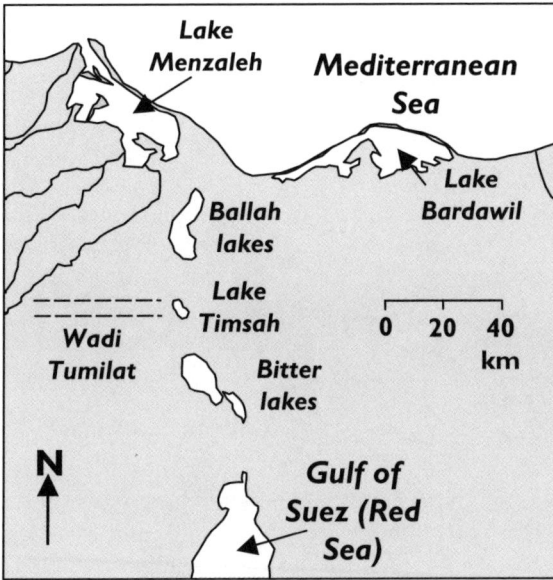

Map of the eastern Nile Delta showing the main bodies of water implicated in the Sea Event. The approximate trace of the Wadi Tumilat is shown schematically by the broken lines. © Mark J. Harris

„Ihr sollt mir ein Königreich von Priestern und ein heiliges Volk sein" Erwägungen zur Funktion von Ex 19,3b–8 innerhalb der Sinaiperikope

von Axel Graupner

Frank-Lothar Hossfeld zum 65. Geburtstag

Nachdem Martin Luther als „Ecclesiast" der Stadtkirche zu Wittenberg im Spätsommer des Jahres 1524 die Auslegung der Genesis abgeschlossen hatte, nahm er am 2. Oktober desselben Jahres, dem 19. Sonntag nach Trinitatis, die Auslegung des Exodusbuches in Angriff, mit der er im Februar 1527 zu Ende kam. Liturgischer Ort blieb der Vespergottesdienst.[1] 1528 erschien bei Hans Weiß in Wittenberg Luthers „Auslegung der Zehen gepot".[2] Wie die Fortsetzung des Titels lehrt, entstammt sie Luthers fortlaufender Predigt über das 2. Buch Mose: „Durch Mart. Luther gepredigt zu Wittemberg, Aus dem xix. und xx. Capitel des andern buchs Mosi". Da die Auslegung an verschiedenen Stellen bereits auf den Bauernkrieg zurückblickt, dürfte sie aus dem Jahr 1526 stammen. Der Schluss des Titels – „sampt einer Unterricht wie Moses zu leren ist" – zeigt an, daß ihr für den Druck eine Einleitung vorangestellt wurde, die Auskunft über die Grundsätze der Auslegung gibt.[3]

In der Predigt über Ex 19 räumt Luther V.6a den mit Abstand breitesten Raum ein. Das ist kaum verwunderlich. Der Halbvers ist – zusammen mit Ex 23,22 G – Quellort für 1 Petr 2,9, Luthers Hauptbeleg für das Priestertum aller Gläubigen. Dieser Zusammenhang bestimmt die Auslegung. Martin Luther übersetzt im Anschluss an die Vulgata,

---

1   M. Brecht, Martin Luther. II. Ordnung und Abgrenzung der Reformation 1521–1532, Stuttgart 1982, 64f.278.
2   J.G. Walch (Hg.), Dr. Martin Luthers sämtliche Schriften III, St. Louis/Missouri ²1894 = Groß Oesingen 1986, 1004–1131.
3   Vgl. dazu auch Luthers „Unterrichtung wie sich die Christen in Mose sollen schicken", die bereits 1526 im Druck erschien (WA 16,363–393).

die ממלכת כהנים als genitivus epexegeticus[4], genauer: als genitivus attributivus[5] auffasst und mit regnum sacerdotale wiedergibt, „ihr sollt mir ein priesterlich Königreich sein" und formuliert unter Berufung auf 1 Petr 2,9 in direkter Anrede an die Gemeinde als Leitsatz: „Ihr sollt alle Priester und Könige sein"[6]. Die Übertragung wird ausdrücklich begründet: Die exklusive Beziehung von Ex 19,6 auf „die Juden" und die Deutung „des Spruchs" „auf alle Christen" 1 Petr 2,9 stehen nicht in Widerspruch zueinander.[7] Da die Verheißung der Gesetzgebung vorangeht, gilt sie auch denen, „so nach dem Gesetze gläubig sind, welchen kein Gesetz gegeben ist. Welcher nun Gott glaubt ohne alles Gesetz, der wird ein Priester und König, er sei Jude oder Heide, vor oder nach dem Gesetz."[8] Im Anschluss an diese Verhältnisbestimmung von alttestamentlicher Verheißung und neutestamentlicher Aufnahme legt Luther die tragenden Begriffe des Leitsatzes aus, wobei er ihre Reihenfolge umkehrt. „König sein" heißt: „Die Gläubigen ..., sie sind Herren über Tod, Teufel, Hölle und alles Unglück."[9] „Priester sein"[10] bedeutet: „Wer mein Wort hat, und dem glaubt, der ist mein Priester"; „wer ihn hört, hört Gott selber".[11] So kann Luther zusammenfassen: „Priester und König sein (ist) nichts anderes, denn den Glauben und den heiligen Geist haben, die Gnade Gottes den anderen zu predigen, und vor Gott zu treten in einem guten Vertrauen, als ein Kind zum Vater."[12] „Also ist ein jeglicher Christ ein König für sich selber, und ein Priester für andere."[13]

4 W. Gesenius / E. Kautzsch, Hebräische Grammatik, Leipzig [28]1909 = Darmstadt 1985, § 128f.
5 Zur Bezeichnung vgl. B.K. Waltke / M. O'Connor, An Introduction to Biblical Hebrew Syntax, Winona Lake/Ind. 1990, 9.5.3b, zur Sache außerdem Gesenius/Kautzsch, Grammatik, § 128o; G. Fohrer, ‚Priesterliches Königtum', Ex 19,6 (1963): ders., Studien zur alttestamentlichen Theologie und Geschichte (1949–1966) (BZAW 115), Berlin 1969, 149–153, hier 151; C. Houtman, Exodus II, Kampen 1990, 399.
6 Walch III, 1013.
7 Ebd.
8 Walch III, 1014.
9 Walch III, 1014.
10 Walch III, 1015.
11 Walch III, 1016.
12 Walch III, 1016.
13 Walch III, 1017. – Zum inneren Zusammenhang und den kontroverstheologischen Bezügen der Aussagen Luthers zum Priestertum aller Gläubigen vgl. H. Goertz / W. Härle, Art. Priester/Priestertum. II. Allgemeines Priestertum. 1. Systematisch-theologisch: TRE 27 (1997) 402–410.

I

Luthers Auslegung hat das Verständnis von Ex 19,6a über Jahrhunderte bestimmt. Noch die historisch-kritische Exegese des 19. Jh. ist von ihr stark beeinflusst. So kommentiert beispielsweise August Dillmann V.6a in implizitem, aber unüberhörbarem Rekurs auf das Ensemble von Luthers Aussagen zum Priestertum aller Gläubigen:

> „*ein Königreich von Priestern*, d.h. ein von mir als König regiertes Gemeinwesen ..., ein Reich, dessen Bürger alle Priester sind", „d.h. ... mir geweihte Diener, die nach meinem Namen sich nennen, bei mir Zutritt haben, mir fortwährend nahe sind, ganz meinem Dienste leben ..., *und* noch kürzer aber im selben Sinn *ein heiliges Volk*, d.h. ein Volk, welches sämtliche ... in die göttliche Heiligkeit ... aufgenommen sich so rein hält, wie es die Gemeinschaft mit dem Heiligen erheischt ..., und hinwiederum durch diese Gemeinschaft geschützt, unantastbar gemacht wird."[14]

---

14 A. Dillmann / V. Ryssel, Die Bücher Exodus und Leviticus (KEH 12), Leipzig ³1897, 214 (Hervorhebungen im Original); vgl. H.L. Strack, Die Bücher Genesis, Exodus, Leviticus und Numeri (KK 1), München u.a. 1894, 223. – Dillmann versteht die Wortfolge ממלכת כהנים als constructus-Verbindung. Vgl. α': βασιλεία ἱερέων. Diese weithin übliche Auffassung ist allerdings nicht ohne Widerspruch geblieben. Nach anderer Auffassung handelt es sich um zwei selbständige, asyndetisch gereihte Substantive. Demnach wäre כהנים Apposition zu ממלכת. Vgl. etwa J.B. Bauer, Könige und Priester, ein heiliges Volk (Ex 19,6): BZ NF 2, 1958, 283–286 und N. Brox, Der erste Petrusbrief (EKK XXI), Köln u. Neukirchen-Vluyn 21986, 98 Anm. 326 im Anschluss an J.H. Elliott, The Elect and the Holy. An exegetical examination of 1 Peter 2:4–10 and the phrase βασίλειον ἱεράτευμα (NT.S 12), Leiden 1966, 50–128. Diese Auffassung beruft sich auf Mi 4,8αβ und die Textgeschichte, jedoch kaum zu Recht. ממלכת ist auch in Mi 4,8 status constructus und fungiert dort als „Verbindungsform" (Gesenius/Kautzsch, Grammatik, § 130a). Vgl. R. Kessler, Micha (HThK.AT), Freiburg u.a. 1999, 199. *G* faßt ממלכת כהנים wie *V.*(s.o.) als genitivus epexegeticus auf, jedoch nicht als genitivus attributivus, sondern als genitivus qualitatis (vgl. Waltke/O'Connor 9.5.1j), bei dem das nomen regens das nomen rectum näher bestimmt, und gewinnt auf diese Weise einen – im Deutschen allerdings nicht wiedergebbaren – Chiasmus: βασίλειον ἱεράτευμα – ἔθνος ἅγιον („eine königliche Priesterschaft – ein heiliges Volk"). J.W. Wevers, Notes on the Greek Text of Exodus (SCS 30), Atlanta 1990, 295; vgl. A. Le Boulluec / P. Sandevoir, La Bible d'Alexandrie. II. L'Exode, Paris 1989, 200 und – im Blick auf 1 Petr 2,9 – (H. Balz /) W. Schrage, Die Briefe des Jakobus, Petrus, Johannes und Judas (NTD 10), Göttingen 21980, 86. Erst *T, S, Syh* sowie σ' und θ' lösen die constructus-Verbindung auf, wobei die Targumim ממלכה als abstractum pro concreto verstehen (H.L. Strack / P. Billerbeck, Kommentar zum Neuen Testament aus Talmud und Midrasch III, München 41965, 788): „Könige, Priester und ein heiliges Volk" (*T^O* und *T^{III}*), „ein Königreich und Priester und ein heiliges Volk" (*S*), „ein Königreich, Priester und ein heiliges Volk" (*Syh*, σ' und θ'). *TJ* gestaltet zudem aus: „Könige, mit einer Krone geschmückt, und diensttuende Priester und ein heiliges Volk". – Zu ἱεράτευμα als Bildung der Übersetzer vgl. G. Schrenk, Art. ἱεράτευμα, ThWNT 3 (1938) 249–251, hier 249; H. Goldstein, Art. ἱεράτευμα, EWNT 2 (1981) 426.

Gegenwärtig wirkt Luthers Auslegung in der Auffassung weiter, daß die constructus-Verbindung ממלכת כהנים als genitivus generis[15] („ein Königreich, das aus Priestern besteht") oder genitivus objectivus[16] („ein Königtum über Priester") aufzufassen ist und zusammen mit der unmittelbar folgenden Bestimmung der Israeliten zu einem גוי קדוש ein Hendiadyoin – in der Sprache der Poetik: einen synonymen parallelismus membrorum – bildet, das Israels Sonderstellung unter den Völkern als סגלה, als „persönliches Eigentum / persönlicher Erwerb" JHWHs umschreibt.[17]

Dabei können Einzelzüge der Kommentierung A. Dillmanns beherrschend in den Vordergrund treten oder gar als ausschließliche Intention erscheinen: die Unmittelbarkeit Israels resp. jedes einzelnen in Israel zu Gott[18] oder – Wechsel der Perspektive – die Unmittelbarkeit der Königsherrschaft JHWHs über Israel[19], Israels Sonderstellung innerhalb der Völkerwelt[20], Israels Absonderung von den Völkern in der ausschließlichen Verehrung JHWHs[21], Israels Verpflichtung zu besonderer Reinheit[22], außerdem Gebotstreue[23], Israels Unan-

---

15　Vgl. Waltke/O'Connor 9.5.3i (genitive of genus).

16　Vgl. Waltke/O'Connor 9.5.2b (objective genitive).

17　Zur Bedeutung von סגלה vgl. HAL 701a und E. Lipiński, סְגֻלָּה, ThWAT 5 (1986) 749–752. Der Vorschlag, das Lexem auf die Bedeutung „Krongut" einzugrenzen (R. Mosis, Ex 19,5b.6a. Syntaktischer Aufbau und lexikalische Semantik, BZ.NF 22 [1978] 1–25, hier 17f), kann sich zwar auf 1 Chr 29,3 und Koh 2,8 berufen. Das ist aber eine zu schmale, außerdem keineswegs eindeutige Basis; denn natürlich hat auch ein König persönliches Eigentum. Erst recht unbefriedigend bleibt die Begründung der These mit der Etymologie (G. Barbiero *mamleket kōhănim* [Ex 19,6a] [1989 ‹ital.›]: Die Priester an die Macht?: Studien zu alttestamentlichen Texten [SBAB 34], Stuttgart 2002, 11–27, hier 22). Sie verkennt die Bedeutungsbreite von akkadisch *sikiltu(m)* / babylonisch *šagiltu(m)* (vgl. Lipiński, ThWAT 5,750f) und reflektiert nicht hinreichend die Differenz zwischen Herkunft und Bedeutung eines Lexems. Vgl. dazu die grundsätzlichen Ausführungen von U. Rüterswörden, Art. Wortforschung. I. Altes Testament, TRE 36 (2004) 329–335, hier 333 im Anschluss an J. Barr, Bibelexegese und moderne Semantik. Theologische und linguistische Methode in der Bibelwissenschaft, München 1965 (1961 [engl.]), 111–113. – Zum relativen Recht, Termini der Poetik auf Ex 19,3b–8 anzuwenden, vgl. M. Noth, Das zweite Buch Mose. Exodus (ATD 5), Göttingen 1959, 126; B.S. Childs, Exodus (OTL), London 1974, 366: Der Stil des Textes ist „elevated", „approaches poetry in its use of parallelism and selected vocabulary".

18　B. Baentsch, Exodus – Leviticus – Numeri (HK I/2), Göttingen 1903, 173; G. Beer, Exodus (HAT I/3), Tübingen 1939, 97.

19　M. Buber, Moses, Heidelberg 21952, 125.

20　P. Heinisch, Das Buch Exodus (HSAT I/2), Bonn 1934, 146; vgl. Bauer, Könige und Priester, 286, der darüber hinaus an eine Erhebung Israels „zum König unter den Völkern" denkt: JHWH gewährt Israel „Teilhabe an seiner unumschränkten Königsherrschaft über alle Welt" (286). Vgl. Offb 5,10; 20,6

21　K. Galling, Die Erwählungstraditionen Israels (BZAW 48), Gießen 1928, 27; vgl. R.B.Y. Scott, A Kingdom of Priests (Exodus XIX 6), OTS 8 (1959) 213–219: „a positive counterpart of the idea of separation from the worship of other gods" (219).

22　Vgl. Jub 33,20 und A.B. Ehrlich, Randglossen zur hebräischen Bibel I, Leipzig 1908, 337.

23　Heinisch, Exodus, 146.

tastbarkeit[24]. Darüber hinaus verbinden nicht wenige Ausleger Ex 19,6 mit tritojesajanischen Aussagen (Jes 61,6; vgl. 62,12; 63,18) und finden – gegen den frühen Einspruch A. Dillmanns[25] – in der Verbindung ממלכת כהנים eine Aufgabenstellung: Israel ist berufen zum Mittler zwischen JHWH und der Völkerwelt.[26] Dagegen betont R. Mosis: V.6a hat „nicht aktiv-funktionalen, sondern passiven Sinn". Zusammen mit V.5bβ beschreibt er „Stand und Würde", die Israel von Gott her zukommen sollen.[27] Gelegentlich wird V.6a auch als Ablehnung des besonderen Priestertums gelesen.[28] Eine Verbindung verschie-

---

24 H. Wildberger, Jahwes Eigentumsvolk (AThANT 37), Zürich 1960, 7ff.80ff.95ff, bes. 82.

25 S.o. Anm. 14.

26 So nach dem Vorgang von H. Holzinger, Exodus (KHC 2), Tübingen u.a. 1900, 67, H. Groß, Weltherrschaft als religiöse Idee im Alten Testament (BBB 6), Bonn 1953, 23f; vgl. 66.127; Noth, Das zweite Buch Mose, 126; H.-J. Kraus, Das heilige Volk. Zur alttestamentlichen Bezeichnung 'am qadoš, in: Freude am Evangelium. FS Alfred de Quervain, München 1966, 50–61, hier 58–60; A.R. Hulst, Art. גּוֹי/עַם, THAT 2 ([2]1979) 290–325, hier 313f; R. Rivard, Pour une relecture d'Ex 19 et 20; analyse sémiotique d'Ex 19,1–8, ScEspr 33 (1981) 335–356; H.F. Fuhs, Heiliges Volk Gottes, in: J. Schreiner (Hg.), Unterwegs zur Kirche. Alttestamentliche Konzeptionen (QD 110), Freiburg 1987, 143–167, hier 158 und – mit besonderem Nachdruck – Barbiero, mamleket kōhǎnîm, 11–27 sowie mit feministischer Zuspitzung T.E. Fretheim, „Because the whole earth is mine". Theme and narrative in Exodus: Interp. 50 (1996) 229–239, hier 236: „All the people of God, not just the (male) clergy, are given this vocation, to function among the nations as a priest functions in worship, as mediators of God's blessing (cf. Isa. 43:21). This is a strike against any form of (male) clericalism". Zuletzt hat G. Vanoni (Wer ist König? Untersuchungen zum Nominalsatztyp von Exodus 19,6a, in: „Wer darf hinaufsteigen zum Berg JHWHs?" Beiträge zur Prophetie und Poesie des Alten Testaments. FS Sigurd O. Steingrimsson (ATS 22), St. Ottilien 2002, 333–339) in explizitem Anschluss an Fuhs dafür plädiert, die Verbindung מַמְלֶכֶת כֹּהֲנִים als eine Funktionszuweisung zu verstehen.

27 Mosis, Aufbau, 24f; vgl. auch B. Renaud, La théophanie du Sinaï Ex 19 – 24. Exégèse et théologie (CRB 30), Paris 1991, 150. – Üblicherweise versteht man das כי zu Beginn von V.5bβ kausal und zieht den Teilvers im Gefolge von M zu V.5abα. Dagegen deutet R. Mosis das כי explikativ, verbindet V.5bβ mit V6a und liest beide Teilverse als antithetischen Parallelismus (Aufbau, 14–17): „D.h.: Mir gehört zwar die ganze Erde. Aber ihr sollt mir als priesterliches Königreich und heiliges Volk gehören". Vgl. auch T.B. Dozeman, God on the Mountain. A Study of Redaction, Theology and Canon in Exodus 19 – 24 (SBL.MS 37), Atlanta 1989, 94–96. Der Vorschlag hat den Vorzug, den Einsatz von V. 6 mit adversativem ואתה erklären zu können. Gleichwohl ist damit noch nicht über den Sinn von V.6a entschieden. Zur Frage des Verhältnisses von V.5bβ und V.6a vgl. auch A. van der Kooij, A Kingdom of Priests: Comments on Exodus 19:6: The Interpretation of Exodus. FS Cornelis Houtman. Contributions to Biblical Exegesis and Theology 44, Leuven u.a. 2006, 171–179, der darauf beharrt, daß V.6 nach V.4 (אתם) und V.5 (ועתה) mit eigenem Thema neu einsetzt.

28 J.E. Park, Exodus (IntB 1), New York / Nashville 1952, 972 (mit Verweis auf Jer 31,34); F. Crüsemann, Die Tora. Theologie und Sozialgeschichte des alttestamentlichen Gesetzes, München 1992, 417; W. Oswald, Israel am Gottesberg. Eine Untersuchung zur Literargeschichte der vorderen Sinaiperikope Ex 19 – 24 und deren historischem Hintergrund (OBO 159), Fribourg und Göttingen 1998, 164ff; vgl. auch E. Schüßler-Fiorenza, Priester für Gott. Studien zum Herrschafts- und Priestermotiv in der Apokalypse (NTA NF 7), Münster 1972, 143–151: Die „Unmittelbarkeit und Nähe Israels zu

dener, durch die Forschungsgeschichte vorgegebener Aspekte vertritt gegenwärtig wieder J.B. Wells. V.6a beschreibt „a status and a standard and a function." „Israel is unique", „belongs to God", „must live for God" und „must relate to others", und zwar als Repräsentant und Mittler von Gottes Gegenwart.[29]

Die Deutung ist jedoch nicht ohne Widerspruch geblieben. Nach
anderer Auffassung ist die constructus-Verbindung ממלכת כהנים als
genitivus subjectivus, genauer als genitivus of agency[30] zu verstehen.
Er bildet mit גוי קדוש kein Hendiadyoin, sondern einen Merismus oder –
wiederum in der Sprache der Poetik – keinen synonymen, sondern
einen synthetischen parallelismus membrorum, der konkretisiert, wie
Israel als Eigentum JHWHs unter den Völkern verfasst sein soll: als
Hierokratie oder – bei stärkerer Verbindung des Begriffs ממלכה mit der
Vorstellung des Königtums Gottes – als sakrale Theokratie.[31]

Jahwe bedarf keiner Mittlerinstitutionen, weder der königlichen noch der priesterlichen" (150).

29 God's Holy People. A Theme in Biblical Theology (JSOT.S 305), Sheffield 2000, 56f.

30 Waltke/O'Connor 9.5.1b.

31 So nach Erwägungen Holzingers, Exodus, 67 („*ein von Priestern geleitetes Gemeinwe-
sen, eine Hierokratie*" [Hervorhebung im Original]) dezidiert W. Caspari, Das priesterliche Königreich, ThBl 8 (1929) 105–110: „Ihr müsst mir die (?) aus Priestern gebildete
Regierung und heilige Nation werden" (107). „Im Alten Testament gibt es kein allgemeines Priestertum der Gläubigen. Jedem Testament das Seine!" (108). Ihm schloss
sich G. von Rad an (Das formgeschichtliche Problem des Hexateuch [1938], in: ders.,
Gesammelte Studien zum Alten Testament (TB 8), München 41971, 9–86, hier 47f). In
der ersten Hälfte des 20. Jh. eher eine Minderheitsmeinung wird die Deutung ab 1960
häufiger vertreten. Vgl. W. Beyerlin, Herkunft und Geschichte der ältesten Sinaitradi-
tionen, Tübingen 1961, 85; W.L. Moran, A Kingdom of Priests, in: J.L. McKenzie
(Hg.), The Bible in Current Catholic Thought, New York 1962, 7–20; R. van de Walle,
An Administrative Body of Priests and a consecreated People – Exod. 19,6: IJT 14
(1965) 57–72; A. Cody, A History of Old Testament Priesthood (AnBib 35), Rom
1969, 178.192; A. Deissler, Das Priestertum im Alten Testament. Ein Blick vom Alten
zum Neuen Bund, in: ders., Der priesterliche Dienst I (QD 46), Freiburg u.a. 1970, 69f;
N. Lohfink, Bundestheologie im Alten Testament. Zum gleichnamigen Buch von Lo-
thar Perlitt (1973), in: ders., Studien zum Deuteronomium und zur deuteronomistischen
Literatur I (SBAB 8), Stuttgart 1990, 325–361, hier 355 („*in nucleo* eine Definition der
Verfassung der späten Jerusalemer Tempelgemeinde: Von Priestern ausgeübte Herrschaft und heiliges Staatsvolk"); H. Cazelles, „Royaume de prêtres et nation consacrée"
(Exode XIX,6) (1976), in: ders., Autour de l'Exode. Études (SBi), Paris 1987, 289–294;
D. Muñoz Léon, Un reino de sacerdotes y una nación santa, EstBib 37 (1978) 149–212,
bes. 163; (H. Ringgren /) K. Seybold (/ H.-J. Fabry), Art. מֶלֶךְ, ThWAT 4 (1984) 926–
957, hier 941; A. Schenker, Drei Mosaiksteinchen: „Königreich von Priestern", „Und
ihre Kinder gehen weg", „Wir tun und wir hören" (Exodus 19,6; 21,22; 24,7) (1996), in:
ders., Recht und Kult im Alten Testament (OBO 172), Fribourg und Göttingen 2000,
90–103; ders., „Ein Königreich von Priestern" (Ex19,6). Welche Priester sind gemeint?,
IKZ 25 (1996) 483–490; ders., Besonderes und allgemeines Priestertum im Alten Bund.
Ex 19,6 und Jes 61,6 im Vergleich, in: Pfarrei in der Postmoderne? Gemeindebildung in
nachchristlicher Zeit. FS Leo Karrer, Freiburg 1997, 111–116; van der Kooij, Kingdom,
171–179. Eine Modifikation dieser Deutung vertrat Fohrer. ‚Priesterliches Königtum':
Ex 19,6a besage, „daß Jahwe eine heilige, ihm geweihte *Nation* mit einem priesterli-

In neuerer Zeit sucht man den Sinn der Prädikationen ממלכת כהנים und גוי קדוש aus den seit längerem erkannten Beziehungen ihres unmittelbaren Kontexts V.3b–8 zum Bundesschluss 24,3–8 zu erheben. Die bedingte Verheißung 19,5f, die die Sinaiperikope programmatisch eröffnet, deutet den Bundesschluss, der mit dem Blutritus V.6.8a an den Blutritus der Priesterweihe 29,20f; Lev 8,22f erinnert, als Konsekration Israels.[32] Innerhalb dieser Deutung kehrt allerdings die oben skizzierte Alternative im Verständnis von Ex 19,6a wieder. So fasst E. Blum V.6a als Hendiadyoin auf und plädiert in explizitem Anschluss an A. Dillmann[33] für ein konkretes Verständnis: „Ohne Frage, in dieser Situation am Sinai *ist* Israel tatsächliche eine ממלכת כהנים, ein גוי קדוש.“[34] Dage-

---

chen Königtum bzw. *König* schaffen wird. Wie der *gój* – die verfasste und regierte Nation – heilig, ausgesondert, gottgeweiht sein wird, so der jeweilige Herrscher priesterlich, d.h. heilig in gesteigerter Weise und in hervorragendem Maße: ‚Und ihr werdet mir ein priesterlich(-heiliger) König (bzw. ein priesterlich-heiliges Königtum) und eine heilige Nation sein'" (152). Widersprüchlich äußert sich J.L. Ska, Exode 19,3b–6 et l'identité de l'Israel postexilique, in: ders., Studies in the Book of Exodus. Redaction – Reception – Interpretation (BEThL 126), Leuven 1996, 289–317, bes. 301.303f; vgl. ders., Ex 19,3–8 et les parénèses deutéronomiques, in: Biblische Theologie und gesellschaftlicher Wandel. FS Norbert Lohfink, Freiburg u.a. 1993, 307–314.

32 E. Blum, Studien zur Komposition des Pentateuch (BZAW 189), Berlin / New York 1990, 51f im Anschluss an E. Ruprecht, Exodus 24,9–11 als Beispiel lebendiger Erzähltradition aus der Zeit des babylonischen Exils, in: Werden und Wirken des Alten Testaments. FS Claus Westermann, Göttingen / Neukirchen-Vluyn 1980, 138–173, hier 167; aufgenommen von C. Dohmen, Der Sinaibund als Neuer Bund nach Ex 19 – 34, in: E. Zenger (Hg.), Der Neue Bund im Alten. Zur Bundestheologie der beiden Testamente (QD 146), Freiburg u.a. 1993, 51–83, hier 72: „Durch die ‚Voraussetzung' von Ex 19,5f wird der Blutritus des Bundesopfers in Ex 24,8 neu interpretiert, und zwar vom Blutritus der Priesterweihe ... her, so daß auf diese Weise Ex 24,8 nur noch insofern ‚Bundesschlussritus' ist, als das Volk in Erfüllung der Verheißung von Ex 19,5f nun geheiligt wird." Vgl. auch G. Steins, Priesterherrschaft, Volk von Priestern oder was sonst? Zur Interpretation von Ex 19,6, BZ 45 (2001) 20–36, hier 28ff. Eine im Ansatz verwandte Auffassung vertritt auch E. Otto, Die nachpriesterschriftliche Pentateuchredaktion im Buch Exodus, in: M. Vervenne (Hg.), Studies in the Book of Exodus. Redaction – Reception – Interpretation (BEThL 126), Leuven 1996, 61–111, hier 78ff; ders., Das Deuteronomium im Pentateuch und Hexateuch. Studien zur Literaturgeschichte von Pentateuch und Hexateuch im Lichte des Deuteronomiums (FAT 30), Tübingen 2000, 70f. 19,3b–9 (!) kündigt an, was sich 24,1–11 vollzieht: „Auf der Basis des von Mose verschrifteten Bundesbuches wird das Volk als heiliges Bundesvolk zur Priesterschaft geweiht, wobei die Jungen als Priester amtierend das Opfer darbringen, während die Ältesten und Führer des Volkes den Gott Israels schauen und vor seinem Angesicht ein Mahl halten" (Pentateuchredaktion, 82; vgl. auch ders., Kritik der Pentateuchkomposition, ThR 60 [1995] 175). Zum Vorschlag, Ex 19,9 zu V.3b–8 hinzuzunehmen, s.u. S. 44.

33 Dillmann, Studien, 51 Anm. 22.

34 Ebd., 52 (Hervorhebung im Original). Vgl. auch Steins, Priesterherrschaft, der ממלכת כהנים jedoch „als Metapher für die am Sinai konstituierte Beziehung zwischen Gott und Israel" liest (31; im Original kursiv). Darüber hinaus entdeckt Steins „in kanonischer Lektüre" Beziehungen zu Tritojesaja: „Die positive Gestaltung des Verhältnisses Israels

gen deutet E. Otto V.6a als Merismus und „amphibolische" Präfiguration des besonderen Priestertums[35], mithin als Verfassungsentwurf: Der
Halbvers „definiert ... die ideale nachexilische Tempelgemeinde"[36].

II

Ursachen dieses Dissenses sind die Bedeutungsbreite des Lexems
ממלכה sowie die semantische Multifunktionalität der constructus-
Verbindung im Hebräischen. Die Abstraktbildung ממלכה ist
„(zusammen mit *malkût*) der gängigste Ausdruck für die monarchische
Staatsform"[37] und kann „Königreich, Königtum, Königswürde,
Königsherrschaft" bedeuten. Dasselbe gilt für das Lexem ממלכות, das
wohl eine aus ממלכה und מלכות gebildete Mischform darstellt.[38] Rein
lexikalisch läßt sich im Blick auf Ex 19,6a keine Klarheit gewinnen.[39]
Die constructus-Verbindung lässt sich – isoliert betrachtet – sowohl als
genitivus attributivus („ein königliches Priestertum"[40]), als genitivus
qualitatis („ein priesterliches Königtum oder Königreich"[41]), als
genitivus generis („ein Königreich, das aus Priestern besteht"[42]), als
genitivus objectivus („ein [nämlich Gottes] Königtum über [ein Volk]
von Priester[n]"[43]) oder als genitivus subjectivus („ein Königreich, das
von Priestern regiert wird"[44]) deuten. Lässt sich Ex 19,6a angesichts
dieser Schwierigkeiten überhaupt auf ein Verständnis festlegen?
    Auszuschließen ist zunächst die jüngste der drei Deutungen. 19,3b–
8 ist zwar – das ist seit langem erkannt – auf den Bundesschluss 24,3–8
bezogen und sucht ihn zu interpretieren[45], jedoch kaum im Sinne einer
Konsekration Israels. Liest man den Zusammenhang in der vorgeschla-

---

zu den Völkern ... wird in Ex 19 nicht näher bestimmt. ... Die Leerstelle wird ... gefüllt
durch einen größeren Abschnitt des Jesajabuches (Kap. 60 – 62)" (33f). Eine „Leerstelle" tut sich allerdings nur dann auf, wenn man den Horizont des Textes überdehnt, indem man an ihn die Frage heranträgt: „Israel ist separiert von den Völkern – aber wo-
zu?" (33).

35 Otto, Pentateuchredaktion, 77 mit Anm. 76.
36 Otto, Deuteronomium, 71.
37 Seybold, ThWAT 4,941.
38 Ebd., 942.
39 „Der Grundfehler vieler Deutungsversuche von Ex 19,6 liegt einfach in den isolierend-
    lexikalischen Beutezügen, die nicht viel eintragen" L. Perlitt, Bundestheologie im Alten
    Testament (WMANT 36), Neukirchen-Vluyn 1969, 175.
40 S.o. Anm. 14.
41 S.o. Anm. 14.
42 S.o. S. 36 mit Anm. 15.
43 S.o. S. 36 mit Anm. 16.
44 S.o. S. 38.
45 S.u. S. 47.

genen Weise, wäre bereits Folge der Absichtserklärung des Volkes „wir wollen tun" (19,8; vgl. 24,3.7) und des Bundesschlusses, was nach 19,5 erst Folge der Bewährung des zugesicherten Bundesgehorsams sein kann: „Wenn ihr wirklich auf meine Stimme hört und meinen Bund bewahrt, dann ...".[46] Diejenigen, die die bedingte Verheißung 19,5f dem Bundesschluss 24,3–8 vorangestellt haben, hätten sich mithin in einen fundamentalen Widerspruch verwickelt.

Die Deutung bereitet auch im Detail erhebliche Probleme. a) Zwischen dem Blutritus 24,6.8a (R[JE]?) und dem Ritus der Priesterweihe 29,20f (P[S]) besteht zwar insofern eine Gemeinsamkeit, als ein Teil des Opferblutes auf Menschen übertragen wird, während der Rest am Altar verbleibt. Beide Rituale sind aber ansonsten sehr verschieden[47], wobei 24,6.8a im Alten Testament ohne Analogie ist.[48] Außerdem fehlen sprachliche Bezugnahmen, die es nahelegen, 24,6.8a von 29,20f her zu lesen.[49] b) Würde 24,3–8 tatsächlich die Weihe Israels zu einem „Königreich von Priestern" schildern, widerspräche der Abschnitt der Unterscheidung zwischen Mose und Aaron, der Priesterschaft und dem Volk in Ex 19,20b–25, dem Vorrang, den 24,1f Mose vor den Vertretern der Priesterschaft und den Ältesten als Repräsentanten des Volkes einräumt und schließlich der Einsetzung des besonderen Priestertums 29,20f; Lev 8,22f. Da E. Otto diesen Widerspruch selbst sieht, ist er zu der Annahme gezwungen, daß Ex 19,6 lediglich eine „amphibolische" Präfiguration jener Differenzierung zwischen Priesterschaft und Volk darstellt[50], die in 24,1f wie ein „Vorzeichen vor der Klammer" aufgenommen und dann in der Folge realisiert wird[51]. Diese Annahme ist jedoch am Wortlaut nicht mehr ausweisbar. Außerdem: Ursache für die Rücknahme des allgemeinen Priestertums sei das Versagen des Volkes in seinem – auf 32,1ff vorausweisenden – Zurückweichen vor Gott 20,18.[52] Der Erzählzug „das Volk erbebte und blieb von Ferne stehen"

---

46   „Das perfektische ‚meinen Bund bewahren' fügt dem imperfektischen ‚auf meine Stimme hören' kein selbständiges, weiteres Moment hinzu, sondern explifiziert lediglich das zuerst Gesagte" (Mosis, Ex 19,5b.6a, 6 Anm. 19 im Anschluss an D. Michel, Tempora und Satzstellung in den Psalmen, Bonn 1960, 90–99).

47   Vgl. zuletzt M. Konkel, Sünde und Vergebung. Eine Rekonstruktion der Redaktionsgeschichte der hinteren Sinaiperikope (Exodus 32 – 34) vor dem Hintergrund aktueller Pentateuchmodelle, Theol. Hab.schr. Bonn 2006, 339f (im Druck für FAT).

48   Dies gilt nach gegenwärtiger Quellenlage auch im Blick auf Israels Umwelt. Analogien finden sich allenfalls bei den vorislamischen Arabern. Vgl. W. Beyerlin, Herkunft und Geschichte der ältesten Sinaitradition, Tübingen 1961, 46 (Lit.!). – Zur Intention des Blutritus im Rahmen des Bundesschlusses Ex 24,3–8 vgl. W.H. Schmidt, Exodus, Sinai und Mose (EdF 191), Darmstadt ³1995, 88f; ders., Wort und Ritus. Beispiele aus dem Alten Testament, PTh 74 (1985) 68–83, hier 72–76.

49   Konkel, Sünde, 340: „Für den berühmten ‚Erstleser' kommt eine Bezugnahme auf die Riten der Priesterweihe nicht in Betracht, weil ihm diese erst in Ex 29; Lev 8 begegnen. Aber auch für den mit der priesterlichen Kultterminologie vertrauten Leser ist die Bezugnahme auf die Riten der Priesterweihe nicht möglich, da die Differenzen zwischen den Ritualen eine Identifikation nicht zulassen."

50   S.o. S. 40 mit Anm. 35.

51   Otto, Pentateuchredaktion, 80.

52   Ebd., 82f.

wird jedoch in 20,20 positiv gewertet. Indem das Volk Abstand hält, beweist es Gottesfurcht und besteht damit die Prüfung, der es unwissentlich von Gott unterzogen wurde.[53]

Auch die Deutung von V.6a als Hendiadyoin oder synonymen Parallelismus lässt sich ausschließen. Sie kann sich zwar darauf berufen, daß ממלכה und גוי sowohl in poetischen Texten[54] als auch in (gehobener) Prosa[55] promiscue gebraucht werden und das Stilmittel des Hendiadyoin gleich mehrfach im unmittelbaren Kontext begegnet[56], erklärt aber nicht die singuläre Formulierung. Sie bleibt unterbestimmt – erst Recht in einem Kontext, der von der Einsetzung des besonderen Priestertums erzählt. Tatsächlich ergibt sich anderes Bild, wenn man mit Adrian Schenker[57] in die semantische Analyse der Lexeme ממלכה und מלכות ihre Funktionalisierung im status constructus einbezieht. Als nomen regens bedeuten ממלכה oder ממלכות stets „Königtum" oder „Königreich", während das nomen rectum den Inhaber der königlichen Gewalt nennt.[58] Bei suffigierten Formen wird auf ihn verwiesen.[59] Ausnahmen bilden lediglich 1 Sam 15,28 und 24,21. An beiden Stellen handelt es sich nicht um einen genitivus subjectivus, sondern um einen genitivus objectivus. Gemeint ist die Königsherrschaft über Israel. Wahrscheinlich ist dies auch in Mi 4,8 der Fall.[60] Angekündigt wird die Restauration der davidischen Herrschaft über Jerusalem.[61] Das Verständnis der constructus-Verbindung in Ex 19,6a als genitivus objectivus ist jedoch

---

53 Zu Ex 20,18–21 vgl. A. Graupner, Der Elohist. Gegenwart und Wirksamkeit des transzendenten Gottes in der Geschichte (WMANT 97), Neukirchen-Vluyn 2002, 126–129.152–154; ders., Vom Sinai zum Horeb oder vom Horeb zum Sinai? Zur Intention der Doppelüberlieferung des Dekalogs, in: Verbindungslinien. FS Werner H. Schmidt, Neukirchen-Vluyn 2000, 85–101, hier 94–98; ders., Die zehn Gebote im Rahmen alttestamentlicher Forschung. Anmerkungen zum gegenwärtigen Stand der Forschung: H. Graf Reventlow (Hg.), Weisheit, Ethos und Gebot. Weisheits- und Dekalogtraditionen in der Bibel und im frühen Judentum (BThSt 43), Neukirchen-Vluyn 2001, 61–95, hier 88–91.

54 Jes 13,4; Jer 51,20.27; Nah 3,5; Zeph 3,8; Ps 46,7; 79,6; 102,23; 105,13 = 1 Chr 16,20.

55 1 Kön 18,10; 2 Chr 32,15; Jes 60,12; Jer 1,10; 18,7.9; 27,8; Ez 29,15; 37,22; vgl. Jer 28,8 („Länder und Königreiche").

56 Vgl. „Haus Jakob ‖ Israeliten" und „sagen ‖ kundtun" in V.3b, die Aufnahme und Weiterführung des Perfekts ראיתם V.4aα durch die beiden parallelen Narrative ואשא und ואבא in V.4b, die Zweizahl sich gegenseitig erläuternder Bedingungssätze in V.5a sowie „antworten ‖ sagen" in V.8aα und dazu Mosis, Ex 19,5b.6a, 21 mit Anm. 63.

57 Schenker, Mosaiksteinchen, 93–96.

58 Num 32,33; Dtn 3,4.10.13; Jer 27,1; 28,1; 2 Chr 13,8; 21,4.

59 Gen 10,10; 20,9; 1 Sam 13,13.14; 2 Sam 3,28; 5,12; 7,12.16; 1 Kön 9,5; Jes 9,6; 1 Chr 29,30; vgl. auch die Formulierung wie „der Thron / die Tage seines Königtums" Dtn 17,18; 2 Sam 7,13 bzw. Dtn 17,20.

60 Zum Anschluss des rectum durch die Präposition ל s.o. Anm 14.

61 Vgl. H.W. Wolff, Dodekapropheton 4. Micha (BK XIV/4), 90.96f; Kessler, Micha, 200f.

durch die Satzkonstruktion ausgeschlossen: „Ihr sollt mir als Königtum über Priester gehören" ergibt wenig Sinn.

Der Befund bestätigt sich, wenn man die Verwendung von ממלכה im status constructus Plural hinzunimmt. Der Plural begegnet zum einen in der geprägten Wendung „alle (die) Königreiche der Erde"[62] wie ihren Abwandlungen „alle Königreiche der Länder"[63] / „alle (die) Königreiche der Völker"[64], zum anderen in Verbindung mit Toponymen als nomina recta, die die jeweiligen Königreiche namentlich identifizieren oder geographisch eingrenzen.[65] Singulär ist die Formulierung „Königreiche der Götzen" Jes 10,10. Wie der Kontext V.9 zeigt, handelt es sich um eine ironisch-pejorative Bezeichnung für Kalne, Karkemisch, Hamat, Samaria und Damaskus. Sie werden als Königreiche verspottet, in denen Götzen herrschen.

Der Befund zeigt: ממלכת כהנים ist als genitivus subjectivus zu verstehen und bedeutet „ein Königreich, das von Priestern regiert wird".[66] Zusammen mit der Bestimmung Israels zu einem גוי קדוש „heiligen Volk" bildet er ein Verfassungsprogramm, das die Israel verheißene Sonderstellung innerhalb der Völkerwelt als JHWHs „Eigentum" konstitutionell konkretisiert. Daß man Ex 19,6 tatsächlich so verstanden hat, zeigen antik-jüdische Rezeptionen, allen voran die Septuaginta, wie Arie van der Kooij in diesem Band zeigt.[67]

Die wegen der Quellenlage schwierige und komplexe Frage, ob das Verfassungsprogramm Ex 19,6 in persischer Zeit Wirklichkeit war[68] oder nicht[69], lässt sich hier nicht diskutieren.[70] Nur: Als Argument gegen die Semantik

---

62 Dtn 28,25; 2 Kön 19,19; Jes 23,17; 37,16.20; Jer 15,4; 24,9; 25,26; 29,18; 34,1.17; Ps 68,33; Esr 1,2 = 2 Chr 36,23.

63 1 Chr 29,30; 2 Chr 17,10; 20,29; vgl. 2 Chr 12,8 („den Dienst der Königreiche der Länder").

64 Hag 2,22; 2 Chr 20,6.

65 Jer 49,28 („die Königreiche von Hazor"); Jer 51,27 („die Königreiche von Ararat, Minni und Aschkenas"); Ps 135,11 („alle Königreiche Kanaans"); vgl. auch Jer 1,15 („alle Geschlechter der Königreiche des Nordens").

66 Der Einwand von Steins, Priesterherrschaft, daß ממלכת כהנים im Unterschied zu allen anderen Genitiv-Verbindungen mit ממלכה / ממלכות als nomen regens nicht determiniert ist, greift zu kurz, da er den ausschlaggebenden Vergleichspunkt, die Funktionalisierung des Lexems im status constructus, nicht betrifft. Im übrigen dürfte der Umstand, daß ממלכת כהנים nicht determiniert ist, durch den Merismus resp. synthetischen (nicht: synonymen!) Parallelismus erzwungen sein: „ein Königreich von Priestern und ein heiliges Volk". Außerdem hält die Verbindung durch die Meidung der Determination die Möglichkeit einer hierarchischen Unterscheidung innerhalb der Priesterschaft offen.

67 S.u. S. 89–98. Vgl. auch ders., Kingdom, 171–179.

68 So Schenker, Königreich, 484.

69 So Steins, Priesterherrschaft, 26f im Gespräch mit A. Schenker.

70 Zum Problem der Verfassung der Provinz Jehud in nachexilischer Zeit vgl. aus der Fülle der Literatur S. Grätz, Das Edikt des Artaxerxes. Eine Untersuchung zum religionspolitischen und historischen Umfeld von Esra 7,12–26 (BZAW 337), Berlin / New York 2004, 266ff, bes. 279–283; M. Bernett, Polis und Politeia. Zur politischen Organisation Jerusalems und Jehuds in der Perserzeit, in: St. Alkier / M. Witte, Die Griechen

taugt sie nicht. Außerdem sei angemerkt, daß man sich m.E. für die Möglichkeit offenhalten muß, daß das Programm nicht mehr aus der Perserzeit, sondern bereits aus frühhellenistischer Zeit stammt oder erst in hellenistischer Zeit realisiert wurde.

III

Ex 19,3b–8 unterbricht zusammen mit V.9 den Zusammenhang zwischen V.3a.10 JE und ist darum – das ist weithin Konsens – ein Einschub.[71]

Strittig ist lediglich, ob die erste Hälfte von V.9 noch zu V.3b–8 hinzuzunehmen ist[72], V.9 insgesamt von derselben Hand wie V.3b–8 stammt[73], V.9 bereits eine Vorgabe für V.3b–8 darstellte[74] oder ein noch jüngerer Nachtrag ist[75]. Da der Vers mit Moses Beglaubigung ein neues Thema anschlägt und durch das Stilmittel der Wiederaufnahme in den Zusammenhang eingebunden wird[76], dürfte letzteres der Fall sein.[77]

Weitgehende Einigkeit besteht auch darüber, daß Diktion und Metaphorik von V.3b–8 das Deuteronomium bereits voraussetzen.[78]

---

und das antike Israel, Fribourg 2004, 73–129, außerdem den Sammelband O. Lipschits / M. Oeming (Hg.), Judah and the Judeans in the Persian Period, Winona Lake, Ind. 2006.

71 A. Jülicher, Die Quellen von Exodus 7,8 – 24,11, JPTh 8 (1881) 79–127.272–315, hier 306ff; Baentsch, Exodus – Leviticus – Numeri, 172; W. Rudolph, Der „Elohist" von Exodus bis Josua (BZAW 68), Berlin 1938, 41f; M. Noth, Überlieferungsgeschichte des Pentateuch, Darmstadt 21960, 33 Anm. 112; ders., Das zweite Buch Mose, 124.126f; Beyerlin, Herkunft, 15f; Perlitt, Bundestheologie, 167–181; J.C. Gertz, Tradition und Redaktion in der Exoduserzählung. Untersuchungen zur Endredaktion des Pentateuch (FRLANT 186), Göttingen 2000, 226; Graupner, Elohist, 116–118. Anders J. van Seters, The Life of Moses. The Yahwist as Historian in Exodus – Numbers, Louisville 1994, 248, der für die Einheitlichkeit von V.2–11 plädiert, sich dabei aber auf die kaum ursprüngliche Lesart von G in V.3 stützen muß. Zu V.3 G vgl. Graupner, Elohist, 118 Anm. 432.

72 Noth, Das zweite Buch Mose, 124.126f; aufgenommen von E. Zenger, Die Sinaitheophanie. Untersuchungen zum jahwistischen und elohistischen Geschichtswerk (FzB 3), Würzburg 1971, 59.

73 Blum, Studien, 47; Otto, Kritik, 172; ders., Pentateuchredaktion, 76 Anm. 68; ders., Deuteronomium, 71.

74 Rudolph, „Elohist", 41f; Perlitt, Bundestheologie, 168.

75 F.-L. Hossfeld, Der Dekalog (OBO 45), Fribourg und Göttingen 1982, 189; C. Levin, Der Dekalog am Sinai, VT 35 (1985) 165–191, hier 185.

76 Vgl. V.9b mit V.8b.

77 Gertz, Tradition, 226f; Graupner, Elohist, 118.

78 Baentsch, Exodus – Leviticus – Numeri, 171f; Noth, Das zweite Buch Mose, 126 u.v.a. Die in der Forschungsgeschichte gelegentlich vertretene Auffassung, daß Ex 19,3b–8 ein aus vormonarchischer Zeit stammendes Traditionsstück darstellt (Wildberger, Jahwes Eigentumsvolk, 10–14; Moran, Kingdom, 20) oder zumindest vordeuteronomisch ist (D.E. Skeweres, Die Rückverweise im Buch Deuteronomium [AnBib 79], Rom

Typisch dtr sind die Wendungen „auf JHWHs Stimme hören"[79] und „den Bund bewahren"[80]. Dasselbe gilt für die Beschreibung der Sonderstellung Israels unter den Völkern mit Hilfe der Vorstellung, daß Israel JHWHs סגלה „Eigentum" ist[81], und die Vorstellung, daß Israel JHWHs „heiliges Volk" ist oder werden soll[82]. Die Metapher, daß JHWH Israel in der Wüste „auf Raubvogelschwingen" getragen hat, scheint den Vergleich Dtn 32,11 aufzunehmen.[83]

1979, 115–117.176–178), wird gegenwärtig nur noch vereinzelt vertreten. Vgl. etwa T.D. Alexander The Composition of the Sinai Narrative in Exodus XIX 1 – XXIV.11, VT 49 (1999) 2–20, hier 20. Zur Forschungsgeschichte vgl. insbesondere A. Reichert, Der Jehowist und die sogenannten deuteronomistischen Erweiterungen im Buch Exodus: Diss. theol. Tübingen 1972, 121–146; Ska, Exode 19,3b–6, 289f.

79   Dtn 4,30; 13,5.19; 15,5; 26,14.17; 27,10; 28,1f.15; negiert, d.h. im Rahmen der Anklage 8,20; 9,23; 28,45–62; im Rahmen der Hoffnung 30,2.8.10.20.

80   Dtn 7,9.12; Dtn 29,8 („die Worte des Bundes"); vgl. 1 Kön 8,23; 11,11; ferner die durchweg postdeuteronomischen (spät- und nachexilischen) Belege Ps 78,10; 103,18; 132,12; Ez 17,14; Dan 9,4; Neh 1,5; 9,32; 2 Chr 6,14.

81   Dtn 7,6; 14,2; 26,18; vgl. außerdem Ps 135,4; Mal 7,6.

82   Dtn 7,6; 14,2.21; 26,19; 28,9; vgl. 23,15; ferner 33,3.

83   Üblicherweise übersetzt man נשֶׁר im Gefolge von G ($\dot{\alpha}\epsilon\tau\acute{o}\varsigma$) und V (aquila) mit „Adler", jedoch kaum zu Recht. Der mit נשֶׁר bezeichnete Raubvogel ist Mi 1,16 zufolge kahlköpfig, Hi 39,29f und Spr 30,17 zufolge ein Aasfresser (vgl. auch KTU 1.19 I 132; 1.19 II 57; ferner 1.18 IV.20.30 und dazu K. Reiterer, Falknerei in Ugarit, UF 22 [1990] 271–278, hier 278). Darum liegt eine Identifikation mit dem Gänsegeier (gypus fulvus) näher. Vgl. T. Kronholm, Art. נשֶׁר, ThWAT 5 (1986) 680–689, hier 682f (Lit.!). Allerdings paßt die Beschreibung אֲשֶׁר־לוֹ הָרִקְמָה „der bunte (Federn) hat" Ez 17,3.7 weder zum Adler noch zum Gänsegeier. Da eine befriedigende Erklärung für diese Charakterisierung bislang nicht gefunden ist (vgl. W. Zimmerli, Ezechiel [BK XIII/1], Neukirchen-Vluyn ²1979, 379), lässt die Übersetzung offen, um welche Raubvogelart es sich handelt. Die Wiedergabe mit $\dot{\alpha}\epsilon\tau\acute{o}\varsigma$ in G dürfte widerspiegeln, daß der Adler im ptolemäischen Ägypten das Emblem königlicher Macht schlechthin war. – Die Metapher in Dtn 32,11 kann man naturkundlich nicht erklären. „No ornithologist has ever been able to verify the above mentioned behaviour of the eagle or the vulture" (H.G.L. Peels, On the Wings of the Eagle [Dtn 32,11]. An Old Misunderstanding, ZAW 106 [1994] 300–303, hier 300); vgl. K. Koenen, „Süßes geht vom Starken aus" (Ri 14,4). Vergleiche zwischen Gott und Tier im Alten Testament: EvTh 55 (1995) 174–197, 180; S. Schroer, „Im Schatten deiner Flügel". Religionsgeschichtliche und feministische Blicke auf die Metaphorik der Flügel in den Psalmen, in Ex 19,4; Dtn 32,11 und in Mal 3,20, in: „Ihr Völker alle, klatscht in die Hände!". FS Erhard S. Gerstenberger (Exegese in unserer Zeit 3), Münster 1997, 296–316, hier 301 Anm. 10. Dies gilt erst recht für Ex 19,4. Handelt es sich um eine durch den Kontext angeregte ad hoc-Bildung, die „the idea of God's watchful protection (‚eagle's wings') with the idea of God's careful leading (‚carrying')" verbindet, dabei betonen will, "that God's protection of Israel is not local or incidential but mobile and permanent" (Peels, a.a.O., 302; ähnlich Koenen, a.a.O., 181), oder nicht doch um ein Mythologem? P.C. Craigie (Deuteronomy [NICOT], Grand Rapids, Mich. 1976, 381 Anm. 30) verweist auf Zl. 38–46 des Lugalbanda-Epos, jedoch kaum zu Recht. Eine entfernte Parallele bietet allenfalls Zl. 65–66: „einen lebenden Wildstier hielt er (sc. Anzu) in seinen Fängen / einen toten Wildstier trug er auf seinem Nacken" (Übersetzung nach C. Wilcke, Das Lugalbandaepos, Wiesbaden 1969, 69; vgl. TUAT III/3, 514). Sehr viel näher liegt es, an Aufnahme und Abwandlung eines Hauptmotivs des im Alten Orient populären Etana-Epos zu denken. Etana steigt

Setzt V.3b–8 außerdem bereits die Priesterschrift voraus?[84] Die bislang dafür vorgetragenen Argumente bleiben entweder mehrdeutig oder sind wenig überzeugend[85]. Ist aber ein Verfassungsentwurf wie der in V.6a formulierte innerhalb einer Sinaiperikope, die noch keine Kultgesetzgebung unter Einschluss der Einsetzung des (besonderen) Priestertums umfasst, überhaupt sinnvoll? Aus dem Deuteronomium lässt sich ein solcher Entwurf jedenfalls nicht gewinnen.

Zu dieser Erwägung stimmt die Beobachtung, daß die Bedingung V.5aβ „wenn ihr meinen Bund bewahrt" ihre engste Parallele im Tetrateuch in der an Abraham gerichteten Mahnung zum Bundesgehorsam Gen 17,9aα.10a hat, die bereits eine Interpretation darstellt und eine Mischung dtr und priesterschriftlicher Sprache aufweist[86]:

> „Meinen Bund sollst du halten, du und deine Nachkommenschaft nach dir, Generation um Generation ..." (V.9)

Tatsächlich erfüllt der Einschub Ex 19,3b–8 in mehrfacher Hinsicht interpretatorische Funktion, wobei er teilweise weitgespannte Beziehungen herstellt und divergente Konzeptionen zu integrieren sucht. Eine – noch grobe – Skizze:

a) V.3b–8 eröffnet, einem Proömium vergleichbar, die Sinaiperikope und ordnet ihrem ursprünglichen Thema, der Theophanie (V.2b.3a. 4–20 JE; vgl. 24,1.2a.15b.16.17.18aα P), und dem Thema „Stiftung des Kultes", das in priesterschriftlicher Konzeption die Sinaiperikope ex-

---

ausgebreitet auf Rücken und Schwingen eines Adlers (*sēru*) zum Himmel auf (späte, neuassyrische, Fassung Tafel IV, Zl. 17ff.85ff; TUAT.E S. 49.50; vgl. mit anderer Aufteilung der Tafeln M. Haul, Das Etana-Epos. Ein Mythos von der Himmelfahrt des Königs von Kiš, Göttinger Arbeitshefte zur Altorientalischen Literatur 1 [2000] 195–197.203–205).

84   Vgl. Lohfink, Bundestheologie, 355f; H. Cazelles, Alliance du Sinai, Alliance de l'Horeb et renouvellement de l'alliance, in: Beiträge zur alttestamentlichen Theologie. FS Walther Zimmerli, Göttingen 1977, 69–79; P. Weimar, Die Berufung des Mose. Literaturwissenschaftliche Analyse von Exodus 2,23 – 5,5 (OBO 32), Fribourg und Göttingen 1980, 148 Anm. 17; 343f Anm. 24; Hossfeld, Dekalog, 186; Dohmen, Sinaibund, 70–72.76f; H.-C. Schmitt, Die Suche nach der Identität des Jahweglaubens im nachexilischen Israel. Bemerkungen zur theologischen Intention der Endredaktion des Pentateuch (1995), in: ders., Theologie in Prophetie und Pentateuch. Gesammelte Schriften (BZAW 310), Berlin / New York 2001, 255–276, hier 261f; Otto, Kritik, 172; ders., Pentateuchredaktion, 76ff; ders., Deuteronomium, 71; Ska, Ex 19,3b–6, 304ff in Aufnahme und Zuspitzung der Einschätzung von Ex 19,3b–8 durch Perlitt, Bundestheologie, 175 als spät-deuteronomistischer Text, der bereits durch „priesterliche und exilisch-prophetische Strömungen" beeinflusst ist.

85   Vgl. Graupner, Elohist, 117f Anm. 431.

86   K. Grünwaldt, Exil und Identität. Beschneidung, Passa und Sabbat in der Priesterschrift (BBB 85), Frankfurt a.M. 1992, 27ff; H. Seebass, Genesis. II/1. Vätergeschichte I (11,27 – 22,24), Neukirchen-Vluyn 1997, 111f; vgl. Gertz, Tradition, 227f; ZAR 1 (1995) 155–159, bes. 157.

klusiv bestimmte, das Thema „Bundesgehorsam" vor und über.[87] In postdtr Perspektive ist das Hauptthema der Sinaiperikope die Verpflichtung des Volkes auf den Gehorsam gegen die Willensoffenbarung JHWHs als Bedingung für die Sonderstellung Israels unter den Völkern als Eigentum JHWHs.

b) V.3b–8 weist mit der bedingten Verheißung V.5 wie der Bereitschaftserklärung des Volkes zum Gehorsam V.8 auf den Bundesschluss 24,3–8 voraus und sucht das Verhältnis von Verpflichtung (V.3.7) und Bundesschluss (V.6.8) zu bestimmen, das in 24,3–8 noch offen bleibt: Auf JHWHs Stimme hören (שמע בקל 24,7; 19,5aα) heißt seinen Bund bewahren (שמר את־ברית V.5aβ). Aus dem Nebeneinander von Verpflichtung und Bundesschluss wird ein Ineins. Darin liegt eine nicht unerhebliche Verschärfung, theologisch gesprochen: eine Vergesetzlichung des Bundesbegriffs. Während ברית „Bund" in 24,8 begriffliche Fassung der Gemeinschaft von Gott und Volk ist, die durch den zweiseitigen Blutritus zur Darstellung gebracht wird und durch die Verpflichtung des Volkes auf Gottes Willensoffenbarung flankiert wird, verstehen die Bearbeiter ברית „Bund" als Inbegriff der unbedingten Inanspruchnahme Israels durch den Gotteswillen.[88]

Darf man dabei die Formulierung 19,5aα („wenn ihr auf meine Stimme hört") wörtlich nehmen? Dann wäre sie ein Hinweis darauf, daß die Bearbeiter bei der Israel verpflichtenden Willensoffenbarung Gottes in erster Linie an den Dekalog 20,1–17 denken; denn nur er wird Israel unmittelbar – ohne Moses Vermittlung – offenbart.[89]

Allerdings bleibt der Vorrang der Zuwendung Gottes durch den Rückblick auf Herausführung und Führung durch die Wüste 19,4 gewahrt.

c) Die Bearbeiter nehmen aus dem Deuteronomium die Zusage der Erwählung Israels zum Eigentumsvolk JHWHs auf (7,6; vgl. 14,2.21), unterstellen sie jedoch ihrer Konzeption des Bundes entsprechend der Bedingung des Gehorsams gegen Gottes Willensoffenbarung: Nur[90] wenn das Volk auf JHWHs Stimme hört und seinen Bund bewahrt, wird es JHWHs Eigentum unter allen Völkern sein. Anders formuliert:

---

87 Zur Theophanie als ursprünglichem Thema der Sinaiperikope vgl. Graupner, Elohist, 146–149; ders., Sinai, 91 Anm. 20.

88 Dass Ex 19,3b–8 derselben Redaktionsschicht wie 24,7 angehört (L. Schmidt, Israel und das Gesetz. Ex 19,3b–8 und 24,3–8 als literarischer und theologischer Rahmen für das Bundesbuch, ZAW 113 [2001] 167–185; Konkel, Sünde, 338f), ist m.E. darum eher unwahrscheinlich.

89 Vgl. dazu W.H. Schmidt / H. Delkurt / A. Graupner, Die zehn Gebote im Rahmen alttestamentlicher Ethik (EdF 281), Darmstadt 1993, 25; Graupner, Sinai, 85f; Konkel, Was hörte Israel am Sinai? Methodische Anmerkungen zur Kontextanalyse des Dekalogs, in: C. Frevel / M. Konkel / J. Schnocks (Hg.), Die Zehn Worte. Der Dekalog als Testfall für die Pentateuchkritik (QD 212), Freiburg u.a. 2005, 11–42.

90 Vgl. die Verstärkung des Prädikats durch den Inf. abs.: אם־שָׁמוֹעַ תִּשְׁמְעוּ.

Israels Sonderstellung unter den Völkern als Eigentum JHWHs realisiert sich erst im Bundesgehorsam. Dieses Verständnis ist bereits in
einer jüngeren Gestalt des Deuteronomiums angebahnt.[91]

Außerdem konkretisieren die Bearbeiter Israels Sonderstellung in
einem Verfassungsprogramm. Als „Eigentum" oder „Krongut" JHWHs
„unter allen Völkern" soll Israel als Hierokratie verfasst sein. Auf diese
Weise verbindet die Bearbeitung dtn / dtr Erbe mit der priesterschriftlichen Konzeption Israels als kultisch verfasster „Gemeinde" (עֵדָה) oder
„Versammlung" (קָהָל). Anders formuliert: Als Proömium der Sinaiperikope bindet Ex 19,3b–8 die an ihr ursprüngliches Thema, die Theophanie, angeschlossenen Themen der Willensoffenbarung Gottes und
der Kultstiftung zusammen. Israels Sonderstellung unter den Völkern
als Eigentumsvolk JHWHs realisiert sich im Bundesgehorsam und gewinnt ihre konstitutionelle Gestalt in der Leitung des Volkes durch die
Priesterschaft.[92]

Daneben kann man V.6a auch als Vorblick auf das Heiligkeitsge-
setz lesen: „Ihr sollt mir als Heilige gehören, denn heilig bin ich, JHWH,
und habe euch aus den Völkern ausgesondert, damit ihr mir gehört"
(Lev 20,26).

d) Blickt Ex 19,3b–8 nicht nur auf den Bundesschluss 24,3–8 voraus, sondern auch auf den Bundesschluss Gen 17 P zurück, um Väter-
bund und Sinaibund miteinander zu verbinden? Der Einsatz der bedingten Verheißung Ex 19,5f mit einer Formulierung, die streng geurteilt
den Bestand des Bundes bereits voraussetzt, und die Gemeinsamkeit in
der Formulierung zwischen V.5 und der Interpretation des Abraham-
bundes Gen 17,9aβb.10a legen dies nahe.[93] Damit stellt sich freilich die
Frage, wie sich die Bearbeitung das Verhältnis zwischen Väter- und
Sinaibund vorstellt. Darf man vermuten: Die Bearbeitung versteht Vä-
ter- und Sinaibund komplementär: Zum Bundeszeichen der Beschneidung, das durch 17,9aβb.10a bereits als Gebot interpretiert wird, tritt
Israels Verpflichtung auf Gottes Willensoffenbarung.

e) Blicken die Bearbeiter mit Ex 19,3b–8 nicht nur innerhalb des
Pentateuch zurück und voraus, sondern sogar über seinen Rand hinaus?

---

91 Vgl. Dtn 26,18f; 28,9 und jeweils U. Rüterswörden, Das Buch Deuteronomium (NSKAT
    4), Stuttgart 2006 z.St.

92 Das Programm einer Hierokratie als konstitutionelle Konkretisierung der Sonderstel-
    lung Israels unter den Völkern mag insbesondere aus protestantischer Perspektive we-
    nig verlockend erscheinen. Daß man dies im antiken Judentum ganz anders sehen konn-
    te, führt A. van der Kooij vor (s.u. S. 89–98).

93 W. Groß, Zukunft für Israel. Alttestamentliche Bundeskonzepte und die aktuelle Debat-
    te um den Neuen Bund (SBS 176), Stuttgart 1998, 131f im Anschluss an Dohmen, Si-
    naibund, 76; vgl. Gertz, Tradition, 228.

Nicht ausgeschlossen ist, daß V.5.8 das Urteil 2 Kön 18,11f hinterlegen möchten[94]:

(11) Und der König von Assur führte Israel gefangen nach Assur fort ..., (12) weil sie auf JHWHs Stimme, ihres Gottes, nicht gehört und seinen Bund übertreten hatten, (nämlich) alles, was Mose, der Knecht JHWHs, geboten hatte. Sie haben nicht gehört und nicht (danach) getan."

Jedenfalls sind mit den sprachlichen Oppositionen Ex 19,5aα / 2 Kön 18,12aα („nur wenn ihr auf meine Stimme hört" / „sie haben nicht auf JHWHs Stimme gehört"), Ex 19,5aβ / 2 Kön 18,12aβ „([nur wenn] ihr meinen Bund haltet" / „sie haben seinen Bund übertreten") und Ex 19,8aβ / 2 Kön 18,12bβ („alles, was JHWH geredet hat, wollen wir tun" / „sie haben nicht [danach] getan") sowie der sachlichen Entsprechung zwischen dem Erzählzug Ex 19,7 und 2 Kön 18,12aγ erhebliche Gemeinsamkeiten gegeben, die die Vermutung nahelegen, daß Ex 19,3b–8 bereits die Abfolge von Pentateuch und Deuteronomistischem Geschichtswerk voraussetzt und beide ursprünglich selbständige Literaturwerke zu verklammern sucht.

---

94 Konkel, Sünde, 343.345 in Aufnahme und Korrektur einer These von E. Aurelius, Zukunft jenseits des Gerichts. Eine redaktionsgeschichtliche Studie zum Enneateuch (BZAW 319), Berlin / New York 2003, 96ff.208ff.

Moses' Last Day

von Udo Rüterswörden

"These be the words which Moses spake unto all Israel on this side Jordan in the wilderness" – this is the beginning of the book of Deuteronomy in the King James version. Although the form "spake" sounds very nice in the ears of a linguist with diachronic interests, the translation is not correct. The American Standard version reads: "These are the words which Moses spake unto all Israel beyond the Jordan in the wilderness". The hebrew text reads: בְּעֵבֶר הַיַּרְדֵּן – so the author of Deut 1,1–5 is not on the same side of the Jordan together with Moses. On the contrary, Moses is on the other side, beyond the Jordan.[1]

Consequently the narrator of these five verses is not identical with the figure of Moses in Deuteronomy. We hear the voice of the omniscient narrator, a voice to be heard in the whole Pentateuch and the deuteronomistic history. Deuteronomy is not the final address of Moses, but it contains it; we have some elements of narration, which form the container of Moses' address.

If we take a closer look, we will see that we do not have one address, may be in several parts, but several addresses, that are interrupted by some activities of Moses. Since Kleinerts Study from 1872,[2] Deuteronomy presents itself as a string of four Mosaic speeches, each introduced by a superscription:[3]

Deut 1,1:   These be the words which Moses spake unto all Israel on this side Jordan.

Deut 4,44–45: And this is the law (הַתּוֹרָה) which Moses set before the children of Israel.

1   L. Perlitt, Deuteronomium (BK V/1), Neukirchen-Vluyn 1990, 10.
2   P. Kleinert, Das Deuteronomium und der Deuteronomiker. Untersuchungen zur alttestamentlichen Rechts- und Literaturgeschichte, Bielefeld und Leipzig 1872, 167.
3   N. Lohfink, Der Bundesschluss im Land Moab. Redaktionsgeschichtliches zu Dt 28,69 – 32,47, in: idem, Studien zum Deuteronomium und zur deuteronomistischen Literatur I (SBAB 8), Stuttgart 1990, 53–56; G. Braulik, in: E. Zenger u.a., Einleitung in das Alte Testament, Stuttgart 2004, 138.

Deut 28,69:   These are the words of the covenant, which the LORD
                   commanded Moses to make with the children of Israel
                   in the land of Moab, besides the covenant which he
                   made with them in Horeb.

Deut 33,1:   And this is the blessing, wherewith Moses the man of
                   God blessed the children of Israel before his death.

These superscriptions are not on the same level. Deut 1,1 is the superscription for a unit that ends in chapter 32.[4] Deut 32,45+46 reads: "And
Moses made an end of speaking all these words to all Israel: And he
said unto them, Set your hearts unto all the words which I testify among
you this day, which ye shall command your children, to observe to do,
all the words of this law." Moses' addresses in their whole extension
are called "words", דברים, but there seems to be a special unit in these
"words", called "this law", הַתּוֹרָה הַזֹּאת.

According to our system of superscriptions, such a unit containing
the Torah would begin in Deut 4,44–45. Deut 28,69 is more a subscrip-
tion to chapter 28 than a superscription[5], and Deut 33,1 is also an introduction to a shorter part of Deuteronomy, whereas the first two superscriptions introduce longer parts of Deuteronomy.

Normally, Deuteronomy is divided along these superscriptions into
four main speeches, but this is not the whole truth. I would count 14
mosaic addresses, a number that would enjoy Norbert Lohfink and
Georg Braulik, because they look for structures that are built up with
the number seven and its multipliers, the septuples.

These addresses are to be found in:

Deut 1,1ff.
Deut 4,44ff.
Deut 27,1ff.
Deut 27,9ff.

---

4   According to S.R. Driver, A Critical and Exegetical Commentary on Deuteronomy
     (ICC), Edinburgh ³1902, 381, Deut 32,44 is a "concluding notice respecting the Song" –
     Vv. 45–47 are to be understood as "Moses' final exhortation to Israel to obey the Deu-
     teronomic law" (382).
     כָּל־יִשְׂרָאֵל in V. 45 alludes to the beginning of Deuteronomy in Deut 1,1 (382). There
     seems to be a close correspondence between Deut 1,1 and 32,45:
     Deut 1,1: אֵלֶּה הַדְּבָרִים אֲשֶׁר דִּבֶּר מֹשֶׁה אֶל־כָּל־יִשְׂרָאֵל
     Deut 32,45: וַיְכַל מֹשֶׁה לְדַבֵּר אֶת־כָּל־הַדְּבָרִים הָאֵלֶּה אֶל־כָּל־יִשְׂרָאֵל
     Cf. L. Perlitt, Deuteronomium, 8. E. Otto, Das Deuteronomium im Pentateuch und
     Hexateuch (FAT 30), Tübingen 2000, 191–196 follows a different approach. I doubt
     that שִׂימוּ לְבַבְכֶם לְכָל־הַדְּבָרִים אֲשֶׁר אָנֹכִי מֵעִיד בָּכֶם הַיּוֹם in V. 46 refers only to ch. 32;
     the use of כל and היום makes it clear that a much longer address is meant.
5   Cf. H.U. Steymans, Deuteronomium 28 und die adê zur Thronfolgeregelung Asarhad-
     dons (OBO 145), Freiburg/Schweiz, Göttingen 1995, 197–201.

Deut 27,11ff.
Deut 28,1ff. with its subscript in 28,69
Deut 29,1ff.
Deut 31,1ff.
Deut 31,7ff.
Deut 31,9ff.
Deut 31,24ff.
Deut 31,30ff.
Deut 32,44ff.
Deut 33,1ff.[6]

The persons Moses addresses are not identical, in most of the cases it is Israel, but also Joshua, the priests and the elders. All these activities take place in one day, "in the fortieth year, in the eleventh month, on the first day of the month", as Deut 1,3 tells. To this date and place, in Moab, the final section of Deuteronomy is related (Deut 32,48ff.):

> "And the LORD spake unto Moses that selfsame day, saying, Get thee up into this mountain of Abarim, unto mount Nebo, which is in the land of Moab, that is over against Jericho; and behold the land of Canaan, which I give unto the children of Israel for a possession: And die in the mount whither thou goest up."

Moses' communication unfolds within a unity of time and within a unity of space.[7] These two unities, of time and space, are in accordance with the theories of classical antiquity – even although one day is too short for all of Moses' activities, these unities lend Deuteronomy the accent of ancient drama.
The unity of time is echoed by the use of "today" (היום or היום הזה) throughout Deuteronomy. The terms occur about 60 times in the book, even in its legal parts, in 13,19 15,5.15 19,9. Mostly the formulation is אֲשֶׁר אָנֹכִי מְצַוְּךָ הַיּוֹם, with a variation in 15,15.
According to Jean-Pierre Sonnett, Deuteronomy makes the most of the "showing" mode of Biblical poetics.

> "The distinction between 'telling' and 'showing' has been highlighted by Wayne Booth in his *Rhetoric of Fiction*. It originates in earlier views, such as this remark by J. Warren Beach: Authors like Thackeray, or Balzac, or H.G. Wells ... are always *telling* the reader what happened instead of showing them the scene, telling them what to think of the characters rather than letting the reader judge for himself or letting the characters do the telling about one an-

---

6   Sifre ad loc. counts ten words of Mose; the reconstruction by D. Hoffmann follows this outline, D. Hoffmann, Das Buch Deuteronomium I, Berlin 1913, 12.
7   J.-P. Sonnet, The Book within the Book. Writing in Deuteronomy (Biblical Interpretation Series 14), Leiden et alii 1997, 34.

other. I like to distinguish between novelists that *tell* and those [...] who *show*."[8]

An example for this kind of showing can be taken from Deut 29:

"Dramatic speech, which unfolds without the support of narrative comments, has its own way of occupying the represented stage. In Deuteronomy 29–30, for instance, most of the situational parameters of Moses' speech are found in the speech itself (see 29:9, 'You stand this day all of you before YHWH your God: the heads of your tribes, your elders, and your officers, all the men of Israel,' etc.). No narrator elaborates the details of the scene; they are provided in the speech itself. Throughout Deuteronomy, Moses alludes to the act, and to the fact, of his own communication: 'this Torah,' 'this <book of the Torah>,' 'these words, which I command you this day,' etc. Reading Deuteronomy will involve granting these expressions their full dramatic import. Facing these phrases, Deuteronomy's reader is not primarily dealing with a text that imparts self-referential hints, but with a speaking character, who refers to communication *realia* in a world endowed with time and space. In other words, reading will amount to interpreting the speeches in the world they project."[9]

According to many authors the content of Moses' speeches seems to be clear, it is to be identified with the Torah.[10] But this is only the content of one of 14 speeches, albeit the longest one, which begins in 4,44ff. The term "Torah" is part of the superscription, and this superscription seems to introduce that special part of Deuteronomy, which deals with the Torah. In Deuteronomy, the term "Torah" seems to be self referent. This seems to be confirmed by the use of this term; it is always accompanied not only by the article, but also with the deictic element הזה. The only exception that confirms the rule is to be found in 17,11: "According to the sentence of the law which they shall teach thee, and according to the judgment which they shall tell thee, thou shalt do: thou shalt not decline from the sentence which they shall shew thee, to the right hand, nor to the left." Here the Torah of the central judicial authorities is meant, not Moses' Torah. So the deictic particle is not used.

But what is the relation between Moses' Torah and his second speech? The clue to a correct understanding seems to lie in Deut 1,5: "On this side Jordan, in the land of Moab, began Moses to declare this law, saying" But what is meant by "declare"? The underlying Hebrew term is באר, a term that has undergone a long lasting discussion. In the 18th edition of the Gesenius dictionary we have opted for "verdeutlichen, erklären"[11], a translation, which is also found HAL: "deutlich

---

8   Sonnet, ibid., 13.
9   Sonnet, ibid., 14f.
10 Sonnet, ibid., 3.
11 W. Gesenius, Hebräisches und Aramäisches Handwörterbuch über das Alte Testament unter verantwortlicher Mitarbeit von U. Rüterswörden bearbeitet und herausgegeben von R. Meyer und H. Donner, 18. Auflage, Berlin et alii, 1. Lieferung 1987, 120.

machen, erläutern (ein Gesetz)".[12] This is conventional wisdom[13], since the Vulgate reads "explanare", Targum Onqelos and Neofiti forms of פרש, and the Septuagint διασαφῆσαι "to make explicit, to explain". Mittmanns view[14], which also has been followed in the German Catholic bible called *Einheitsübersetzung*, cannot be sustained; the translation "to write" does not fit the contexts of the Old Testament.[15] This is also true for the new Lohfink-Braulik proposal "to give it legal authority"[16]. There seems to be a trend towards legalistic interpretation, perhaps on a confessional bias, but I do not think, this is a good idea in Deut 1,5.[17] As I said, the versions opt for another direction, the following term לאמר demands a verbum dicendi before it[18] and the other occurencies, in Deut 27,8 and Hab 2,2[19] make this understanding impossible. So it is a good idea to remain with Sonnets proposal to translate this verb with "expound"[20], in German "auslegen".

The consequence ist far-reaching: What follows is the expounding of the Torah, but not the Torah itself.[21] But the question arises: What do we have to understand by an expounded Torah?

An example is Deut 15,1–11; the passage begins with:

"At the end of every seven years thou shalt make a release. And this is the manner of the release: Every creditor that lendeth ought unto his neighbour shall release it; he shall not exact it of his neighbour, or of his brother; because it is called the LORD's release. Of a foreigner thou mayest exact it again: but that which is thine with thy brother thine hand shall release; Save when there shall be no poor among you; for the LORD shall greatly bless thee in the land which the LORD thy God giveth thee for an inheritance to possess it: Only if thou carefully hearken unto the voice of the LORD thy God, to observe to do all these commandments which I command thee this day."

The core of this passage consists of V.1–3[22]; it is expanded by the following verses. From the formal aspect, the core is a law in the third

---

12   L. Köhler / W. Baumgartner, Hebräisches und Aramäisches Lexikon zum Alten Testament I, Leiden et alii 1995, 102.

13   Cf. K. Finsterbusch, Weisung für Israel (FAT 44), Tübingen 2005, 120f.

14   S. Mittmann, Deuteronomium 1,1 – 6,3 literarkritisch und traditionsgeschichtlich untersucht (BZAW 139), Berlin / New York 1975, 14f.

15   Cf. L. Perlitt, Deuteronomium, 22f.

16   N. Lohfink, Prolegomena zu einer Rechtshermeneutik des Pentateuchs, in: idem, Studien zum Deuteronomium und zur deuteronomistischen Literatur V (SBAB 38), Stuttgart 2005, 181–231, here 202–204.

17   Cf. the excellent treatment of Deut 1,5 by E. Otto, Mose, der erste Schriftgelehrte. Deuteronomium 1,5 in der Fabel des Pentateuch, in: D. Böhler et alii (ed.), L'Écrit et l'Esprit (OBO 214), Freiburg, Schw. / Göttingen 2005, 273–284.

18   Cf. Sonnet, The Book within the Book, 31.

19   Otto, Mose, 277ff.

20   Sonnet, The Book within the Book, 31.

21   Sonnet, ibid., 31 n. 17.

person, whereas the expansion is addressed to the second person. Gerhard von Rad took this as a kind of preaching, so he argued, that Deuteronomy was a preached law.[23] In the following discussion the question arose, whether we have any kind of preaching in the Old Testament.[24] But what is meant by preaching? Is it not the application or expounding of a foregoing text?[25] So the verb באר can reflect the special character of Deuteronomy, with its mixture of law and adhortation or parenesis. There must be something in the wording of Deuteronomy that leads to the concept of an expounded Torah.

So what we have now in Deuteronomy is not Moses' Torah, but Moses' expounding of the Torah. Moses' Torah is hidden behind his teaching. In a diachronic reading it is possible to reconstruct laws that lie behind the text of this book by the means of the form-critical or redactional-critic method. But this is not the Torah meant by the expression התורה הזה.

In his stimulating study Jean Pierre Sonnet comes to the conclusion:

"On the other hand, the content of Moses' Torah 'book' is not accessible elsewhere than within Deuteronomy. One could argue that the people (Moses' addressees, once arrived in the land, and their descendants) would know the Deuteronomy's Torah, thanks to its periodical reading and its daily learning – in other words, thanks to channels independent of Deuteronomy. For whomever exists in history, however, as against represented history, the Book of Deuteronomy is the unique channel through which the Torah 'book' may be apprehended. In the readers' world, Moses' Torah 'book' is never 'read' outside of the Book of Deuteronomy. The aim of the inset 'book' – to be read to the sons – is thus fulfilled by the reading of the framing book. Deuteronomy therefore achieves the *tour de force* of enabling its reader to peruse the content of a book which one would assume to be out of the reader's range. The Torah 'book' to which Moses points within Deuteronomy's represented world – 'If you obey the voice of YHWH your God, to keep his commandments and his statutes which are written in this 'book' of the Torah' (30:10); 'Take this 'book' of the Torah' (31:26) – is a record on the narrative scene, and, as such, it is not 'open' (or, rather, 'unrolled') to the eyes of the reader. Elsewhere,

---

22 Cf. T. Veijola, Das 5. Buch Mose. Deuteronomium Kapitel 1,1 – 16,17 (ATD 8/1), Göttingen 2004, 310ff.; U. Rüterswörden, Das Buch Deuteronomium (NSK.AT 5), Stuttgart 2006 ad. loc.

23 G. v. Rad, Deuteronomium-Studien, in: idem, Gesammelte Studien zum Alten Testament II (TB 48), München 1973, 112.

24 D. Mathias, 'Levitische Predigt' und Deuteronomismus. ZAW 96 (1984) 23–49; E. Bons, Art. Predigt, NBL 3 (1997) 164f; U. Rüterswörden, Bemerkungen zu Gerhard von Rad als Ausleger des Deuteronomiums, in: B.M. Levinson / E. Otto (ed.), Recht und Ehik im Alten Testament: Beiträge des Symposiums "Das Alte Testament und die Kultur der Moderne" anlässlich des 100. Geburtstags Gerhard von Rads (1901–1971) Heidelberg, 18–21. Oktober 2001 (Altes Testament und Moderne 13), Münster 2004, 51–55.

25 Cf. the critical remarks by Otto, Mose, 277, n. 14.

such a designation on stage in the character's domain would be the reader's despair – the book becoming inaccessible, as far as its content is concerned, precisely when exhibited. Yet in Deuteronomy the aporia is overcome by the narrative's architectonics. The reader makes his acquaintance with the Torah *as spoken* by Moses, before it is committed to writing. As much as Moses' addressees on stage, the reader finds himself in the know. Far from being an opaque record, 'this 'book'' is fully revealed to all. Deuteronomy's paradox goes even further. Deuteronomy is the *surrogate* of another 'book,' disclosing the content of the latter while not assuming its formal identity. But Deuteronomy does so in being a surrogate *book*. The reader comes to know the Torah as spoken by Moses, but Moses's spoken word is, from the outset, a written word within the book of Deuteronomy. If irony is to be found in Deuteronomy, it is that irony of the unavoidable character of the written form. Deuteronomy makes a powerful virtue of such an ironical necessity."[26]

As a consequence, Moses is not a lawgiver, but a law-interpreter. We have to face the paradoxical situation, that Deuteronomy often refers to "this Torah", Moses' Torah, but it does not tell its wording. Does Torah only exist in the mode of its explanation and application and is Moses its first hermeneutic?

Another question arises from this highly sophisticated presentation of the Torah within the book of Deuteronomy: Is it possible to reconstruct foregoing strata, or did the author take his materials, *Wissensmaterialien*, to form a new entity?

The conventional approach in the exegesis of Deuteronomy is characterized by Sonnet: "That there is in Deuteronomy's represented world an autonomous issue of communication, conditioning the consistency of the work, is not sufficiently emphasized even in modern Deuteronomic studies. These studies favor a hermeneutical, reader-oriented perspective. In this view, the Book of Deuteronomy primarily aims to help its reader face historical and existential challenges by rehearsing the paradigmatic scene of the entry into the land. The situation of Israel in Moab, receiving YHWH's ultimate Torah on the eastern bank of the Jordan river, mirrors the historical and existential situation of the people in exile, called to a new bond with YHWH and to a new 'inheriting' of the land. The book is therefore tailored, in its speeches, legal teaching, and narrative, to fit the hermeneutical task of such a reader. The 'fusion of horizons,' to take over Gadamer's concept, combining the work's semantic proposition and the reader's existential project, represents the achievement of Deuteronomy's purport."[27]

This older paradigm would lead itself to the reconstruction of Vorlagen. The most recent example is the Habilitationsschrift of Ansgar

---

26   Sonnet, The Book within the Book, 260f.
27   Sonnet, ibid., 4.

Moenikes.[28] He defines Moses' Torah in the following way "Die wesentlichen Merkmale der Mose-Tora bestehen darin, daß diese ein
schriftliches Dokument darstellt, das den *göttlichen Gesamtwillen* zum
Ausdruck bringt, der das *menschliche Verhalten* betrifft, aber *keine
Einzel*weisung bzw. *kein Einzel*gebot ist; sie gilt *abstrakt und generell*,
bezieht sich auf eine *unbestimmte Vielzahl von Sachverhalten* und rich-
tet sich an eine *unbestimmte Vielzahl von Personen*, hat von daher *Gesetz*escharakter."[29]

The supposed legal character of Deuteronomy leads Moenikes to
the reconstruction of a form of Deuteronomy in the time of Hezekiah.
The existence of such an older stage is derived from the informations
given by the Books of Kings, by text-external data. The starting point
for his analysis is Deut 6,17 and 28,45. In Deut 6,17 we read:

> "Ye shall diligently keep the commandments of the LORD your God, and his
> testimonies, and his statutes, which he hath commanded thee."

God does not speak in the first person, but an author speaks about God
in the third person; God commands the law, not Moses. Besides these
criteria, one main point is derived from archaeology: Hezekiah only
brought the local sanctuaries to an end – Josia destroyed them. On the
one hand, Moenikes acknowledges the problems of archaeology, on the
other hand, he uses this highly disputable criterion.[30] There is no application of the classical methods of redactional criticism to be found in
Moenikes' book; the laws of Deuteronomy are only tested against these
criteria; texts that fulfill these criteria are supposed to derive from the
time of Hezekiah.

From the standpoint of method, this procedure is problematic, because it applies text-external criteria and it cannot escape the problems
of circular argumentation.[31] Deut 6,17 has an address formulated in
plural and singular; according to most exegetes this verse – as well as
Deut 28,45 – cannot belong to the oldest stratum of Deuteronomy.[32]

---

28   A. Moenikes, Tora ohne Moses. Zur Vorgeschichte der Mose-Tora (BBB 149), Ber-
     lin/Wien 2004.
29   Moenikes, ibid., 45: "The essential characteristics of Moses' Torah are: It is a written
     document, that expresses God's will, his will concerns man's conduct, but it is not an
     individual commandment; the Torah is abstract and general; it refers to a indefinite mul-
     titude of matters and it addresses an indefinite multitude of persons; therefore it has the
     character of a law."
30   Moenikes, Tora ohne Moses, 73f.90.
31   Moenikes, Tora ohne Moses, 183.
32   According to T. Veijola, Deuteronomium, 176f Deut 6,17 is an addition to DtrB; Deut
     28,45 is also late: G. Seitz, Redaktionsgeschichtliche Studien zum Deuteronomium
     (BWANT 93), Stuttgart et alii 1971, 263f.

We may doubt, whether it is appropriate to get criteria for the shaping of *Vorstufen* of the book of Deuteronomy from the deuteronomistic history – but the question remains in the perspective of the omniscient narrator: What happens to Moses' Torah after the end of Deuteronomy and how is it related to the book found in Josiah's times? This question is to be asked not in the historical sense, but in the sense of narration. Or is this question illegitimate, because Deuteronomy is a unit of its own, with its unity of time and place?

„Einen Propheten wie mich wird dir der Herr, dein Gott, erwecken." Der Berufungsbericht Jeremias und seine Rückbindung an das Amt des Mose

von Sebastian Grätz

I. Einführung

Das Jeremiabuch ist von Auseinandersetzungen geprägt. Der Prophet begegnet im Verlauf des Buches zahlreichen offenkundigen Gegnern, die ihm das Leben schwer machen, ihn misshandeln, gefangen setzen und sogar nach dem Leben trachten. Aufgrund der eindeutigen Botschaft des Jeremia, der Beamte, Priester, andere Propheten und sogar Könige kritisiert, erscheint dies auch eine logische Konsequenz zu sein, die den Propheten schließlich zu einer sprichwörtlichen Leidensgestalt werden lässt.[1] Doch das Jeremiabuch ist mehr als eine Wiedergabe der Taten und Worte eines Propheten kurz vor dem Untergang des Staates

---

[1] Die kritische Botschaft des Jeremia findet sich sowohl in den Fremdberichten als auch in den prophetischen Worten des Jeremiabuches. Gerade angesichts der Prosastücke ist die Frage nach einer deuteronomistischen Gestaltung dieser Texte unterschiedlich beantwortet worden. A. Graupner, Auftrag und Geschick des Propheten Jeremia. Literarische Eigenart und Intention vordeuteronomistischer Prosa im Jeremiabuch (BThSt 15), Neukirchen-Vluyn 1991, bspw. vermutet für die Fremdberichte ein hohes Maß an historischer Verlässlichkeit (185), v.a. aufgrund der Kontinuität zu der ursprünglichen prophetischen Botschaft. Diese ist indes nicht leicht zu erheben. Besteht sie, um bei dem Beispiel der Fremdberichte zu bleiben, etwa aus einem Kern unbedingter Gerichtsbotschaft, wie er z.B. im Rahmen der Tempelrede Jer 26,6 begegnet (vgl. Graupner, Auftrag, 47), so kann auch diese Kernbotschaft noch einmal kritisch nach ihrer Herkunft befragt werden, zumal sie im gegenwärtigen Text durch den Anschluss mit *wqatal* (ונתתי) doch einen bedingenden Vordersatz benötigt, der die Gesamtbotschaft dann wieder in das Licht des deuteronomistischen Tat-Folge-Zusammenhangs rücken würde. Hierfür könnte auch die möglicherweise Dtn 28,15ff entlehnte Formulierung des vor aller Augen wirksam werdenden Fluchs (קללה) sprechen. H.J. Stipp, Jeremia im Parteienstreit. Studien zur Textentwicklung von Jer 26,36-43 und 45 als Beitrag zur Geschichte Jeremias, seines Buches und judäischer Parteien im 6. Jahrhundert (BBB 82), Frankfurt a.M. 1992, 17ff, legt eine Analyse von Jer 26 vor, die bereits dem Grundbestand des Kapitels eine deuteronomistische Entstehung zuweist.

Juda. Durch redaktionelle Überarbeitungen bekommt es theologische Schwerpunkte und Ansichten, die z.T. aus der Verkündigung des Jeremia gewonnen, die aber eben auch später, nach dem Tod des Propheten, abgefasst sind und bereits den Untergang des Staates Juda und die Zerstörung des Tempels voraussetzen und deshalb die neu aufkommenden Fragen nach dem „Warum?", dem „Wie geht es weiter?" und nicht zuletzt nach der Bewahrheitung der prophetischen Botschaft zu beantworten suchen.[2] Ein wichtiger Text, der sich der letztgenannten Perspektive widmet, ist der Berufungsbericht Jeremias, der dem Buch gewissermaßen eine perspektivische Einleitung verleiht. Anhand von Jer 1,4–10 soll der Frage nachgegangen werden, inwieweit hier auf ein bestimmtes Mosebild zurückgegriffen wird und mit welcher theologischen Zielsetzung dies geschieht. Es wird dabei deutlich, dass bereits der gestaltete Buchanfang des Jeremiabuches keine biographische oder autobiographische Mitteilung ist, sondern eine theologische Positionserklärung und damit auch eine Perspektive für das gesamte Buch. Diese theologische Positionserklärung soll anhand von drei Beobachtungen zu dem Text Jer 1,4–10 und dessen Rückbindungen an u.a. Texte des Pentateuchs deutlich gemacht und daran anschließend sollen die erzielten Ergebnisse kurz ausgewertet werden.

Der Text Jer 1,4–10, lässt sich aus seinem Zusammenhang als eigener Abschnitt gut ausgrenzen: Die ersten drei Verse des Jeremiabuches sind die Überschrift des Buches, die Informationen über den Propheten und seine Wirksamkeit enthält, ehe in V.4 mit der Wortereignisformel: „Und das Wort des Herrn geschah zu mir" die Berufungsszene eröffnet wird. In V.11 begegnet wiederum die Wortereignisformel, die nun auf die erste Vision des Jeremiabuches hinführt. Das Gliederungsprinzip durch die Wortereignisformel zeigt, dass Jer 1,4–10 zumindest als eigener Abschnitt innerhalb des größeren Zusammenhangs V.4–19 verstanden werden kann, auch wenn in Jer 1,17–19 vor allem auf V.4–10 in vielfacher Weise zurückgreift.[3]

II. Erste Beobachtung

Das Deuteronomium kennt innerhalb seiner Vorstellungen vom Zusammenleben der Israeliten im verheißenen Land vier Ämter, die sich

---

2   In der Stellungnahme zu diesen Fragen liegen sicher auch die Anfänge der Überlieferung der Jeremiatradition begründet. Vgl. Stipp, Jeremia, 287ff.
3   Vgl. S. Herrmann, Jeremia (BK.AT 12), Neukirchen-Vluyn 1986, 43f.48ff. Dass auch der nicht selten als sekundär zu V.4–9 eingestufte V.10 zu der Szene gehört, wird im Rahmen der dritten Beobachtung noch näher begründet.

in den Ämtergesetzen ab Kap. 16,18 finden: die Richter mitsamt ihren Helfern sowie einem zentralen Oberrichter für schwierige Fälle, den König, die Priester und schließlich, mit einem Achtergewicht, den Propheten.

Mose selbst, der das Deuteronomium ja in der ersten grammatischen Person predigend verkündet, ist das Vorbild für diesen Propheten, wie Dtn 18,15 festhält:

> „Einen Propheten wie mich (nämlich Mose) wird dir der Herr, dein Gott, erwecken aus dir und aus deinen Brüdern; auf ihn sollt ihr hören."

Die Lektüre der anderen Ämtergesetze zeigt deutlich einen Unterschied: Weder Priester noch Richter oder selbst der König werden hier in die direkte Nachfolge des Mose gestellt. Dem angekündigten Nachfolger des Mose schuldet man zuallererst Gehorsam – ein Merkmal das dem Königsgesetz bezeichnenderweise abgeht. Der jeweilige Nachfolger wird in eine prophetische Sukzession zu Mose gestellt, wie sie sich als Vorstellung etwa auch im Jeremiabuch (26,5 mit der prononcierten Aufnahme der Wurzel שמע) sowie im Hoseabuch (6,5; 12,11) oder, wohl am signifikantesten, bei den Propheten Elia und Elischa findet (1.Kön 19,19–21).[4] Die Idee der Sukzession macht in Dtn 18,15 auch der hebräische Terminus קום hif. „erstehen lassen" deutlich und ist wahrscheinlich dem Sprachgebrauch der königlichen Dynastiebeschreibung entlehnt. So wird er in der Natanverheißung einer ewigen Dynastie Davids in 2.Sam 7,12 ebenso verwendet wie in der Ankündigung eines neuen Herrschers nach der Ausrottung des Hauses Jerobeam in 1.Kön 14,14. Hinzu treten zahlreiche Ankündigungen des messianischen Herrschers (wie Jer 23,4; Ez 34,23; Sach 11,16), wo קום hif. ebenfalls Verwendung findet.[5] Der Eindruck einer starken Aufwertung des Prophetenamtes – bei gleichzeitiger Depotenzierung des Königtums im Königsgesetz[6] – drängt sich angesichts der Ämtergesetze auf. Es wird daher, wie es sich für eine Sukzession gehört, immer nur ein einziger, *der* Prophet, angekündigt, und man ahnt, welche der vier Amtspersonen die Ämtergesetze in einer zentralen Rolle sehen wollen.

Der zitierte Vers Dtn 18,15 stammt aus einem Teil des Deuteronomiums, der häufig seinem älteren Bestand, dem deuteronomischen, zugerechnet wird.[7] Dieser Bestand hat in der Folge des zitierten Verses eine deuteronomistische Bearbeitung erfahren. Diese Bearbeitung setzt

---

4 Vgl. U. Rüterswörden, Von der politischen Gemeinschaft zur Gemeinde. Studien zu Dt 16,18 – 18,22 (BBB 65), Frankfurt a.M. 1987, 84f.
5 Auch Ex 1,8 mit Bezug auf den ägyptischen König. Vgl. J. Gamberoni, Art. קום, ThWAT VI, 1259–1274, hier 1259f.
6 Vgl. Rüterswörden, Gemeinschaft, 95ff.
7 Vgl. Rüterswörden, ebd., 85ff.

direkt nach V.15 in V.16ff ein und macht durch ein klassisches Kriteri-
um der Literarkritik auf sich aufmerksam: die teilweise Wiederholung
von V.15 in V.18. Hinzu kommt ein Perspektivwechsel ab V.17. V. 18
ist keine Mose-Rede mehr, sondern JHWH-Rede:

> „Ich will ihnen einen Propheten, wie du bist, erwecken aus ihren Brüdern und
> meine Worte in seinen Mund geben (ונתתי דברי בפיו); der soll zu ihnen sagen
> alles, was ich ihm gebiete."

Die Erweiterung gegenüber V.15 im zweiten Teil dieses Verses,
dass dem Propheten nämlich die Worte JHWHs in den Mund gelegt
werden sollen, bildet nun eine eindeutige und in der Forschung längst
erkannte Brücke zum Berufungsbericht Jeremias.[8] Die engste Berüh-
rung mit dem Prophetengesetz besteht sicher in der Formulierung Jer
1,9:

> „Siehe, ich lege/gebe meine Worte in deinen Mund (הני ונתתי דברי בפיך)."

Es scheint also eine Wechselbeziehung zwischen dem bereits deuteronomistisch redigierten Prophetengesetz und der Berufung Jeremias
beabsichtigt zu sein. Hierzu fügt sich auch die Aufnahme des Endes
von Dtn 18,18 (ודבר אליהם את כל אשר אצונו) in Jer 1,7:

> „Alles, was ich dir gebiete, sollst du sagen (ואת כל אשר אצוך תדבר)."

Der Text Jer 1,4–10 zeigt weiterhin Beziehungen zu den sog. Berufungsgeschichten des Mose (Ex 3f) und des Gideon (Ri 6), auf die nun
näher eingegangen werden soll.

III. Zweite Beobachtung

Die Bezeichnung „Berufungsbericht" für Jer 1,4–10 ist aus der Sekun-
därliteratur übernommen und enthält ein gattungskritisches Urteil: Eine
Berufung zu einem besonderen Amt laufe, so die klassische Argumentation, nach einem bestimmten formalen Schema ab. Dieses Schema sei
folgendermaßen auf Jer 1,4–10 übertragbar:

I.   Auftrag (V.5)
II. Einwand (V.6)
III. Abweisung des Einwands (V.7–8)
IV. Zeichen (V.9)[9]

---

8 Vgl. u.a. B. Renaud, Jer 1: Structure et Théologie de la Rédaction, in: P.-M. Bogaert
   (Hg.), Le Livre de Jérémie. Le Prophète et son Milieu, les Oracles et leur Transmission
   (BEThL 54), Leuven ²1997, 177–196, hier 192.
9 Vgl. Herrmann, Jeremia, 44. Das Schema erarbeitet hat W. Richter, Die sogenannten
   prophetischen Berufungsberichte. Eine literaturwissenschaftliche Studie zu 1.Sam 9,1 –
   10,16, Ex 3f und Ri 11b–17 (FRLANT 101), Göttingen 1970, 136ff. Vgl. auch die Ap-

Als weiteres prominentes Beispiel dieser mutmaßlichen Gattung „Berufungsbericht" werden zumeist auch Ri 6 (Gideon) und 1.Sam 9 (Saul) genannt.[10] Es lohnt sich, einen näheren Blick auf die beiden engsten Paralleltexte[11] Ex 3,9–12 und Ri 6,14–21 zu werfen:

Ex 3,9–12	Ri 6,14–21	Jer 1,5–9
I. (9)Weil nun das Geschrei der Israeliten vor mich gekommen ist und ich dazu ihre Not gesehen habe, wie die Ägypter sie bedrängen, (10) so geh nun hin, ich will dich zum Pharao senden, damit du mein Volk, die Israeliten, aus Ägypten führst.	(14) Der Herr aber wandte sich zu ihm und sprach; Geh hin in dieser deiner Kraft; du sollst Israel erretten aus den Händen der Midianiter. Siehe, ich habe dich gesandt	(5) Ich kannte dich, ehe ich dich im Mutterleib bereitete, und sonderte dich aus, ehe du von deiner Mutter geboren wurdest, und bestellte dich zum Propheten für die Völker.
II. (11) Mose sprach zu Gott: Wer bin ich, dass ich zum Pharao gehe und führe die Israeliten aus Ägypten?	(15) Er aber sprach zu ihm: Ach mein Herr, womit soll ich Israel erretten? Siehe, mein Geschlecht ist das Geringste in Manasse, und ich bin der Jüngste in meines Vaters Hause.	(6) Ich aber sprach: Ach, Herr, ich tauge nicht zu predigen; denn ich bin zu jung.
III. (12) Er aber sprach: Ich will mit dir sein.	(16) Der Herr aber sprach zu ihm: Ich will mit dir sein, dass du die Midianiter schlagen sollst wie einen Mann.	(7) Der Herr sprach aber zu mir: Sage nicht: „Ich bin zu jung", sondern du sollst gehen, wohin ich dich sende, und

plikation auf Jer 1,4–9 von W.H. Schmidt, Jeremias Berufung. Aspekte der Erzählung Jer 1,4–9 und offene Fragen der Auslegung, in: W. Zwickel (Hg.), Biblische Welten. FS Martin Metzger (OBO 123), Freiburg (Schweiz) / Göttingen 1993, 183–198.

10   Ausführlich: Richter, Berufungsberichte, 13ff134ff.

11   Der im Zusammenhang eines Berufungsschemas z.T. genannte Text 1.Sam 9,1 – 10,6 ist nach Auskunft von P. Weimar, Die Berufung des Mose. Literarwissenschaftliche Analyse von Exodus 2,23 – 5,5 (OBO 32), Freiburg (Schweiz) / Göttingen 1980, 154ff, nicht von vornherein als Berufungsgeschichte konzipiert gewesen, sondern deuteronomistisch gestaltet. Dieser Text wird hier nicht weiter in die Untersuchung einbezogen.

		predigen alles, was ich dir gebiete. (8) Fürchte dich nicht vor ihnen; denn ich bin bei dir und will dich erretten, spricht der Herr.
IV. Und das soll dir ein Zeichen sein, dass ich dich gesandt habe: Wenn du mein Volk aus Ägypten geführt hast, werdet ihr Gott dienen auf diesem Berge.	(17–21) Zeichen: Feuer aus Fels verzehrt Opfergabe	(9) Und der Herr streckte seine Hand aus und rührte meinen Mund an und sprach zu mir: Siehe ich lege meine Worte in deinen Mund.

Schon der erste Eindruck zeigt die zahlreichen Gemeinsamkeiten der drei Texte, die sich auch am hebräischen Text belegen lassen. Die neben dem Gesamtschema größten und z.T. wörtlichen Übereinstimmungen finden sich unter III., wo das Mitsein (Präp. את od. עם) Gottes/JHWHs mit dem Berufenen ausgedrückt wird. In allen Fällen wird die Sendung des Betroffenen mit dem hebr. Verbum שלח „senden" bezeichnet. Im Folgenden sollen nun die drei Texte unter dem Gesichtspunkt ihrer Gemeinsamkeiten kurz näher betrachtet werden.

1. Ex 3,9–12

In der gegenwärtigen Forschung herrscht wenig Einigkeit über die literarische Herkunft von Ex 3,9–12. Der Gesamtzusammenhang der Moseberufung erstreckt sich über die beiden Kapitel Ex 3,1 – 4,18, deren Literarkritik zu den vieldiskutierten Fragen der Pentateuchexegese zählt; aus diesem Grunde ist nun etwas weiter auszuholen. Die klassische Lösung bietet einen jahwistischen und einen elohistischen Erzählfaden. W.H. Schmidt z.B. weist in seinem Kommentar Ex 3,9–12 der elohistischen Quelle zu[12], was auch in der Verwendung der Gottesbezeichnung אלהים deutlich werde. Diese Position ist in jüngerer Zeit mit

---

12   Vgl. die jüngste ausführliche Untersuchung zur vermuteten elohistischen Pentateuchquelle von A. Graupner, Der Elohist. Gegenwart und Wirksamkeit des transzendenten Gottes in der Geschichte (WMANT 97), Neukirchen-Vluyn 2002, 18ff, die mit der Untersuchung von Ex 3f einsetzt.

teilweise substanziellen Anfragen konfrontiert worden. Gerade das Grundkriterium der Quellenscheidung, der Wechsel der Gottesnamen, bereitet bei der Rekonstruktion von konsistenten Erzählfäden innerhalb des zu besprechenden Passus Schwierigkeiten. In Ex 3,4 wechselt die Gottesbezeichnung unvermittelt, was bereits den um Glättung bemühten antiken Textzeugen aufgefallen ist.[13] Hinzu kommt, dass Ex 3,4b (E) den „Busch" erwähnt, obwohl der „brennende Busch" ein Konzept des Jahwisten ist[14], da der Elohist das Ereignis der Moseberufung am „Gottesberg" (Ex 3,1b) verortet und bis auf Ex 3,4b den „Busch" nicht kennt. Gravierender noch als die teilweise schwierige Rekonstruktion der literarischen Fäden aber sind die Probleme, die sich bei den inhaltlichen Anschlüssen der je rekonstruierten Erzählfäden in das Gesamt der jeweiligen postulierten Quellen ergeben: Die Selbstvorstellung Gottes in Ex 3,6 (E)[15] zielt wahrscheinlich auf eine Tradition, die sich in der Vätergeschichte der Genesis findet[16], die aber für den konkreten Zusammenhang von Ex 3 kaum einen geeigneten literarischen Anknüpfungspunkt bietet. Die Notlage der Israeliten, ausgedrückt in deren „Elend" (עני) und Geschrei" (צעקה) in Ex 3,7.9 wird im Quellenmodell klassisch jeweils J und E zugewiesen. Doch wo ist der Anschlusspunkt für eine entsprechende Situation im vorangehenden Zusammenhang zu finden? Sieht man einmal von Ex 2,23f ab, ein Passus, der der priesterschriftlichen Tradition zugerechnet wird[17], bleibt nur die Beschreibung der Unterdrückung in Ex 1,11–14 übrig.[18] Diese jedoch erfährt in der Geschichte von den Hebammen eine Lösung (Ex 1,20b), wobei diese Geschichte, v.a. durch den redaktionellen Vers 1,22[19], gleichzeitig die Geburts- und Jugendgeschichte des Mose (Ex 2,1–22) vorbereitet, die als solche zumindest nicht explizit auf die Not der Israeliten zielt. Ein terminologischer Anschluss von Ex 3,7b[20] lässt sich hingegen über den seltenen Terminus נגש („bedrängen") nach Ex 5,6.10.13f belegen, so

---

13 Vgl. Graupner, ebd., 19f.
14 Weimar, Berufung, 199ff, rekonstruiert eine eigene „Dornstrauch-Geschichte" in Ex 3,1–6; 4,2–4, die auf der einen Seite einige Spannungen innerhalb von Ex 3 zu lösen vermag, die aber auf der anderen Seite den Berufungsgeschichten nach E und J eine Exposition nimmt.
15 Vgl. Graupner, Elohist, 22.
16 Vgl. Graupner, ebd., 28.
17 Vgl. J.C. Gertz, Tradition und Redaktion in der Exoduserzählung. Untersuchungen zur Endredaktion des Pentateuchs (FRLANT 186), Göttingen 2000, 352ff; vgl. aber K. Schmid, Erzväter und Exodus. Untersuchungen zur doppelten Begründung der Ursprünge Israels innerhalb der Geschichtsbücher des Alten Testaments (WMANT 81), Neukirchen-Vluyn 1999, 193.
18 Vgl. Schmid, Erzväter, 193, der einen Rückbezug von Ex 3,7 auf 2,23f annimmt.
19 Vgl. Graupner, Elohist, 48.
20 Zur Literarkritik von Ex 3,7 vgl. Gertz, Tradition, 284f.

dass diese Passagen wohl zusammenhängend zu interpretieren sind. Da das in Ex 3 berichtete Geschrei der Israeliten aber im vorausgehenden Zusammenhang keinen Haftpunkt – außer an den priesterschriftlichen Versen Ex 2,23f – findet und sozusagen in der Luft hängt[21], dürfte, literaturgeschichtlich betrachtet, eher eine Vorbereitung der erst in Ex 5 entfalteten Problematik der Unterdrückung der Israeliten in Ägypten vorliegen.[22] Schließlich ist zu bedenken, dass Ex 4,19ff die eben erst in Ex 3f erzählten Begebenheiten gar nicht zu kennen scheint, sondern nahtlos an die Flucht des Mose nach Midian und sein dortiges Verweilen in Ex 2,11–20 anschließt.[23] Auch dieser Gesichtspunkt weist darauf hin, dass die Verbindung von Ex 3f mit seinem literarischen Zusammenhang zur Nachfrage Anlass gibt.[24]

Abgesehen von einer möglichen Grunderzählung in Ex 3(f)[25] sind nun diejenigen Passagen für eine Zuordnung des Textes unter den hier interessierenden Gesichtspunkten am signifikantesten, die tatsächlich tendenzkritisch auswertbar sind. So weisen der Zusammenhang Ex 3,7a.8 deuteronomistisches Kolorit auf: Die Vorstellung, des Landes, „darin Milch und Honig fließt", ist ebenso dem deuteronomistischen Vorstellungskreis zuzuordnen wie die Aufzählung der Fremdvölker, die das zu besiedelnde Land noch bewohnen.[26] Diese Beobachtung ist, auch wenn es sich um eine redaktionelle Bearbeitung in Ex 3,8aδ.b handeln sollte, umso wichtiger, als die Deuteronomismen direkt den hier interessierenden Versen Ex 3,9–12 vorausgehen und gleichzeitig mit Ex 3,9(ff) eine Dublette bilden. Die beiden Aussagen haben leicht voneinander abweichende Inhalte: Während der Text Ex 3,7a.8 den Exodus aus Ägypten ankündigt und erst in 3,16f bzw. 3,20f eine Fort-

---

21 Das gilt insbesondere auch im Sinne des Quellenmodells für den elohistischen Stoff, der, für sich betrachtet, seinen nächsten Bezugspunkt in Ex 1,15–20 hat. Vgl. Graupner, Elohist, 42.

22 Vgl. Gertz, Tradition, 337f. Die Herkunft von Ex 3,7a sei dagegen von der vorausschauenden Bearbeitung nicht betroffen.

23 Vgl. E. Blum, Studien zur Komposition des Pentateuch (BZAW 189), Berlin / New York 1990, 20ff, mit der bündigen Zusammenfassung der literarkritischen Argumente.

24 Die Vermutung von M. Noth, Überlieferungsgeschichte des Pentateuch, Darmstadt ²1960, 31f. mit Anm. 103, bei Ex 3,1 – 4,18 handele es sich um einen späteren Einschub in einen vorliegenden jahwistischen Zusammenhang, wird z.B. von Schmid, Erzväter, 186ff, aufgenommen und weitergeführt. Schmid vermutet für die Moseberufung eine späte Entstehung, die bereits auf den priesterschriftlichen Erzählzusammenhang zwischen Genesis und Exodus zurückblicke.

25 Im Rahmen eines jeweiligen redaktionsgeschichtlichen Modells vgl. Schmid, Erzväter, 186ff; Gertz, Tradition, 254ff; R.G. Kratz, Die Komposition der erzählenden Bücher des Alten Testaments. Grundwissen der Bibelkritik, Göttingen 2000, 295ff.

26 Vgl. Weimar, Berufung, 319ff, der der Wendung ארץ זבת חלב ודבש (spät-)deuteronomistische Provenienz zuweist. Für Aufzählung der sechs Völker, die mit den Kanaanäern einsetzt, nimmt Weimar ebenfalls eine spätdeuteronomistische Herkunft an.

setzung findet[27], bereitet Ex 3,9ff zusätzlich die Sendung des Mose zum Pharao und damit auch den Plagenzyklus vor. Da jedoch ein möglicher Zielpunkt von Ex 3,9ff für eine postulierte Pentateuchquelle E im Plagenzyklus kaum zu erheben ist[28], wird man hier am wahrscheinlichsten tatsächlich die redaktionelle Vorbereitung einer nichtpriesterschriftlichen Plagenerzählung zu vermuten haben, die die ursprüngliche Offenbarungsszene in Ex 3, deren Grundbestand wohl in Ex 3,1–8(aα–γ) mit einer Fortsetzung in Ex 3,16f bzw. 3,20f zu finden ist, mit der Sendung des Mose vor den Pharao verbinden soll.[29] Konsequenterweise ist zu folgern, dass die Schilderung von Not und Elend in Ex 3,7a.8aα–γ, die der nichtpriesterschriftlichen Exodusgeschichte einen Anlass gibt, die Einfügung von Ex 3,9–12 mit der initialen Wiederaufnahme der Notlage und dem weiterhin dazugehörigen literarischen Bestand motiviert zu haben scheint. Den erwähnten deuteronomistischen Anteil von V.8 wird man dann sinnvollerweise der Redaktion zuschreiben, die auch für die Einfügung von Ex 3,9ff verantwortlich ist. Dieses vorläufige Ergebnis lenkt das Augenmerk auf den Text aus Ri 6.

2. Ri 6,14–21

Der Text Ri 6,14–21 ist Bestandteil eines größeren literarischen Zusammenhangs, der nach dem deuteronomistischen Richterschema in Ri 6,1–6 in Ri 6,11 einsetzt und mit Ri 6,24 schließt. Eine Grunderzählung lässt sich möglicherweise in V.11a.18.19aα.b.21–24a finden[30], während die eigentliche Berufungserzählung die Perspektive ausweitet. Interessant ist in diesem Zusammenhang die Verbindung der Herausführung Israels aus Ägypten mit seiner Bedrohung durch die Midianiter in Ri 6,13f, die den Eindruck erweckt, ganz Israel sei durch die Midianiter bedroht. Es liegt auf der Hand, dass Ri 6,13f und damit auch die organische Fortsetzung in V.15–18 Gideon als Erretter von ganz Israel analog des Exodusgeschehens präsentieren möchte. Das deuteronomistische Schema in Ri 6,1–6 liefert dafür den Vorbau, wenn auch hier die Perspektive auf ganz Israel liegt und das Geschrei des Volkes zu JHWH

---

27 Möchte man in Ex 3,20 die literarische Fortsetzung von Ex 3,1ff sehen, kann die Zäsur sinnvollerweise erst frühestens mit V.8aγ erfolgen; vgl. Kratz, Komposition, 298ff Gertz, Tradition, 289f, vermutet, der mit Ex 3,7f verlassene Erzählfaden werde in V.16f wieder aufgenommen.

28 Vgl. Gertz, Tradition, 290f; Graupner, Elohist, 70f.

29 Vgl. Kratz, Komposition, 296.

30 Vgl. U. Becker, Richterzeit und Königtum. Redaktionsgeschichtliche Studien zum Richterbuch (BZAW 192), Berlin / New York 1990, 145ff; ähnlich: Kratz, Komposition, 211.

den Abschluss bildet.[31] Hinzu kommt, dass Ri 6,11b mit der unvermittelten Nennung der Midianiter, V.13f (כל זאת) und der Feststellung, dass sich Israel in den Händen der Midianiter befindet, auf eine Bedrohung hinweist, die als bekannt vorausgesetzt wird und damit nur in Ri 6,1–6(10) berichtet sein kann. Aus diesem Grunde fällt es schwer, Ri 6,11b–18 unabhängig von der deuteronomistischen Gestaltung Ri 6,1–6 zu verstehen.[32]

Das in Ri 6 zu findende Zusammenspiel der Motive des Notschreis und der Errettung Israels aus der Hand der Feinde lässt sich auch in Ex 3 finden:

Ri 6,6b	„Da schrien (זעק) die Israeliten zu JHWH"	Ex 3,9a	„Weil denn nun das Geschrei (צעקה) der Israeliten vor mich gekommen ist"
Ri 6,14a	„(...) und er sprach: Geh in deiner Kraft; du wirst Israel aus der Hand Midians erretten."	Ex 3,10	„so geh nun hin, ich will dich zum Pharao senden, damit du mein Volk, die Israeliten, aus Ägypten führst."

Der Ablauf in Ri 6 erscheint plausibel: Die Not der Israeliten führt zur Berufung der Rettergestalt Gideon, der mit der Errettung der Israeliten aus der Hand der Feinde beauftragt wird. Dieses Schema ist typisch für das deuteronomistisch redigierte Richterbuch, wie die Abläufe in Ri 3,7–11; 3,12–30; 4,1–24 zeigen, und es findet sich nun auch partiell in Ex 3,9ff wieder. Im Unterschied zu Ri 6 fehlt jedoch in Ex 3 die Motivation der Berufung des Mose, die in einer Notlage der Israeliten bestehen sollte. Denn, wie gesagt, abgesehen von dem priesterschriftlichen Text Ex 2,23f findet sich im Vorlauf zu Ex 3 keine Schilderung der ägyptischen Bedrängung, auf die der Text dezidiert reagieren könnte. Es hat daher den Anschein, als sei das Motiv des Geschreis in Ex 3 (V.7b.9) topologisch in den Zusammenhang gerückt, um eine Notsitua-

---

31 Die Wiederholung von Ri 3,6 in V.7 signalisiert den Beginn der Erweiterung V.7–10.

32 A. Scherer, Überlieferungen von Religion und Krieg. Exegetische und religionsgeschichtliche Untersuchungen zu Richter 3 – 8 und verwandten Texten (WMANT 105), Neukirchen-Vluyn 2005, 189ff, rekonstruiert mit Ri 6,2b–5 vordeuteronomistisches Material innerhalb von Ri 6,1–6, das dann natürlich einen Ausgangspunkt für Ri 6,11bff liefern könnte. Man kann jedoch fragen, ob erstens mit Ri 6,2b ein sinnvoller erzählerischer Beginn vorliegt und ob zweitens die umfassende Perspektive auf ganz Israel, die durch die Notiz „bis nach Gaza" in V.4a bestätigt wird, für eine vordtr. Rettergeschichte mit entsprechendem Lokalkolorit angemessen ist. Vgl. Kratz, Komposition, 211.

tion analog dem Richterschema zu konstruieren, in die Mose dann als Retter geschickt wird. Dies wird besonders in dem Abschnitt der Mose-berufung Ex 3,9ff deutlich. Der formale Aufbau, die engen literarischen Berührungen und das zugrunde liegende gemeinsame Schema von Not und Errettung sprechen hier für ein literarisches Wechselverhältnis der beiden Texte.[33] Dies scheint umso wahrscheinlicher zu sein, als sich beide Texte bereits fortgeschrittener redaktioneller Arbeit innerhalb von vorgegebenen größeren literarischen Zusammenhängen verdanken: Ex 3,9–12 als vorbereitender und von vornherein unselbständiger Bestand-teil der nichtpriesterschriftlichen Plagenerzählung, die sekundär in die nichtpriesterschriftliche Exoduserzählung eingearbeitet wurde, Ri 6,14ff als Bestandteil der deuteronomistischen Gideon-Erzählung. Ein literarisches Wechselspiel zwischen Ex 3f und Ri 6 lässt sich weiterhin auch in Ex 3,20 und Ri 6,13 mit der gemeinsamen Verwendung des seltenen Begriffs נפלאת im Zusammenhang des Exodusgeschehens sowie der deutlichen Reflexion von Ex 3,8f in Ri 6,8f feststellen. Es hat daher den Anschein, dass beide Abschnitte nicht unabhängig voneinan-der konzipiert und abgefasst worden sind, also wohl auch nicht formge-schichtlich im klassischen Sinne zu erheben sind. Aufgrund des nur angespielten Retterschemas in Ex 3 dürfte der deuteronomistische Zu-sammenhang in Ri 6,1–6.11b–18 der literarische Ausgangsort für die Gestaltung der Szene in Ex 3,9–12 sein. Mose wird damit als charisma-tischer Retter Israels im Sinne des Richterschemas stilisiert.[34]

3. Jer 1,4–10

Dass auch der Text Jer 1,4–10 literarisch mit dem bereits deuterono-mistisch redigierten Deuteronomium verwoben wurde, ist bereits ge-zeigt worden. Auch die Nähe zu den beiden eben beschriebenen Texten ist auffallend. Zunächst weist Jer 1,8 mit der Ankündigung כי אתך אני eine erkennbare Nähe zu Ex 3,12/Ri 6,16 (כי אהיה עמך) auf. Der göttli-che Beistand ist jedoch in Jer 1,8 nicht auf eine Rettungstat eines cha-rismatischen Anführers bezogen, sondern gilt der Person des Propheten als demjenigen, der selbst gerettet (נצל) werden muss. Die Gegnerschaft bleibt vorerst im Dunkel, sie ist nur im enklitischen Personalpronomen in מפניהם enthalten und dürfte, ebenso wie das Moment der Bewahrung Jeremias, in Jer 1,17–19 wiederum reflektiert werden.[35] Die Perspektive

---

33   Vgl. auch Weimar, Berufung, 178.
34   Vgl. a.a.O.
35   Vgl. Herrmann, Jeremia, 79ff.

ist damit die Auseinandersetzung Jeremias mit seinen Gegnern, die erst
in bestimmten Partien des bereits gestalteten Buches, vor allem den
Prosastücken, Konkretion erfährt.[36] Damit erfährt das in Ri 6 grundge-
legte und in Ex 3 bereits abgewandelte Schema hier eine weitere Vari-
ante, die sehr wahrscheinlich auf die Bedürfnisse des Jeremiabuchs hin
adaptiert worden ist. Dass dabei weitere literarische Interdependenzen
vorliegen, zeigen die Anspielungen auf die Berufung des Mose. Innerhalb dem gegenüber dem älteren Bestand in Ex 3 späteren Passus Ex
4,10–16 begegnet in Ex 4,12 eine Ausgestaltung[37] von Ex 3,12 (כי אהיה
עמך), wenn der göttliche Beistand auf das Sprechen hin konkretisiert
wird: ואנכי אהיה עם פיך. Auch in Jer 1,9 wird die göttliche Hilfe auf
das Sprechen hin spezifiziert, indem, wie bereits oben erläutert, auf das
deuteronomistisch redigierte Prophetengesetz zurückgegriffen wird. Es
spricht stark für die wechselseitige Benutzung dieser Texte, wenn bei
diesem Beispiel das literarische Gefälle sehr wahrscheinlich von Jer
1,4–10 nach Ex 4,10–16 verläuft, wie J.C. Gertz gezeigt hat.[38]

Zusammenfassend lässt sich sagen, dass alle besprochenen „Berufungsberichte" Funktionen für größere literarische Zusammenhänge
erfüllen. Der wahrscheinlich älteste Text, Ri 6,11b–18 stammt bereits
aus deuteronomistischer Feder und wendet das Schema von Not und
Rettung auf Israel an. Auf dieses Schema greift auch Ex 3,9–12 zurück,
wenn Mose als Retter Israels vor den Pharao gesandt wird. Die
Notschilderung, die der vorausgehende nichtpriesterschriftliche Zusammenhang nicht bietet, wird mit dem Motiv des notschreienden Volkes
eingeholt, was schriftstellerische Varianz erklärt. Zusätzlich zu dieser
Übereinstimmung im Schema lassen sich auch literarische Berüh-
rungspunkte zwischen den beiden Texten feststellen. Auch der Text Jer
1,4–10 partizipiert an dem ihm – augenscheinlich literarisch bekannten
– Grundschema, wenn göttlicher Beistand in Aussicht gestellt wird.
Weil es nun erstens sehr wahrscheinlich ist, dass Jer 1,4–10 auf das
deuteronomistisch redigierte Prophetengesetz Bezug nimmt und
gleichzeitig auch literarische Affinitäten zu Ex 3f aufweist, dürfte ein
literarischer Rückgriff auf beide Texte im Rahmen einer Rezeption der
Mosetradition zu vermuten sein. Eine Varianz der Vorlagen ergibt sich
für die topische Notsituation in Jer 1,4–10: Die Not betrifft anscheinend
den Propheten selbst, da er vor seinen Gegnern gerettet werden muss.
Die Gegner werden nicht benannt, sie treten erst im Verlauf des

---

36 Vgl. die Zusammenfassung bei Stipp, Jeremia, 294ff.
37 Vgl. Schmid, Erzväter, 205; Gertz, Tradition, 318ff.
38 Vgl. Gertz, Tradition, 318ff.

Jeremiabuches in Erscheinung, was den literarischen Charakter der Berufungsszene unterstreicht.

IV. Dritte Beobachtung

Diese Beobachtung bezieht sich auf Jer 1,5, wo JHWH zu Jeremia spricht:

> „Ich kannte dich, ehe ich dich im Mutterleib bereitete, und sonderte dich aus, ehe du von der Mutter geboren wurdest, und setzte dich zum Propheten für die Völker ein."

Dieser Vers bildet den feierlichen Auftakt der Berufung Jeremias. Auf den ersten Blick scheint der angesprochene Gedanke der Sukzession im Sinne von Dtn 18 bereits hier realisiert zu sein: Der von JHWH ausersehene Prophet in der Nachfolge Moses steht bereits vor seiner eigenen Geburt fest. Der Vers beantwortet damit die in Dtn 18,15 offen formulierte Ankündigung, dass JHWH einen Propheten wie Mose erstehen lassen werde. Doch Jer 1,5 ist noch auf einer anderen Ebene interessant: Er formuliert ein sehr eigenständiges Prophetenbild, das so in Dtn 18 nicht expliziert wird. Zunächst erinnert Jer 1,5a deutlich an Ps 2,7, die Legitimation eines Königs als Sohn Gottes: „Du bist mein Sohn, heute habe ich dich gezeugt." Oder an das zweite Lied des hier königliche Züge tragenden Gottesknechts[39] in Jes 49,1: „Der Herr hat mich berufen von Mutterleibe an, er hat meines Namens gedacht, als ich noch im Schoß meiner Mutter war." Und weiter in Jes 49,5: „Und nun spricht der Herr, der mich von Mutterleib an zu seinem Knecht bereitet hat." In diesem zuletzt genannten Text findet – wie in Jer 1,5 – das hebräische Verbum יצר „formen, erschaffen, bereiten" Verwendung: Der von JHWH Auserwählte ist sein Geschöpf. Wie bereits Ps 2 nahe legt, verweist das Motiv der Geschöpflichkeit oder Zeugung durch JHWH weniger auf das biblische Prophetenbild als vielmehr auf die altorientalische Königsideologie. Dies kann durch zahlreiche Beispiele aus neuassyrischer und neubabylonischer Zeit illustriert werden. So z.B. in den Einleitungen der Prismeninschriften Assurbanipals A und J, der in dieser Hinsicht auch einen besonders sprechenden Namen trägt:

> „Ich, Assurbanipal (Assur ist der Erzeuger des Erbsohnes), Erzeugnis des Assur und der Mulissu (...)."

---

39   Vgl. O. Kaiser, Der königliche Knecht. Eine traditionsgeschichtlich-exegetische Studie über die Ebed-Jahwe-Lieder bei Deuterojesaja (FRLANT 70), Göttingen ²1962, 56f; H.-J. Hermisson, Deuterojesaja (BKAT 11), Neukirchen-Vluyn 2003, 341ff, macht ebenfalls darauf aufmerksam, dass die präexistente Berufung ein Anspruch sei, wie ihn Großkönige geltend machen.

„Ich, Assurbanipal, großer König, [mächtiger König], König der Welt, König von Assyrien, König der [vier Weltsektoren], Erzeugnis der Hände des Assur und der Mulissu (...)"[40]

Die Gottesgeschöpflichkeit des Königs ist ein Topos der Selbstvorstellung altorientalischer Herrscher, der in Jer 1,5a auf den Propheten übertragen ist. Zu der Prädikation eines Königs als göttliches Geschöpf gehört selbstverständlich auch der Nachweis der göttlichen Vollmacht, der sich in den legitimatorischen Tatenberichten der Könige niederschlägt. Diese toposhaften Tatenberichte sind aus dem altorientalischen Raum sehr zahlreich überliefert[41] und auch biblisch belegt: Könige wie Saul, David oder Salomo erringen toposhaft zur Bestätigung ihrer göttlichen Berufung zum König militärische Siege und sorgen gleichzeitig für die Prosperität des Landes (u.a. 1.Sam 11; 2.Sam 5,17ff; 8; 10). Zu der speziellen Gottesgeschöpflichkeit des Erwählten tritt also seine Befähigung in der Ausführung des anvertrauten Amtes, was etwa auch Jer 1,10 nahelegen könnte:

„Siehe, ich setze dich heute über Völker und Königreiche, dass du ausreißen und einreißen, zerstören und verderben sollst und bauen und pflanzen."

Dieser Vers wird in der Forschung gern als gegenüber V.4–9 sekundär eingestuft, weil die Reihe der Infinitive im Jeremiabuch auch als finite Formen andernorts mit dem Subjekt JHWH begegnet (Jer 12,14; 18,7.9; 24,6; 31,28.40; 42,10) und die Gestalt Jeremias so sehr stark in den Vordergrund rückt.[42] Doch dieses Argument hat vor allem dann Gewicht, wenn der Berufungsbericht in seinem Kern auf den Propheten selbst zurückgeführt wird. Ist dieser insgesamt eine spätere literarische Gestaltung, dann sind Vorausgriffe auf das Jeremiabuch und seine Inhalte zu erwarten. Hinzu kommt, dass der Vers, wie gesagt, V.5a in sinnvoller Weise nach dem Schema von (königlicher) Erwählung und Investitur weiterführt, also keinen grundsätzlich neuen Gedanken in den Text einträgt.[43] Denn auch V.10 schildert mit dem Verbum פקד *hif.* + על[44] („Aufsicht führen über") eine Investitur zum Aufseher über Völker und Königreiche, die ebenfalls wenig in das Bild eines Propheten zu

---

40   Übersetzung: R. Borger, Beiträge zum Inschriftenwerk Assurbanipals. Die Prismenklassen A, B, C = K, D, E, F, G, H, J und T sowie andere Inschriften. Mit einem Beitrag von A. Fuchs, Wiesbaden 1996, 208f.

41   Vgl. G. Ahn, Religiöse Herrscherlegitimation im achämenidischen Iran. Die Voraussetzungen und die Struktur ihrer Argumentation (AcIr 31), Leiden/Louvain 1992, 65ff.

42   Vgl. B. Duhm, Das Buch Jeremia (KHC 11), Tübingen, Leipzig 1901, 10, dessen Auffassung, dass Jeremia hier zum „Stellvertreter Gottes auf Erden" werde, nicht wenige Nachfolger gefunden hat.

43   Auch Herrmann, Jeremia, 61, hält die inhaltliche Verbindung von V.5 und V.10 für wahrscheinlich.

44   Vgl. G. André, Art. פקד, ThWAT VI, 708-723, hier 715.

passen scheint.[45] Es wird vielmehr wiederum Königsideologie transpor-
tiert[46], die sich an dem königlichen Amt des erfolgreichen zerstöreri-
schen Kriegsherren, aber auch am Bild des pflanzenden (נטע) Gärtners[47]
orientiert. Bezeichnend ist, dass Jeremia als Subjekt des Geschehens
angesprochen ist, während sonst im Jeremiabuch (Ausnahme Jer 31,40:
passivisch) die zerstörende und aufbauende Tätigkeit eine göttliche ist.
Es erscheint nicht wahrscheinlich, dass hier Jeremia als der „König der
Propheten", wie teilweise vermutet wird[48], vorgestellt werden soll.
Denn diese Bezeichnung benötigte eine weitere inhaltliche Füllung, die
im Alten Testament sonst nicht zu finden ist. Vielmehr dürften auch
hier die Spuren zunächst nach Dtn 18 führen. Im ersten Abschnitt wurde darauf hingewiesen, dass die prophetische Sukzession analog einer
königlichen mit קום hif., „erstehen lassen, erwecken", formuliert ist. Da
das Amt des Propheten an das mosaische inklusive der Anweisung, auf
ihn zu hören – bei gleichzeitiger Depotenzierung des Königtums –,
gebunden wird, lässt sich eine Ablösung der Gewichtung der beiden
Ämter folgern. Genau dieser Gewichtung trägt nun Jer 1,4–10 Rech-
nung, indem der Prophet mit seiner Beamtung Züge der Königsideologie zugeeignet bekommt. Jeremia ist nicht „König der Propheten", sondern er bekleidet ein Amt, das bereits nach dem Prophetengesetz des
Deuteronomiums das höchste ist und das in Jer 1 mit hergebrachten
königsideologischen Zügen beschrieben und ausgestaltet wird. Mit der
expliziten Eintragung dieser Züge in das Jeremiabild übersteigt Jer 1,4–
10 allerdings auch den Referenztext in Dtn 18, da hier eine solche Aus-
deutung des Sukzessiongedankens nicht erfolgt. Es kann damit
festgehalten werden: Die Verfasser von Jer 1,4–10 stehen dem deutero-
nomisch-deuteronomistischen Prophetenbild einerseits sehr nahe, andererseits werten sie dieses noch stärker auf, sie weisen ihm sogar eine
königliche Dimension zu. Wie ein König in der altorientalischen
Vorstellung wird nun der Prophet Jeremia zum Mittler zwischen Gott
und Mensch und für seine Gegner kaum antastbar. Diese Entwicklung,
die sich in den Ämtergesetzen des Deuteronomiums bereits im
Gedanken der Sukzession und der Verkündigung des göttlichen Wortes
bei gleichzeitiger Abwertung des Königtums abzeichnete, nimmt damit
in Jer 1,4–10 weiter Gestalt an.

---

45 In diesem Zusammenhang wird jedoch Jer 1,5b mit der Wendung נביא לגוים als sekun-
    där einzustufen sein, da die Einsetzung des Propheten für die Völker (נתן ל) vgl. GK, §
    119t) mit dem Gedanken der Oberaufsicht (פקד על) aus V.10 semantisch nur schwer
    vereinbar ist.

46 Vgl. Herrmann, Jeremia, 67.

47 Vgl. W. Fauth, Der König als Gärtner und Jäger im Paradeisos. Beobachtungen zur
    Rolle des Herrschers in der vorderasiatischen Hortikultur, Persica 8 (1979) 1–53.

48 Beispiele bei Herrmann, Jeremia, 67.

Hieraus lässt sich zweierlei entnehmen. Zunächst rückt die indivi-
duelle Person des Propheten Jeremia stark in den Mittelpunkt der Verkündigung des Jeremiabuches. Genau dieser Befund wird durch die
Zeichenhandlungen und die Prosaberichte, die die Person des Jeremia
und sein Geschick in das Zentrum rücken, eingelöst.[49] Zudem erfolgt
gleichzeitig eine Beglaubigung der Worte und Taten des in seiner Zeit
umstrittenen Jeremia in einer späteren Perspektive: Das göttliche Wort
im Munde Jeremias (Jer 1,9) macht ihn zum bevollmächtigten Mittler,
dessen Verkündigung Niedergang, aber auch Aufbau bewirkt (hat). Die
Zuspitzung auf den Propheten als Subjekt des Zerstörens und Bauens
am Anfang des Buches macht es wahrscheinlich, dass für die Träger-
kreise des Jeremiabuchs[50] das göttliche Wort seine maßgebliche und
autoritative Gestalt in der Verkündigung des Jeremia gewann. Dies
dürfte auch der Grund gewesen sein, weshalb die Autoren von Jer 1,4–
10 die Anklänge an die Mosetradition eingearbeitet haben.

V. Fazit

Der Berufungsbericht Jeremias nimmt literarisch Bezug auf das
deuteronomistisch gestaltete Prophetengesetz in Dtn 18 und stellt
bereits damit Jeremia als legitimen Nachfolger des Mose vor. Um dies
zu unterstreichen, begegnen ebenfalls Anspielungen auf die Berufung
des Mose in Ex 3, die ihrerseits die Berufungsszene anhand des aus Ri
6 übernommenen Retterschemas gestaltet. Zusammen mit einer königsideologischen Perspektive in Jer 1,5.10, die die Berufungsszene gewissermaßen rahmt, entsteht der Eindruck einer starken Aufwertung von
Person und Verkündigung des Propheten Jeremia zu Beginn des Buches. Der entscheidende Punkt dürfte dabei in der Autorisierung Jeremias als dem Verkünder des JHWH-Wortes bestehen, das nunmehr in
einem Jeremiabuch schriftlich vorliegt. Die Legitimierung der Person
und der Verkündigung Jeremias mithilfe der schriftlich vorliegenden
Mosetradition dürfte in einem zu vermutenden nachexilischen Kontext

---

49 Vgl. R.G. Kratz, Die Propheten Israels, München 2003, 79.

50 Die deuteronomistische Beeinflussung des Jeremiabuchs wird in der Forschung unter-
    schiedlich beurteilt, da der Prophet Jeremia sich dezidiert gegen die Kreise der Nota-
    beln, in deren Horizont aber die Überlieferung des deuteronomisch-deuteronomi-
    stischen Gedankenguts gepflegt wurde, gewandt hat. Vgl. Stipp, Jeremia, 294ff; T.
    Römer, La conversion du prophète Jérémie à la théologie deutéronomiste, in: A.H.W.
    Curtis / T. Römer (Hg.), The Book of Jeremiah and its Reception (BEThL 128), Leuven
    1997, 27–50, der sich für eine Beurteilung des Deuteronomismus im Jeremiabuch in
    enger Beziehung zum Geschichtswerk ausspricht.

in einer zunehmenden Beschäftigung mit der (Mose-)Tora ihren Grund gehabt haben, da nun natürlich die Frage nach dem verbindlichen und gültigen Wort JHWHs vor dem Hintergrund der Tora gestellt wurde.[51] In dem hier diskutierten Zusammenhang bedeutet dies nichts anderes, als dass das Jeremiabuch in ein enges Verhältnis zur Tora gestellt wird. Das Buch ist anscheinend in dieser Perspektive auch andernorts redigiert worden[52], so dass die Berufungsgeschichte auch hierin eine vorausweisende Position einnimmt und zugleich eine literarische Beschäftigung mit der Tora bestätigt. Ist Jeremia nach dem Berufungsbericht der legitime Nachfolger des Mose gewesen, dessen Verkündigung gegen jeden Zweifel und gegen jede zeitgenössische Anfeindung bewahrheitet worden ist, dann kann und soll auch sein schriftlich niedergelegtes Wort in Kontinuität zur Tora verstanden werden – auch wenn dies die ursprüngliche jeremianische Verkündigung noch nicht beabsichtigt haben konnte.

---

51 Die von T. Willi, „Wie geschrieben steht" – Schriftbezug und Schrift. Überlegungen zur frühjüdischen Literaturwerdung im perserzeitlichen Kontext, in: R.G. Kratz (Hg.), Religion und Religionskontakte im Zeitalter der Achämeniden (VWGTh 22), Gütersloh 2002, 257–277, hier 271, für die spätpersische und frühhellenistische Zeit konstatierte kulturelle Atmosphäre mit einem neuen Verständnis von Bildung und Lehre dürfte der produktiven Beschäftigung mit einer schriftlichen Tora (und den mit ihr verbundenen Ansprüchen wie sie etwa Esr 7 vermittelt) sehr förderlich gewesen sein, so dass eine Abgleichung der unterschiedlichen (schriftlichen) Traditionen, wie z.B. einem älteren Jeremiabuch, mit der Tora nicht ungewöhnlich erscheint.

52 Dies gilt nicht nur für die Aufnahmen von einzelnen Toratraditionen im Rahmen einer innerbiblischen Exegese, auf die auch explizit für das Jeremiabuch M. Fishbane, Biblical Interpretation in Ancient Israel, Oxford 2004 (Nachdr.), 292ff, aufmerksam macht, sondern möglicherweise auch weitergehend für eine redaktionelle Konzeption, die Jeremia als Lehrer der Tora darstellt. Vgl. hierzu die Ergebnisse von C. Maier, Jeremia als Lehrer der Tora. Soziale Gebote des Deuteronomiums in Fortschreibungen des Jeremiabuches (FRLANT 196), Göttingen 2002, die für die von ihr untersuchten Belege im wesentlichen eine schriftlich niedergelegte Tora-Urkunde erhebt, deren Bedeutsamkeit für das Konzept der literarische Figur des Jeremia als „Lehrer der Tora" dann folglich auch in nachexilische Zeit zu datieren sei. Vgl. die Auswertung 353ff.

Mose im Psalter

von Johannes Schnocks

Unter den Mosebelegen der Hebräischen Bibel außerhalb des Hexateuch nimmt das Psalmenbuch eine Sonderstellung ein. Das gilt zunächst wegen der relativ hohen Anzahl der Belege.[1] Die 8 Mosenennungen des Psalters[2] werden nur von 1./2.Kön und dem Bereich Esra/Neh/Chr übertroffen. Eine Durchsicht dieser Belege zeigt, dass es hier, abgesehen von den Genealogien in 1.Chr, ganz überwiegend um den Bezug auf Mose als Gesetzgeber geht.[3] Gerade dieser Aspekt scheint im Psalter völlig zu fehlen.[4] Die Mosebelege im Psalter konzentrieren sich zudem fast ausschließlich auf den Bereich der Psalmen 90 – 106, also das vierte Psalmenbuch, das zudem von Ps 90 eröffnet wird, dem einzigen Psalm, den seine Überschrift als Gebet des Mose bezeichnet. Die außergewöhnliche Dichte von Mosebelegen in diesem strukturell abgegrenzten Psalterbereich ist insbesondere von Exegeten, die Psalmen auch in Bezug auf ihre Stellung im Psalmenbuch auslegen, schon lange wahrgenommen und unterschiedlich stark akzentuiert worden.[5] In diesem Beitrag möchte ich die Mosebelege im Psalter kurz

---

1   Zur Verteilung der Belege vgl. G. Fischer, Das Mosebild der Hebräischen Bibel, in: E. Otto (Hg.), Mose. Ägypten und das Alte Testament (SBS 189), Stuttgart 2000, 84–120, hier 88.
2   Ps 77,21; 90,1; 99,6; 103,7; 105,26; 106,16.23.32.
3   Typisch sind Fügungen mit dem Verb צוה oder dem Substantiv תורה.
4   Vgl. etwa E. Ballhorn, Zum Telos des Psalters. Der Textzusammenhang des Vierten und Fünften Psalmenbuches (Ps 90 – 150) (BBB 138), Berlin/Wien 2004, 74, der nach einer Besprechung der Überschrift Ps 90,1 die Frage nach der Gestalt des Mose im Vorgriff auf seine Bedeutung in Ps 90 – 106 stellt und festhält, „daß die Gleichung ‚Mose = Tora' nicht ohne weiteres zutrifft, sondern die Assoziationen vielmehr im Bereich des Fürbittgebetes und auch in Fragen des Kultes zu suchen sind."
5   Eine Ausnahme stellt hier die Studie von M. Leuenberger dar. Einerseits gesteht er in Anschluß an E. Zenger eine durch die Überschrift von Ps 90 eingeleitete „Mose-Dimension" zu, „die sich in IV (dem vierten Psalmenbuch, J.S.) partiell durchhält" (M. Leuenberger, Konzeptionen des Königtums Gottes im Psalter. Untersuchungen zu Komposition und Redaktion der theokratischen Bücher IV – V im Psalter (AThANT 83), Zürich 2004, 86), hält aber die von M.E. Tate (und vielen anderen) vertretene Charakterisierung von Ps 90 – 106 als „Moses-book" für „stark übertrieben" (ebd. Anm. 64). Entsprechend schreibt er ohne erkennbare Begründung die Moseüberschrift diachron der letzten Redaktionsstufe des vierten Psalmenbuchs zu (ebd., 239 Anm. 362) und erwähnt

einzeln besprechen und ihr Verhältnis zu Konzeptionen im Pentateuch untersuchen, um dann die Bedeutung Moses für das Verständnis insbesondere des vierten Psalmenbuchs zu bestimmen.

1. Ps 77,21: Geführt hast Du wie Kleinvieh dein Volk / durch die Hand von Mose und Aaron

Die erste Erwähnung Moses im Psalter am Ende von Ps 77 hat nach B. Weber eine Schlüsselfunktion für das Verständnis des gesamten Textes.[6] Wenn hier Mose – zusammen mit Aaron – als Mittler des göttlichen Handelns am Volk eingeführt wird, so wirft das ein Licht auch auf die gattungskritisch schwer zu fassende Struktur des Psalms, die Momente der Volksklage mit denen einer Individualklage verbindet. Webers Lösung besteht darin, „dass der Psalmist sich in eine von Mose her legitimierte ‚Mittlerfunktion' gestellt weiss, die ihn die Not des Volkes als seine persönliche erleben und beklagen läßt".[7] Entsprechend charakterisiert er den Psalm insgesamt als „(theologisierende) ‚Mittlerklage'".[8] Mose wird damit in diesem Psalm zum Paradigma für das theologische Selbstverständnis des Psalmisten bzw. des Beters. Dabei ist die Formulierung „[göttliche Aktivität] durch die Hand Moses (und Aarons)" zwar im Psalter singulär, ansonsten aber innerhalb und außerhalb des Pentateuch ausgesprochen weit verbreitet.[9]

---

in derselben Fußnote die „diversen Mosereminiszenzen in IV: 90,1; 99,6; 103,7; 105,26; 106,16.23.32 (sonst nur noch 77,21), die man aber kompositionell nicht übergewichten sollte". Diese Abwehrhaltung ist wohl der Vorentscheidung geschuldet, das vierte Psalmenbuch synchron durch eine aus Ps 89 abgeleitete exilische Brille wahrzunehmen, so dass hier konzeptionell und theologisch für Mose kein Platz ist: „In der Perspektive einer historisierenden Ablauflesung [...] schließt also Buch IV nahtlos an den Prätext an und präsentiert sich als tiefgreifende Bearbeitung der geschichtlichen Notlage des Exils, die mit der großen Rettungsbitte 106,47 schließt und literarisch resp. für eine historisierende Synchronlesung dann konsequent in V für die nachexilische Epoche weitergeführt und zu einem Abschluß gebracht wird" (ebd., 217; Kursivierung im Original). M.E. wird eine solche Lektüre dem komplexen textlichen Befund nicht gerecht.

6   Vgl. B. Weber, Psalm 77 und sein Umfeld. Eine poetologische Studie (BBB 103), Weinheim 1995, 191–198.
7   Ebd., 192.
8   Ebd., 191 u.ö.
9   Die Belege – oft in Formen wie על־פי יהוה ביד־משה oder auch צוה יהוה / כאשר דבר יהוה ביד־משה – sind: Ex 9,35; 35,29; Lev 8,36; 10,11; 26,46; Num 4,37.45.49; 9,23; 10,13; 15,23; 17,5; 27,23; 36,13; Jos 14,2; 20,2; 21,2.8; 22,9; Ri 3,4; 1.Kön 8,53.56; 2.Chr 33,8; 34,14; 35,6; Neh 8,14; 9,14; 10,30. Aaron wird hier interessanterweise nicht genannt, so daß der Psalm zumindest innovativ formuliert. Nicht die Mittlerschaft, sondern die gemeinsame Führung des Auszuges wird in Num 33,1durch ביד־משה ואהרן ausgedrückt; vgl. auch den einzigen Beleg für ביד־אהרן in 1.Chr 24,19.

Neben dieser Funktion des Mose als Mittler zwischen JHWH und Volk, die zudem hier auf die literarische Gestaltung des Textes zurückwirkt, sind weitere Momente festzuhalten. So sind es gerade die mit Mose verbundenen Exodustraditionen, die der Psalm auslegt, um seine theologischen Fragen, die um ein offenbar gestörtes Gottesverhältnis ringen (V.8–10)[10], zu bearbeiten. Die Nennung des Mose gemeinsam mit Aaron als Protagonisten des Exodusgeschehens erinnert an die priesterschriftliche Konzeption der Moseberufung (Ex 7). „Eine Spezifizierung ihrer Führungsfunktionen in den *Propheten* Mose und den *Priester* Aaron sowie eine Angabe zum Binnenverhältnis beider Funktionen überstrapaziert den Text."[11]

2. Ps 90,1a: Ein Gebet des Mose, des Gottesmannes

Die Überschrift des 90. Psalms[12] hat ihre Bedeutung nicht einmal so sehr wegen der Singularität, dass Mose nur hier mit einem Gebet des Psalmenbuches verbunden wird – etwa Salomo werden lediglich zwei Psalmen, Ps 72 und 127, zugeschrieben. Äußerst ungewöhnlich im Konzept der Psalmenüberschriften ist aber, dass hier eine Persönlichkeit, die lange vor David ihren Ort in der Geschichte Israels hat, als Autor eines Psalms genannt wird. Zusätzliches Gewicht bekommt diese Angabe dadurch, dass nach der großen Zäsur des Psalters in Ps 89[13] die Überschriften generell und die Autorenangaben im besonderen stark abnehmen. Die nächste Autorenzuschreibung findet sich erst in Ps 101 (David), so dass die jüdische Tradition für die gesamte Psalmenstrecke Ps 90 – 100 Mose als Autor angibt.[14] Diese Spur wird mit Blick auf das vierte Psalmenbuch weiter zu verfolgen sein.

Fragt man aber zunächst nach dem Mosebild, das hier gezeichnet wird, so ist einerseits die Gestalt der Überschrift, andererseits das Psalmkorpus aufschlussreich. Was die Gattungsangabe תפלה im Zu-

---

10 Vgl. zu den Fragen im strukturellen Zentrum des (Grund-)Psalms F.-L. Hossfeld/E. Zenger, Psalmen 51 – 100 (HThK.AT), Freiburg u.a. 2000, 408f (Hossfeld).

11 Ebd., 412 (Hossfeld; Kusivierung im Original).

12 Zu Ps 90 vgl. J. Schnocks, Vergänglichkeit und Gottesherrschaft. Studien zu Psalm 90 und dem vierten Psalmenbuch (BBB 140), Berlin/Wien 2002, 17–177.

13 Vgl. F.-L. Hossfeld, Von der Klage zum Lob – die Dynamik des Gebets in den Psalmen, BiKi 56 (2001) 16–20, hier 18.

14 Das legt eine Passage im Midrash Tehillim nahe, in der es heißt, Mose habe den elf Stämmen entsprechend elf Psalmen verfaßt. Die Psalmen 90 – 95 werden dann Stämmen zugeordnet, worauf die Anforderung folgt, man möge diese Zuordnung fortsetzen; vgl. W.G. Braude, The Midrash on Psalms (Midrash Tehillim) II (YJS 13), New Haven 1959, 87.

sammenhang mit Mose betrifft[15], so ist zwar das Substantiv singulär, die Verbwurzel פלל begegnet dagegen in Num 11,2; 21,7; Dtn 9,20.26, immer im Zusammenhang mit Fürbittsituationen, wenn das Volk – in Dtn 9,20 Aaron – durch göttliche Strafen bedroht wird. Gemeinsam ist diesen Gebeten wie auch den anderen im Pentateuch ausführlich zitierten Fürbitten des Mose in Ex 32,11–13.31f; Num 14,13–19; Dtn 9,26–29, dass eine Vernichtung Israels immer abgewendet wird. Insofern akzentuiert bereits die Formulierung תפלה למשה Mose als *den* „Fürbitter Israels"[16] und damit als eine paradigmatische Betergestalt höchsten Ranges.

Die Bezeichnung des Mose als Gottesmann – zudem am Beginn eines ihm zugeschriebenen Textes – entspricht exakt der Einleitung des Mosesegens Dtn 33,1. Der Titel begegnet häufig für prophetische Persönlichkeiten im DtrGW und wird für Mose noch in Jos 14,6; 1.Chr 23,14; Esra 3,2 verwendet.

Egbert Ballhorn hat zu Recht darauf hingewiesen, dass die Gattungsangabe תפלה in Verbindung mit der Beigabe eines Titels zum Personennamen (hier „der Gottesmann") die Überschrift am Beginn des vierten Psalmenbuchs mit einem anderen Metatext im Psalter verbindet, dem Kolophon in Ps 72,20, der sowohl den zweiten Davidpsalter als auch, im Anschluss an die Doxologie, das zweite Psalmenbuch abschließt:

כלו תפלות דוד בן־ישי – Zuende sind die Gebete Davids, des Isai-Sohnes.

„Daher wirkt es von der Überschrift her, als sollte in Ps 90 Mose David in der vom Psalter bisher als ausschließlich davidisch eingeführten Gattung der תפלה beerben."[17]

Vor diesem Hintergrund kann man fragen, ob sich auch im Psalmkorpus dieses „mosaische" Beten greifen lässt. Für Ps 90 ist hier die eindringliche Bitte in V.13 besonders interessant. Sie stellt mit der Abfolge Imperativ von שוב, Imperativ Nifal von נחם mit Präposition על die engste Parallele zu Ex 32,12 in der Hebräischen Bibel dar. Damit knüpft der Psalm an die entscheidende Fürsprache des Mose für das Volk an, nachdem es das goldene Kalb angefertigt hat und dafür von JHWH vernichtet werden soll. Ein weiteres Beispiel ergibt sich, wenn man wahrnimmt, dass die Psalmen 90 – 92 auf vielfache Weise mitein-

---

15 Mit der Bezeichnung תפלה werden sonst lediglich Ps 17; 86; 102; 142 überschrieben; vgl. dazu Schnocks, Vergänglichkeit und Gottesherrschaft, 171 und zum Folgenden ebd., 185–191.

16 Vgl. den Titel der Studie von E. Aurelius, Der Fürbitter Israels. Eine Studie zum Mosebild im Alten Testament (CB.OT 27), Stockholm 1988.

17 Ballhorn, Telos, 71.

ander verknüpft sind.[18] Ps 92 endet im Duktus der drei Psalmen damit, dass der Gerechte dafür dankt, dass die in Ps 90 geäußerten Bitten nach einer Heilszusage (Ps 91) in Ps 92 erfüllt sind. Aus dieser Erfahrung heraus erwächst die Verkündigung: „Ja, gerecht ist JHWH, er ist mein Fels, und kein Unrecht ist an ihm" (Ps 92,16). Dieser Schlusspunkt des Psalms ist seinerseits aber eine Mischung aus Elementen von Dtn 32,4, verweist also auf das Moselied am Ende des Pentateuch.

Damit ist Mose in Ps 90 und wohl zumindest auch für Ps 90–92 als wirkmächtiger Fürsprecher und – was auf den ersten Blick erstaunlich ist – als paradigmatischer Psalmenbeter eingeführt.

3. Ps 99,6: Mose und Aaron sind unter seinen Priestern und Samuel unter denen, die seinen Namen (an)rufen / sie rufen zu JHWH und er antwortet ihnen.

Wie schon in Ps 77 begegnet Mose hier zusammen mit seinem Bruder Aaron. Dass beide unterschiedslos zu den Priestern gerechnet werden, ist mit Blick auf Mose singulär.[19] Ebenso wie die ungewöhnliche Kombination mit Samuel ist dieser Umstand wohl dem Umfeld eines Psalms zu verdanken[20], den Norbert Lohfink als „bewusste und dichte Zusammenfassung der gesamten Theologie der Tempelgemeinde"[21] bezeichnet hat. Interessant ist nun, dass trotz aller kult- und gesetzestheologischer Akzente, die der Psalm auch setzt, der Schwerpunkt seiner „historischen" Begründung auf dem Gottesverhältnis dieser großen Persönlichkeiten liegt. Wenn sich dieses in Anrufung und Erhörung manifestiert, so besteht etwa im Blick auf die Wüstenwanderung (V.7f) gerade darin der Gründungsmythos der Tempelgemeinde, der sich im Kult und in der Gesetzesobservanz entfaltet.

Im Vergleich zu Ps 90 ist also eine Neuerung im Mosebild festzuhalten. Während ebenfalls auf die Qualitäten Moses als paradigmatischer Beter Wert gelegt wird, so zielt die Kombination mit Aaron und Samuel doch deutlich darauf ab, dass sich dieses Paradigma in der Gegenwart der Beter am Jerusalemer Tempel mit seinen priesterlichen Institutionen aktualisiert.

---

18 Vgl. Schnocks, Vergänglichkeit und Gottesherrschaft, 191–196.
19 Vgl. R. Scoralick, Trishagion und Gottesherrschaft. Psalm 99 als Neuinterpretation von Tora und Propheten (SBS 138), Stuttgart 1989, 86–89.
20 Vgl. Hossfeld/Zenger, Psalmen 51 – 100, 702 (Zenger).
21 N. Lohfink, Der Begriff des Gottesreichs vom Alten Testament her gesehen, in: J. Schreiner (Hg.), Unterwegs zur Kirche. Alttestamentliche Konzeptionen (QD 110), Freiburg u.a. 1987, 33–86, hier 74 Anm. 108.

4. Ps 103,7: Erkennen ließ er seine Wege den Mose / den Kindern Israels seine Taten.

Wenn nun in Ps 103 Mose wieder allein begegnet, so geschieht das zunächst, um sein exklusives Gottesverhältnis zu betonen. Es liegt nahe, hier Ex 33,13 angespielt zu sehen, wo Mose JHWH gerade darum bittet, ihn seine Wege erkennen zu lassen.[22] Als Auszeichnung einer überragenden Persönlichkeit, die ebenfalls ihren Platz im Bundesgeschehen JHWHs mit Israel hat, findet sich die Kenntnis und Vermittlung der „Wege" JHWHs auch bei Abraham in Gen 18,17–19. Wenn nun die Kinder Israels die Taten JHWHs in der Geschichte erleben, so besteht ein großer Unterschied gegenüber dem, der mit der Kenntnis der „Wege" JHWHs geradezu den Interpretationsschlüssel in Händen hält und evtl. sogar fürbittend auf die Vorhaben Gottes einwirken kann.[23] Damit ist es aber unwahrscheinlich, dass hier „Mose nicht mehr Fürbitter oder Protagonist seines Volkes, sondern nur noch erster unter Gleichen"[24] ist. Sein bereits in Ps 90 benanntes Gottesverhältnis erhält vielmehr eine Steigerung ins Exklusive. Diese Kenntnis Moses um Wege und Wesen JHWHs kommt bereits im folgenden Vers zum Tragen, wenn die sog. Gnadenformel (vgl. Ex 34,6) aufgegriffen wird. In Num 14,18 hat Mose selbst diese Formel in einer Fürbitte als *argumentum ad deum* zitiert. Im Psalm wird sie der Ausgangspunkt[25] für umfassende Aussagen zum Verzeihen Gottes.

5. Ps 105,26: Er sandte Mose, seinen Knecht, / Aaron, den er erwählt hatte.

Wie in Ps 77 und 99 steht Mose wieder neben seinem Bruder Aaron. Verglichen mit der ausführlichen Darstellungen von Ägyptenaufenthalt, Plagen, Auszug und Wüstenwanderung ist es fast erstaunlich, dass Mo-

---

22 Zur Verbindung von ידע mit dem Weg Gottes vgl. nur noch Gen 18,19; Hiob 21,14; Ps 25,4; 67,3; 95,10; Jer 5,4f.
23 Zu einer solchen Deutung der „Wege JHWHs" als Gottes rechte Ordnung, als seine Grundsätze, die in seinem Wesen begründet liegen, vgl. C. Dohmen, Vom Sinai nach Galiläa. Psalm 103 als Brücke zwischen Juden und Christen, in: R. Scoralick (Hg.), Das Drama der Barmherzigkeit Gottes. Studien zur biblischen Gottesrede und ihrer Wirkungsgeschichte in Judentum und Christentum (SBS 183), Stuttgart 2000, 92–106, hier 95f, der neben den genannten Parallelen auch auf den Talmud verweist.
24 Ballhorn, Telos, 122.
25 Vgl. ebd., 122. – Ballhorn erblickt hier den Aussagekern und im Anschluß an Martin Metzger das strukturelle Zentrum des Psalms.

se in dem langen Text nur hier erwähnt wird. Dieser Umstand ist wohl der konsequenten Theozentrik des Psalms geschuldet.[26] Auffällig bei der Sendung Moses und Aarons ist allerdings, dass „die Ehrentitel Davids aus Ps 78,70 und 89,4 nun auf die beiden Volksführer übertragen"[27] werden. Dies geschieht zuvor bereits in V.6, wo Abraham als Knecht JHWHs und die Söhne Jakobs als seine Erwählten bezeichnet werden. Verglichen mit den bereits besprochenen Psalmen bleibt aber das hier gezeichnete Mosebild relativ blass.

6. Ps 106,16.23.32(f): 16 Sie eiferten gegen Mose im Lager / gegen Aaron, den Heiligen JHWHs.

23 Und er sprach, sie zu vernichten, wenn nicht Mose, sein Erwählter, in die Bresche vor ihn getreten wäre, / um umzuwenden seinen Zorn vom Verderben.

32 Und sie reizten zum Zorn am Wasser von Meriba / und es war schlecht für Mose ihretwegen,

33 denn sie waren widerspenstig gegen seinen Geist / und er schwatzte mit seinen Lippen.

Der Schlusspsalm des vierten Psalmenbuchs kann gleich mit drei Mosebelegen aufwarten. Recht unspezifisch erscheinen zunächst die Erwähnungen in V.16.32. Für V.16 ist zu notieren, dass hier wieder Mose und Aaron gemeinsam genannt werden, wobei auffällt, dass Aaron, nicht aber Mose mit einem Ehrentitel bedacht wird. Diese Tendenz, den Priester Aaron in ein besonders gutes Licht zu stellen, verstärkt sich mit Blick auf V.32f, wo der Konflikt von Massa und Meriba mit der Voranzeige des Mosetodes referiert wird. Während nach V.32 Mose die Kollektivschuld tragen muss, haftet er in V.33 eher individuell. Von Aaron ist diesmal nicht die Rede. „Nun sind an den priesterlichen Vergleichsstellen Num 20,12.24; 27,14 und Dtn 32,51 immer Aaron und Mose für ihren Tod verantwortlich. [...] Wiederum wird wie in der Horeb-Passage VV 19–23 Aarons Mitschuld verschwiegen. Das entspricht der prokultisch-priesterlichen Linie des Gesamtpsalms, die Korachs Aufstand übergeht, Aaron zum „Heiligen JHWHs" ernennt und den

---

26 Vgl. ebenso ebd., 129.
27 F.-L. Hossfeld, Eine poetische Universalgeschichte. Ps 105 im Kontext der Psalmentrias 104–106, in: ders. / L. Schwienhorst-Schönberger (Hg.), Das Manna fällt auch heute noch. Beiträge zur Geschichte und Theologie des Alten, Ersten Testaments. FS Erich Zenger (HBS 44), Freiburg i.Br. 2004, 294–311, hier 300.

Aaronenkel Pinhas zur Gründungsfigur eines mittlerischen Priestertums stilisiert."[28]

V.23 ist dagegen für das Mosebild des Psalms interessanter. Es geht um die Mose-Fürbitte schlechthin, die im Kontext des goldenen Kalbs steht. Die Wortwahl zeigt allerdings ezechielische Prägung. Ez 13,5; 22,30 sprechen ebenfalls davon, dass der Vernichtungswille JHWHs von Israel auf diese Weise abgewendet werden könnte. Ez 13 wirft den (falschen) Propheten Israels vor, gerade diesen interzessorischen Dienst nicht geleistet zu haben.

Damit kehrt Ps 106 einerseits zur Hauptfunktion Moses, der wirkmächtigen Fürbitte zurück, wie sie schon in Ps 90 nachweisbar war. Andererseits wird er, wenn er in Ps 106 die Bühne des Psalters wieder verlässt, in seiner Bedeutung für Israel von priesterlichen Persönlichkeiten wenn nicht verdrängt, so doch zumindest eingeholt.

7. Mose im vierten Buchband

Auf der Basis der gemachten Beobachtungen kann nun die Frage bearbeitet werden, welche Konzepte im Blick auf Mose im vierten Psalmenbuch sichtbar werden. Dies soll zunächst auf der Ebene des Endtextes der Ps 90–106 geschehen, bevor noch einige wenige Bemerkungen mit Blick auf die Redaktionsgeschichte formuliert werden.

Nach dem Durchgang durch die Einzelstellen lässt sich auf synchroner Ebene bereits der deutliche Wechsel festhalten, der durch die Moseüberschrift in Ps 90 angezeigt wird. Wenn auch bis Ps 89 David der überragende Vorbeter war, dem man im Psalter bis hierher meditierend folgen konnte, so stellt doch der in Ps 89 beklagte Untergang seiner Dynastie eine Zäsur dar. Die Monarchie als Symbol der Gottesbeziehung Israels im Davidbund hat Schiffbruch erlitten. Unter dem Schock des Verlustes wird es notwendig, innezuhalten und nach anderen Identitätsmomenten für Israel als der Monarchie und nach anderen Betergestalten als dem Dynastiegründer Ausschau zu halten. Bei der Wahl eines paradigmatischen Beters wählt das vierte Psalmenbuch mit Mose eine Persönlichkeit, die bereits in Ps 77 als Mittler zum Vorbild des Psalmenbeters geworden ist. Anders als bei Personen, die genealogisch bis in die jeweilige Gegenwart hineinwirken, verbinden sich mit

28 F.-L. Hossfeld, Ps 106 und die priesterliche Überlieferung des Pentateuch, in: K. Kiesow / T. Meurer (Hg.), Textarbeit. Studien zu Texten und ihrer Rezeption aus dem Alten Testament und der Umwelt Israels. FS Peter Weimar zur Vollendung seines 60. Lebensjahres mit Beiträgen von Freunden, Schülern und Kollegen (AOAT 294), Münster 2003, 257–266, hier 261f.

Mose einerseits keine Gruppeninteressen, so dass er für ganz Israel eine Identifikationsgröße sein kann. Andererseits bietet das betende Israel nun, wo es sich der Vernichtung nahe glaubt, den wirkmächtigsten Fürsprecher auf, den seine Überlieferung zu bieten hat. Die Gebetslinie führt also von der Katastrophe der Zerstörung des Jerusalems der Königszeit nicht nach Babylon, sondern in die Wüste zurück, damit das gestört erscheinende Gottesverhältnis neu bedacht werden kann.

Dieser Rückbesinnung auf die grundlegenden Problemstellungen entspricht auch, dass das vierte Psalmenbuch die Spur von Ps 89,48f aufnimmt und sich zunächst (besonders in Ps 90; 102; 103, aber auch in Ps 91; 92) ganz grundsätzlich anthropologischen Fragen zuwendet. Damit wird die Fokussierung auf den König in Ps 89 durch eine allgemein menschliche Perspektive und die Frage nach dem Gottesverhältnis der Beter abgelöst. Mit Händen greifen lässt sich dieser Vorgang der Kollektivierung etwa bei der Bezeichnung Davids als עבד JHWHs in Ps 89,4.21.40 (immer mit enklitischen Personalpronomen), während am Ende des Psalms (Ps 89,51) wie auch in Ps 90,13.16 die Beter die Selbstbezeichnung „deine Knechte" (ebenso mit enklitischen Personalpronomen) wählen.

Ballhorn resümiert völlig zu Recht: „Damit nimmt Ps 90 gegenüber Ps 89 eine doppelte Position ein: zum einen wird die darin zumindest angebotene Kollektivierung vollends fortgeführt. Gleichzeitig wird jedoch eine energische Entdavidisierung betrieben, die nicht im Horizont von Ps 89 lag. Vom Davidkonzept wird auf das Mosekonzept umgestellt."[29]

Die oben angestellten Überlegungen haben gezeigt, dass dieses Konzept in synchroner, linearer Lesung sicher Ps 90–92 umfasst. Mit Ps 93–100 tritt eine andere Bewältigungsstrategie für das untergegangene Königtum hinzu: das Konzept des Königtums JHWHs, erfahrbar in der Schöpfung und in der Theologie des Tempels. Wichtig ist aber auch hier, dass es um ein grundlegendes Konzept geht. Es geht weniger um den von Salomo oder den nach dem Exil errichteten konkreten historischen Bau, sondern um das grundsätzlich-urzeitliche Aufrichten des Kosmos und Bannung des Chaos, um das Thronen und Richten JHWHs und damit um eine Weltordnung, die universale Geltung beansprucht und am Tempel in Jerusalem lediglich ihren irdischen Haftpunkt hat. Wenn in diesem Konzept in Ps 99 auch Mose als Priester auftaucht, so verbinden sich hier Mosekonzept und JHWH-Königkonzept.

Um so mehr erstaunt es, wenn Ps 103 – noch dazu unter einer David-Überschrift – noch einmal mosaische und anthropologische Ele-

---

29 Ballhorn, Telos, 77.

mente zu einer umfassenden Lösung führt, bevor dann ein kleiner theokratischer Hymnus in V.19–22 folgt.

In den Ps 105f ist deutlich die theokratische und besonders auch in Ps 106 eine priesterliche Handschrift zu erkennen. Mose wird nun viel stärker als zuvor zu einer nationalen Gestalt aus vergangenen Zeiten. Wurden in Ps 100 die Völker noch zum Tempelkult eingeladen, so warnt Ps 106 vor einer Vermischung mit ihnen (V.35) und erwartet zukünftiges Heil durch eine Sammlung Israels aus den Nationen (V.47) unter die Fittiche der priesterlichen Nachfahren des Pinhas.

Dieses etwas verwirrende Bild erhält mehr Tiefenschärfe, wenn man die Entstehung des vierten Psalmenbuches in die Überlegungen einbezieht.[30] Demnach gehören Ps 90 – 92; 102 und 103 zur ältesten Schicht des vierten Psalmenbuchs und sind so die erste Antwort auf Ps 89. Dabei ist es sehr wahrscheinlich, dass die Davidüberschrift in Ps 103 erst später eingetragen wurde. Nach dem Einbau der JHWH-Königpsalmen Ps 93 – 100* gehört Ps 99 zu drei Psalmen, die hier wiederum nachträglich eingeschoben wurden[31]. Die Verbindung der tempeltheologischen mit der mosaischen Konzeption in diesem Psalm könnte also ein Hinweis darauf sein, dass er bewusst für diesen Kontext geschrieben oder – dann allerdings sehr geschickt – überarbeitet wurde. Die Psalmen 104 – 106 schließen das vierte Psalmenbuch auch entstehungsgeschichtlich ab. Gerade Ps 106 zieht die vorgegebenen Linien im Sinne einer priesterlich geprägten Theokratie aus. Dabei wird die prophetisch-interzessorische Bedeutung des Mose von der richtenden Funktion der Priesterschaft genauso abgelöst, wie die universale Offenheit gegenüber den Völkern von eher engen Sammlungsbestrebungen.

---

30 Die redaktionsgeschichtlichen Analysen können hier nicht dargestellt werden; vgl. zum Ergebnis Schnocks Vergänglichkeit und Gottesherrschaft, 265–276. Das konkurrierende Konzept von Leuenberger, Konzeptionen, 221–264 hat mich nicht überzeugen können: vgl. die Rezension von J. Schnocks, ThRev 102 (2006) 113–116.
31 Hierher gehört auch Ps 103,19–22.

Moses and the Septuagint of the Pentateuch

by Arie van der Kooij

I

Moses and the laws dominate the scene in the Pentateuch, particularly so in the books Exodus up to and including Deuteronomy. Hence one can imagine that the books which constitute the Pentateuch were designated as 'the law', with Moses as lawgiver. We have explicit evidence of this designation from the second century BC onwards. A well-known example is to be found in the Prologue to the Wisdom of Ben Sira where 'the Law' (ὁ νόμος) is a clear reference to the five books of Moses. According to F. García Lopez (ThWAT VIII, 634), this instance is 'die erste klare Bezeichnung des Pent. als ›Gesetz‹', but this is questionable. There are other sources of the time, in particular the Letter of Aristeas, dating roughly speaking of the same time as the Prologue, and the work of Aristobulus, dating presumably to the first half of the second century BC. Unlike the author of the Prologue who came from Judea, Aristeas, the alleged author of the Letter, and Aristobulus – both Jewish scholars in Egypt, Alexandria –, have the Greek version in mind.

In the Letter of Aristeas the term ὁ νόμος as designation of the Pentateuch in Greek is very common. Related words used are νομοθεσία, 'legislation', νομοθέτης, lawgiver, – Moses our wise lawgiver (§ 139) –, and the verb νομοθετέω, 'to give laws'. Also the expression 'the books of the Law' (§ 30) occurs. The Law is called 'holy' (§ 45; cf. § 313), and the legislation 'divine' (§ 31; cf. the expression 'the divine law' in § 3). The name of Moses is mentioned explicitly only once (§ 144), but at other places he is referred to as 'lawgiver', and in one instance, he is called, by Eleazar the high priest, 'our wise lawgiver' (§ 139).

The fragments of Aristobulus, exegete and philosopher in Alexandria, testify to the same terminology. Moses is called 'our lawgiver', the Greek Pentateuch ('our books') is designated as 'the Law' and 'our legislation'. Moses is the great wise man (due to the div-

ine spirit). The Law is presented as the source of wisdom, or philosophy. Aristobulus claims that this philosophy is both prior and
superior to any Greek philosophy.[1]

Thus, in the Alexandrinian tradition, the Pentateuch – in Greek – is
called 'the Law', or 'our legislation' which is considered the personal
achievement of Moses, the wise man.[2]

The books of the Pentateuch have been translated in Alexandria,
presumably in the first half of the third century BC. According to the
Letter of Aristeas the work was carried out by Jewish scholars from
Judea. The fact that only these books have been translated at that time
indicates that they were considered a specific set of literature. It has
been suggested that the translation of just these books was made because they were held to be the most important part of the canon of the
Hebrew Bible, but the difficulty is that the assumption of a canon of the
Hebrew Bible at that early stage is very questionable indeed. In my
view, the reason that the books involved were rendered into Greek is
somehow related to the fact that they contain the laws of the Jews. The
matter of who took the initiave to the translation is disputed – was it
the Jewish community in Alexandria, or the Ptolemaic court? However,
one should also take into serious consideration the possibility that the
authorities in Jerusalem were involved in the project, in particular if
this project is to be seen as an official one.[3] Judea and Jerusalem were
part of the Ptolemaic empire, and furthermore, the experts and scholars
of the literature concerned were to be found, first of all, in temple
circles in Jerusalem. Hence, it may well be that the translators came
from Palestine as is depicted in the Letter of Aristeas.

It is not my intention to deal here with this complicated issue[4], nor
with the question of whether the books of the Pentateuch were
designated as 'the law' at the time of the translation.

---

1   See J.M.G. Barclay, Jews in the Mediterranean Diaspora from Alexander to Trajan (323
    BCE – 117 CE), Edinburgh 1996, 150.

2   Cf. Eupolemus, a Jewish author in Jerusalem (ca 160 BC), who speaks about Moses as
    'the first wise (man)'.

3   For the view that the translation of the Law is to be seen as an official project, see e.g.
    N. Fernández Marcos, The Septuagint in Context. Introduction to the Greek Version of
    the Bible. Tr. by W.G.E. Watson, Leiden 2000, 63.

4   For recent contributions, see e.g. N.L. Collins, The Library in Alexandria and the Bible
    in Greek (VT.S 82), Leiden 2000; W. Orth, Ptolemaios II. und die Septuaginta-
    Übersetzung, in: H. Fabry / U. Offerhaus (Hg.), Im Brennpunkt: Die Septuaginta.
    Studien zur Entstehung und Bedeutung der Griechischen Bibel (BWANT 153),
    Stuttgart 2001, 97–114; S. Honigman, The Septuagint and Homeric Scholarship in
    Alexandria. A study in the narrative of the Letter of Aristeas. London / New York 2003;
    A. van der Kooij, The Septuagint of the Pentateuch and Ptolemaic Rule, in: G.N.

The focus of this contribution is on Moses and the laws in the Pentateuch. By discussing a few passages in LXX Pentateuch (Exod 24,12; Lev 26,46, and Deut 17,18), I will try to find out which ideas on Moses and the laws this version might reflect, particularly regarding the issue of the laws as related to the political constitution of the Jewish nation of the time. As an illustration of the interest taken in the connection between the laws of Moses and the matter of the constitution, or polity, the following statement by Hecataeus of Abdera (ca 300 BC) may suffice:

'Moses, outstanding both for his kindness and for his courage ... (he) drew up their laws (i.e., of the Jews) and ordered their political institution (καὶ τὰ κατὰ τὴν πολιτείαν ἐνομοθέτησέ τε καὶ διέταξε)'.[5]

II

Let us start with Lev 26,46[LXX], which reads as follows,

ταῦτα τὰ κρίματα καὶ τὰ προστάγματα καὶ ὁ νόμος,
ὃν ἔδωκεν κύριος ... ἐν τῷ ὄρει Σινα ἐν χειρὶ Μωϋσῆ

This passage is a summary statement, although there is an extra chapter, ch. 27, which has a similar statement of its own (27,34). It is about the 'judgements' (κρίματα) and the 'ordinances' (προστάγματα), terms usually the equivalent of Hebrew משפט and of חק respectively. So the order of both words in Greek is not the same as in MT (החקים והמשפטים). In addition to these terms the LXX offers the expression ὁ νόμος, 'the law', where MT has a plural reading, 'the laws' (התורת). Like in the Hebrew text, the Greek equivalent in many instances, particularly so in Leviticus, designates particular laws (e.g. the law of leprosy, etc...), but in our text the singular ὁ νόμος is used in an encompassing sense – the law as a whole consisting of judgements and ordinances. In this statement at the end of the book the term ὁ νόμος is best understood as referring to the whole of Leviticus – in line with the name of the book in the Mishnah (Meg. 3,5), תורת כהנים.[6]

Knoppers / B.M. Levinson (ed.), The Pentateuch as Torah: New Models for Understanding Its Promulgation and Acceptance (forthcoming).

5 See M. Stern (ed.), Greek and Latin Authors on Jews and Judaism. I. From Herodotus to Plutarch, Jerusalem 1974, 28.

6 Cf. P. Harlé / D. Pralon, Le Lévitique (La Bible d'Alexandrie 3), Paris 1988, 210. For another view, see L. Monsengwo Pasinya, La notion de nomos dans le Pentateuque grec (AnB 52), Rome 1973, 120. I leave aside Lev 27,34 and Num 36,13 which also are meant as summary statements – the former apparently of Lev 27 on its own –, because both texts do not display any specific usage of the term ὁ νόμος.

We now turn to Exod 24,12[LXX] which, together with the passage in
Deuteronomy, is of particular interest to our topic. It reads,

καὶ εἶπεν κύριος πρὸς Μωϋσῆν· ἀνάβηθι πρός με εἰς τὸ ὄρος καὶ ἴσθι ἐκεῖ καὶ
δώσω σοι τὰ πυξία τὰ λίθινα τὸν νόμον καὶ τὰς ἐντολὰς ἃς ἔγραψα
νομοθετῆσαι αὐτοῖς

According to this passage Moses is ordered to go to God on the
mountain and to be there in order to receive from God

'the tablets of stone, the law and the commandments
which I have written to give them laws'.

This text, in Hebrew, is well known because of the exegetical issue
regarding the relationship between 'the tablets of stone' and 'the law
and the commandment'. The former expression (לחת האבן) clearly
evokes the idea of the Decalogue (see Exod 31,18; 32,15f.19; 34,1.4.
28), whilst the latter (והתורה והמצוה) is never used as referring to the
Decalogue, but rather reflects a word usage which is typical of the book
of Deuteronomy.

One wonders how this text has been understood by the translator of
the verse. From the point of view of word order his rendering of the
Hebrew is a literal one, but there are a few observations to make which
may give us a clue.

First, it is to be noted that the expression 'the law and the
commandment(s)' is taken as an apposition to 'the tablets of stone'.[7]
Apparently, the *waw* before התורה – if part of the underlying Hebrew
text[8] – was interpreted as an explicative one, and not as a conjunction.

Secondly, the lexical choice made for the rendering of Hebrew לוח
is not the one which one would expect. As stated above, the expression
is easily understood in light of other places, both in Exodus (see above)
and in Deuteronomy (9,9–11; 10,1–4), as referring to the tablets on
which the Ten Words were put in writing. However, the rendering in
our verse is not the same as in all the places just mentioned. In all these
instances, the Greek πλάξ is used consistently, whereas in Exod 24,12
the Greek πυξίον is found. It thus seems that the translator did not take
our verse as referring to the two tablets of the Decalogue which indeed
would not fit the following expression 'the law and the command-

---

7   Cf. J.W. Wevers, Notes on the Greek Text of Exodus (SCSS 30), Atlanta 1990, 386.
8   The reading *hattorah* without *waw* is attested in: 4Q216 I,6 (quote of Exod 24,12 in Jub
     1,1; see DJD XIII, 5), 4Q364 14,4 (Reworked Pentateuch; see DJD XIII, 221), and
     SamPent. For Jub 1,1, see C. Werman, "The תורה and the תעודה" engraved on the
     Tablets, DSD 9 (2002) 77f.

ments'.[9] This raises the question to which law, or laws, our text then may refer.

The terminology involved is of a rather general nature and it therefore could allude to any legal section of the Pentateuch (compare, e.g., Lev 26,46 and 27,34), or alternatively to all laws which have been given to Moses in addition to the Decalogue.[10] However, it may well be that the expression 'the law and the commandments' envisages the law of Deuteronomy. It is noteworthy that both terms are found in a passage which refers to this law, namely Deut 27,1–3[LXX]: for ἐντολαί see v.1 and for νόμος see v.3. Furthermore, such an understanding of Exod 24,12 is plausible in light of the relationship between Exod 20,18–20 and 24,12, on the one hand, and Deut 5,23–31, on the other.

Interestingly, the literature of the time seems to contain a passage which reflects the same idea – Wisdom of Ben Sira 45,5 (Hebrew), beginning second century BC. It reads as follows:

> He permitted him to hear his voice,
> and led him into the cloud (ויגישהו לערפל);
> he put in his hand the commandments (וישם בידו מצוה),
> the law of life and understanding (תורת חיים ותבונה),
> that he (Moses) might teach his precepts to Jacob (ללמד ביעקב חקיו),
> and his testimonies and his judgements to Israel (ועדותיו ומשפטיו לישראל).

This verse is part of the passage devoted to Moses (44,23[final clause]–45,5), which by the way is short in comparison to the one about Aaron (45,6–22). Reading this passage from an intertextual point of view the following observations can be made: The phrase 'he led him into the cloud' is clearly based on Exod 20,21 (but see also 24,18).[11] The words that follow – 'he put in his hand the commandments, the law ...' – is related to Ex 24,12 because both texts have two elements in common, (a) the notion of God's giving to Moses, and (b) the terms תורה and מצוה.[12] The wording of the rest of the passage, however, is best understood in the light of Deuteronomy: As to the notion of 'life' related to 'the law', see 30,15 ('See, I have set before you this day life and good, ...'), and for the idea of understanding and wisdom as characterization of the law, see 4,6 ('for that [i.e. the law of Deuteronomy] will be your wisdom and your understanding'). Finally, the idea that Moses might 'teach the precepts, the testimonies and judgments' to Israel is based on

---

9   It is further to be noted that Exod 24,12 does not speak of *two* tablets of stone, as is usual the case elsewhere. Hence, the text is open to an alternative interpretation.

10   Mongingwo Pasinya (Notion, 114) suggests that 'the law' in LXX Exod 24,12 might refer to Exod 25,1 – 31,17.

11   Cf. P.C. Beentjes, Jesus Sirach en Tenach, Diss., Nieuwegein 1981, 115.

12   Di Lella is of the opinion that "the commandments" are the Decalogue (see P.W. Skehan / A.A. di Lella, The Wisdom of Ben Sira [AncB 39], New York 1987, 511).

Deut 5,31 ('I will tell you all the commandments and the precepts and the judgments which you shall teach them'). This last passage has not only the verb למד in common with Sir 45,5, but also a triple expression as designation of the law. The three words involved in both passages differ in one instance – מצוה in Deut and עדותיו in Ben Sira –, but it is noteworthy that the wording of Sir 45,5 has a complete parallel in Deut 4,45; 6,20. Thus, Sir 45,5 presents a picture of Moses as the one who received 'the law' which turns out to be based on a combination of Exod 20,21; 24,12 and Deut 5,31.

It thus seems that the choice of πυξίον in Exod 24,12, instead of πλάξ, has to do with the understanding of the verse as alluding to the law of Deuteronomy – an interpretation which also makes perfect sense as far as the Hebrew text is concerned. The fact that the expression 'the law and the commandments' is taken as apposition to 'the tablets of stone' on which God had written the law, underscores its authority in a way similar to the idea of heavenly tablets known from other sources of the time, such as Jubilees.[13]

If indeed Deuteronomy is envisaged in Exod 24,12[LXX], one wonders how the law of Deuteronomy was seen, by the team of scholars responsible for the Greek version of the Pentateuch, in relation to the other laws in the Pentateuch which, according to several passages (e.g. Lev 26,46[LXX]), were also given to Moses. As to this issue the third text, Deut 17,18[LXX], deserves our attention. It reads as follows:

καὶ ἔσται ὅταν καθίσῃ ἐπὶ τοῦ δίφρου τῆς ἀρχῆς αὐτοῦ καὶ γράψει ἑαυτῷ τὸ δευτερονόμιον τοῦτο εἰς βιβλίον παρὰ τῶν ἱερέων τῶν Λευιτῶν.

This verse is part of the passage on the king, 17,14–20, in MT. Unlike the latter, the Greek version does not speak of a king (βασιλεύς), but of a leader, a ruler, ἄρχων. As a result the Hebrew כסא has not been rendered θρόνος, but δίφρος (so with the Göttingen edition); cf. ἀρχή for ממלכה instead of βασιλεία. I will not deal with the question what might be the reason of all this, but will concentrate on another interesting piece – the phrase τὸ δευτερονόμιον τοῦτο as rendering of the phrase משנה התורה הזאת. The Hebrew is about a 'copy' of 'this law', i.e. the law of Deuteronomy, but the wording in Greek seems to convey another meaning. Opinions differ as to the meaning of δευτερονόμιον, which actually is a neologism (see also Josh 9,2c[LXX] [MT 8,32]). The question is whether this term should be understood as 'repeated' law, or

---

13   On the heavenly tablets in Jubilees, see F. García Martínez, The Heavenly Tablets in the Book of Jubilees, in: M. Albani et al. (ed.), Studies in the Book of Jubilees, Tübingen 1997, 243–260.

as 'second' law.[14] Dogniez/Harl have advanced the view that, on the one hand, the translator wanted to express the idea of repetition in the sense of a copy, – 'un double de la loi (de cette loi, celle de ce livre)'[15], but that, on the other, the ambiguity of the word led Greek speaking Christians to the idea of a second law (that of Christ, so Origen).[16] However, if it was intended to express the idea of a repetition of this law, then one would expect a rendering such as τὴν δευτέρωσιν τοῦ νόμου τούτου, or, more elegantly, τὸ ἀντίγραφον etc. As a matter of fact, the actual Greek rendering (δευτερονόμιον) represents a designation of the law involved. The Hebrew מִשְׁנֶה has not been taken in the sense of 'copy of (this law)', but as a reference to the name of the book. Of course, the fact that the ruler will write 'this deuteronomion' into a book implies that he will make a copy of it, but the term itself does not denote this element, as does the Hebrew. Like other δευτερο–words as substantives in Greek, the term as it stands is best understood as 'second law'.[17] This is not to deny that in one way or another repetition may be involved, – this depends on the relationship between what is considered first and what is considered second –, but this is not the primary meaning of the word.

According to the Greek of our verse, the law called 'deuteronomion' which the ruler has to write for himself into a book, was given to him by the priests (Levites). The law referred to is supposed to be in their possession. This reminds one of Deut 31,9 where it is stated that, according to the LXX,

> Moses wrote the words of this law into a book
> (εἰς βιβλίον [not in MT, but see 31,24])
> and gave it to the priests, the sons of Levi …
> and to the elders of the sons of Israel.

This passage refers to the law of Deuteronomy. Hence the phrase 'the second law' is to be understood as a designation of the law of Deuteronomy – in line with later tradition.

This raises the intriguing question of what this naming of the law of Deuteronomy may imply. In his Notes on LXX Deuteronomy Wevers

---

14 See J. Lust et al., Greek-English Lexicon of the Septuagint. Revised edition, Stuttgart 2003, 133: 'second or repeated law'.

15 See C. Dogniez / M. Harl, Le Deutéronome (La Bible d'Alexandrie 5), Paris 1992, 22.27.

16 For the view of Origen, see ibid., 27f.

17 Cf. Monsengwo-Pasinya, Notion, 136; Wevers, Notes on the Greek Text of Deuteronomy, Atlanta 1995, 289; T. Muraoka, A Greek-English Lexicon of the Septuagint. Chiefly of the Pentateuch and the Twelve Prophets, Louvain 2002, 111. Deuterowords which are verbs, – to do something a second time – of course imply the notion of repetition.

makes the following statement: 'Deut is a second law over against the
תורה of Exodus – Numbers, a repetition of the law by God to Moses in
Transjordan' (p. 289f). Long ago a similar idea was advanced by Theodoretus of Cyrrhus. In his view, the law of Deut is a recapitulation – not
a repetition – of the legislation in the books of Exodus – Numbers, for a
new generation. He further suggested that it constitutes a recapitulation
which includes elements of explication.[18] For this latter aspect, he
points to Deut 1,5[LXX] where one reads,

> ἐν τῷ πέραν τοῦ Ἰορδάνου ἐν γῇ Μωαβ ἤρξατο Μωϋσῆς διασαφῆσαι τὸν
> νόμον τοῦτον λέγων.

The issue at stake here is the meaning of the verb διασαφέω (as
rendering of באר). Does this verb mean 'to present clearly', 'to instruct
plainly', or does it carry the notion of interpretation, as Theodoretus
assumes? The latter meaning does not seem to be plausible because the
point is not to explain, or clarify 'this law', the law of Deuteronomy,
but to present it in a clear way in public (cf. σαφῶς for באר in 27,8).

I agree with Wevers that the Greek δευτερονόμιον reflects the idea
that Deut is the second law over against the laws of Exodus – Numbers,
but I don't think that, although an element of some repetition may be
involved, the second law is simply 'a repetition' of these laws. There is
a difference between the two sets of laws. Roughly speaking, one can
say that the laws in Exodus – Numbers are mainly dealing with the
priesthood, the cult and related matters, whereas those of Deut are
particularly concerned with the life of the people, both in religious and
in moral affairs.

Here I would like to come back to the issue of the political
institution mentioned above. In the third and second century BC the
Jewish nation was ruled by priests, under the supreme direction of the
high priest. According to sources of the time, such as Hecataeus of Abdera and the Wisdom of Ben Sira[19], this type of leadership was in line
with the laws of Moses.

> Hecataeus of Abdera: He (Moses) picked out the men of most refinement and
> with the greatest ability to head the entire nation, and appointed them
> priests.... These same men he appointed to be judges ...the Jews never have a
> king, and authority over the people is regularly vested in whichever priest is
> regarded as superior to his colleagues in wisdom and virtue. They call this
> man the high priest ...[20]

---

18   See Le Deutéronome, 28.
19   See also the Letter of Aristeas, and the Letter of Antiochus III (Ant. 12,142).
20   Stern, Greek and Latin Authors I, 28.

Exod 19,6[LXX] is an important passage in this respect. As I have argued elsewhere, the phrase βασίλειον ἱεράτευμα, 'a royal priesthood', as rendering of Hebrew ממלכת כהנים, does not refer to the people as a whole, but to a particular form of government of the people, namely, that of (high-)priestly rule.[21] This text testifies to an interpretation which served as a legitimation of the leadership of the Jewish nation of the time.

Strictly speaking, however, priestly rule is part of the picture. As is clear for instance from the letter of Antiochus III to his governor Ptolemy, dating to about 200 BC, the government of the Jewish nation also consisted of a 'council of elders', ἡ γερουσία[22], – a term also attested in LXX Pentateuch (e.g. Exod 3,16; 24,9; Deut 5,23). The government thus consisted of two elements, first of all the priesthood of the temple, and secondly, the council of elders, the representatives of what is called 'the people'. Cf. for instance 1 Macc 7,33 where one reads about 'some of the priests from the temple' (ἀπὸ τῶν ἱερέων ἐκ τῶν ἁγίων) and 'some of the elders of the people'(ἀπὸ τῶν πρεσβυτέρων τοῦ λαοῦ).[23]

It is my proposal to understand the distinction between the first and the second law in LXX Pentateuch against the background of the twofold rule, that is to say, the first law in Exodus – Numbers as containing the laws of the priests[24], and the second law in Deut as the law of (the representatives of) the people, civic law so to speak. As far as the the latter is concerned, this idea is in line with the statement that it should be made public to the people, and that it should be read in public, at the feast of booths, once in seven years (Deut 31,10–11).[25] Moreover, it is the second law that is to be copied by the ruler, not the laws of Exodus – Numbers.

21 A. van der Kooij, A Kingdom of Priests: Comment on Exodus 19:6, in: R. Roukema (ed.), The Interpretation of Exodus. Studies in Honour of Cornelis Houtman (CBET 44), Leuven 2006, 173–175.
22 See Josephus, Ant. 12,142.
23 See also 1 Macc 14,28. Cf. the expression 'Aaron' and 'Israel' in writings of Qumran (e.g. CD VI 2; 1QSa II 13–14).
24 Compare the expression 'the law of the priests' as the designation of Leviticus in mMeg 3,5.
25 Deut 31,10–11 does only refer to the law of Deuteronomy; cf. Josephus, Ant. 4,209, and mSota 7,8.

III

In conclusion, the distinction evoked by the name 'the second law' as designation of the book of Deuteronomy makes good sense if understood in light of the constitution of the Jewish nation of the time – that of priestly rule accompanied with the senate. Hence, it might be stated that LXX Pentateuch mirrors a picture of Moses who, as lawgiver, introduced this constitution of the Jews – a picture fully in line with that of Hecataeus of Abdera (ca 300 BC). The deuteronomic law has its own place in being considered the law of 'the people', i.e. 'the people' distinct from 'the temple', or like in Qumran documents, 'Israel' distinguished from 'Aaron'. According to Exod 24,12^{LXX} this law was given to Moses on mount Sinai, written by God on 'stone tablets' which greatly underscores the authority of this part of the laws of the Pentateuch.

Finally, a short remark on the figure Moses as depicted in the Wisdom of Ben Sira (Hebrew). As argued above, Sir 45,5 strongly suggests that it was the law of Deuteronomy only which was given to Moses. If so, the significance of Moses as lawgiver is limited here in a remarkable way. In his long presentation of Aaron, Ben Sira states, among other things, that God 'gave' him, Aaron, his commandments (45,17). One could argue that Aaron is presented here as the one to whom the remaining laws, the laws of the priests, had been given.[26]

---

26 See also the discussion of Sira 45,5.17 by H. Stadelmann, Ben Sira als Schriftgelehrter (WUNT 2/6), Tübingen 1980, 279.

Who was standing on the mountain?
The portrait of Moses in 4Q377

by Wido van Peursen

1. Introduction[1]

The Qumran document 4Q377 appeared in Volume 28 of the DJD series under the name '4QApocryphal Pentateuch B'.[2] This designation relates the document to 4Q368 ('4QApocryphal Pentateuch A'), because 'both clearly reflect and rework materials from various parts of the Pentateuch, especially Exodus (the Sinai sections), Numbers, and Deuteronomy', although the two texts differ in that '4Q368 includes text in which God and Moses are conversing (…) and which contain exhortations (…), while 4Q377 differs in having more about Moses the man.'[3]

An earlier name of the document was 4QApocryphon of Moses C, which relates it to 4Q374–375 (4QApocryphon of Moses A-B), but that designation has been abandoned because the text is a 'Joshua-Apocryphon' or 'Pseudo-Joshua' rather than a 'Moses Apocryphon'[4] or 'Moses-Pseudepigraphon'[5], since Moses is spoken of in the third person, and the events at Sinai are described in the first person plural. Calling 4Q377 a Joshua Apocryphon links it with 4Q378–379 (4QApocryphon of Joshua[a-b], also called 'Psalms of Joshua').[6]

---

1 The investigations have been supported by the Netherlands Organisation for Scientific Research (NWO).

2 J. VanderKam / M. Brady, 377. 4QApocryphal Pentateuch B, in: M. Bernstein et al., Qumran Cave 4. Miscellanea Part 2, Oxford 2001, 205–217; similarly F. García Martínez / E.J.C. Tigchelaar, The Dead Sea Scrolls. Study Edition, 2 vols., Leiden 1997–98, II, 743.

3 VanderKam/Brady, 4QApocryphal Pentateuch B, 207.

4 This designation is used in G. Vermes, The Complete Dead Sea Scrolls in English, London 1997, 542 and M. Wise / M. Abegg / E. Cook, The Dead Sea Scrolls. A New Translation, San Francisco 1996, 337–338.

5 Thus G.G. Xeravits, King, Priest, Prophet. Positive Eschatological Protagonists of the Qumran Library (STDJ 47), Leiden 2003, 124.

6 J. Zimmermann, Messianische Texte aus Qumran. Königliche, priesterliche und prophetische Messiasvorstellungen in den Schriftfunden von Qumran (WUNT 104), Tübingen 1998, 340–341; similarly VanderKam/Brady, 4QApocryphal Pentateuch B,

The names 'Apocryphal Pentateuch', 'Moses Apocryphon' and
'Joshua Apocryphon' share the characterisation of our document as
'apocryphal'. It should be remembered, however, that designations like
'Rewritten Bible', 'Apocryphon' and the like are problematic because
they suggest a kind of secondary status of these documents compared
with the so-called 'canonical' Bible which they reworked or paraphrased.[7]

In the present paper we will focus on the *relecture*[8] or retelling of
the Sinai and Horeb stories from Exodus and Deuteronomy in the second half of 4Q377 2 II[9], but it should be remembered that in the context
of this Qumran document these stories play only a subsidiary role. The
main issue is the observation of the commandments, rather than God's
revelation at Sinai or Moses' glorification.[10] The Sinai/Horeb traditions
function to strengthen the encouragement to obey God's command-

---

Tübingen 1998, 340–341; similarly VanderKam/Brady, 4QApocryphal Pentateuch B,
207. Also the references to the tribes in col. I suggest that the text dealt with regulations
analogous to the land division in Josh 13–19 (Zimmermann, Messianische Texte, 341).

7   Cf. J.P. Meier, The Historical Jesus and the Historical Law: Some Problems within the
Problem, CBQ 65 (2003) 52–59, esp. 57 n. 10: 'The phrase "rewritten Bible" has become common in discussions about the intertestamental writings that, in one way or another, reworked, paraphrased, or added to books that later formed the canon of Scripture. However, the phrase is, technically speaking, inaccurate since no "Bible" with an
agreed-upon list of all the books accepted as inspired and normative existed in the latter
centuries B.C.; hence, there was no Bible to "rewrite" (...) Especially problematic are
the fragments from Cave 4 of Qumran that are given telling labels such as Reworked
Pentateuch (4Q158; 4Q364.365.366.367), Apocryphon Pentateuch A (4Q368), Apocryphon Pentateuch B (4Q377), and the Apocryphon of Moses (4Q375, 376). To what extent these texts should be considered variant textual traditions of the Pentateuch, early
targums of the Pentateuch, or attempts to replace the traditional version(s) of the Pentateuch with a new version remains unclear; the fragmentary nature of the evidence
makes a final decision very difficult.' See also B. Chiesa, Biblical Texts from Qumran,
Henoch 20 (1998) 131–151, esp. 132.

8   Thus Zimmermann, Messianische Texte, 341.

9   This text has also attracted attention because of the epithets given to Moses: משיחו (line
5; cf. Xeravits, King, Prophet, Priest, 125, 130–132.136.179; Zimmermann, Messianische Texte, 339–340 איש האלוהים (line 10; cf. Xeravits, ibid., 178; Zimmermann,
ibid., 339), איש חסדים (line 12; cf. Zimmermann, ibid., 336.339; VanderKam/Brady,
4QApocryphal Pentateuch B, 212 [on 2 I 8]) and according to some interpreters also
מבשר (line 11; see below). These epithets will be discussed by other contributors to the
present volume.

10 Cf. Zimmermann, Messianische Texte, 341: 'Auch wenn für den heutigen Ausleger von
4Q377 die Aussagen über Mose zum Interessantesten des Textes gehören, hat der Text
nicht in erster Linie die Absicht, eine Darstellung der Person Moses zu bieten. Die
einleitende Fluchformel gibt zu erkennen, daß er vor allem um das Einhalten der
Gebote geht. Die Hervorhebung der Einzigartigkeit des Sinaiereignisses und der Unver-
gleichlichkeit Moses dienen dazu, die besondere Autorität der Gebote Gottes hervor-
zuheben und die Zuhörer bzw. Leser zum Bewahren dieser Gebote zu bewegen'.

ments. In the beginning of 2 II, a certain אליבח[11] curses those who do not obey Moses' commandments (חוקות מושה[12]) in a language that is reminiscent of curse formulae in Deuteronomy and Jeremiah (see especially Deut 27,26; Jer 11,3).[13] This is followed by a reference to, and a retelling of the Sinai and Horeb stories.[14]

2. 4Q377 and the Sinai and Horeb traditions

The second half of 4Q377 2 II deals with the people's experiences at Sinai. The author of our text draws from both Exodus and Deuteronomy. The direct 'face to face' communication between God and the people stands closer to Deuteronomy than Exodus, but the idiom 'as a man speaks to his friend', which is used to describe this communication, comes from Exod 33,11, where it occurs in relation to Moses.[15] Also the name 'Sinai' rather than 'Horeb' comes from Exodus[16], as does the 'priestly' term כבוד, but קהל as a designation for the people of Israel is favoured by Deuteronomy, although not completely absent from Exodus. There are also some reminiscences to the theophany in Exodus 24. Taking a closer look at the words and expressions in 4Q377 and their use in the Hebrew Bible, we can discern eight passages in which a concentration of them occurs.

1. Exod 19,16–19. Parallels with 4Q377 include the thunders (קלת; the singular קל is used for the trumpet blast and the thunder in which God answers Moses), the cloud (ענן) on Mount Sinai (על הר סיני), the trembling of the people (חרד; cf. רעדודיה אחזתם in 4Q377) , the LORD descending upon the mountain in fire (באש), and Moses speaking (דבר) with God.

---

11   Thus VanderKam/Brady, 4QApocryphal Pentateuch B, 213; Zimmermann (Messianische Texte, 334) reads אליכה; E. Puech (Le fragment 2 de 4Q377, Pentateuque apocryphe B : L'exaltation de Moïse, RdQ 21 [2004] 469–475, esp. 471) has אליבוא, which he interprets as אל יבוא 'Qu'il n'entre/vienne pas!'). The proper name אליבה does not occur in the Hebrew Bible; VanderKam/Brady, 4QApocryphal Pentateuch B, 214, compare KAI 183,6 אלבא.

12   This phrase is not attested in the Hebrew Bible (VanderKam/Brady, 4QApocryphal Pentateuch B, 215).

13   Thus Zimmermann, Messianische Texte, 341; VanderKam/Brady, 4QApocryphal Pentateuch B, 215. Note that also the curse formula in Jer 11,3 is followed by a retelling of the Exodus and Sinai stories (Zimmermann, ibid.).

14   Cf. Zimmermann, Messianische Texte, 337.341.

15   For details see below, Section 3.

16   Cf. Zimmermann, Messianische Texte, 338.

2. Exod 20,18–22. Parallels with 4Q377 include the mountain (הר), the thunder (קולת; the singular קל is used for the sound of the trumpet), the people seeing (ראה Qal; cf. הראנו in 4Q377), and their trembling and fear (נוע & ירא; cf. רעדודיה אחזתם in 4Q377). This passage mentions God speaking with the people (דבר עם) from heaven (מן השמים) as well as their request that God might not speak with (דבר עם) them anymore and that, instead, Moses might speak to them. A contrast is made between the people, who stand at a distance (twice מרחק ויעמדו/ויעמד), and Moses, who draws near to God (compare the contrastive ומשה in 20,21 with that in 4Q377 2 II 10).

3. Exod 24,15–18. Parallels with 4Q377 include the cloud that covers the mountain (ויכס הענן את ההר and ויכסהו הענן; if the suffix of ויכסהו is taken as referring to Moses, the parallel with 4Q377 becomes even closer), the appearance of the glory of the LORD (מראה כבוד יהוה; cf. כבוד אלוהים and הראנו in 4Q377), which is like a fire (אש) on Mount Sinai (על הר סיני), and Moses abiding on the mountain.[17]

4. Exod 33,9–11. Unlike 4Q377, this passage deals with the communication between God and Moses in the Tent of Meeting. The people saw (ראה Qal; cf. הראנו in 4Q377) the pillar of cloud (ענן) standing (עמד) at the door of the tent when the LORD spoke with (דבר עם; also דבר אל) Moses 'face to face, as a man speaks to his friend' (אל רעהו פנים אל פנים כאשר ידבר איש).

5. Deut 4,10–15. Parallels with 4Q377 include the mountain (הר) that burned (בער), the fire (אש), the heavens (שמים), the cloud (ענן), and the sound (קול; cf. קולות in 4Q377). God commanded Moses to gather (קהל Hifil; cf. קהל in 4Q377) the people and they stood (עמד) at the foot of the mountain and the LORD spoke (דבר) to them. Moses was further commanded to teach (ללמד; cf. להודיע in 4Q377) the statutes (חקים; cf. חוקות in 4Q377).

6. Deut 4,33–40. Parallels with 4Q377 include the fire (אש), the sound (קול; cf. קולות in 4Q377), God speaking (דבר) to the people, his statutes (חקיו; cf. חוקות in 4Q377) and the expressions 'out of heaven' (מן השמים) and 'and on earth' (ועל הארץ).[18] The phrases 'to you it was shown' (ראה Hofal) and 'He let you see his great fire' (את אשו הגדולה הראך) can be compared with הראנו באש בעורה in 4Q377, and 'that you

---

17   Note also עצם השמים in Exod 24,10 and 4Q377 1 I 2.
18   Note that in 4Q377 the fire is 'from heaven', while in Deut 4,36 it is 'on the earth'.

might know that the LORD is God; there is no other besides him' (מלבדו
עוד אין האלהים הוא יהוה כי לדעת) and 'know (...) that the LORD is
God' (וידעת [···] כי יהוה הוא האלהים) with כיא אין אלוה מבלעדיו
להודיע.

7. Deut 5,4–6. In this passage we find the mountain (הר), the fire
(אש), the LORD speaking with (דבר עם) the people 'face to face' (בפנים
פנים), the people's reaction of fear (ירא; cf. רעדודיה אחזתם), Moses
standing (עמד) between the LORD and the people, and his task of de-
claring (להגיד; cf. להודיע in 4Q377) to them the word of the LORD.
God's words 'I am the LORD your God' (אנכי יהוה אלהיך) can be compared with כיא אין אלוה מבלעדיו in 4Q377.[19]

8. Deut 5,22–27. Parallels with 4Q377 include the burning (בער)
mountain (הר), the fire (אש), the cloud (ענן), the voice (קול; cf. קולות in
4Q377), the assembly (קהל), God speaking (דבר) with the people and
with Moses, and his act of showing (ראה Hifil) his glory (כבוד) to the
people, who are flesh (בשר).

3. God and the people

In line 6 we find the expression פנים עם אל פנים. This is equivalent to
פנים אל פנים[20] which is used twice in the Hebrew Bible for the communication between God and Moses, in Exod 33,11 and Deut 34,10. The
former is the closest parallel to 4Q377 2 II 6–7, because it also contains
כאשר ידבר איש אל רעהו 'as a man speaks to his friend'.[21] An expression equivalent to פנים אל פנים is פה אל פה, which occurs together with
the verb דבר in Num 12,8.[22] The phrase פנים אל פנים is also used in
relation to Jacob (Gen 32,31) and Gideon (Judg 6,22).

19 According to Zimmermann, Messianische Texte, 338, כיא אין אלוה מבלעדיו in 4Q377
   reflects a reworking of Deut 5,6 אנכי יהוה אלהיך: this *monolatric* command of the
   Decalogue (cf. Deut 5,4–22) has been coloured by *monotheistic* passages such as Deut
   4,35; 1 Sam 2,2; 2 Sam 22,32 = Ps 18,23; Isa 44,8 and other passages in Deutero-Isaiah.
20 Since פנים עם אל פנים occurs also in 4Q377 1 II 5, we prefer to regard it as a reflection
   of the tendency to heap up prepositions, which is also attested in Late Biblical Hebrew
   and Rabbinic Hebrew, and occasionally elsewhere in Qumran Hebrew, rather than a
   scribal error; cf. R. Polzin, Late Biblical Hebrew. Toward a Historical Typology of Biblical Hebrew Prose (HSM 12), Missoula 1976, 69; A. Bendavid, לשון מקרא ולשון חכמים
   (Biblical Hebrew and Mishnaic Hebrew), 2 vols., Tel Aviv 21967–71), I, 66; M. Pérez
   Fernández, An Introductory Grammar of Rabbinic Hebrew (transl. from Spanish by
   John F. Elwolde), Leiden 1997, 160.
21 Cf. above, Section 2 (4).
22 Targum Onqelos renders both פה אל פה and פנים אל פנים with ממלל עם ממלל.

Since the biblical passages quoted describe God speaking with Moses פנים אל פנים as an extraordinary event, demonstrating Moses' incomparability, it is remarkable that 4Q377 says that He spoke in this manner to the congregation of Israel.[23] But there are some passages in the Hebrew Bible where it is said that God spoke face to face with the people. The exact phrase פנים אל פנים is used for the communication between God and the people in Ezek 20,35–36, where God says that He will enter into judgement (שפט Nifal) with the people פנים אל פנים as He did with their fathers 'in the wilderness of the land of Egypt'.[24] In Deut 5,4 Moses says that God spoke (דבר) with the children of Israel פנים בפנים. Although the preposition is different, the use of the verb דבר agrees with the 4Q377 passage.[25]

Line 7 continues by telling that God showed a burning fire (reading הראנו as a Hifil)[26] or appeared as a burning fire (reading הראנו as a Hofal)[27] in the heaven above.[28]

4. Who was standing upon the mountain?

Opinions differ about the subject of עמד in line 8: is it God or Moses? The understanding that God is the subject of עמד is supported by the

---

23 Considering Moses, rather than God as the subject of ויִדבר does not give more sense to this passage; cf. Zimmermann, Messianische Texte, 337: 'Zwar ware auch Mose als Redener denkbar, aber die Theophanieaussagen (Z. 7) und das Sehen-Lassen' (הראנו) sprechen für Gott als Subjekt.'

24 Neither Zimmermann, nor VanderKam/Brady, nor Puech mentions this parallel, perhaps because they focus too much on the parallels in the books of Exodus or Deuteronomy.

25 Here too Targum Onqelos has ממלל עם ממלל.

26 Thus Zimmermann, Messianische Texte, 335; VanderKam/Brady, 4QApocryphal Pentateuch B, 214; Puech, 4Q377, 470; Vermes, Dead Sea Scrolls, 542.

27 Thus Wise/Abegg/Cook, Dead Sea Scrolls, 338; García Martínez / Tigchelaar, Study Edition II, 745.

28 According to VanderKam/Brady, 4QApocryphal Pentateuch B, 215, הראנו could be either Hifil or Hofal, although a suffix would be unexpected with a Hophal. Note however, that 'many Hebrew verbs take a suffix pronoun where such a pronoun has "datival" force and therefore is normally capable of being rewritten by means of a preposition other than את', according to P. Joüon / T. Muraoka, A Grammar of Biblical Hebrew, 2 Vols. (SubBi 14), Rome 1993, §125ba. In the Hebrew Bible the Hofal with a suffix is, according to some, attested in the form תָּעׇבְדֵם (Exod 20,5; 23,24; Deut 5,9; 13,3) (thus e.g. the parsing of the Accordance Bible software), but this form should be interpreted as a Peal; cf. Joüon/Muraoka, Grammar, §63; compare the forms of the type יקוטלנו with a vowel letter after the first radical in Qumran Hebrew; E. Qimron, Hebrew of the Dead Sea Scrolls (HSS 29), Atlanta 1986, 51–53.

subsequent 'trembling' in reaction to God's glory[29], as well as passages
from Exodus and Deuteronomy to which these lines seem to refer, such
as Exod 19,20 וירד יהוה על הר סיני אל ראש ההר.[30] One could object
that such an anthropomorphic remark about God standing is unusual[31],
but there are some parallels in the Hebrew Bible. In Hab 3,6, which is
part of a description of a theophany, God standing there causes the
mountains and people to tremble. God standing 'on the mountain' occurs in Sach 14,4 ועמדו רגליו ביום ההוא על הר הזתים and God 'standing
on the rock' in Exod 17,6 הנני עמד לפניך שם על הצור בחרב. In Ezek
11,23 the כבוד יהוה is standing on a mountain.[32]

Crispin Fletcher-Louis has proposed a different interpretation, in
which Moses is the subject of עמד. He gives the following arguments
for this interpretation:[33]

1.   The subject of this verb 'teaches that there "is no God apart
from *him* and no rock like *him*" this might imply that he is, in fact,
someone other than God.'

2.   The 'literary and conceptual structure of the text' in 4Q377 2 II
6–8 has been provided by Deut 5,4–6, and in these verses it is Moses
who stands.

3.   'The standing theme is important for the text as a whole. Line
10a refers to the assembly of the people standing at Sinai and in line 4
we already have יעמוד.'

In our view, however, these arguments are not convincing. The first
argument is only valid if the following כיא clause is considered as direct speech. It is also possible, however, to interpret כיא as a particle
introducing indirect speech, in which case the reference to God in the
third person is not irregular.[34] Moreover, the parallel to this כיא clause

---

29   Zimmermann, Messianische Texte, 338: 'Bei עמד ist offen, wer Subjekt ist. Der Duktus
des Textes spricht zusammen mit der sich anschließenden und von "Zittern" begleiteten
כבוד-Erscheinung (Z. 9) für Gott als Subjekt.'
30   Cf. VanderKam/Brady, 4QApocryphal Pentateuch B, 215.
31   Cf. Zimmermann, Messianische Texte, 338.
32   Other examples of the verb עמד with God as subject (Isa 3,13; Ps 10,1; 102,27; 109,31)
are less relevant for our purpose, although we cannot rule out that these cases, in which
צמד seems to be used metaphorically, inspired the author of the Qumran document to
use צמד with God as subject.
33   C.H.T. Fletcher-Louis, All the Glory of Adam. Liturgical Anthropology in the Dead
Sea Scrolls (STDJ 42), Leiden 2002, 141–148; these pages are a slightly revised version
of idem, Some Reflections on Angelomorphic Humanity Texts among the Dead Sea
Scrolls, DSD 7 (2000) 292–312.
34   The use of indirect speech instead of direct speech increases in Late Biblical Hebrew;
see W. van Peursen / E. Talstra, Computer-Assisted Analysis of Parallel Texts in the
Bible. The Case of 2 Kings 18–19 and Its Parallels in Isaiah and Chronicles, forthcoming in VT 57 (2007) 45–72, esp. 70.

in Deut 5,6 (cf. Fletcher-Louis' second argument) is pronounced by God.

The second argument is not compelling because Deut 5,4–6 cannot be singled out as the most important source of this part of 4Q377. As we have seen in Section 2, there are quite a number of biblical passages containing parallels to 4Q377. An attempt to answer the question as to the subject of עמד in 4Q377 II 8 on the basis of parallels from Exodus and Deuteronomy, may even tip the balance towards the interpretation in which God is the subject of עמד. That it is God who stood 'on the earth... the mountain' is supported by e.g. Exod 19,20, quoted above, and Deut 4,36, where מן השמים ··· ועל הארץ is used to locate two actions of God (cf. Section 2). Even the parallel in Deut 5,4–6 argues in two directions: Moses is the one who stands, but God is the one who speaks (cf. Fletcher-Louis' first argument).

The third argument is not convincing either. The verb עמד occurs three times in 4Q377, including the disputed example under discussion. In the two other cases it is used in two rather different ways. In line 4 it refers to the keeping of God's commands, in line 10 to the people standing at a distance from Mount Sinai. The conclusion that עמד has thematic significance in 4Q377 and that therefore the subject of the third, disputed occurrence of עמד must be Moses, is unfounded.

The question arises as to whether more can be said about the subject of עמד on the basis of syntactical or text-hierarchical considerations. Fletcher-Louis assumes that a change of subject is unlikely and since he takes Moses as the subject of עמד, he goes so far as to assume that Moses is also the subject of the preceding verbs. However, if he cannot convince us that Moses is the subject of the preceding lines, his assumption that a subject change is unlikely becomes an argument against his view that Moses is the subject of עמד.

If we agree with Fletcher-Louis that it is unlikely that the subject of עמד is different from that of the preceding clauses, two interpretations are possible:

a. The subject is Moses, who is also the subject of the preceding lines.[35]

b. The subject is God, who is also the subject of the preceding verbs.[36]

---

35   Thus Fletcher-Louis; but note that in his view the subject is at the same time God, since 'God's standing and that of Moses is deliberately blurred because 4Q377 wants to say that in Moses' standing there is God's standing' (Glory of Adam, 145; Some Reflections, 302).

36   This interpretation is found in the following translations (as appears from the use of capital letters): Wise/Abegg/Cook, Dead Sea Scrolls, 338; Vermes, Dead Sea Scrolls, 542; Puech, 4Q377, 470.

If we consider it possible that the subject of עמד is different from that of the preceding lines, there are two other options.

    c. The subject of עמד is Moses; the subject of the preceding lines is God.[37]

    d. The subject of עמד is God; the subject of the preceding lines is Moses.[38]

To our best knowledge, Fletcher-Louis is the only advocate of the view that the subject of the preceding lines is Moses, but he needs to assume deliberate ambiguity (i.e. the borderline between God and Moses has been blurred) to maintain this theory. In our view, the character of the actions described and the mass of biblical parallels leave little doubt that the subject of these lines is God. This eliminates options b and d. What is essential for the choice between a and c is to ascertain whether it is possible from a syntactic and text-hierarchical perspective to take God as the subject of the preceding lines and Moses as the subject of עמד. Fletcher-Louis' argument for considering a subject change unlikely is that 'there is no grammatical indication of a change of subject at the beginning of line 8 (...), but rather the last of a string of paratactic clauses sharing the same divine subject.' However, if it is formulated in this way, we cannot agree with his argument, because there are many examples in the Bible where there is a change of subject without any 'grammatical indication'.[39] Well known are those dialogues between two persons in which ויאמר without any explicit subject marks the shift from one speaker to the other without mention of the changed subject.[40]

    To decide whether עמד can have a subject that is different from that of the preceding lines we should have a closer look to see under what conditions the explicit reference to a new subject by a common noun or a proper noun is required. Although a subject change can take place without any grammatical indication, there are certain circumstances that require the explicit reference of a new subject.

    1. If the participant is new in the context, they are referred to by a common noun or a proper noun. If they have been mentioned in the

---

37   This possibility is mentioned, but not preferred by Zimmermann; see above, n. 22. We would also arrive at this interpretation if we were to follow Fletcher-Louis in considering Moses as the subject of עמד, but disagree with his more controversial view that Moses is also the subject of the preceding lines.

38   This option is only theoretical. To our best knowledge there are no advocates of this interpretation.

39   Cf. L.J. de Regt, Participants in Old Testament Texts and the Translator. Reference Devices and their Rhetorical Impact (SSN 39), Assen 1999, 43: 'There are many cases where the referent of a pronominal or inflectional element can only be determined through interpretation of the context and knowledge of the world'.

40   De Regt, Participants, 23–32.

directly preceding lines or earlier in the text, a pronoun or affix suf-
fices.[41] Since Moses has been mentioned in line 5, this observation does
not argue against Moses' being the subject of עמד.

2. If the participant is a minor character, they are referred to by a
common noun or a proper noun; if they are a major participant, they are
more likely to receive pronominal or inflectional reference, because of
its status as old information.[42] This observation too is not an objection
to considering Moses the subject of עמד. If God is the subject of עמד,
Moses becomes a major participant only in the final lines of this col-
umn, but if Moses is the subject of עמד, he can be considered a major
participant throughout the text. In other words: It is hard to maintain at
one and the same time that Moses is the subject of עמד *and* that he is a
minor participant (which would require an explicit reference).

3. Explicit reference to a participant by a full noun phrase rather
than by a pronoun or affix is preferred in the opening or closing lines of
a paragraph.[43] In these positions the explicit marking of a participant
serves the logical division of the text into smaller literary units. In
4Q377 this device has indeed been used to structure the text. In line 9
the change from a singular to a plural verb would have been enough to
mark the subject change and the subject of this verb, the קהל ישראל, is
mentioned previously in line 6, but the explicit noun phrase {העד[ר]ה}
הקהל marks the beginning of the subsection about the people's reaction.
In line 10 the noun phrase מושה איש האלוהים re-identifies Moses, who
is the major participant of lines 10–12. Since this observation concerns
reference to a participant as a means of structuring a text, rather than
the identification of a participant, it does not help us identify the subject
of עמד.

4. A common noun or a proper noun is used to avoid ambiguity. In
the line under discussion there seems to be ambiguity regarding the
subject of עמד, but that observation as such does not help us resolve the
ambiguity. Moreover, there is indeed a tendency to avoid ambiguity,

---

41   In his discussion of cases in which a participant is reactivated that has not been men-
     tioned in the immediately preceding clauses but somewhere earlier in the context, De
     Regt, Participants, 44, speaks of 'global strategy' (as against 'local strategy'): The pro-
     noun or affix is assigned to one of the major participants early in the story and is re-
     tained throughout the discourse as referring to this entity, even if there are intervening
     local instances of other potential referents'; see idem, Participant Reference in Some
     Biblical Hebrew Texts, JEOL 32 (1991–92) 150–172, esp. 161–162.
42   De Regt, Participants, 23–27; idem, Participant Reference, 158–161.
43   De Regt, Participants, 13–20; idem, Participant Reference, 156–158.

but there remain many examples in which ambiguity does occur.[44] Note
especially the following example where, as in 4Q377, the question
arises as to whether God or Moses was standing on the mountain: Exod
34,5–6 ויקרא ויהוה פני על יהוה ויעבר יהוה בשם ויקרא שם עמו ויתיצב בענן
ויהוה וירד 'And the LORD descended in the cloud; and he (the LORD or
Moses?) stood with him (the LORD or Moses?) there; and he (the LORD
or Moses?) proclaimed the name of the LORD; and the LORD passed
before him; and he (the LORD or Moses?) proclaimed...'.[45]

5. If two subjects are contrasted, they are referred to explicitly.
Whereas the four preceding observations did not compel us to reject the
interpretation of Moses as the subject of עמד, this final observation
strongly argues against it. If God were the subject of וממ[שמים ממעלה
הראנו באש בעורה and Moses that of ועל הארץ עמד על ההר, there would
be a sharp contrast between God and Moses: the first appeared *from
heaven*, the second stood *on the earth*. In such cases where two elements are contrasted with two other elements, the explicit mention of
the entities in question is the rule. Compare, for example, 1 Sam 15,34
וילך שמואל הרמתה ושאול עלה אל ביתו גבעת שאול 'Then Samuel left for
Ramah, but Saul went up to his home in Gibeah of Saul'. In this case
there is a contrast between 'Samuel' + 'going to Ramah' versus 'Saul'
+ 'going to Gibeah'. The explicit reference to Saul seems obligatory for
the expression of this contrast.[46]

Since we do not have a native informant who can tell us what is
possible and what is not in Classical Hebrew, we should be careful in
drawing conclusions. However, if we do what we can do, namely carefully analyse the way participants are referred to in the Hebrew Bible
and the patterns that can be discerned, and try to establish what from
that perspective is a coherent and reasonable interpretation of our text,
the interpretation that takes God as the subject of עמד appears by far to
be the most preferable. Line 8, like the preceding lines, deals with
God's appearance to the people. This is followed by a subsection in
lines 9–10 describing the reaction of the people, who receive explicit

---

44 De Regt, Participants, 48–54; idem, Participant Reference, 162–164.
45 On the basis of the preceding context, in which God promises '...and I will proclaim
    the name of the LORD' (33,19) and the following context, which describes Moses' reac-
    tion (34,8), De Regt (Participants, 49–50) argues that the inflectional affixes in the sec-
    ond, third and fifth clause refer to the LORD, even though in 33,21 and 34,2 Moses is
    asked 'to stand on the rock' (Nifal of נצב, instead of the Hitpael in 34,5).
46 Compare the contrastive ומושה in Exod 20,21 and ומושה איש האלוהים in 4Q377 2 II 10,
    mentioned above, Section 2.

participant reference at the beginning of this section.[47] It is only in lines 10–12 that Moses becomes the major participant.[48]

5. Moses in the cloud

Lines 9–10 describe the people's reaction to the appearance of God's glory in a way that contains many parallels to passages from Exodus and Deuteronomy, especially Exod 19–20, 24:[49] They answered[50] and were seized with trembling because of God's glory and the wondrous thunder and they stood at a distance.

From the second half of line 10 till the end, the focus is entirely on Moses. He was with God in the cloud, which covered him; he was sanctified; and he spoke 'from the mouth of God' as a מלאך. The meeting of God and Moses in the cloud reminds us of Exod 24,15–18 and 33,7–11.[51] The motif of the cloud is also found in other contexts, which deal with angelic or divine beings, such as the Son of Man in Dan 7,13 and Jesus at the Transfiguration. However, there is no indication that the author of our text wanted to go beyond the description of Moses in the Exodus passages by trying to depict him as an 'angelomorphic'[52] or 'angelified'[53] being.

The suffix of בהקדשו refers in all likelihood to Moses, although we cannot rule out the possibility that its referent is the mountain. In Exodus we read that the people are sanctified (Exod 19,10,14,22) as well as the mountain (19,23); the sanctification of Moses has a parallel in Sir 45,2.[54]

---

47   In Vermes' translation (Dead Sea Scrolls, 338) the direct speech that started in line 3 ends here; on the contrary VanderKam/Brady, 4QApocryphal Pentateuch B, 214, do not give a match to the quotation mark in line 3, apparently because they consider all that follows the content of the direct speech.

48   On the contrast between Moses and the trembling people in this passage see Xeravits, King, Priest, Prophet, 127.

49   For details see above, Section 2.

50   We interpret ענה as 'to answer' (thus VanderKam/Brady, 4QApocryphal Pentateuch B, 214; Puech, 4Q377, 470; cf. Exod 19,8; 24,3) rather than 'to be bent, oppressed' (thus Zimmermann, Messianische Texte, 335–336).

51   For details see above, Section 2.

52   Thus Fletcher-Louis, Glory of Adam, 142; idem, Some Reflections, 298–305; he also speaks of Moses becoming a 'divine' figure.

53   Thus Xeravits, King, Priest, Prophet, 122.128.174.201.

54   Fletcher-Louis, Glory of Adam, 142; idem, Some Reflections, 293. The parallel from b. Yoma 4a, in which Moses is sanctified (ונתקדש בענן כדי לקבל תורה לישראל בקדושה משה עלה בענן ונתכסה בענן) mentioned by the DJD editors (VanderKam/Brady, 4QApocryphal Pentateuch B, 216) is interesting, but too late to help us in the interpretation of this Qumran text.

In the second half of line 11 we read that Moses spoke God's words like a 'messenger' or 'angel'.[55] However, since a comparison does not imply complete overlap, this does not mean that Moses is elevated to the level of being 'God's angel' or that this passage 'align[s] the law-giver with the Angel of the LORD tradition'.[56] It indicates rather his role as a trustworthy messenger who passed God's words on to the people.[57] Moses' incomparability (cf. Deut 34,10–12; AssMos 11,16–17) is further expressed by the rhetoric question כמוהו] מי מבשׁנר 'who from all flesh is like him?'[58] (cf. Sir 45,4 [MS B] בחר בו מכל בנשׁר[59]) or 'who was a messenger like him?'[60] The interpretation of the last line is difficult because of the lacunae. Perhaps it refers to the 'wonders never done before in any nation in the whole world' in Exod 34,10.[61]

6. Conclusions

The results of our investigation, both for the interpretation of 4Q377 2 II and for the methodological question of how the analysis of such a *relecture* of a biblical story should proceed, can be summarised as follows:

– 4Q377 contains a retelling of the Sinai and Horeb stories from Exodus and Deuteronomy. The author takes phrases from or alludes to these various traditions, sources and books indiscriminately. This means that the interpretation of the text cannot depend solely on

---

55   Thus VanderKam/Brady, 4QApocryphal Pentateuch B, 214 (they translate מלאך with 'messenger'); Wise/Abegg/Cook (Dead Sea Scrolls, 338) translate 'God would speak through his mouth as though he were an angel', which is possible as well; cf. AssMos 11,17, where Moses is called the magnus nuntius, on which see J. Tromp, The Assumption of Moses. A Critical Edition with Commentary (SVTP 10), Leiden 1993, 257.
56   Cf. VanderKam/Brady, 4QApocryphal Pentateuch B, 216; *pace* Fletcher-Louis, Glory of Adam, 146; idem, Some Reflections 302–303.
57   Cf. Deut 18,18 ונתתי דברי בפיו (concerning the 'prophet like Moses').
58   Thus VanderKam/Brady, 4QApocryphal Pentateuch B, 214; Zimmermann, Messianische Texte, 335; Fletcher-Louis, Glory of Adam, 141.
59   Cf. Fletcher-Louis, Glory of Adam, 142: 'The interrogative expression "who from flesh…" would tie up well with Ben Sira 45,4; Jub 31,14 and other DSS texts where angelomorphism is expressed in terms of a transcendence of that realm'.
60   Thus García Martínez / Tigchelaar, Study Edition II, 745; Vermes, Dead Sea Scrolls, 542; similarly Xeravits, King, Priest, Prophet, 179: 'Moses, according to 4Q377, is a "messenger" (מבשר). The author considers this title to be important: he emphasizes it stylistically by inserting an interrogative form'; see also ibid. 126, where Xeravits argues that מבשר denotes 'a figure with prophetic characteristics'; cf. VanderKam/Brady, 4QApocryphal Pentateuch B, 216; Fletcher-Louis, Glory of Adam, 142; Zimmermann, Messianische Texte, 336.
61   Cf. Zimmermann, Messianische Texte, 339.

one out of many parallel biblical passages. For this reason, we rejected that view that Deut 5,4–6 has provided the 'literary and conceptual structure of the text' in 4Q377 2 II 6–8 and that therefore
Moses should be taken as the subject of עמד in line 8.

–   As long as the text does not go beyond the biblical language, we
should not read into it more than what is found in the biblical parallels. Thus the cloud that covered Moses on the mountain in 4Q377
2 II can be accounted for sufficiently by the parallels from Exodus
and Deuteronomy. It does not support the claim that Moses is depicted here as an angelic or divine being, such as the Son of Man in
Daniel or Jesus in the Transfiguration stories.

–   For the composition of this text the author apparently drew not only
from parallel texts that tell 'the same story'. Thus the closest parallel for the expression פנים עם אל פנים for the communication between God and the people occurs in Ezekiel. Likewise, the epithets
given to Moses, משיחו and perhaps מבשר, do not come from Exodus
or Deuteronomy, but rather from Deutero- and Trito-Isaiah.[62] Taking into account these Old Testament parallels and observing that
4Q377 does not surpass them, again prevent us from claiming that
these titles are used to elevate Moses to the realm of the angelic and
the divine. We should be even more careful in drawing conclusions
on the basis of the terminology used, if that terminology occurs in a
comparison. In 4Q377 Moses' speech is compared with that of an
angel (or just a messenger!), but that does not imply that Moses has
become a מלאך.

–   Sometimes the author seems to re-use biblical phraseology. Thus
the expression 'as a man speaks to his friend', which in the Bible
describes Moses' incomparability, is in 4Q377 applied to the people. The question whether this indicates a deliberate re-use of biblical phraseology, thus creating a 'patchwork of biblical language
and allusions'[63] (i.e. the author deliberately applies to the whole
congregation an expression that in the Bible is reserved for Moses)
or an indiscriminate use of the stock of Biblical Hebrew – or, even
more general: 'Classical Hebrew' – words and idioms (i.e. the author was acquainted with 'face to face' and 'as a man speaks to his
friend' as expressions that indicate an intimate relationship) is beyond the scope of the present paper. The tacit assumption of the
first option in much scholarly literature can be questioned.

62   Elsewhere we have argued that the notion of 'parallel texts' is very complex, because it
may refer to a large range of different phenomena; see Van Peursen / Talstra, Parallel
Texts.
63   Fletcher-Louis, Glory of Adam, 141; idem, Some Reflections, 299.

– A meticulous study of biblical and extra-biblical parallels should
  accompany, but never overrule, the syntactic, text-hierarchical and
  literary analysis of a text in its own right. In our investigation, observations on syntactical structure and participant reference were
  decisive for answering the question as to the subject of עמד in line
  8. This line belongs to a description of the encounter between God
  and the people (lines 6–8), followed by the people's reaction of
  trembling and standing at a distance (lines 8–10), which is contrasted with Moses' ascent of the mountain and his sojourn with
  God (lines 10–12).

According to Fletcher-Louis 'The Qumran sectarians knew and evidently whole-heartedly approved of the tradition that Moses was a divine man and that, in particular, upon his ascent up Mount Sinai, he
was transfigured to an angelic and glorious form.'[64] As to 4Q377,
which plays a major role in Fletcher-Louis' argument, we agree that the
text reflects a high esteem of Moses, the man of God who ascended
Mount Sinai whereas the people stood at a distance. However, the portrayal of Moses in this text is similar but not superior to that in the Sinai
and Horeb stories in the Pentateuch. It is enriched by designations such
as בפי משה and משיח, which reflect the understanding of Moses as a
prophet, but it does not elevate him to the level of being an angelic or
divine being.

---

64 Glory of Adam, 137.

Was Moses considered to be an angel by those at Qumran?

by Phoebe Makiello

1. Introduction

Two fragmentary manuscripts in particular, 4Q374 and 4Q377 have raised speculations that Moses was accorded a "divine and angelic"[1] status by those at Qumran. Given the revelatory role of angels in Second Temple Jewish apocalypses, as well as Moses' traditional status as mediator of the Torah, the idea that he was considered to be an angel by those at Qumran has potentially groundbreaking implications for the role and nature of divine revelation at Qumran.

Whilst investigating whether Moses was considered to be an angel in these two texts, I shall also be enquiring whether he was portrayed as an angelomorphic figure. In line with the work by Rowland[2], D. Hannah[3] and Sullivan[4] I shall be using the term 'angelomorphic' to denote descriptions of humans as appearing in the form ($\mu o\rho\phi\acute{\eta}$) of angels. This term does not imply that the human being was identified with "that created order [the angels]"[5], and so may enable a more cautious consideration of the evidence, where no clear identification with or transformation into an angel is implied. This in no way entails that the human in question ought to be considered as ontologically transformed. At the same time this term shall be used to imply something more than

---

1   C. Fletcher-Louis, All the Glory of Adam, Leiden 2002, Chapter Five: The Divine and Angelic Moses at Qumran, 137–149.
2   C. Rowland, The Open Heaven: A Study of Apocalyptic in Judaism and Early Christianity, New York 1982; idem, A Man Clothed in Linen: Daniel 10.6ff and Jewish Angelology, JSNT 24 (1985) 99–110.
3   D.D. Hannah, Michael and Christ: Michael Traditions and Angel Christology in Early Christianity, Tübingen 1999, 13. – Hannah, though he focuses on portrayals of Christ, confines the use of the term "angelomorphic" to visual phenomena.
4   K.P. Sullivan, Wrestling with Angels: A Study of the Relationship between Angels and Humans in Ancient Jewish Literature and the New Testament, Leiden 2004.
5   Rowland, A Man Clothed in Linen, 100.

simple analogy. The term 'angelic' is avoided as potentially confusing except when used in quotations.

Following Michael Mach's criticism of those who concentrate solely on passages containing the word מלאך in their studies of angels[6], evidence shall also be considered which might seem to suggest that Moses appeared as a supernatural being, even where other terms are employed. This especially justifies the inclusion of 4Q374 in our discussion, as it contains no instance of the word מלאך. Nonetheless, this should not be taken to imply any sort of fluidity between the categories of human, angel and God.

An angel shall be understood as a heavenly being who mediated between the human and the divine, and belongs to a quite separate ontological category from humans and from God in Second Temple writings, as Sullivan's collection of relevant data and commentary thereof has demonstrated[7]. Of course, in both Hebrew and Greek, the most common terms, מלאך and ἄγγελος had the flexibility to refer to either human or divine messengers. However, as Sullivan has shown, this does not necessarily imply any blurring between angels and humans[8].

The provenance of both fragments, 4Q374 and 4Q377, must be ascertained before one is able to proceed to a detailed analysis of the texts themselves: were they composed by a group based at Qumran or are they to be considered pre-Qumranic? The relationship between the two documents must also be questioned: are they both fragments of a larger coherent document, or were they composed as separate texts? Both these points bear upon the relevance of the documents to our understanding of beliefs about Moses at Qumran.

2. Provenance and Relatedness

4Q374 contains, according to Newsom[9], "no indications of Qumran authorship". This is also the case with 4Q377. Furthermore, both documents freely use the Tetragrammaton, which argues against a Qumran origin as it is avoided in sectarian literature. The physical manuscripts however are dated to different periods, as the script used in 4Q374 is early Herodian semiformal, dating the scroll to 30–1 BCE,

---

6   M. Mach, Entwicklungsstadien des jüdischen Engelglaubens in vorrabbinischer Zeit, Tübingen, 1992, 1–6.
7   Sullivan, Wrestling, 1–145.227– 237.
8   Sullivan, ibidem, 27–145.
9   C. Newsom, 4Q374: A Discourse on the Exodus/Conquest Tradition, in: D. Dimant / U. Rappaport (eds.), The Dead Sea Scrolls, Forty Years of Research, Leiden 1992, 40–52.

whilst 4Q377 was written in the Hasmonean period, between 100–50 BCE, with a date earlier in this 50 year period considered more likely by VanderKam and Brady in DJD XXVIII. This in itself does not preclude a close relationship between the texts, but, while 4Q377 prefers the fuller spelling familiar with Qumran texts, 4Q374 is orthographically conservative, with even לא and כל spelt without waw.

There is no a priori indication that the fragments belong to a single work, and since they appear to cover similar themes and events, it is unlikely that they belonged to a larger document but ought rather to be considered separate compositions.

It is nevertheless quite possible that both these texts derive from a very similar milieu. The authors, however, do not appear to have been members of the Qumran yahad. Nonetheless, given the importance accorded to Moses in texts such as 1QS 5,8 and the pre-sectarian CD 15,9.12; 16,1–2.5, where joining the community is tantamount to "taking upon oneself to return to the Torah of Moses"[10], the presence of an angelomorphic Moses in a non-biblical manuscript found at Qumran might provide an insight into conceptions of Moses by those who formed the Qumran yahad, or at the very least inform us concerning texts potentially influential to those who authored the sectarian scrolls.

3. Textual Analysis

Fletcher-Louis sees both 4Q374 and 4Q377 as describing "the divine and angelic Moses"[11]. Here, the texts will be examined separately in order to test this claim.

a) 4Q374[12]

4Q374 appears to recount traditions of the Exodus and settlement in Canaan. The largest fragment, fragment 2 ii, has been interpreted by Fletcher-Louis as recording the "deification of Moses at Sinai"[13]. Lines 6–11 are particularly pertinent to this question:

---

10   האיש על נפשך לשוב אל תורת משה.

11   Fletcher-Louis, All the Glory of Adam, 137. He goes so far as to posit the existence, at Qumran, of a "tradition that Moses is *elohim*", 140–141.

12   Text to be found in DJD XIX, ed. with notes by C. Newsom, Oxford 1995.

13   Fletcher-Louis, All the Glory of Adam, 137–141.

יחדו ויח[ּ]₀ 2 [— —] ויֿרוֿממו גוים בָּאָף[ֿ] 3 [— —] במעלליהם ובנדת
מעשי הֿ[ֿ]. [— —] 4 ואין ל[כם] שרית ופליטה ולצאצאיהֿם מ[]₀
[— —] .[— —] 5 ויטע ל[נ]ֿוֿ בחירו בארץ חמדות כל הארצות ברי [— —]
[6 .[וֿ]יֿתננו לאלוהים על אדירים ומחינ[ה]לפרעה עבֿ[ן — —].
7 [יֿ]ֿתמוֿגֿגֿו ויתנועעו לבם וימסו קרבֿיֿ[ה]ֿם [וֿ]יֿרחם בכֿ[]₀ — —].
8 ובהאירו פנֿו אליהם [ ]למרפֿאֿוֿיֿגֿבֿירו לב[ם] עוֿד ודֿעֿתֿ[— —]
[9. וכֿל לא ידעוך ויתמוגגו ויתנֿ[וֿ]ֿעֿוֿ חֿנֿוֿ לק[וֿל] 10 [— —]
[להם] לֿ [ ] להושיע יבעֿ[ֿ] [שֿ]₀₀₀ וֿ]₀ 11 [— —] [לֿ [— —]].

Fletcher-Louis insists that the agent in lines 6–10 is Moses, and so argues that he assimilates the role of the divine warrior. He also believes that the non-recognition in line 9 "is also an element of the theophanic constellation ...". This, he contends, is a "recurrent feature of the angelophony form" and it has been "transferred to the angelomorphic human"[14]. However, this point alone cannot justify the identification of Moses as either an angel or as angelomorphic. All the more so since it is not clear that Moses is in fact the cause of fear in lines 7–9.

Indeed, though there is little doubt that line 6 refers to Moses, two points need to be clarified. Firstly, what are we to make of [וֿ]יֿתננו לאלוהים? Secondly, who is the subject of the singular verbs in lines 7–9?

Fletcher-Louis argues that line 6 is a midrashic expansion of Exod 7,1 and that the text as a whole combines "the statement in Exodus that God 'made Moses as God to Pharaoh' with the description of Moses' glorious appearance on his descent from Mount Sinai in Exodus 34"[15]. Although the reference to Exod 7,1 in line 6 is unquestionable, it does not include any mention of Moses' appearance. Moreover, לאלוהים would seem to imply an analogy with God, rather than a deification. Indeed, the phrase which follows, על אדירים ומחינ[ה]לפרעה, appears to designate those to whom Moses becomes "as God", thus qualifying and restricting the scope of לאלוהים.

Is there any reason, nonetheless, to understand the subject of the verbs in lines 7–10 as Moses? If there were, this might strengthen the case for calling him a "divine Moses"[16], since the passage appears to describe the effects of the divine presence upon humans. The first singular verb, in line 7, [וֿ]יֿרחם is generally used of God, especially with relation to his people[17]. It is never used of Moses and if used of a hu-

---

14   Fletcher-Louis, ibid., 139.
15   Fletcher-Louis, ibid., 136.
16   Fletcher-Louis, ibid., 137.
17   For instance in Exod 33,19; Deut 30,3. See also F. Brown / S. Driver / C. Briggs, The Brown-Driver-Briggs Hebrew and English Lexicon, 1906, 933.

man, the latter is generally a conqueror[18]. This appears to be confirmed
by Newsom's point concerning ויתמוגגו and ויתנועעו, that though melting
and trembling is usually associated with the effect of the divine warrior
on Israel's enemies, "in this case it may be better to interpret the ones
who are afraid as the Israelites themselves"[19] as this seems better to
account for the references to compassion and healing. Thus, she interprets the references as possible allusions to the sin and redemption pattern in Israel's history: "the rhetorical point is an evocation of the loss
of courage and its recovery through the graciousness of God"[20]. Needless to say, this loss of courage would then not be caused by the sight of
a deified or angelomorphic Moses. Furthermore, it would be rather
strange if the subject were to change without explicitly being mentioned, from God in line 6 to Moses in line 7.

It therefore appears that fragment 2 of 4Q374 does not refer to a divine or angelomorphic Moses. It simply implies his elevated status over
the אדירים and reaffirms his biblical role as ומחינ[ה] לפרעה, whilst the
subject of the actions in lines 7–9 is God. Indeed, though the word
ומחינ[ה] is damaged and uncertain, Strugnell[21] has suggested that it may
be associated with the verb חגג which occurs in Ps 107,27 in a simile
about drunkenness and which parallels וינועו from נוע ("to stagger"),
whilst in verse 26, the verb תתמוגג from מוג ("to melt") occurs. Similarly, in line 7 of our document, both נוע and מוג are found, strengthen-
ing the likelyhood of Strugnell's association. Interestingly, in Isa 19,17:
והיתה אדמת יהודה למצרים לחגא, Judah is described as *becoming to
Egypt a reeling*, using a verb חגא which the Brown-Driver-Briggs Lexicon judges to be derived from an original sense of חגג[22]. Moreover, in
Isa 19,16, it is before the Lord of Hosts that the Egyptians will tremble
although the verbs used – חרד and פתד – are different from those in
4Q374. In Isa 19,1 however, the oracle insists that the idols of Egypt
will tremble in the presence of the Lord and, in a passage reminiscent,
both in content and in vocabulary of line 7, says that the heart of the
Egyptians will tremble within them: ובא מצרים ונעו אלילי מצרים מפניו
ולבב מצרים ימס בקרבו. This does not necessarily mean that we ought to
reject Newsom's understanding of line 7 as referring to the fear of Israel. Indeed, this oracle which shares a significant amount of terminology with 4Q374 ends in verse 25 with a remarkably universalistic

---

18 For instance in 1Kings 8,50; Jer 42,12; 6,23; 21,7; 50,42. See also Brown/Driver/
    Briggs, Lexicon, 933.
19 Newsom, 4Q374, 46.
20 Newsom, ibid., 46.
21 J. Strugnell, Preliminary notes on 4Q374 cited in Newsom, 4Q374, 46.
22 Brown/Driver/Briggs, Lexicon, 290–291.

אשר ברכו יהוה צבאות לאמר ברוך עמי מצרים ידי אשור statement that
ונחלתי ישראל. Given the mention of Heliopolis in verse 18 and the mention of מצבא אצל גבולה ליהוה in verses 19–22 where it is also said that
the Lord will be worshiped in Egypt, one might seek to understand the
judgment on Egypt in Isa 19,1–17 as part of a sin and redemption pattern familiar from Israel's history. The entire oracle makes no mention
of any intermediary or angel, bar one reference to the hand of the Lord
in verse 16 and certainly does not refer to Moses. Given the contrast, in
4Q374, between verse 2, which describes the nations as lifted up in an-
ger, and verse 5 where the chosen are mentioned, it is highly unlikely
that 4Q374 shares the universalist tendencies of Isa 19. However, this
oracle does exhibit some marked similarities to our text both in vocabulary and in its setting in Egypt. These affinities, coupled with the focus
of Isa 19 on God as the sole cause both of fear and of redemption, render more likely that in 4Q374 it is also God alone, and not a deified
Moses, who causes the reaction in verse 7 and effects compassion and
healing upon his chosen ones in verses 7–8.

Moreover, ובהאירו פנו אלוהים in line 8 most likely refers to God's
causing someone's face to shine, and not to Moses making his own face
shine. Indeed, in the Hebrew Bible there is no instance of a human
agent causing anyone's face to shine. The closest parallel may be found
in Eccles 8,1, and even here, it is wisdom and not a human who causes
man to shine: חכמת אדם תאיר פניו. Furthermore, אלוהים is undoubtedly
intended as the subject of ובהאירו. However, the question then turns to
the object of the verb: whose face is being referred to: God's or
Moses'? Although we cannot be certain, it seems likely that it is the
face of God which the author of this text had in mind. Indeed, though
God is mentioned, there appears to be no allusion to Moses in this line.
Furthermore, in Jer 33, מרפא is mentioned in verse 6 after a reference
in verse 5 to God hiding his face from Jerusalem:

(5) ... חסתרתי פני מהעיר הזאת על כל רעתם: (6)הנני מעלה לה ארכה ומרפא...

This prophecy, where healing is associated with a shining face provides a
precedent for that face being God's rather than the prophet's, although
there is no firm indication that the author of 4Q374 drew upon Jer 33.

In fact, it is 4Q374 fragment 7 which might, though consisting of
only 4 very broken lines, provide us with an answer concerning the
conception of Moses' person and his role in 4Q374 fr. 2 ii.

4Q374 fr. 7:] -- [בֿך] [ ] [--] 2 [--] מֿליץ לעמך [--]
-- 4 [--]שֿחקים ומעלֹה[--] 3 [--
.[--]סֿ∞[

Indeed, although no mention of his name is made, line 2 reads: ‫מליץ ם[-‬
‫]לעמך‬ "a mediator for your people". The ‫מליץ‬, which is best translated
as 'mediator', 'intermediary', or 'magistrate' appears as a recognised
leader in Israelite society in Isa 43,27 and in Sir 10,2[23]. The term is not
applied to Moses in the Hebrew Bible, however given the focus on
Exodus/Conquest traditions elsewhere in 4Q374 and the fairly transpa-
rent references to Moses in fragment 2 ii, it is probable that he is the
mediator in question, especially given the stress upon his mediatorial
role in Exod 32–34 in the incident of the golden calf and in Deut 9–10
(especially 10,10). In 4Q374 fr. 7, it is significant that where an epithet
probably applied to Moses is not preceded by a preposition such as ‫כיא‬
or ‫ל‬, that appellation has no supernatural connotations, unlike ‫לאלוהים‬,
and as we shall find in 4Q377, ‫כמלאך‬. Nonetheless, it may possible to
associate the term ‫מליץ‬ with angelomorphic descriptions. Indeed, it is
used in 4Q368[24] in a fragmentary passage which runs as follows:

3 ‫בשר נהפך‬ "flesh was changed"
4 ‫ת ואעמוד‬ ".t and I stood"
5 ‫רים קרן‬ "rym shone"
6 ‫עם השכנתה‬ "'m you caused to live"
7 ‫לך מליץ‬ "for you a mediator"

It is noteworthy that line 3 is reminiscent of the change in Moses' face
described in Exod 34,29–35, although neither of the words used here
appear in the biblical text. This impression is reinforced by line 5 since
forms of ‫קרן‬ are used for the shining of Moses' face in Exod
34,29.30.35 and these are the only passages in the Hebrew Bible where
this verb occurs. Despite the very fragmentary nature of this passage,
we can thus not only be fairly sure that it is Moses who is being referred to as ‫מליץ‬ here[25], but also that the change in flesh described in
line 3 is probably connected to his appointment to this role. Nevertheless, rather than leading one to conclude that the term ‫מליץ‬ was after all
used with supernatural connotations, and that, by extension, this was its
meaning in 4Q374, one ought rather to consider that ‫בשר נהפך‬ in no
way necessarily indicates an ontological transformation, but rather denotes a change in *appearance* commensurate with the taking on of a
new role. Moreover, although it is not impossible that Moses was por-

23 As Newsom points out in her commentary on 4Q374 in DJD XIX, 107.
24 Text to be found in DJD XXVIII, ed. with notes by J. VanderKam / M. Brady, Oxford,
2001, 131–150. Though its content does not exactly overlap with that of 4Q377, 4Q368
also focuses on the person of Moses.
25 Moreover, 4Q368 as a whole belongs to the group of texts from Qumran that centre
around or are otherwise directly related to Moses. For details see text and commentary
in DJD XXVIII, esp. 133–134.

trayed as an angel or in an angelomorphic manner in 4Q374 fragment 7,
the poor condition of this manuscript allows us to draw no such firm
conclusions. Furthermore, whilst 4Q368 may perhaps have linked a
changed appearance with Moses possible appointment as מליץ, this
term is mentioned nowhere in 4Q374 fragment 2, which, as we have
seen, offers no indication that Moses was considered anything other
than an exceptional man.

b) 4Q377[26]

The other text which has been considered by Fletcher-Louis as envisag-
ing a divine, angelic or angelomorphic Moses (he consistently fails to
draw distinctions between these categories) is 4Q377 fragment 1 col-
umn ii:

```
۰[ -- ] ⟦ ⟧ ۰۰۰[ -- ] יבינו בחוקות מושה. 2 [ -- ]۰۰۰ומופתיכה[ -- ]۰
3 ויען אליבח۫ וי۟[א]מר שמ۫[עי ]עד۫ת יהוה והקשב כול חקהל
۰۰۰۰[ ]۰ש۟[ ]۰۰[ ]۟י۟[ ]. [ ⟧ ⟦ ]. אלור۫ האיש אשר ל۰[ ]۰ל 4 [ -- ]۰ם[ ]۰
۰۰[ -- ]۰מ۫ בפי מושה ]۰۰ לכול מ۫[ 5 [ -- ]שה۫]לוא יעמוד וישמור ויע۫[
משיחו וללכת אהר יהוה אלוהי אבותינו המ۫[ -- ]۰۰[ 6 לנו מהר
סינ۫[י -- ]. [ ⟧ ⟦ ]. וי۫ד۫ב۫ר۫ ע۫[ם ]קהל ישראל פנים עם אל פנים
כאשו ידבר۫ 7 איש עם רעהו וכא[ש[ר۟۰ ש۟۰ ]ר۫ ]۰ הראנו באש
בעורה ממעלה [מ]שמים. ⟦ ⟧ [ -- ] 8 ועל האָרץ עמד על
ההר להודיע כיא אין אלוה מבלעדיו ואין צור כמוהו [ -- ] 9
הקהל ⟨⟨ה۫ע۫ד]ה⟩⟩ [ ]ע۫נו. ורעדודיה אחזתם מלפני כבוד
אלוהים ומקולות הפלא۟[ -- ] 10 ויעמודו מרוחק. ⟦ ⟧ ומושה
איש האלוהים עם אלוהים בעֵנן. ויכס 11 עליו ה۫ענן כיא۰[ --
]בהקדשו וכמלאכ ידבר מפיהו כיא מי מבש[ר ]כמ۫וה۫ו. 12
איש חֵסדים ויו۰[ -- ]۰ם אשר לוא נבר۫או ⟨⟨ל⟩⟩{{מעולם ולעֵד
.۰۰۰[ ]۰۰۰
```

Two main arguments are used in order to advance this thesis. Firstly, he
perceives "an angelic description of Moses" in this passage. Secondly,
he claims that the distinction between Moses and God is blurred in lines
8–10, "because 4Q377 wants to say that in Moses' standing there is God's
standing", because Moses is regarded by the author of this text as a divine or angelic being. I shall thus scrutinise these two elements in order
to determine the author's understanding of Moses' nature and role.

α) The Description of Moses in 4Q377

Lines 4–5 exhort all to carry out "the la[ws of y]hwh by the mouth of
Moses his anointed one (משיחו)". Moses is again explicitly mentioned in

---

26   Text to be found in DJD XXVIII, 205–218.

lines 10–12 where he is called איש האלוהים and איש חסדים. Furthermore, in line 11 he is compared to an angel as it is said that וכמלאך ידבר
מפיהו. The question is whether any of these epithets might indicate that
Moses was considered to be an angel, or whether they imply that he is
angelomorphic.

The commands in line 5 are given through the mouth of Moses who
is called משיחו. It is unlikely that Moses is being ascribed a Messianic
character here, let alone anything more supernatural, since, whilst
Moses himself is not characterised as God's anointed in the Hebrew
Bible, other prophets are in 1Kings 19,16; Isa 61,1; Ps 105,15 = 1Chron
16,22. This appellation is also a feature of the Dead Sea Scrolls as it is
found in CD 2,12; 6,1 which refers to those "anointed ones" who had
taught Israel throughout her history by God's Holy Spirit; 1QM 11,7–8
which reads: "By the hand of your anointed ones, seers of decrees, you
taught us the times of the wars of your hands, to fight to cover you with
glory, with our enemies to fell the hordes of Belial..." That Moses is
simply understood as a prophet here appears to be confirmed by the
expression בפי מושה, which, though not applied to Moses in the Hebrew
Bible is used for other prophets, for instance Balaam in Num 23,5 and
Jeremiah in 2Chron 36,21–22.

The designation of Moses as איש האלוהים in line 10 is no indication
that he is understood as anything more than human. Indeed, it is by no
means an unusual appellation for Moses in the Hebrew Bible as it is
found in Deut 33,1; Jos 14,6; Ps 90,1; Ezra 3,2. It is also used in 1Sam
9,6f; 1Kings 12,13f for Elijah and Elisha. In fact this term does not
have the same aspect associated with receiving and delivering divine
messages as does the term נביא, neither does it imply the same media-
tory role as does the word מליץ.

Neither can איש חסדים in line 12 be taken to indicate anything other
than that Moses was an exceptional *man*, despite the likelihood that he
is described in line 11 as being sanctified, since sanctification has no
connotations in the Pentateuch with ontological transformation or even
with a changed appearance. Indeed, in Exod 19,10 it is the people who
are described as being sanctified: ויאמר יהוה אל משה לך אל העם וקדשתם
היום ומחר. There is therefore nothing to indicate that an angelic nature
is being imputed to Moses in this passage. The focus of our investigation must then shift to the question of his presentation as an angelomorphic figure.

Indeed, in line 11 Moses is said to speak כמלאך from the mouth of
God. However this ought not to be taken as anything more than a comparison, and gives no indication that Moses has taken on the form of an
angel. Rather, it seems that the phrase is designed to single him out as

an exceptional human messenger of God: he is so exalted that he is comparable to an angel. One might liken this point to the discussion surrounding Gal 4,14, where Paul writes: "and though my condition was a trial to you, you did not scorn me but received me as an angel of God, as Christ Jesus" (ὡς ἄγγελον θεοῦ ἐδέξασθέ με, ὡς Χριστὸν Ἰησοῦν). Despite Betz's[27] belief that "in antiquity there was not a great difference between [humans and angels] because one could never be sure whether one was encountering a divine or a human messenger", not only has this statement been found dubious, but the word ὡς would seem redundant and out of place if Paul was really identifying himself as an angel. In the same way, the כ in verse 11 is unnecessary if Moses is considered as having transformed into an angel.

One must however also account for the slightly ambiguous ending to line 11: מי מבש[ר] כמוהו. Which can be translated as either "for who was a messenger like him" or as "who from flesh was like him". Fletcher-Louis argues that "it is possible that Moses is viewed as a transformed human who is no longer confined to the realm of flesh"[28]. It is true that the context should perhaps lead us to favour the latter translation rather than understanding מבש[ר] as a Piel participle. However, his conclusion that "the interrogative expression 'who from flesh...?' would tie in well with Sir 45,4, Jub 31,14 and other Dead Sea Scroll texts where angelomorphism is expressed in terms of a transcendence of that realm"[29] does not follow. On the contrary, Ben Sira makes it clear that Moses is chosen *from* all humankind: ἐν πίστει καὶ πραΰτητι αὐτὸν ἡγίασεν ἐξελέξατο αὐτὸν ἐκ πάσης σαρκός. Similarly, Jub 31,14 "May he draw you and your seed near to him from all flesh to serve in his sanctuary as the angels of the presence and the holy ones." assumes that Levi and his descendants are human as they are singled out *from* all flesh – in the sense that the preposition מן does not imply transfer from one state to another but is used, as Brown/Driver/Briggs[30] clearly finds, in comparisons. So one might compare the use of מבש[ר] in line 11 to expressions such as Lev 21,10: הכהן הגדול מאחיו – here, the priest is great above his brethren, but does not stop being one of them. This is perhaps even more clear in Jubilees, which Fletcher-Louis believes clarifies 4Q377 since מכל is a common Biblical expression used "when an object is compared with a group or multitude of

27   H.D. Betz, Galatians: A Commentary on Paul's Letters to the Churches in Galatia, Philadelphia 1979, 226.
28   Fletcher-Louis, All the Glory of Adam, 142.
29   Ibidem, 142.
30   Brown/Driver/Briggs, Lexicon, 577–578.

which it forms one"[31], for instance in Gen 37,3 Israel loved Joseph מכל בניו, which does not imply that Joseph stopped being his son. These points also apply to Fletcher-Louis' insistence that Sir 45,4 implies a real ontological transfer from one realm of being to the other, with the new realm of being characterized in particular by "glory". Sir 45,2 does indeed mention that God made Moses equal in glory to the holy ones: ὡμοίωσεν αὐτὸν δόξῃ ἁγίων, however, there is no reason why this should necessarily be taken to imply that Moses became an angel in a full and literal sense, and stopped being a man; the text makes no such explicit identification. Simply, he was so exalted a man that he attained the rank of an angel with regard to glory, not only without becoming an angel, but without necessarily resembling one in his outward appearance either. This is the sense in which one should interpret line 11 of our text: the rhetorical question underlines the uniqueness of Moses, the man of God. There is no interest here in portraying Moses as an angel, even less does the author of 4Q377 conceive him as such a being.

β) Who is subject of 3. sg verbs in lines 6–9?

Although the epithets ascribed to Moses in 4Q377 do not indicate either that he was considered as an angel or that he was portrayed as angelomorphic by the author, one might still contend that lines 6–9 refer to Moses as the subject who speaks with the assembly of Israel, stands on the mountain, and teaches them that there is no God apart from him. The description of the reaction to the sight of the Glory of God in line 9, ורעדודיה אחזתם מלפני כבוד אלהים would then be a reference to Moses, at least as a mediator of God's glory to the people and as such, possibly denote an angelomorphic or divine character. Three salient points appear to militate against this hypothesis.

First of all, if it is Moses who is speaking with the assembly of Israel face to face in lines 6 and 7, why is it necessary to precise that he speaks פנים עם אל פנים כאשר ידבר איש עם רעהו. Why point out that he speaks as a man does to his neighbour if the speaker is human? In fact, as pointed out in DJD, the purpose of this passage is to extend the Mosaic privilege from Exod 33,11 to the entire community, especially given its similarity to the expression in lines 6–7:

ודבר יהוה אל משה פנים אל פנים כאשר ידבר איש אל רעהו

---

31 Ibidem, 583.

This may be based on Deut 5,4 where the Lord speaks with the entire people. As the document is addressed in line 3 to the עדת יהוה in a passage emphasising the privilege granted to their forefathers in speaking face to face with God would seem a fitting encouragement following the exhortation in lines 3–5.

Secondly, the reason for the standing on the mountain is clarified in line 8 as follows: להודיע כיא אין אלוה מבלעדיו ואין צור כמוהו. If this is not done by God revealing himself to the people in order that they may behold his glory, it is surprising that no further detail is provided, since, as indicated by the use of להודיע, standing on the mountain is the mechanism by which the glory of God is revealed.

Nonetheless, both points might be challenged on the grounds given by Fletcher-Louis[32] that Deut 5,5 has Moses standing between the Lord and the people, and that with this text in mind, the author of 4Q377 is attempting to reconcile differences between the Exodus and Deuteronomy accounts by blurring the distinction between God and Moses: "4Q377 wants to say that in Moses' standing there is God's standing". However, even if this were the case, it would not necessarily follow that Moses was considered to be an angel. But one could still object that if line 9 describes the trembling of the people in the face of God's glory, and if it is in fact Moses who is standing on the mountain, then surely given the theophanic effect upon the congregation, he is understood in this passage as a theomorphic personage. In fact, Fletcher-Louis wishes to argue that "as is perhaps the case in 4Q374, where Moses fulfills Num 6,25, God's face is seen in Moses' face"[33]. However, as demonstrated above, it is not at all clear that it is Moses' face which is caused to shine, and there is nothing concrete in line 9 which would indicate that "the author perhaps has in mind the shining of Moses' face in Exod 34,30"[34]. If one still presses the point, the most that can be said of this passage is that Moses is the instrument of God's glory – which still does not warrant the epithet of theomorphic.

Even if we were to consider that Moses is the one standing on the mountain, mediating God's word to the assembly of Israel, this does not necessarily entail that he was considered an angel or even an angelomorphic figure either by the author of this text or by those who preserved and copied it at Qumran. Even the reaction of the people is to the Glory of God, whether revealed directly or through Moses, and in no way entails that he was understood as theomorphic or angelomorphic.

---

32 Fletcher-Louis, All the Glory of Adam, 144–145.
33 Ibidem, 145–146.
34 Ibidem, 146.

4. Conclusion

The fact that Moses has been described in both these manuscripts in ways sometimes associated with angels, sometimes associated with the Angel of the Lord, and sometimes associated with God does not mean that he was considered as anything other than a human being. Using an example provided by Sullivan, his description is "analogous to the way in which God can be described in anthropomorphic terms without being human"[35]. No identification to the angels is implied by either manuscript. In fact, we have seen that in some ways the description of Moses is more theomorphic than angelomorphic, and this with no implication that Moses can in any way be identified with God.

Not only have we concluded that Moses was neither an angelomorphic figure nor a divine figure for the Qumran community, this paper has also demonstrated the difficulty of concluding that great heroes of the past, though able to approach the divine in privileged ways, were thereby considered in Hellenistic Jewish texts as deified or transformed into angels as a result of that process.

To conclude, it is appropriate to cite an unrelated Qumran sectarian text: 1QS 1,2–3 in which the mission of the community is "to do what is good and right before him as he commanded by the hand of Moses and by the hand of all his servants the prophets"[36]. This encompasses the most salient aspect of the texts analysed above: Moses is an instrument, and a quite human one, of the Lord, as are all prophets, yet at the same time he is exalted above these. It is this sentiment which transpires from the manuscripts which we have examined. There was no understanding of Moses as an angel at Qumran, and where he was described in exalted terms, even approaching angelomorphic portrayals, this did not imply that he was believed to have taken on the form of an angel.

---

35   Sullivan, Wrestling, 34.
36   לעשות הטוב והישר לפניו כאשר צוה ביד מושה וביד כול
     עבדיו הנביאים.

Mose, der "Gesalbte JHWHs".
Messianische Aspekte der Mose-Interpretation in Qumran

von Heinz-Josef Fabry

Ein erster Blick in die *Encyclopedia of the Dead Sea Scrolls*[1] vermittelt den Eindruck, dass Mose in Qumran überraschend wenig bedeutsam war. Der knapp zweispaltige Beitrag von D.K. Falk lässt zu Person und Gestalt des Mose in den Schriften von Qumran kaum Substantielles erwarten. Der wesentlich längere Beitrag über „Moses, Texts of"[2] dagegen lässt erahnen, dass der Hauptzugang zu dieser Gestalt über Schriften, die dem Mose zugeschrieben werden, gesucht werden muss. Aus Gründen der Arbeitsteilung im Blick auf die Beiträge von Phoebe Makiello und Wido van Peursen will sich die vorliegende Untersuchung lediglich auf einen Aspekt konzentrieren, auf Mose als den Gesalbten in den Schriften von Qumran. Mose wird in den gesamten Qumrantexten nur in 4Q377 so bezeichnet. Deshalb ist dieser Beleg gesondert zu analysieren. Es sind die Vorstellungen, die mit der Salbung verbunden werden, zu sichten und zu selektieren. Erhält Mose in 4Q377 eine königliche, priesterliche, prophetische oder gar messianische Qualifikation? Oder vielleicht sogar alles zusammen?

1. Mose in den Texten von Qumran

1.1. Der lexikalische Befund

Ein kurzer Durchgang der Belege außerhalb der eigentlichen Mose-Texte zeigt uns Mose
a) als Priester in einmaliger Funktionszuweisung im Zusammenhang eines Bußrituals (4Q504[DibHam^a] 1–2,II,9f);

---

1   L.H. Shiffman / J.C. VanderKam (Hg.), Encyclopedia of the Dead Sea Scrolls, Oxford 2000, hier 576–577.
2   D.K. Falk, ebd. 577–581.

b) dann als der Geber der Tora schlechthin. Die „Tora des Mose"
gilt dem Empfinden nach als einer der meistverbreiteten Ausdrücke im
Qumran-Schrifttum, begegnet interessanterweise aber nur 15mal in
nicht-biblischen Texten[3], die Wendung „Tora, die er befohlen hat durch
die Hand des Mose" sogar nur 5 mal[4]. Mose gilt aber nicht nur als Pro-
mulgator der Tora, sondern auch der Rechtsordnungen, welche die Gemeinde von Qumran im Besonderen betreffen (CD 5,8.18; 8,14; 1QS;
Toharot, Mišmarot etc.), sowie der „verborgenen Dinge" (4QMMT, TR
und 4QRP). Vom „Buch des Mose" wird gesprochen in 2Q25,1,3;
4Q174,1–3,III,3; von der „Stimme des Mose" in 4Q266,1a–b,16;

c) als das Offenbarungsmedium besonders in der parabiblischen Literatur[5]. In solchen Texten begegnet Mose als „Gottesmann", „Gerech-
ter", „dessen Stimme in der Versammlung der himmlischen Wesen
gehört wird" (4Q378,3,26);

d) als Prophet, dem die Auflage obliegt, das Volk zur Umkehr von
seinen Sünden zu bewegen[6]. Als solcher bildet er den Prototyp für den
„Lehrer der Gerechtigkeit" (מורה הצדק) und den „Anweiser der Tora"
(דורש התורה), die ihre Legitimation direkt aus Dtn 18,18 ableiten;

e) als eschatologische Gestalt in Begleitung der/s Messias/se aus
Aaron und Israel[7] und schließlich

f) als der Gesalbte (nur 4Q377,2,II).

Dieser Überblick zeigt bereits, dass Mose weder in Qumran, noch
im Alten Testament königliche Züge erhält. Die Zeichnung Moses als
König ist ausschließlich der späteren Rezeption überlassen. Philo stilisiert in seiner *Vita Mosis* (ähnlich wie Josephus) den Propheten zum
königlichen Hirten (1,60ff), der auch den Titel „König" trägt (1,150ff).
Nach dem Targum Jeruschalmi I zu Dtn 34,5 trägt Mose vier Kronen:
die des Gesetzes, des Priestertums, des Königtums und des guten Namens.

Auch die einmalige priesterliche Qualifikation des Mose scheint
eher eine Randerscheinung zu sein.

---

3   Nahezu ausschließlich in CD 15,2.9.12; 16,2.5 und 1QS 5,8; 8,22, sowie in 4QD und
    4QS.
4   1QS 8,15; 4Q255,1,3; 4Q258,VI,7; 4Q266,11,2; 4Q270,7,I,17.
5   4Q158,6,4; 7–8,3; 7–8,5; RP u.ö.
6   CD 8,14; 19,26; 1QS 1,3; 5,8; 1QM 10,6; 4Q504; 1Q22; 4Q216 u.ö.
7   4Q175; 1QS 9; 11Q13 u.ö.

1.2. Die Mose-Texte im Überblick

Daniel K. Falk weist darauf hin, dass Mose „as the greatest figure within the Judaism ... inspired an extensive body of extrabiblical literature". In diesen Schriften wird Mose durchaus unterschiedlich gewertet, so z.B. als der große Offenbarungsempfänger am Sinai in den vielen Handschriften des Jubiläenbuches und in den sog. Reworked Pentateuch-Texten (4Q158; 4Q364–367). Auch die viel diskutierte 1. Person in der Tempelrolle (11Q19) bezieht sich im ganzen Text nicht automatisch auf Gott als offenbarendes Subjekt, sondern könnte auch Mose als Offenbarungsempfänger meinen (z.B. TR 44; 51).

1.2.1. Zu den eigentlichen Mose-Pseudepigraphen sind zu rechnen:

– 1Q22 (1QDibre Mošæh): ein „reworked" Dtn-Text mit Jubiläen-Zitaten und Legitimation der Aaroniden über die Gestalt des Eleasar. Soeben hat E. Tigchelaar[8] ein bisher nicht identifiziertes Fragment aus Höhle 4[9] als zum Text der Dibre Mošæh gehörig nachgewiesen, das er entsprechend 4QDM zu nennen vorschlägt. Zugleich hat er eine neue Lesung von 1Q22,1,7–10 vorgeschlagen, die in dem Text eine direkte Rede Gottes an Mose sieht, in der diesem die zukünftigen Vergehen Israels angekündigt werden:

7) I (announce) that they will abandon [me and follow] the [abominations of the]nati[ons, and their] offenses [and their I]dols; [and they will worship]

8) their g[od]s and they will be a sna[re and a] trap; and they will ab[andon me and forget n]ew moon and Sabbath and [jubilee] and covenant; [and they will break] what

9) I[ ] command you today [to ke]ep them, [so that I shall stri]ke them with a great [blow] in the midst[of the]land whi[ch th]ey cross

10) the [Jo]rdan [to pos]sess. And w[hen] all the curses happen to t[he]m, [and] overtake them t[o]destory them an to

Tigchelaar zeigt synoptisch die Übereinstimmungen mit Jub 1,9 und 1,14 im Vergleich mit 4Q216, II, wobei deutlich wird, dass 1Q22 eine Texttradition bewahrt hat, die älter als Jub 1,9–14 ist. Hier aber ist die Deutungsmöglichkeit der wenigen erhaltenen Worte von 4QDM bereits erheblich überschritten. Sicher ist für Tigchelaar, dass sich dieses Fragment nicht mit den sonstigen Mose-Apokrypha (s.u.) in Verbindung bringen lässt.

---

8   E. Tigchelaar, A Cave 4 Fragment of Divre Mosheh (4QDM) and the Text of 1Q22 1:7–10 and Jubilees 1:9,14, DSD 12/3 (2005) 303–312.
9   DJD XXX, PAM 43.686. Fragm. 30.

- 1Q29 (1QLiturgy of the Three Tongues of Fire)[10]: Ritual um das hohepriesterliche Pektorale; die Zuordnung zu Mose ist unsicher;

- 2Q 21 (Mose-Apokryphon A): Rede des Mose an sein Volk; Betonung der Aaron-Söhne;

- 4Q375 (4QApocrMos B[a]): Aufnahme einer priesterlichen Sondertradition mit der Vorstellung eines „priesterlichen" Messias oder Zeichnung des Mose als Prototyp des wahren Propheten[11];

- 4Q376 (4QApocrMos B[b]): es geht um die Entscheidung des gesalbten Priesters in einem Streit zwischen einem wahren und einem falschen Propheten; ein zwingender Mose-Bezug ist nicht erkennbar;

- 4Q374: ein weiteres Mose-Apokryphon? In dem stark fragmentierten Text (16 Fragmente; nur Fragment 2 enthält noch zusammenhängenden Text) sah C.A. Newsom in ihrer „preliminary edition"[12] das Mose-Apokryphon A. Die Schrift ist frühherodianisch, der Text stammt aus spät-vorqumranischer oder frühqumranischer Zeit.

1) zusammen und [

2) Und Völker wurden erhoben im Zorn [

3) wegen ihrer Taten und wegen der Unreinheit ihrer Handlungen von [

4) Und [du] wirst weder einen Rest noch einen Überlebenden haben; aber für ihre Nachkommen [

5) Und er errichtete eine Pflanzung für [u]ns, seine Erwählten, in dem Land, das das am meisten begehrenswerte aller Länder ist [

6) [Und] er machte ihn wie einen Gott über die Mächtigen und zu einem Grund für das Schwan[ken] des Pharao [

7) [<Und>] sie schmolzen dahin und ihre Herzen zitterten und ihr Innerstes löste sich auf. [Aber] er erbarmte sich [

8) Und als er leuchten ließ sein Angesicht über sie zur Heilung, da erstarkten [ihre Herzen wieder, und Erkenntnis [

9) Und obwohl sie dich nicht erkannt haben, schmolzen sie dahin und zitt[er]ten. Sie schwankten beim K[lang der

10)] für sie [ ] zur Befreiung [ ] [

---

10 Zur Datierung dieser Texte in die vormakkabäische Zeit vgl. jetzt A. Lange, Pre-Maccabean Literature from the Qumran Library and the Hebrew Bible, DSD 13/3 (2006) 277–305, bes. 286.

11 M. Broshi, 375. 4QApocryphon of Moses[a], in: J. Strugnell, DJD XIX, Oxford 1995, 107–119; vgl. dazu G. Brin, The Laws of the Prophets in the Sect of the Judaean Desert. Studies in 4Q375, JSPE 16 (1992) 19–51.

12 C.A. Newsom, 4Q374: A Discourse on the Exodus/Conquest Tradition, in: D. Dimant / U. Rappaport (Hg.), The Dead Sea Scrolls. Forty Years of Research (StTDJ 10), Leiden 1992, 40–52.

Durch die Fragmente hindurch zieht sich die „Du"–Anrede in der 2. Person Sg. Es ist von einer Erhebung der Völker im Zorn die Rede. Daneben lassen sich Anspielungen an den Exodus und an die Landnahme erkennen. Der Pharao wird einmal genannt. Der Text scheint keine Erzählung zu sein, eher eine Rede, in der Gott oder Mose oder Josua jemand an die göttliche Heilstat der Herausführung aus Ägypten und der Hineinführung in ein Land voller Köstlichkeiten erinnern. Versteht man die Verbformen imperfektivisch, dann scheint der Text auf die Landnahme zurückzublicken. In diesem Falle könnte Mose kaum der Sprecher sein. Diese Ansicht hat sich wohl durchgesetzt, denn die offizielle Edition in DJD XIX (1995) nennt nach dem Vorschlag von Carol A. Newsom den Text „4QDiscourse on the Exodus/Conquest Tradition".

Dem aber wurde widersprochen von Crispin Fletcher-Louis[13], der in diesem Text (d.h. Fragm. 2,II) primär die Schilderung von Ereignissen am Sinai, darin zentral „the divinization of Moses at Sinai" sieht[14]. Er geht aus von dem auch von Newsom beobachteten theophanischen Kolorit in Z. 6–8, akzeptiert aber ihre Textrekonstruktion nicht. Aus der Klage Josuas über den Tod des Mose wird bei Fletcher-Louis die Klage des Mose über das Schicksal des Volkes u.s.w. Das starke Auftreten des Mose vor dem Pharao wird hier seiner Meinung nach aufgenommen und ausgeweitet zu einem Midrasch über eine Deifikation des Mose am Sinai. Gerade das Aufstrahlen seines Gesichtes in Z. 8 sei ein untrüglicher Hinweis (vgl. 34,29–35).

1.2.2. Die Pseudo-Mose-Texte sind nach J. Strugnell 4Q385a; 387a; 388–389 und 390, nach der Editorin D. Dimant[15] jedoch nur 4Q389–390:

– 4QpsMose^e : es handelt sich um eine Geschichtsdarstellung in der Form einer Offenbarung an Mose, in der besonders die Umkehr-

---

13 C. Fletcher-Louis, 4Q374: A Discourse on the Sinai Tradition: The Deification of Moses and Early Christology, DSD 3 (1996), 236–252.
14 Ebd. 236. Die Vorstellung einer Vergöttlichung des Mose in den Qumranschriften derart, dass Mose als „Engel" anzusehen sei, wird von Phoebe Makiello untersucht (S. 115–127). Soeben ist von R. Duke, Moses' Hebrew Name: The Evidence of the Vision of Amran, DSD 14 (2007) 34–48 die Meinung vertreten worden, aus 4Q545 (4QAmram^c) Z. 9 sei der ursprüngliche hebräische Name des Mose, nämlich *Malakijah* zu erschließen (vgl. auch Ps.Philo, Lib.Ant. 9,16 „Melchiel"). Der erste Eindruck ist der, dass man solches aus dem sehr fragmentarischen Text von 4Q545 kaum überzeugend herauslesen kann. Würde es sich als richtig erweisen, dann würde dies mancher „Engel"–These den Boden entziehen.
15 D. Dimant, DJD XXX, Oxford 2001.

Verweigerung des Volkes beklagt wird, das deshalb Belial und
den Mächten des Mastemah ausgeliefert wird.

– 4QpsMose^{a-d}: es handelt sich um 4Q389, der in der Edition als
   4QApocrJer C^d bezeichnet wird, aber wohl eine Gottesrede an
   Mose und andere Führer des Volkes unmittelbar vor der Über-
   schreitung des Jordan enthält.

Die schematisierte Geschichtsdarstellung beider Pseudo-Mose-Werke
stimmt darin überein, dass beide von einer sehr langen Dauer des Exils
ausgehen, das unter der Herrschaft von bösen Engeln steht. Das ist
nicht neu in der frühjüdischen Literatur, denn Dan 9,20–27; die Tier-
Apokalypse in 1Hen 89; 11QMelch und vielleicht auch 4Q180–181
(4QAges of Creation) sprechen auch von 10 Jubiläen oder 70 Jahrwo-
chen (= 490 Jahre). Ein ähnliches Schema begegnet im Jubiläenbuch, in
der Wochen-Apokalypse (äthHen 93) und im TestLevi. Selbst der Kata-
log der Sünden findet sich ähnlich in Jubiläen und in CD und – etwas
weniger umfangreich – in TestLevi und TestMos. Die Pseudo-Mose-
Texte zeigen keinerlei Anzeichen dafür, dass sie etwa in Qumran entstanden sind. Alle Anzeichen sprechen für eine präqumranische Herkunft. D. Dimant denkt wegen diverser historischer Anspielungen an
die Zeit des Hasmonäers Johannes Hyrkan (134–104 v.Chr.).

2. Mose als der Gesalbte in den Qumrantexten

Mit Rücksicht auf den Beitrag von Wido van Peursen in diesem Band
soll nur kurz auf den Text 4Q377 Text eingegangen werden, wobei die
Aufmerksamkeit auf die Mose-Titulatur konzentriert werden soll.

2.1. Die Handschrift 4Q377

4Q377 (4QApocrPentateuch B) sollte eher mit 4QApocrMos C bezeichnet werden. Der Text galt lange Zeit als verschollen oder nicht
entzifferbar. Nach einer vorläufigen Transkription ist er inzwischen von
J.C. VanderKam und M. Brady offiziell publiziert[16]. Die Schrift ist
paläographisch der hasmonäischen Zeit (100–50 v. Chr.) zuzuweisen,
der Text muss aber aus vorqumranischer Zeit stammen[17]. In den erhaltenen 6 Fragmenten ist nur der Text von Fragment 2, Kol. 2 noch eini-

---

16   J.C. VanderKam / M. Brady, 377. 4QApocryphal Pentateuch B (DJD XXVIII), Oxford
     2001, 205–217.
17   Vgl. Lange, Pre-Maccabean Literature, 286.

germaßen erhalten. Es handelt sich insgesamt um einen „reworked text" von Teilen aus Exodus und Numeri. Der Text bezieht sich wohl auf die Offenbarungen am Sinai. Im 1. Fragment sind Reste einer Gottesrede erhalten, in der Gott auf seine Gerechtigkeit verweist, mit der er Recht spricht zwischen einem Mann und seinem Nächsten, zwischen Vater und Sohn und Mann und Frau. Eine folgende Völkerliste ist typisch für die dtn/dtr Literatur des AT, obwohl die hier vorliegende Liste mit keiner im Alten Testament übereinstimmt, aber doch Gemeinsamkeiten hat mit den Listen in Ex 34,11 und Jos 3,10; 24,11. Das 2. Fragment beginnt in der 1. Kolumne mit einer Liste von Spähern aus Num 13, eine weitere Zeile erinnert an den Levi-Segen in Dtn 33,8; es ist von einem „Mann der Frommen" und von jemandem, der seine Stimme erhebt, die Rede; dann wird Mirjam (?) genannt.

Kolumne II beschäftigt sich nun primär mit Mose.

1) [ ] und deine Wunder ...[

2) [...] und sie sollen aufmerken auf die Satzungen des Mose <vacat> [

3) und 'lybh[ ] er antwortete [und] sagte: Hö[re], Gemeinde JHWHs, und merke auf, ganze Versammlung ... [ ]m[

4) l [   ]..[ ]..š [ ]y[ ] <vacat> Verflucht ist der Mann, der nicht steht und festhält und t[ut]

5) alle m.[ ].. durch den Mund des Mose, seines Gesalbten, und zu folgen JHWH, dem Gott unserer Väter, der m...[

6) zu uns vom Berg Sin[ai]<vacat> Und er sprach mi[t]der Versammlung Israels von Angesicht zu Angesicht, wie ein Mann spricht

7) mit seinem Freund und al[s]r ..š.[ ]r Er zeigte uns in einem Feuer, brennend oben [vom] Himmel her <vacat> [ ]

8) und auf der Erde; er stand auf einem Berg, um bekannt zu geben, dass es außer ihm keinen Gott gibt und dass es keinen Felsen gibt wie ihn [

9) die Versammlung (die Gemein[schaft]) sie antworteten. Zittern befiel sie vor der Herrlichkeit Gottes und wegen der wunderbaren Geräusche, [

10) und sie standen von ferne. <vacat> Und Mose, der Gottesmann, war mit Gott in der Wolke. Und die Wolke bedeckte

11) ihn, denn [ ]als er geheiligt wurde, und gleich einem Boten begann er zu sprechen aus seinem Mund, denn wer aus Flei[sch] ist wie er,

12) ein Mann der Frommen und yw.[ ].m (wie sie) nicht geschaffen geschaffen sind {für} von Ewigkeit zu Ewigkeit ... [

Ohne Zweifel ist in diesem Mischtext von Mose die Rede: er ist vielleicht der „Mann der Frommen" (איש חסידים)[18], „sein Gesalbter" und „der Gottesmann". Vielleicht ist es seine Fürsprache, auf die hin der

---

18 Auch in 4Q378,26 begegnen die Titel „Gottesmann" und „Mann (?) der Frommen" und sind wohl auf Mose bezogen.

Zorn Gottes (?) zurückgeht (2,I,9). Aber in Z. 3 wird eine Person namentlich – aber unvollständig – genannt, die im Folgetext eine Rede an
die JHWH-Gemeinde hält. Sie kann kaum jemand anders als Mose
sein, der Vermittler der göttlichen Tora (vgl. Ex 20,19; Dtn 5,24–27).
Es folgt eine Erinnerung an die Sinai-Offenbarung, in der Mose als
Gottesmann Gott von Angesicht zu Angesicht sehe konnte.

2.2. Mose als der „Gesalbte" in 4Q377,2,II und die alttestamentliche Salbung

Mit Johann Maier[19] ist grundsätzlich daran festzuhalten, dass der Ter-
minus משיח zuerst einmal nicht notwendig messianische Vorstellungen
impliziert. Dies wird schon gleich an einer markanten Stelle deutlich:
CD 5,21–6,1 erinnert daran, dass zur Zeit der Verwüstung des Landes
Leute aufgestanden sind, die die Grenze des Landes verrückten und
Israel in die Irre führten. Das führte zur Verwüstung des Landes, „denn
sie predigten Aufruhr gegen die Gebote Gottes durch die Hand des
Mose und auch durch die heiligen Gesalbten[20] und sie prophezeiten
Lüge ...". Da es sich eindeutig um einen geschichtlichen Rückblick
handelt, können hier neben Mose nur die Hohenpriester gemeint sein.
Das wird dadurch gestützt, dass im folgenden Vers von den Aaroniden
gesprochen wird, die „den Brunnen gegraben", d.h. in der Tora ge-
forscht haben.

Was nun ist in 4Q377 mit der Bezeichnung „sein Gesalbter" gemeint? Es ist festzuhalten, dass diese Bezeichnung für Mose absolut
singulär ist, also wohl nur durch die kontextuelle Einbindung gedeutet
werden kann. Weiter ist festzuhalten, dass die Texte von Qumran in
enger Sukzession zu den alttestamentlichen Vorgaben den Mose weder
in einer königlichen, noch in einer priesterlichen Funktion kennen.
Wenn der aktuelle Kontext es nicht anders erfordert, dann kann man
diese beiden Funktionen des Gesalbten aus der näheren Deutung he-
rausnehmen.

Eine schon oberflächliche Abschreitung des sicher fragmentarischen Kontextes ergibt, dass hier die Verkündigungsfunktion des Mose
angesprochen ist. Der in Z. 4 vielleicht mit fragmentarischem Namen
Genannte (?) spricht einen Fluch aus. Dieser Fluch hat seine Vorlage in
Dtn 27,26 und verflucht den, der – so müsste man den Text rekonstruie-

---

19 J. Maier, Messias oder Gesalbter? Zu einem Übersetzungs- und Deutungsproblem in
den Qumrantexten, in: F. García Martínez / É. Puëch (Hg.), Hommage à Józef T. Milik,
RdQ 17 (1996) 585–612.
20 Der Text liest במשיחי הקודש.

ren – die Tora JHWHs nicht befolgt, *die aus dem Mund des Mose, seines Gesalbten kommt.* Solche Textkonstellationen begegnen häufig im Deuteronomium (z.B. Dtn 4,2; 6,17; 8,6 u.ö.). Moses Rede ist dadurch autorisiert, dass Gott durch ihn spricht. Dazu bedarf es aber zuerst einmal nicht der Salbung, sondern lediglich der göttlichen Beauftragung und Sendung.

Wenn der Verfasser die – biblisch nicht bekannte – Salbung Moses hier memoriert, dann will er auf eine besondere Qualität des Mose hinweisen, die ihm durch eine Salbung zugekommen sein muss. Solche Qualitäten sind nun aber unter dem Stichwort „Salbung" allseits bekannt: Entweder sollte Mose durch die Salbung als gereinigt und gepflegt charakterisiert werden, oder er sollte als königliche oder priesterliche Gestalt ausgewiesen werden, da Salbung im Alten Testament und im Alten Orient primär ein königliches Privileg[21], nach dem Ende der Monarchie ein hohepriesterliches[22], noch später[23] ein priesterliches Privileg war. Alle diese Elemente – s.o. – sind aber für das qumranische Mosebild ungewöhnlich. Was also bleibt dann noch?

Die Salbung signalisierte die Übertragung eines Amtes[24] und sollte die Befähigung zur Ausübung dieses Amtes vermitteln. Durch das Subjekt der Salbung (Älteste des Volkes, Charismatiker, Propheten) wurde der Gesalbte für seine Aufgabe ausgesondert und legitimiert. Eine lapidare Notiz im Zusammenhang der Salbung Davids durch Samuel stellt fest, dass von nun an der Geist JHWHs über David war (1.Sam 16,13). Von da an wurde die Salbung als Geistbegabung verstanden und wurde deshalb auch – aber nicht notwendig – mit dem Prophetenamt verbunden. In 1.Kön 19,16 beauftragt JHWH den Elija, den Jehu zum König über Israel und Elischa zum Propheten zu salben. Die etwas rätselhafte Begleitnotiz deutet in einem gestuften Parallelismus diesen Vorgang so, dass Elischa eine größere Macht erhält als der König. In Jes 61,1 heißt es: „Der Geist des Herrn JHWH ruht auf mir, denn JHWH hat mich gesalbt". Man wird kaum anzweifeln können, dass das „Ich" sich hier auf den Propheten bezieht, wenn auch starke kontextuelle Bezüge zu den Ich-Worten in Jes 40–55, näherhin zu Liedern vom Gottesknecht deutlich sind, der nach Jes 42,1 auch vom Geist Gottes erfüllt war. So kann nach Ausschluss einer königlichen und priesterlichen Salbung die in 4Q377 dem Mose verliehene Bezeichnung „sein Gesalbter" nur besagen, dass er durch die Salbung als prophetischer Geistträger ausgewiesen ist.

---

21 Vgl. 2.Sam 2,4; 5,3; 2.Kön 9,3.6.12; 23,30 u.ö.
22 Vgl. Ex 29,7; Lev 8,12; Sach 4,14.
23 Vgl. Ex 40,15.
24 Vgl. K. Seybold, Art. משח I, ThWAT 5 (1986) 46–59, bes. 49f.

Nun ist jedoch die Salbung zum Propheten zumindest alttestament-
lich keineswegs die Regel, denn sie wird nur nebenbei erwähnt: Ps
105,15 (vgl. 1.Chr 16,22) spricht im Blick auf die Patriarchen von Propheten und Gesalbten und scheint dabei zumindest im Blick auf Letzteres eine sonst unbekannte Tradition bewahrt zu haben. Sir 48,8 stellt
einen Rückbezug auf 1.Kön 19,16 dar. Die Belege sind also denkbar
knapp und z.T. voneinander abhängig. Möglicherweise war diese Tradition einmal weit umfangreicher, aber es ist kaum noch etwas von ihr
erhalten geblieben. Die wenigen Belege haben aber offensichtlich ge-
nügt, messianische Erwartungen in nachalttestamentlicher Zeit auch auf
Propheten zu applizieren (CD 2,12; 6,1). „Das hat vornehmlich seinen
Grund darin, dass der Prophetie im Alten Testament selbst bereits eine
zeitliche Entgrenzung zugesprochen wird, wenn Gott dem Volk »immer
einen Propheten wie Mose aus dem Kreis der Brüder entstehen lassen
wird« (Dtn 18,15ff). Daraus entstand die Vorstellung eines Moses redivivus und eine ähnliche Erwartung um Elija, der von Gott erneut zu
seinem Volk gesandt wird, »bevor der Tag JHWHs kommt« (Mal 3,23).
Nach Sir 48,10 »steht er bereit für die Endzeit«, um Gottes Zorn zu
beschwichtigen. Eine solche Erwartung ist eschatologisch, aber nicht
eindeutig auch messianisch."[25]

3. Der engere Kontext:
Die qumranische Vorstellung vom „gesalbten Propheten"

Die in 4Q377 auf Mose bezogene Salbungsnotiz scheint nun von sich
aus keine eschatologische oder gar messianische Valenz zu haben. In
diese Richtung werden wir aber geleitet durch eine weitere Beobachtung.

3.1. 11Q13(11QMelch)

Der apokalyptisch orientierte Midrasch 11Q13(11QMelch)[26] aus der
Hasmonäerzeit (paläographisch: späthasmonäisch: 1. Jh. v. Chr.) sieht
Melchisedek als אלהים „göttliches Wesen" im endzeitlichen Geschehen
involviert. Im eschatologischen Erlassjahr (vgl. Lev 25) fungiert Melchisedek als Priester, König und Richter (vgl. Ps 82,1) und verrichtet

---

25 H.-J. Fabry / K. Scholtissek, Messias. Perspektiven des Alten und Neuen Testaments
    (NEB.Th 5), Würzburg 2002, 25.
26 Dazu P.J. Kobelski, Melchizedek and Melchireša' (CBQ.MS 10), Washington 1981.

die Sühneriten im Himmel; er tritt als Anführer der himmlischen Heerscharen auf, kämpft gegen Belial und führt damit den Anbruch der Heilszeit herbei (Aufnahme von Jes 49,8; 52,7). Dieser Anbruch der Heilszeit wird von einem „Gesalbten des Geistes" (משיח הרוח) angesagt. Er ist der „Freudenbote" (11Q13, II,16–18) und sein Auftreten erinnert dabei an den „Gesalbten" in Jes 61,1–3. Da auch in Z. 17 von den „Propheten" gesprochen wird, ist trotz fragmentarischem Kontext eine Deutung des Geistgesalbten auf den Propheten naheliegend. Man kann also 11Q13 als Zeugnis für das Auftreten eines Propheten werten, der einer priesterlichen messianischen Figur assistiert und im Rückgriff auf die Verheißung der Sendung eines „Propheten wie Mose" (Dtn 18,15ff) zur bevollmächtigten Auslegung der göttlichen Freudenbotschaft berufen ist. Die meist verhandelte Frage, ob dieser „Gesalbte des Geistes" eine menschliche Gestalt, den Vorläufer-Prophet, einen inspirierten Ausleger prophetischer Botschaft, den Prophet Daniel oder den prophetisch verstandenen Messias meine[27], lässt sich nicht beantworten.

3.2. 4Q558 (4QVision[b] ar)[28]

Man muss konstatieren, dass die Erwartung eines messianischen Propheten eher als eine eigenständige Sonderentwicklung anzusehen ist und erst nach dem Tod des Lehrers der Gerechtigkeit auch für Qumran wichtig wurde. War der „Geistgesalbte" in 11QMelch eher ein Mediator des himmlischen eschatologischen Hohenpriesters, so scheint Qumran schließlich auch die Vorstellung eines Vorläufer-Propheten zu kennen. Der fragmentarische Text 4Q558 aus vor-chassidischer Zeit hat einen solchen im Blick, wenn er unter Zitierung von Mal 3,23 von der Sendung des Elija spricht (Fragm. 1,4). Der Text ist „zwar nicht sicher, aber mit einiger Wahrscheinlichkeit ein Beleg für die Erwartung des wiederkommenden Elia in vorchristlicher Zeit"[29].

---

27 Zur Diskussion vgl. bereits A.S. van der Woude, Melchisedek als himmlische Erlösergestalt in den neugefundenen eschatologischen Midraschim aus Qumran Höhle XI, OTS 14 (1965) 354–373; É. Puëch, Notes sur le manuscrit de XIMelkîsédeq, RdQ 12 (1987) 483–523 und F. Manzi, La figura di Melchisedek: Saggio di bibliografia aggiornata, EphLit 109 (1995) 331–349.

28 K. Beyer, Aramäische Texte vom Toten Meer. Ergänzungsband, Göttingen 1994, 93f.

29 J. Zimmermann, Messianische Texte aus Qumran (WUNT 2/104), Tübingen 1998, 415.

3.3. 4Q521 (4QMessianic Apocalypse)[30]

Der aus hasmonäischer Zeit stammende Text 4Q521 wurde vom Herausgeber als „apocalypse messianique" bezeichnet, wird aber inzwischen auch als ein „sapiential poem" verstanden, weil doch bedeutende Elemente einer Apokalypse fehlen[31]. G. Xeravits[32] spricht deshalb von einem „apocalyptic poem containing eschatological wisdom material", weil er alle futurischen Verbformen als weisheitliche Exhortative wertet. Die 2. Kolumne beginnt mit dem Satz: „Himmel und Erde werden auf *seine/n Gesalbten* hören und alles, was in ihnen ist, wird nicht abweichen von den Geboten der Heiligen". Die Frage nach der Identität dieses/dieser Gesalbten ist ungelöst. Der Text spricht die neue Heilszeit an, denn es werden die Wunder und Zeichen genannt, die (vgl. Mt 11,2 par. Lk 7,19) das klassische Repertoire der messianischen Großtaten bilden: Befreiung der Gefangenen, Heilung der Blinden und Aufrichtung der Gebeugten (vgl. Ps 146,7f; Jes 35,5), Heilung der Geschlagenen, Wiederbelebung der Toten und die Verkündigung der frohen Botschaft (vgl. Jes 61,1). Das eigentlich handelnde Subjekt hinter diesen Großtaten bleibt unklar, aber die Verkündigung der frohen Botschaft ist Aufgabe des gesalbten Propheten. Damit legt sich nahe, dass an die Großtaten eines prophetischen Messias gedacht ist, wobei die Bezüge zu Elijas Totenerweckung (1.Kön 17; vgl. Sir 48,3) offensichtlich sind. Die Kombination der beiden Jesaja-Zitate in Qumran hat mit dem NT das Textplus der Wiederbelebung der Toten gemeinsam.

3.4. 4Q174 und 175

Zur eigentlichen Ausprägung der prophetischen Messiaserwartung kommt es jedoch erst später in der Hochphase der apokalyptischen Naherwartung. Der eschatologische Midrasch 4Q174[33] (nach 71 v. Chr.)

---

30 É. Puëch, Une apocalypse messianique (4Q521), RdQ 15 (1990–92) 475–522; ders., DJD XXV, Oxford 1998, 1–38.
31 Vgl. R. Bergmeier, Beobachtungen zu 4Q521 f 2,II,1–13, ZDMG 145 (1995) 38–48; G.J. Brooke, Shared Intertextual Interpretations in the Dead Sea Scrolls and the New Testament, in: M.E. Stone / E.G. Chazon (Hg.), Biblical Perspectives: Early Use and Interpretation of the Bible in Light of the Dead Sea Scrolls (StTDJ 28), Leiden 1998, 35–58, bes. 44f.
32 G. Xeravits, Moses Redivivus in Qumran?, Qumran Chronicle 11 (2003) 91–105.
33 A. Steudel, Der Midrasch zur Eschatologie aus der Qumrangemeinde (4QMidrEschata.b). Materielle Rekonstruktion, Textbestand, Gattung und traditionsgeschichtliche Einordnung des durch 4Q174 („Florilegium") und 4Q177 („Catena A") repräsentierten Werkes aus den Qumranfunden (StTDJ 13), Leiden 1994.

erwartet den prophetischen „Anweiser der Tora" zusammen mit dem „Sproß Davids". Der Text 4Q175 denkt wie 1QS 9,11 an eine prophetische Gestalt („der Prophet"), die Gottes Wort vermitteln soll. Dann springt der Text zur doppelten Messiaserwartung („Stern und Szepter", nach Num 24,15–17) und zum Zitat des Levi-Segens aus Dtn 33,8–11, das als Ankündigung eines priesterlichen Messias zu deuten ist. Jedenfalls scheint dieser Text den endzeitlichen Propheten selbst nicht als messianische Gestalt verstanden zu haben.

4. Schlussfolgerung und Ausblick

4.1. Erste These

Die in 4Q377 dem Mose verliehene Bezeichnung „sein Gesalbter" besagt weder eine königliche noch eine priesterliche Funktion des Mose. Sie ist nach allem nur als Attribut des Mose zu verstehen, das ihn als prophetischen Geistträger ausweisen soll.

Die mehrfach gebrauchte Titulatur „Gesalbter des heiligen Geistes" (CD 2,12; 1QM 11,7; 4Q270[4QD^e], Fragm. 2,II [frühherodianisch]) 4Q287,10,13 „die Gesalbten seines Heiligen Geistes" (leider in einem völlig zerstörten Kontext einer Berakot-Handschrift aus den ersten Jahrzehnten n. Chr.) und 4Q377 könnte eine prophetische Gestalt meinen, über eine messianische Funktion wird jedoch nichts gesagt. Nicht uninteressant ist die Beobachtung, dass die Vorstellungen eines messianischen Propheten literarisch mittels eschatologisch-apokalyptischen und besonders auch weisheitlichen Elementen ausgedrückt werden. Das ermöglicht die vorsichtige Hypothese, dass die prophetisch geprägte Messiaserwartung primär in einem weisheitlichen Kontext entstanden ist.

4.2. Zweite These

Der Titel „Gesalbter" für prophetische Gestalten ist demnach in Qumran bezeugt und steht auch für den endzeitlich erwarteten prophetischen Boten, der die Ankunft des eigentlichen Messias ansagt.

Diese Konnotation ist möglicherweise zu trennen von der Ankündigung der Entsendung eines „Propheten wie Mose" (Dtn 18,15.18) und der Betonung von Geistbesitz und Salbung, was dann in Qumran auf den דורש התורה, „Anweiser der Tora", übertragen werden kann.

4.3. Dritte These

Das Auftreten dieses Amtsinhabers wird mit den eschatologischen Pro-
phetengestalten verbunden (4Q174). Da er in der Gemeinschaft selbst
eine entscheidende Rolle spielt (1QS 6,6; CD 6,2–11), ist die Erwartung seines Auftretens auch in der Endzeit zugleich Äußerung der endzeitlichen Kontinuität zurück bis auf den Anfang der Prophetie, auf
Mose.

In dieser Hinsicht steht Qumran in einer breiten rezeptionsge-
schichtlichen Linie: Die Zeichnung des Mose als Prophet begann in der
früh-dtr Literatur des Alten Testaments, in der ihm auch erste weisheitliche Züge verliehen wurden. So ist er für das Dtn der prophetische
Ausleger des von Gott selbst verkündeten Gotteswillens. Mit dem deuteronomistischen Geschichtswerk ist die Rolle des Mose als prophetischer Verkündiger fest etabliert, indem von ihm aus über Josua eine
feste Linie zu den Propheten gezogen wird, wie dann umgekehrt Mal
3,22–24 am Ende der Prophetie eine Rückbindung des Corpus prophe-
ticum zu Mose herstellt. Die *Assumptio Mosis* (um 30 n. Chr.) schließlich sieht in Mose den „göttlichen Propheten über die ganze Erde"
(11,16f).[34]

„Mose, sein Gesalbter" in 4Q377 lässt sich aus dem Kontext der
qumranischen Handschriften heraus erklären als Hinweis auf die Qualifikation des Mose als Geistbegabter und Berufener Gottes. Mit dem
Titel schwingen zweifellos auch königliche und priesterliche Aspekte
der Unantastbarkeit und Heiligkeit mit. Erst recht wird Mose durch
dieses Epitheton zum Urbild des eschatologisch-messianischen Vorläufer-Propheten, was sich dann in Qumran auswirkt auf die kanonische
Institution des „Lehrers der Gerechtigkeit", der als התורה דורש beansprucht, der in Dtn 18,18 angekündigte „Prophet wie Mose", der von
Gott berufene und eingesetzte rechtmäßige Vermittler der Offenbarung
zu sein. In der Bezeichnung als Gesalbter Gottes schwingt dann auch
die Vorstellung vom Geistgesalbten mit, die dem Qumraner gleich die
Perspektive zum eschatologischen Urpriester und Urkönig Melchisedek
eröffnet, mit dem er die Erwartung des endzeitlichen Heiles schlechthin
verbindet: Er wird die Unterdrückten Zions trösten und über die Epo-
chen der Weltzeit belehren.

---

34 Vgl. dazu den Beitrag von John Muddiman in diesem Band (S. 169–180).

Reminiscences of Ezekiel's *Exagoge* in Philo's *De vita Mosis*

by Pierluigi Lanfranchi

In the incipit of his biography of Moses, Philo of Alexandria throws a hard invective at the Greek men of letters who have composed comedies and sybaritical pieces about subjects unworthy of attention, instead of treating the life of the legislator of the Jews. Philo does not want to follow their example, but intends to make up the deficiency by offering his audience a detailed account of Moses' biography, treating important events of his life in a first book and his qualities as law-giver, high priest and prophet in a second. In an almost Thucydidian way, Philo announces he will tell the story of his hero as he has learned it from both the sacred books and some of the elders of the nation (Mos. 1.4: τὰ περὶ τὸν ἄνδρα μηνύσω μαθὼν αὐτὰ κἀκ βίβλων τῶν ἱερῶν, ἃς θαυμάσια μνημεῖα τῆς αὐτοῦ σοφίας ἀπολέλοιπε, καὶ παρά τινων ἀπὸ τοῦ ἔθνους πρεσβυτέρων). Scholars often think that by this reference to the oral testimony (τὰ λεγόμενα) of the Jewish elders, the Alexandrian philosopher alludes to midrashic traditions which find their origins in the synagogue. According to them, the elders mentioned in the passage cited above would be the same as the anonymous sages of whom Philo talks in Spec. Leg. 1.8: "divinely gifted men who made deep research into the writings of Moses".[1] But a more careful analysis of the language Philo used in *De vita Mosis* enables us to see that his sources do not only derive from homiletic synagogal traditions. In this contribution I will show that Philo knew and made use of a Greek tragedy on the exodus from Egypt called *Exagoge* and written by Ezekiel, a Jewish poet – maybe Philo's fellow-citizen, who lived some decades before him.[2] The *Exagoge* is partially lost, but some fragments (269 lines in

---

1 The translations of Philo's works are taken from Philo: in ten volumes with an English transl. by F.H. Colson and G.H. Whitaker (LCL), London/Cambridge, 1929–1962.

2 The date of the *Exagoge* is uncertain. The *terminus post quem* is the translation of the Septuagint (mid 3rd century BCE) which Ezekiel used, the *terminus ante quem* is Alexander Polyhistor's ethnographical work Περὶ Ἰουδαίων (mid 1st century BCE), which contains quotations from the *Exagoge*. For the discussion on Ezekiel's chronology see

him where the marshland growth was very thick (Mos. 1.14: ἐν τῷ δασυτάτῳ τῶν ἑλῶν): this is an almost literal quote from Exag. 16 (εἰς ἕλος δασύ).[4] We read in the Septuagint that Pharaoh's daughter sees (2.6: ὁρᾷ) that Moses is a Jew. Philo and Ezekiel use the verb γιγνώσκω (Mos. 1.15: γνοῦσαν δ᾽ ὅτι τῶν Ἑβραίων ἐστὶ καταδεισάν-των τοῦ βασιλέως τὸ πρόσταγμα; Exag. 22: ἔγνω δ᾽ Ἐραῖον ὄντα), which suggests that she recognizes (as a cognitive process) Moses' Jewishness: she does not see any specific external feature (circumcision or possible objects), but deduces that the child must have been exposed in order to escape the decree against the male Jewish children. Being weaned, Moses is brought to Pharaoh's palace, where he received, ac-cording to Philo, a royal education (Mos. 1.20: τροφῆς ... βασιλικῆς). Philo formulates this idea with the same words in Exag. 37: τροφαῖσι βασιλικαῖσι. In the section on exegetical parallels, I will discuss the meaning of Moses' education more elaborately.

Besides this remarkable number of lexical echoes in the story of the birth and childhood of Moses, we can also find numerous unexpected lexical analogies between the *De vita Mosis* and the *Exagoge* in the account of Moses' stay in Midian (b). Whereas the Septuagint mentions the seven daughters of Raguel (2.16: ἑπτὰ θυγατέρες), Philo and Eze-kiel both call them παρθένοι (Mos. 1.53 and Exag. 59; see also Jose-phus, AJ 2.258). Moreover, the Greek translation of the Bible says that Raguel's daughters were watering their father's flock, πρόβατα, while in the same context Philo uses the word θρέμματα (see also Josephus, AJ 2.258). Although this word does not appear in the remaining frag-ments of the *Exagoge*, Alexander Polyhistor employs it in his summary which links two different passages of Ezekiel's *Exagoge*, namely the passage of the encounter between Moses and Sepphora (Exag. 60–65) and the passage on their wedding (Exag. 66–67). It is likely that Alex-ander, when he informs us that Ezekiel tells the story of the watering (περὶ τοῦ ποτισμοῦ τῶν θρεμμάτων), borrows an expression from Eze-kiel's text. The fact that in both Philo and Ezekiel Raguel addresses Moses by calling him ξένος, stranger (Mos. 1.58; Exag. 67), is another interesting coincidence.

More parallels are to be found in the burning bush episode (c), where Philo and Ezekiel expand the concise passage of Exod 3,2 and describe how the bramble-bush suddenly took fire and how huge the flame was. The first idea is expressed by two similar adverbs: ἐξαίφνης in Mos. 1.65 and ἄφνω in Exag. 92; the second contains a small varia-tion (Exag. 92: πολλῷ πυρί; Mos. 1.65: πολλῇ φλογί: see also, Jose-

---

4　The same 'iunctura' ἕλη δασύτατα is found in Philo, *Abr.* 138.

phus AJ 2.266). The miracle of the burning bush is said to be a "great sight" (τὸ ὅραμα τὸ μέγα) in Exod 3,3 and a "great wonder" (τεράσ-τιον μέγιστον) in the *Exagoge* (vv. 91, 93–94). It is meaningful that Philo uses the same word as Ezekiel to stress the miraculous nature of this event (Mos. 1.71). Ezekiel and Philo also use τεράστιον to describe the prodigious cloud which guides the Jews throughout the crossing of the Red Sea (Exag. 220 and Mos. 1.165). Moreover, in Philo and in Ezekiel, when justifying his refusal to accept the mission assigned to him by God, Moses says he is οὐκ εὔλογος (Mos. 1.83; Exag. 113). This is a variation on the biblical expressions οὐχ ἱκανός (Exod 4,10) and ἄλογος (Exod 6,12), present in most of the manuscripts of the Septua-gint. Philo could have been inspired by Ezekiel, but it is also possible that, in this case, he followed, like Ezekiel, a different manuscript tradi-tion of Exod 4,10, which contained the reading οὐκ εὔλογος.[5] A passage from Det. 38 seems to confirm this hypothesis: "Moses' plea is that he is not 'eloquent' (οὐκ εὔλογος), which is equivalent to saying that he has no gift for the oratory which is but specious guess work at what seems probable". Philo and Ezekiel certainly preferred the litotes οὐκ εὔλογος, because it avoids the ambiguous ἄλογος of the other manu-scripts, as it means not only 'speechless', but also 'irrational', 'unrea-soning'. Elsewhere, Philo feels the need to explain the word ἄλογος in Exod 6,12 in the following way: "He (i.e. Moses) calls himself 'speech-less' (ἄλογος) not in the sense in which we use the word of animals without reason, but of him who fails to find a fitting instrument in the language uttered by the organs of speech and prints and impresses on his understanding the lessons of true wisdom, the direct opposite of false sophistry" (Det. 38).

Another verbal echo is found in the account of Moses' rod becom-ing a serpent (d). In Ezekiel and Philo the rod became a δράκων, whereas in the corresponding passage of the Exodus the serpent is called ὄφις (Exod 4,3). In applying his typical technique of 'télésco-page', Ezekiel seems to merge two different episodes: the transforma-tion of the rod at the burning bush and the transformation of the rod before Pharaoh (Exod 7,10), where indeed there is no question of an ὄφις, but of a δράκων. Furthermore, the Greek Bible says that Moses took the serpent by the κέρκος (Exod 4,4), a term meaning 'tail', which is replaced by οὐρά in Exag. 128, as well as in Mos. 1, 77.

Further remarkable lexical similarities between *De vita Mosis* and the *Exagoge* are to be found in the account of the ten plagues of Egypt (e). Exag. 133 (πρῶτον μὲν αἷμα ποτάμιον ῥύσεται) is problematic for

---

5   See J.W. Wevers, Exodus, Göttingen 1991, 93 (apparatus ad loc.).

scholars because of the syntactical function of ποτάμιον: this word can be taken as an adjective referring to an understood ὕδωρ, or as a substantive, subject of ῥύσεται. The first solution seems to be accepted by Philo, who, telling the same episode, writes: "The water which thou dost draw from the river (τοῦ ποταμίου ... ὕδατος) and pour on the land will be blood quite ruddy (αἷμα ξανθότατον ἔσται)" (Mos. 1.81). The plagues of the sores are caused by furnace dust in Ezekiel (Exag. 136: τέφραν ... καμιναίαν) and in Philo (with a very similar wording, Mos. 1.127: τέφραν ἀπὸ καμίνου), while the Bible has αἰθάλη καμιναία (Exod 9,8). The expression βατράχων πλῆθος occurs in Ezekiel (Exag. 135) and in Philo (Mos. 1.103), but also in other Greek-Jewish texts (Josephus, AJ 2.293; Wis 19.10). Therefore, it cannot be numbered with certainty among the possible quotations from the *Exagoge*.

I conclude this long list of parallels with two short but telling examples, one from the account of the pursuit of the Jewish people by the Egyptians (f), the other from the crossing of the Red Sea (g). In order to describe Pharaoh's army, Ezekiel uses a *hapax*, φαλαγγικοί, which could very well have suggested to Philo the expression φάλαγγες ἐχθρῶν, referring to the Egyptian infantry. Finally, Ezekiel replaces the biblical expression κατὰ τὸ ξηρόν, the dry way through the sea, by the Homeric word ἀταρπός, 'path', which is used in the exact same context by Philo (Mos. 2.254).

Thus, given this large number of lexical parallels we can safely assume that Philo, while composing his biography of Moses, exploited several literary reminiscences from the poetic tradition of the Hellenistic-Jewish literature, namely from Ezekiel's tragedy.

2. Exegetical parallels between Ezekiel and Philo

Besides lexical echoes, the *Exagoge* and *De vita Mosis* have also exegetical traditions in common. Let me take some of them into consideration, starting not with what is significant by its presence, but with what is significant by its absence. Philo, for instance, skips the story of two Hebrew midwives, Shiph'rah and Pu'ah, to whom Pharaoh orders to kill the male children of their people (Exod 1,15–21). The same omission is found in Ezekiel, the *Book of Jubilees* and Josephus.

Another interesting element is the omission of the basket in which Moses is deposited (Exod 2,3) in Philo and Ezekiel. Because of the elimination of this element, neither of them can accept the version of the story according to which Moses was deposited in waters of the river, but they have to leave the baby on the river banks, in a well pro-

tected space (Exag. 17; Mos. 1,10). Philo seems to share Ezekiel's preoccupation in wanting to show that Moses' mother has done her utmost
best to ward off any possible danger and to save her son. The indication
of the position of Miriam has to be interpreted in the same way: according to Exodus, Moses' sister observes the scene from far away (Exod
2,4), but in Ezekiel and Philo she was nearby (Exag. 18; Mos. 1,12).
The *Book of Jubilees* shows the same preoccupation with the safety of
Moses, when affirming: "Your mother would come at night and nurse
you, and during the day your sister Miriam would protect you from the
birds" (47.7; trans. VanderKam).

One of the most significant analogies between Philo and Ezekiel
concerns the education of Moses. The *Exagoge* is the first source to
mention his pagan education, a theme that has been picked up later on
by Philo and by the Acts of the Apostles (7.22). Actually, Ezekiel does
not tell us the exact content of Moses' education, but it is obvious that
he is talking about pagan education. The public of the *Exagoge* could
have imagined Egyptian wisdom, but it also could have actualized the
story of the Exodus, thinking of the Greek paideia of the Ptolemaic
court. These aspects are implied by Ezekiel, but made explicit by Philo,
who describes the education of Moses in detail (Mos. 1.21–24). According to him, the Egyptians taught Moses the sciences based on numbers (arithmetic, geometric, music, astronomy), hieroglyphs and their
philosophy. The wise men of the neighbouring regions instructed him
in the Syrian language and astronomy, while the Greeks initiated him
into the ἐγκύκλιος παιδεία.

As has been observed by Ton Hilhorst, the initiation into the Egyptian wisdom is absent from the Hebrew and Aramaic texts of the Second Temple and in the Rabbinic literature.[6] In the *Book of Jubilees*, for
example, Moses receives his education exclusively from his father Am-
ram. Ezekiel and Philo talk not only about pagan education, but also
about traditional Hebrew education. However, the two authors do not
agree on which moment Moses received his Hebrew education. According to Ezekiel it took place before Moses was conducted to the
palace of Pharaoh, according to Philo after he had finished his profane
studies. Ezekiel and Philo do not share the radical position of Artapan,
who identifies Moses with Hermes and considers him the founder of the
Egyptian religion and culture. The Moses of Artapan assimilates into a
foreign culture and makes an essential contribution to the formation of

---

6   A. Hilhorst, 'And Moses Was Instructed in All the Wisdom of the Egyptians' (Acts
     7.22), in: idem / G.H. van Kooten (eds.), The Wisdom of Egypt. Jewish, Early Christian
     and Gnostic Essays in Honour of Gerard P. Luttikhuizen, Leiden 2005, 153–176.

this culture. To put it more strongly: he founds it. Contrary to Artapan, Ezekiel and Philo do not have any "dream of assimilation", to use the words of Jan Assmann.[7] They assign an Egyptian education to Moses, because they are aware of the cultural prestige which the Egyptian culture enjoyed among the Greeks since Homer and because they knew the stories about Greek wise men travelling to Egypt for educational purposes (see Diodorus Siculus 1.96.2). In short, they both acknowledge the richness of the pagan education and the profane sciences in which they themselves have been instructed, but at the same time confirm the superiority of the traditional education based on the Scripture.[8]

Yet another element of Ezekiel's *Exagoge* can be found in Philo's *Vita*: Ezekiel tells us that during its flight from Egypt, the Egyptian army catches up with the Jews when they are feeding their wives and children (Exag. 207). An echo of this pathetic amplification of the biblical narrative is also present in Philo, because in his *Vita* the Egyptians arrive at the encampment of the Jews when they are having their supper (Mos. 1.169).

3. Conclusion

In spite of the lexical and exegetical convergences between the *Exagoge* and *De vita Mosis* discussed in the preceding paragraphs, there are many differences between these two works due to the fact that they belong to different literary genres and, consequently, serve different purposes. Philo does not only accept exegetical traditions from outside the *Exagoge*, but sometimes openly differs from Ezechiel. For example, when amplifying Exod 14,28, he confirms that from Pharaoh's army "not even a torchbearer survived to announce to the people of Egypt the sudden disaster" (Mos. 1.179), whereas in the *Exagoge* the messenger speech is precisely uttered by a rescued Egyptian soldier who describes the crossing of the Red Sea and the catastrophe of his own army.

Nevertheless, Philo seems to have appreciated the eulogistic presentation of Moses in Ezekiel's play, as has been observed by David Runia.[9] In fact, Philo's insistence on the role of Moses as guide of the

---

7   J. Assmann, Moses the Egyptian, Cambridge (Mass.) / London 1997, 36.

8   On the ἐγκύκλιος παιδεία and the pagan education of Philo in particular, cf. the "Introduction" of M. Alexandre to Philon d'Alexandrie, De congressu eruditionis gratia, Paris 1967 (esp. 29–46).

9   D. Runia, God and Man in Philo of Alexandria, JThS 39 (1988) 48–75, here 52. In the same article, Runia says that he is not persuaded that "we can be at all confident that

Jewish people and as prophet, a central motif in his biography, reflects the representation of the protagonist in Ezekiel's tragedy.

Besides this laudatory presentation shared by both authors, we may assume that the *Exagoge* also inspired Philo with the idea of giving a particular theatrical dimension to some of the episodes of his biography of Moses. I am thinking especially of the description of the song started by Moses after the crossing of the Red Sea (Exod 15), presented by Philo in terms of a choral performance: "He (i.e. Moses) divides the nation into two choirs (δύο χορούς), one of men, the other of women, and he himself leads (ἐξάρχει) the men while he appoints his sister to lead the women, that the two in concert might sing hymns to the Father and Creator in tuneful response (ἀντιφθόγγοις), with a blending both of temperaments and melody – temperaments eager to render to each other like for like (ἐπὶ τὴν αὐτὴν ... ἀμοιβήν); melody produced by the concord of treble and bass (...). All these myriads were persuaded by Moses to sing with hearts in accord the same song, telling of those mighty and marvelous works which I have recorded just above. And the prophet, rejoicing at this, seeing the people also overjoyed, and himself no longer able to contain his delight, led off the song, and his hearers massed in two choirs sang with him the story of these same deeds (Mos. 2.256–257; cf. also Mos. 1.180)". In his Vit.Cont. 85–88, Philo affirms that the choirs and the dances by which the Therapeutae celebrate the eve of the festival of the Weeks are an imitation of the events of the crossing of the Red Sea. In this case the songs accompanying the mimetic dance of the two choirs are composed according to the metric and the structure of the choral passages in Greek theatre. Unfortunately, not one of the choral passages of the *Exagoge* (if they ever existed) has been transmitted, so that we will never know how Ezekiel dramatized the song of Moses, nor if Philo's representation of the choirs is an echo of Ezekiel's *Exagoge*. We may argue, however, that Philo was aware of how Ezekiel exploited the mimetic and dramatic possibilities of Exodus in his *Exagoge* and that he found them particularly suitable for his own representation of the life of Moses.

Philo was acquainted with the play" (53). But his observations are based exclusively on the parallels between the *Exagoge* and *De vita Mosis* discussed by Jacobson, Exagoge.

Moses as Philosopher-Sage in Philo

by Hywel Clifford

The conference that gave rise to this volume occurred in the fiftieth anniversary year of Cecil B. DeMille's successful and lavish biblical epic, *The Ten Commandments*. The film begins with the director stepping out from behind stage curtains to say that ancient historians' writings (Philo, Josephus) were used to fill in the early years of Moses' life, on which the Bible is silent. The construal of Moses as a philosopher-sage in Philo's writings is not just supplementation in this sense but a radically idealised transformation. Indeed, it is a fine example of what can happen to a biblical figure in extra-biblical tradition. Philo does not use this dual title, but the terms φιλοσοφέω/φιλοσοφία/φιλόσοφος and σοφός do appear in passages in which Moses also features.[1] In order to understand how these word groups relate, this study treats them separately, and then together; a critical assessment follows thereafter. Besides exemplifying the themes of the conference, this investigation reflects an on-going interest in the relationship between Jewish wisdom and Greek philosophy. The case of Philo is especially instructive in this regard because his writings represent, in a paradigmatic way, their creative combination within Hellenistic Judaism.

1. Moses as Philosopher

It needs to be established, first of all, that Philo viewed Moses as a philosopher. At the start of his second biographical volume of *The Life of*

---

1 For a list of Moses' epithets, F.H. Colson, Philo X (LCL), Cambridge, Mass. 1962, 386–389. Philo does not discuss or present these systematically, unlike Moses' four principal offices (Mos. 2,2ff; Praem. 53–55), so the entire corpus must be consulted to determine their significance. All of the occurrences are listed alphabetically in P. Borgen / K. Fuglseth / R. Skarsten, The Philo Index: A Complete Greek Word Index to the Writings of Philo of Alexandria, Grand Rapids / Leiden 2000. The abbreviations for Philo's works used in this study follow the latter publication, and the excerpts of text are taken from F.H. Colson et alii, Philo with an English Translation (LCL), 10 vols., Cambridge, Mass. 1929–1962.

Moses Philo refers to the first, in which he had presented Moses as king, and then enhances it by suggesting that Moses displayed what all states ideally require: leaders who are philosopher-kings (Mos. 2,2), recalling Plato's influential ideal. Moses as philosopher can be inferred from other indirect comments. Moses is compared with 'other philosophers' (Gig. 6; cf. Plant. 14), implying that he was one himself. On another occasion, Philo uses the form φιλοσοφεῖ 'philosophises' (Her. 257), rather than a standard citation formula, to characterise the nature of Moses' writing. Moving beyond these merely functional observations, we shall now consider the various ways in which Philo accounts for Moses' philosophical persona.

In the first place, philosophy was a part of Moses' education, which was the best available in his day, and in which he excelled as the ideal student. Raised by Pharaoh's daughter, Moses presumably benefited from a royal education, although Exodus is silent on this (Exod 2,10–11). Philo amply fills in the narrative gap, describing how Moses' education was both thorough and international by listing the branches of knowledge he was taught and the variety of cultures that his teachers represented (Mos. 1,18–24; cf. Acts 7,22). Philosophy is included here, not as a separate discipline, but in reference to the system of thought in ancient Egyptian religion:

> These [Egyptians] further instructed him in the philosophy [φιλοσοφίαν] conveyed in symbols, as displayed in the so-called holy inscriptions and in the regard paid to animals, to which they even pay divine honours. He had Greeks to teach him the rest of the regular school course, and the inhabitants of the neighbouring countries for Assyrian letters and the Chaldean science of the heavenly bodies. This he also acquired from Egyptians, who gave special attention to astrology (Mos. 1,23).

It is not entirely clear what is meant by 'the philosophy conveyed in symbols'.[2] Philo's predecessor Artapanus had already spoken of the godlike honour that Moses received from Egyptian priests because of his ability to read their sacred texts (presumably hieroglyphics), as well as his patronage of animal cults.[3] With such a tradition 'in the air', Philo seems to have deduced that Moses must have been well-educated in this foreign philosophy, although he is careful to distance Moses

---

2   J.M.G. Barclay, Manipulating Moses: Exodus 2.10–15 in Egyptian Judaism and the New Testament, in: R.P. Carroll (ed.), Text as Pretext. Essays in Honour of Robert Davidson (JSOT.S 138), Sheffield 1992, 38 notes its obscurity; whereas S. Pearce, King Moses: Notes on Philo's Portrait of Moses as an Ideal Leader in the Life of Moses, Mélanges de l'Université Saint-Joseph 57 (2004) 37–74, here 52 suggests either the study of hieroglyphics or the symbolic interpretation of animal cults known in Hellenistic philosophy.

3   Eusebius, PE 9,27,4–6.9–12. J.H. Charlesworth, OTP I, 1985, 898–899.

from its associated theriomorphic cultic activity ('to which they even pay divine honours'). This would have prepared Moses to be an expert interpreter of sacred letters generally; and it also traces, back to the prince of Egypt, and his ancient hero, Philo's proclivity for allegorising Moses' own sacred texts so that philosophy might be conveyed through their symbols.[4]

The other aspect of Moses' formation that explains his capacities as a philosopher was his innate ability. With immense natural gifting he surpassed all of his teachers, posing problems that they could not easily solve. Indeed, the master-pupil relationship was somewhat unfair because, 'his seemed a case rather of recollection than of learning' (1,21).[5] Moses was also unusually advantaged because, concerned only with the truth, he was incapable of accepting any falsehood (1,24)[6], and he also happened to have a semi-divine mind (1,27).[7] Expressing such adulation regarding his formative years, Philo was thus able to portray Moses' emergent leadership in similarly glowing terms, and in which philosophy had an on-going role to play. For instance, while in the wilderness of Arabia, after killing the Egyptian taskmaster, but before God visited Egypt with plagues:

> Moses was carrying out the exercises of virtue with an admirable trainer, the reason within him, under whose discipline he laboured to fit himself for life in its highest forms, the theoretical and the practical. He was ever opening the scroll of philosophical doctrines [φιλοσοφίας ... δόγματα], digested them inwardly with quick understanding, committed them to memory never to be forgotten, and straightaway brought his personal conduct, praiseworthy in all respects, into conformity with them; for he desired truth rather than seeming, because the one mark he set before him was nature's right reason, the sole source and fountain of virtues (Mos. 1,48).

This passage shows various Classical and Hellenistic philosophical influences: reason's assistance of the athlete of virtue, the distinction between theoretical and practical virtue, quick apprehension and an exceptional memory, and conformity to nature's 'right reason', to name but some of them.[8] But Philo primarily wants his audience to realise that Moses' regular, disciplined reading of philosophy, coupled with his natural gifts, enabled him very quickly to live a life of virtue led by

---

4   It is worth noting that philosophy was not part of 'the regular school course [ἐγκύκλιον παιδείαν]', the traditional Greek diet of 'grammar, geometry, astronomy, rhetoric, music, and all the other branches of intellectual study' (Cong. 11; cf. 140–150; Spec. 2,30; Prov. 2,4–46), which was good preparation for it as a higher discipline.

5   Cf. Plato, Meno 82a.86b.

6   Cf. Plato, Rep. 485d; SVF 3,55.

7   Cf. Leg. 1,40; Sacr. 9; Mos. 1,158.

8   Cf. Plato, Rep. 431c.487a; Diogenes Laertius 6,24; SVF 3,4.265.

reason. In this way, reason successfully trained Moses for life with a fruitfulness that thrived in the soil of natural brilliance.

Second, Moses was the supreme philosopher of contemplation. This quality was already evident during his tender years. Even though he was allowed to make sport and laughter just like other children, Moses tended to act differently: he had an unusual level of dedication to things that would only profit the soul (Mos. 1,20).[9] This reverence for weighty matters continued into his adult life: when confronted by the divine commission to rebuke Pharaoh, Moses considered himself to be a poor public speaker, partly because of hearing God's overwhelmingly superior speech (Mos. 1,83–84). Moses' eventual exit from the land of Egypt also had contemplative significance, as this was but an allegory of the philosophical mind that loves wisdom coming out of the body (Mut. 207–209). Moses then encountered God at Sinai:

> A seeker was also the prophet himself, to know the cause of successful achievement, and he found that it was the presence with him of the only God. ... by reason of His gracious nature, He comes to meet us with His pure and virgin graces, and shews himself to those who yearn to see Him, not as He is, which is a thing impossible, since even Moses "turned away his face, for he was afraid to look upon God" (Exod iii.6), but so far as it was allowable that created nature should gaze towards the Power that is beyond conception (Fug. 140–141).

Those who 'yearn to see Him', whether Moses and the wandering Hebrews or Philo and his fellow Jews, were seeking after intelligible realities.[10] Yet 'even Moses' had to turn his face away from God, whose essence is inaccessible to humans.[11] Philo nevertheless lauds the end-product of Moses' visionary experiences. Since Moses represented the mind at its purest, with rationality integral to it, the revealed and written Law, which Philo calls the 'Mosaic philosophy', amounted to nothing less than a 'faithful impress of the divine image' (Mut. 223). Moses' various contemplative journeys had thus prepared him for the ultimate: to receive, and then impart to posterity, a written reflection of the divine will that carries with it philosophical significance.

Third, the mature Moses was a consummate philosopher, and this made him a suitable source of truth in subsequent Greek philosophy. Philo claims that unlike those who simply dictate laws or invent myths, Moses saw the value of combining both: he prefaced the law with creation in Genesis, thereby indicating a harmonious unity of the law in its

---

9   Cf. Plato, Rep. 485d–e; Josephus, AJ 2,230.
10   This Platonic thread is dominant in Philo's writings. See Plato, Phdr. 248a.253 along with Philo, Opif. 71; Det. 89; Post. 14; Ebr. 124; Her. 76; Fug. 164; Spec. 1,37.207; 2,165; 3,4; Contempl. 35.
11   Cf. Her. 219–220.293–297.

natural and written modes of revelation (Opif. 1–3).[12] Another instance
of this unitary view of knowledge was Moses' insight that thought and
action, or the theoretical and the practical (cf. Mos. 1,48 above), should
not be separated:

> He [Moses] exemplified his philosophical creed [φιλοσοφίας δόγματα] by his
> daily actions. His words expressed his feelings, and his actions accorded with
> his words, so that speech and life were in harmony, and thus through their mu-
> tual agreement were found to make melody as on a musical instrument (Mos.
> 1,29).

Philo portrays this mature fusion as more than just functional; that is, he
likens it to an aesthetically pleasing enterprise. What is most noteworthy, however, is the belief that the union of theory and practice was
entirely natural. Why was this so obvious to Philo? It must be rooted in
Philo's conviction that the Law, which guides behaviour, is also by
nature philosophical: Moses followed the 'royal road' of philosophy
that leads to God by means of an unswerving obedience to the Law
(Post. 100–102). In other words, the Mosaic Law *is* philosophy. If true,
and given the fact that Moses had lived long before the Greeks, then
Moses' role and status as the fount of truth was assured:

> For the two opposites together form a single whole, by the division of which
> the opposites are known. Is not this the truth which according to the Greeks
> Heracleitus, whose greatness they celebrate so loudly, put in the fore front of
> his philosophy and vaunted it as a new discovery? Actually, as has been
> clearly shewn, it was Moses who long ago discovered the truth that opposites
> are formed from the same whole, to which they stand in the relation of sec-
> tions or divisions (Her. 213–14).

Philo, just before this excerpt, cites from Gen 15, which describes the
covenant rite that required Abraham to cut sacrificial animals in two
and place them opposite each other; then Philo lists all kinds of opposition within nature, such as hot-cold, dry-wet, light-heavy. It is these that
Philo takes to be evidence in Moses' writings for a pre-Heraclitean
awareness of unity and opposition (Her. 207–212). Armed with the
apparently knock-down argument of chronological priority, Philo thus
confidently asserts that the best of the Greeks was already contained in
the Jewish Scriptures; that is, for those with the allegorical eyes to see
it.[13] This approach to the history of ideas, that identifies and privileges

---

12 Cf. Opif. 131; Mos. 2,51–52; Josephus, AJ 1,18–26.
13 Her. 213–214 does not cite Heraclitus, although it recalls the theme of unity in oppo-
    sites that pervades the surviving fragments: 'Graspings: wholes and not wholes, con-
    vergent divergent, consonant dissonant, from all things one and from one thing all' (DK
    B10) in C. Kahn, The Art and Thought of Heraclitus. An Edition of the Fragments with
    Translation and Commentary, Cambridge 1979, 281. For other examples of Moses'

the 'first inventor', was frequently employed in Hellenistic Judaism, and then in the newer Christianity, to demonstrate antiquity and truth, over against accusations of novelty and imitation.[14] Philo's simple, albeit speculative, exegesis and historical convictions led to the obvious conclusion that later thinkers, who expounded similar ideas, were but 'broken lights' of Moses, the greater light.[15]

2. Moses as Sage

Wisdom in Philo's writings is both a generic quality that impressive figures already have, or that to which others should aspire.[16] He attributes it to many biblical heroes, but none more so than Moses. Indeed, judging by epithets alone, Moses as a sage, or wise man, is more prominent than his description as philosopher. Philo uses mostly 'the wise (man)'[17], and, less commonly 'wise'[18], 'the perfect wise man'[19], 'all-wise'[20], and the 'wise legislator of the Jews'[21].

---

supposed prior knowledge of Greek philosophy, see Aet. 17–19; Opif. 128; Abr. 13; Leg. 1,108; Cher. 128–130; Her. 300–301; Mos. 1,158.

14 Cf. Josephus, Ap. 2,134.168.257.286. For a general discussion, see N. Roth, 'The "theft of philosophy" by the Greeks from the Jews', ClF 32 (1978) 53–67. Clement of Alexandria inherited this apologetic stance: 'And Numenius, the Pythagorean philosopher, write explicitly: for what is Plato but Moses speaking in Attic Greek?' (Strom. 1,150). See A. van den Hoek, Clement of Alexandria and the Use of Philo in the Stromateis. An Early Christian Reshaping of a Jewish Model, Leiden 1988, 49–50.

15 F.H. Colson, Philo I (LCL), Cambridge, Mass. 1962, xvii, note b. Philo claims that the Stoic Zeno used the 'law book of the Jews' for his views of slavery (Prob. 57; cf. Spec. 4,61; Aet. 147ff). This attempt at historical explanation is a telling rarity in Philo (cf. Josephus, Ap. 1,162–165), even though its chronological possibility is more sober than Aristobulus' claim that biblical texts were translated before the Septuagint, and already used, in a corrupted form, by the Greeks. Eusebius, PE 13,12,1f; 13,13,3–8. Charlesworth, OTP I, 839–841. The earliest references in Greek authors to Jewish culture are from the Hellenistic period, which renders Philo's apologetic historically problematic (cf. Isa 66,19). For the sources, see M. Stern, Greek and Latin authors on Jews and Judaism. Edited, with Introductions, Translations, and Commentary, Jerusalem 1974–84), and the brief but pointed comments in E.J. Bickerman, The Jews in the Greek Age, Cambridge, Mass. 1988, 13–14. On the 'first inventor' motif in Hellenistic Jewish authors, see M. Hengel, Judaism and Hellenism: Studies in their Encounter in Palestine during the Early Hellenistic Period, London 1974; original Judentum und Hellenismus: Studien zu ihrer Begegnung unter besonderer Berücksichtigung Palästinas bis zur Mitte des 2. Jh. v. Chr, Tübingen 1969 (ET J. Bowden), 90–92.95.129.

16 Plant. 138; Ebr. 86; Conf. 49; Fug. 112.
17 Leg. 2,87.89; 3,140–141; Gig. 48; Ebr. 100; Cher. 15; Sacr. 8; Agr. 99; Migr. 168.
18 Migr. 201; Mut. 19.
19 Leg. 3,147; cf. 3,207–208; 2,91.
20 Post. 28.
21 Prob. 68.

Moses' wisdom was characterised, most importantly, by virtue. This was the main quality of the Hellenistic and especially the Stoic sage. The 'aretalogy', a recitation of the deeds and qualities of a god, sage, divine man, and hero or athlete of virtue, was a component of ethical instruction in the Hellenistic schools. A variety of figures served as moral exemplars, the most famous among them Pythagoras, Socrates, Diogenes, Zeno and Hercules.[22] They scaled the heights of virtue in a range of ways: they set the standard for virtue itself; they possessed virtues required for heroism, or specific roles such as priest or diviner; they were models of moral progress; and they ended their lives with a noble or courageous death. Philo held that Moses had shown all of these qualities.

(a) Moses had all of the virtues, like all true sages, because the virtues exist as a unity.[23] Virtue is also an essential characteristic of the sage because of its value in leadership: like a benevolent king, the sage rules over all affairs with a virtue that generates authority.[24] Moses was able to assume this task naturally as a 'lover of virtue [φιλάρετος]'.[25]

(b) Moses had the virtues required for his principal offices: as king, exercising this God-given role with nobility[26]; as lawgiver, comprehending and articulating virtue in the written law[27]; as priest, for which the primary virtue is piety[28]; and as prophet, inspired to proclaim God's words, a role that befits the virtuous, but not the wicked[29].

(c) Moses' moral progress climaxed with the divine encounter at Sinai's summit.[30] Among Israel's own collection of sages, the scale that had began with the antediluvians ascended, *via* the Patriarchs, toward Moses, the human summit.[31] Indeed, to be a sage such as Moses, with the quality of immutability, signalled having moved beyond gradual progress so as to exist third in rank only to God and his Logos.[32]

---

22 D.L. Tiede, The Charismatic Figure as Miracle Worker (SBLDS 1), Missoula, Mont. 1972 discusses the main evidence for each, and their relevance to understanding Philo.

23 Mos. 2,7; Abr. 54; Praem. 53.56; Mos. 1,148–159; 2,187; cf. Plato, Prot. 329c–d.349a; Meno 72c; Diogenes Laertius 6,72; SVF 3,295; Josephus, Ap. 2,158–160.163; 2,286; AJ 1,22–24.

24 Somn. 2,244; Mut. 152–153; Migr. 197; Agr. 66; Mos. 1,328; cf. SVF 3,81.108.158. 173.617.

25 Opif. 128; Leg. 2,90; 3,130.147.

26 Mos. 1,148.154; Mut. 152; Somn. 2,243–244; Virt. 154.

27 Opif. 128; Mos. 2,9–10.

28 Mos. 2,66–68; Praem. 53.56; Post. 133; cf. SVF 3,157.604–610.

29 Her. 259–260; Spec. 1,64–65.

30 Mos. 2,66–70; cf. SVF 443–445.448.644.

31 Jos. 1; Decal. 1; Leg 3,131–132.140.144; Mut. 24–25; Somn. 2,234; Post. 173–74.

32 Somn. 2,237; Det. 162.

(d) Moses' death was impressive: translated to heaven, he was drawn away from earthly things to stand with God, who prizes the sage like the world.[33] Moses' departure was, as with his ascent of Sinai, like a pilgrimage from mortality to immortality, since, at death, his transformed unity of soul and body became mind alone, as pure as sunlight.[34]

Philo's understanding of Moses' virtue cannot, however, be simply equated with Stoic ideals.[35] For the Stoic sage, complete virtue was a true human achievement, whereas Philo was clear that the sage's virtue is a divine gift alone; although this antithesis should not be drawn too sharply.[36] Moreover, Moses' virtue was not just a composite of the best available features: he also superseded the Stoic sages.[37] Moses, the godlike man, 'given as a loan to earthlings' (Sacr. 9), belonged to the category of rational souls that never properly leave the heavenly realm. Untroubled by human feelings all his passions were eliminated, all except pure joy; indeed, Moses' body was led by a purely rational soul.[38] As a 'super-sage', guided by perfect rationality, Moses was closest of all human beings to the Divine Mind. This leads neatly to the next point.

Second, Moses' wisdom was a kind of *imitatio Dei*. Philo describes God as 'alone wise'[39], such that for Moses to be declared especially wise he must have been godlike in some way. For instance, just as

---

33 Sacr. 8.
34 Mos. 2,288.291. As well as the evident Platonic influences, Philo's imagination was prompted by Jewish traditions: ignorance about the location of Moses' grave (Deut 34,6), traditional interpretations of his translation, and the experiences of Enoch (the proto-prophet), Abraham, Isaac, Jacob and Elijah (QG 1,86; Sacr. 8–10). W.A. Meeks, The Prophet-King: Moses Traditions and the Johannine Christology (NT.S 14), Leiden, 1967, 124.
35 Nor does it mean that Philo's *Life of Moses* was intended as an aretalogy. P. Sigal, Manifestations of Hellenistic historiography in select Judaic literature, SBLSPS 23 (1984) 170–174. Philo calls his work a βίος (Mos. 1,1), a genre used to describe a person's life from beginning to end (cf. Suetonius, Plutarch). This explains why Moses' education is described at the start and climaxes with an apotheosis.
36 Immut. 49–50; Post. 69.73; Fug. 58; Her. 85.89.123; cf. Plato, Meno 100b. See G.B. Kerferd, The Sage in Hellenistic Philosophical Literature (399 B.C.E.–199 C.E.), in: J.G. Gammie / L.G. Perdue (eds.), The Sage in Israel and the Ancient Near East, Winona Lake 1990, 319–328, here 320–322, and D. Winston, The Sage as Mystic in the Wisdom of Solomon, in: ibid., 383–397, here 391–393.
37 D. Winston, Judaism and Hellenism: Hidden Tensions in Philo's Thought StPhil 2 (1990) 1–19, here 10–12; and idem, Sage and Super-sage in Philo of Alexandria, in: G. Sterling (ed.), The Ancestral Philosophy in Second Temple Judaism: Essays in Honour of David Winston (SPM 331/4), Providence 2001, 171–180.
38 Mos. 2,68.164; Leg. 2,91; 3,129; 3,134; Migr. 67.
39 Plant. 38.46; Conf. 39.94; Cong. 114. Cf. Heraclitus, B 32; Plato, Phdr. 278d; Sir 1,8.

God's nature is unchanging, so were Moses' wisdom and virtue.[40] The
following sets out a theological and exegetical basis for this:

> God, since His fullness is everywhere, is near us, and since His eye beholds us,
> since He is close beside us, let us refrain from evil-doing. ... Thus may the di-
> vine spirit of wisdom not lightly shine His dwelling and be gone, but long
> abide with us, since He did thus abide with Moses the wise [σοφῷ]. For the
> posture and carriage of Moses whether he stand or sit is ever of the most tran-
> quil and serene, and his nature averse to change and mutability. For we read
> "Moses and the ark were not moved" (Numb. xiv. 44). The reason may be ei-
> ther that the wise man [σοφός] cannot be parted from virtue, or that neither is
> virtue subject to movement nor the good man to change, but both are stayed on
> the firm foundation of right reason. ...true stability and immutable tranquillity
> is that which we experience at the side of God, who Himself stands always
> immutable. For when the measuring line is true all that is set beside must
> needs be set straight (Gig. 47–49).

The concept of immutability receives particular attention in Philo's
discussions of Moses at Sinai: invited to stand with and partake in
God's unchanging nature, Moses received laws that are like immutable
Platonic Ideas and Pythagorean numbers. Moses was also, through this
experience, stamped with God's unchanging nature.[41] Indeed, Philo
claims that his ascent of Sinai and vision of God were, in essence, about
leaving the body to know wisdom in soul and mind.[42] It is in this rare-
fied realm that Philo interprets Moses' biblical title 'god' (Exod 7,1).
His passage up God's holy mountain symbolised the rule of the mind
over the body, and the virtual identification of his mind and prophetic
office with the Logos, the very image of God.[43]

Third, Moses' status as a sage was more important than his miracle-
working. The popularity of certain Oriental cults in the Hellenistic
period reintroduced the religious imagination to divine or prophetic
miracle-workers such as Asclepius, Isis and Imhotep. This provoked
discomfort among the educated classes, including the Hellenised Jewish
aristocracy of Alexandria. Aware of the attendant dangers of
sensationalism, Philo rationalised some biblical episodes that contain
strong supernatural content. For example, Philo proposes that earth, fire,
air and water (constituents in Greek cosmology) were responsible for
the attack on Egypt, grouping his discussion of the plagues according to
these elements; in so doing Philo abandons the narrative sequence of

---

40 Gig. 47–50; Post 27–31; Somn. 2,219; Migr. 130–131.
41 Post. 27–31 cf. Det. 49. See M.A. Williams, The Immovable Race: A Gnostic Designa-
    tion and the Theme of Stability in Late Antiquity, Leiden, 1985, 13–15.39–43.
42 Conf. 81–82; Migr. 168–169; cf. Spec. 4,31; Ebr. 100; Det. 135–138.
43 Leg. 1,40; Migr. 84; Sacr. 9–10. The definite 'the god' is reserved for God (Somn.
    1,227–230; Mos. 1,75–76). Meeks Prophet-King, 371; D.T. Runia, God and Man in
    Philo of Alexandria, JThS 39 (1988) 48–75, here 60.

Exodus.[44] Before describing Moses' role in Egypt, Philo theorises on
the Nile's flooding (another traditional Greek interest), and then goes
on to attribute the plagues of hail and lightning, locusts and darkness to
unusual meteorological conditions, yet another naturalistic strategy.[45]

It should be observed that Philo neither rules out the miraculous nor
Moses' ability to perform miracles. Still, Philo is careful to ensure that
Moses is not seen as a sensationalist wonder-worker, preferring to focus
on the natural causality that God's power directs. So, the water-emitting
desert rock that Moses struck, albeit under prophetic inspiration, might
have contained a spring or water channels. The miraculous is still important: to disbelieve it signals a person does not know or seek God, for
whom such events are but 'child's play'. What should really invite our
admiration, however, is not this local desert event, but, taking a lead
from it, what we too often take for granted: the great marvels of nature
such as the seas, rivers, springs, torrents and fountains in the world at
large.[46] In such ways, the cultivated image of the virtuous sage provided, for Philo, a useful control against the sensationalist potential of
the biblical Moses: an acceptable mantle with which to clothe the Jewish hero.[47]

3. Moses as Philosopher-Sage

Having considered aspects of Philo's portrayal of Moses as both philosopher and sage, we shall now consider their combination. Given the
extent to which philosophy and wisdom were important for Philo, it
comes as no surprise that they were both integral to Moses' fourfold
offices of king, law-giver, priest and prophet. Philo's discussion of his
priestly office is particularly interesting in this regard, and serves as a
useful example:

> We have now fully treated of two sides of the life of Moses, the royal and the
> legislative. We must proceed to give an account of the third, which concerns
> his priesthood. The chief and most essential quality required by a priest is pi-
> ety, and this he practised in a very high degree, and at the same time made use
> of his great natural gifts. In these philosophy [φιλοσοφία] found a good soil,

---

44 Mos. 1,90–146, esp. 96.
45 Mos. 1,113–118, cf. 201–202. For a recent attempt to defend the plagues in naturalistic
    terms, see K. Kitchen, On the Reliability of the Old Testament, Grand Rapids 2003,
    249–252. W. Johnstone, Exodus, Sheffield 1990, 31–34 proposes, by contrast, that the
    Exodus narrative was intended not as historiography, in this rationalistic sense, but as
    an appeal to the theological imagination.
46 Mos. 1,212–213.
47 Meeks, Prophet-King, 104; Tiede, Charismatic Figure, 100.215.235.

which she improved still further by the admirable truths which she brought before his eyes, nor did she cease until the fruits of virtue shewn in word and
deed were brought to perfection. Thus he came to love God and be loved by
Him as have been few others. A heaven-sent rapture inspired him, so markedly
did he honour the Ruler of the All and was honoured in return by Him. An
honour well-becoming the wise [σοφῷ] is to serve the Being Who truly IS,
and the service of God is ever the business of priesthood. This privilege, a
blessing which none in the world can surpass, was given to him as his due, and
oracles instructed him in all that pertains to rites of worship and the sacred
tasks of his ministry (Mos. 2,66–67).

Philosophy, personified here as a nurturing woman, exercised a formative role in the development of Moses' virtue. This is a development of
the identity of the biblical Lady Wisdom.[48] Indeed, it seems as if, for
Philo, Lady Wisdom and Lady Philosophy were one and the same; if so,
this represents useful evidence for the confluence of Hebrew and Greek
ideas in Philo's thought: to speak of one was to speak of the other. The
philosophical elaboration concerning 'the wise', in what follows, sup-
ports this interpretation. Wisdom characterises those who serve God,
especially priests, for whom divine service is their *raison d'être* (cf.
Praem. 56), but in a way that is remarkably abstract: 'to serve the Being
Who truly IS'. This suggests that, in Moses' exemplary experience of
his priestly office, wisdom was philosophy, and that the wise thing he
did was to be philosophical; not for its own sake, but because of the
roles that wisdom and philosophy played in divine service at Sinai.[49]

Second, the mystical vision of God at Sinai was the foundation for
philosophy and wisdom. In his analysis of the tower of Babel episode
(Conf. 91–98), Philo allegorises brick-making as the shaping of evil
thoughts. This, in turn, prompts recollection of the Hebrew slaves making bricks in Egypt, and then the climactic vision of God at Sinai,
which includes a description of the brickwork under God's feet:

> What then is the liberty which is really sure and stable? Aye, what? It is the
> service of the only wise [σοφοῦ] Being, as the oracles testify, in which it is
> said, "Send forth the people that they may serve me" (Ex. viii. 1). But it is the
> special mark of those who serve the Existent, that theirs are not the tasks of
> cupbearers or bakers or cooks, or any other tasks of the earth earthy, nor do
> they mould or fashion material forms like the brick-makers, but in their
> thoughts ascend to the heavenly height, setting before them Moses, the nature
> beloved of God, to lead them on the way. For then they shall behold the place
> which in fact is the Word, where stands God the never changing, never swerv-

---

48 It is not obvious in this passage that philosophy, as with Sophia elsewhere, was a wife
    to Moses, on which see K.-G. Sandelin, Wisdom as Nourisher: A Study of an Old Tes-
    tament Theme, its Development within Early Judaism and its Impact on Early
    Christianity, Abo 1986, 98–100.
49 Cf. Cong. 114–115; Mos. 2,68ff.108.

ing, and also what lies beneath his feet like "the work of a brick of sapphire,
like the form of the firmament of the heaven" (Ex. xxiv. 10), even the world of
our senses, which he indicates in this mystery. For it well befits those who
have entered into comradeship with knowledge to see the Existent if they may,
but, if they cannot, to see at any rate his image, the most holy Word, and after
the Word its most perfect work of all that our senses know, even this world.
For by philosophy [$\phi\iota\lambda o\sigma o\phi\epsilon\hat{\iota}\nu$] nothing else has ever been meant, than the
earnest desire to see these things exactly as they are (Conf. 94–97).

There is much here that echoes features already mentioned. What is
new is the definition of philosophy as the desire to perceive reality correctly.[50] Philo leads up to this with a philosophical allegory on the experience at Sinai (God, Logos, Sense)[51], and an abstract approach toward God that complements it ('the Existent', 'the never changing'). As
for wisdom, rather than it describing ideal humans, as in the previous
citation, here wisdom is uniquely true of God ('the only wise Being').
What, then, is the relationship between philosophy and wisdom in this
passage? The answer is similar to before: they meet in divine service.
True enough, there are some differences in emphasis. Philo envisages
not individual but a corporate priesthood, since all the people wor-
shipped at Sinai; and this implies, for Philo, that they were all philoso-
phically engaged. Yet divine service remains the key: the disposition of
worship invites recognition of God as alone wise, in a unique sense;
and it also encourages a certain humility, that it is 'wise' (i.e. prudent)
to consider certain kinds of knowledge as inaccessible, given the limits
of experience: even during the most exalted religious visions.[52]

Third, and finally, the Mosaic Law *is* philosophy and wisdom. In a
discussion of the Sabbath, Philo has a lengthy section on the ideal properties of the number seven, which he claims are recognised by all in the
main branches of education (Opif. 89–127). Philo completes and then
continues this discourse as follows:

> On these grounds I hold that those who originally fitted names to things, being
> wise men [$\sigma o\phi o\iota$], called this number "seven" because of the "reverence" ($\sigma\epsilon$-
> $\beta\alpha\sigma\mu\acute{o}\varsigma$) which it deserves, and the heavenly "dignity" ($\sigma\epsilon\mu\nu\acute{o}\tau\eta\varsigma$) pertaining

---

50   Philo has various comments about the nature and meaning of philosophy. See A.M.
     Malingrey, 'Philosophia': étude d'un groupe de mots dans la littérature grecque de Pré-
     socratiques au IVe siècle après J.-C., Paris 1961, 77–91, and V. Nikiprowetzky,
     Le Commentaire de l'Écriture chez Philon d'Alexandrie. Son Caractère et sa Portée, Lei-
     den 1977, 97–116.

51   Philo follows the reserved Exod 24,10 LXX, which states that the people saw the place
     ($\tau\acute{o}\pi o\varsigma$) where God stood, and not God himself, as in MT. In distinguishing God and lo-
     cation, this tradition lent itself to the hierarchy of divine transcendence and the media-
     tion of the Logos. Cf. Somn. 1,62, Conf. 136; J.G. Kahn, De Confusione Linguarum.
     Introduction, Traduction et Notes (OPA 13), Paris 1963, 163–164.

52   Cf. Post. 12–21.

to it. The Romans, who add the letter *s* left out by the Greeks, make this appear still more clearly, since they, with greater accuracy, call the number *septem*, owing to its derivation, as I have said, from σεμνός ("reverend") and σεβασμός ("reverence"). These and yet more than these are the statements and reflections of men on the number 7, showing the reasons for the very high honour which that number has attained in Nature, the honour in which it is held by the most approved investigators of Mathematics and Astronomy among Greeks and other peoples, and the special honour accorded to it by that lover of virtue Moses. He inscribed its beauty on the most holy tables of the Law, and impressed it on the minds of all who were set under him, by bidding them at intervals of six days to keep a seventh day holy, abstaining from other work that has to do with seeking and gaining a livelihood, and giving their time to the one sole object of philosophy [φιλοσοφεῖν] with a view to the improvement of character and submission to the scrutiny of conscience (Opif. 127–128).

The wisdom aspect of this excerpt requires awareness of Philo's apologetic intent. It was a traditional view that ancient sages had given objects their names.[53] Yet, according to Philo, the Greek language (and culture) remains deficient because its morphology of this number (i.e. ἑπτά) obscures an etymological insight about its moral value; although the later Romans did perceive it.[54] But Moses, who lived long before the renowned and legendary Seven Sages of Greece, and therefore the Romans after them, already knew of its ideal properties that all now recognise, and gave it special honour by placing its beauty on the holy tablets of the Law in the form of the Sabbath.[55] The implication is clear: because the ancient Sabbath represents the number seven, Moses was the fount of what is now agreed to be universal wisdom. This allows Philo to commend the Jewish Law as the primary source of ancient wisdom, and also of practical philosophy: the Sabbath day is now given over by sagacious Jews to philosophical learning, which has moral progress, or virtue, as its clear, defining purpose.[56] In sum, Philo presents

---

53 Plato, Cratyl. 401b; Cicero, Tusc. 1,62.
54 The original Indo-European root word had 's': *sapta* (Sanskrit), *sibun* (Gothic). D.T. Runia, On the Creation of the Cosmos according to Moses, Leiden 2001, 296.
55 Elsewhere Philo even trumps the sages' traditional role in naming objects by claiming that Moses ascribed the task of naming to Adam on whom *all* humans depend for their language (Leg. 2,15).
56 Mos. 2,185; Leg. 3,156; Agr. 101.106; cf. Josephus, Ap. 2,170. While Philo is willing to commend philosophers for teaching that humans should live in accordance with nature and its laws, this is best achieved by following God's laws, since they are at one. See Migr. 127–128; Mos. 2,14.48, and H. Koester, ΝΟΜΟΣ ΦΥΣΕΩΣ: The Concept of Natural Law in Greek Thought, in: J. Neusner (ed.), Religions in Antiquity: Essays in Memory of Erwin Ramsdell Goodenough, Leiden 1968, 521–541, here 533.

students of the Mosaic Law, in following their ancient guide, as both philosophers and sages.[57]

4. Assessment

It is striking that Philo makes virtue the hallmark of all true philosophy and wisdom. This is the theme that recurs in the evidence considered thus far, and it is useful at this point to recapitulate in order to draw this thread together. Even though Moses learned Egyptian religious philosophy, he did not involve himself in theriomorphic cults; in the Arabian wilderness he brought his conduct into conformity with philosophical doctrines that reflect nature's reason; his contemplation of God at Sinai was the climax of a reverential life; and his daily fusion of theoretical and practical knowledge generated a harmonious unity. Virtue was the defining feature of Moses the super-sage; at Sinai he gained the godlike virtue of immutability; and his later wonder-working was not sensationalist but showed the activity of God who works through natural causality. Moses' priestly service, for which piety is the primary virtue, is the goal of philosophy and wisdom. The vision of God at Sinai was their foundation, and the revealed and written Law their expression.

What motivated Philo to construe Moses as this virtuous philosopher-sage? A key factor was the contested reputation of Moses and, by association, those who revered the Mosaic Law. Philo had inherited from his 3rd – 2nd century Hellenistic Jewish predecessors (Artapanus, Eupolemus, Aristobulus) the view that Moses was the fount of philosophy and a sage.[58] But their diverse portraits were at times excessive, and while Philo claims the direct influence of 'the elders of the nations' (Mos. 1,4), that is, Jewish legends, he did not follow them in every respect.[59] Moreover, the complexity of opinions about Moses among

---

57 The actions of the sage are the words of God, that is, the enactment of the Mosaic Law (Migr. 127–132); and the sense of φιλοσοφία is the Law (Post. 101–102; Mos. 2,36), which echoes a common Stoic definition, 'the art of life', and not, therefore, analytical philosophy. Runia, On the Creation, 297.

58 Eusebius, PE 7,32; 9,26.27; 8,9–10; 13,12. Charlesworth, OTP I, 839–840.865.898–899. On this evidence, see the recent S. Inowlocki, Eusebius and the Jewish Authors: His Citation Technique in an Apologetic Context (AJEC 64), Leiden 2006.

59 Philo did not push the 'first inventor' motif as far as Artapanus, who had claimed that Moses, whom he identified with the Greco-Egyptian god Hermes-Thoth, had taught Orpheus, the founder of Greek culture. Philo's allegories are more fully developed and nuanced than those of Aristobulus (such as we have), by distinguishing both literal and allegorical meanings and allowing their co-existence in exegesis (Migr. 89–93). On these

non-Jewish opponents (Manetho, Apion; and later Tacitus, Juvenal), which must have depended to some degree on Jewish sources, indicates just how much Moses had become a disputed figure.[60] What unites the Jewish tradition is an apologetic concern to champion their divinely-gifted individual, and Philo's own defence of Moses fits into that trend (Mos. 1,4).[61] The emphasis that Philo places on virtue can, thus, be seen in this context: the ancient hero of the Jews, as philosopher-sage, gives pride to and adorns the Jewish community.[62] Philo's description of students of the Jewish Law as those who seek to improve character through the scrutiny of conscience, an exercise in practical virtue, echoes this as well, in that they were but following their esteemed founder along the same noble path.

The other major factor was the intellectual climate within which Philo operated. From his thorough classical education, Philo had learned the creative potential of allegory as a means of embellishing and defending the sacred text, especially if it was available to the purview of all, sympathiser and critic alike.[63] Philo's re-reading of the biblical texts with new meaning for a new age was thus to be expected; indeed, Philo saw himself as belonging to a tradition comprising not only religious teachers and disciples of Moses' writings, but also philosophers in the Greek manner.[64] It is easy to criticise this from the standpoint of historical criticism: Philo's manipulation of the Greek Bible lacked the literary-critical disciplines that moderns prize; and his eclectic philosophical, moral and mystic fusion, driven by apologetic interests, tells us more about him and his times. The pressure to present an ideal Moses who represents everything that intellectual Greeks and Romans, as well as cultured Jews, could ever wish for, by developing and accumulating roles that the biblical Moses clearly does not have, had led to the free adaptation of biblical texts; and in the process, Philo omits to mention, for instance, the less flattering incident of the two

---

portraits, see the survey in J.M.G. Barclay, Jews in the Mediterranean Diaspora. From Alexander to Trajan (323 BCE – 117 CE), Edinburgh 1996, 125–180. See also D.M. Hay, Philo's References to Other Allegorists, StPhil 6 (1979–80) 41–75.

60 J.G. Gager, Moses in Greco-Roman Paganism, Nashville 1972.

61 Cf. Tiede, Charismatic Figure, 105.237–239.

62 Barclay, Jews in the Mediterranean, 176–177 writes: 'His [Philo's] norms and values are the common coinage of Hellenism: an admirable *paideia*, a life of piety and the pursuit of virtue in accordance with nature. But for Philo nowhere are such norms attained or such values cherished as among the Jews, where they are to be found embedded in their sacred text and practised in their ancestral customs.' Moses' virtue is also a leitmotif in Josephus, AJ 2,205.257.262; 3,12.65.69.74.97.187.188.192.317.322; 4,331.

63 For representative statements, see Jos. 28; Abr. 147.236; Cont. 78. For the rationale and motives lying behind allegory, see Barclay, Jews in the Mediterranean, 165ff.

64 Her. 291; Spec. 1,8.344–345.

Hebrew disputants and their rejection of Moses' leadership. This hermeneutical state of affairs may be seen as an ancient example of the
modern genre classification 're-written Bible'.[65]

But if we are prepared to admit that all interpretations are ideologi-
cally located, and that texts are therefore polyvalent in the hands of all
readers, we may begin to see some enduring value in Philo's approach,
despite its particularities. The central place that Philo gives to virtue
points in this direction; and here we can refer, once more, to Philo's
intellectual milieu, as it presents us with another important reason for
understanding Philo's methods:

> And the wisdom must not be that of the systems hatched by the word-catchers
> and sophists who sell their tenets and arguments like any bit of merchandise in
> the market, men who for ever pit philosophy against philosophy without a
> blush, O earth and sun, but the true philosophy which is woven from three
> strands – thoughts, words and deeds – united into a single piece for the attain-
> ment and enjoyment of happiness (Mos. 2,212).

Just beforehand Philo lauds the high festival of the Sabbath that Moses
had set up. After commenting on its joyous practice, he warns that its
happiness should be appropriately conceived, and not characterised by
superficial and sensual leisure. This prompts Philo to comment on the
irresponsible trading in wisdom by the Sophists.[66] Given the context of
this excerpt, Philo makes clear that the integration of 'thoughts, words
and deeds' is a test of the practical responsibility of a given philosophy
or wisdom. In this, the Sophists were found wanting: the selling of
ideas without a thought for the consequences, quite apart from its
commercialism, is profoundly dangerous (cf. Mos. 2,215–216). Whereas
Philo's attribution to Moses of an integrationist approach, which has
biblical echoes (Deut 6,5) and virtue as its guide, implies that attention
to an idea and its moral consequence was, for Philo, crucial to society's
well-being; indeed, the proper enactment of justice requires it (Mos.
1,24). This also suggests that virtue was not only important in Philo's
portrait of Moses, since, arguably, it transcends him in having public

---

65   P. Borgen, Philo, John and Paul. New Perspectives on Judaism and Early Christianity,
     (BJS 131), Atlanta 1987, 18–20; A. Salvesen, Early Jewish Bible Interpretation, in: J.
     Barton (ed.), The Biblical World I, London 2002, 323–332, here 327. The portrayal of
     Moses in early Christianity, and comparisons between him and Jesus, are naturally rele-
     vant in this context: John 1,17; 1 Cor 10,2; Heb 3,1–6.

66   Philo makes the Sophists the target of a number of exegetical manoeuvres. Moses'
     humble speech impediment contrasts the eloquence and persuasiveness of the Sophists
     (Sacr. 11). Moses' battle with the magicians of Egypt was a contest with the intellectual
     sorcery of the Sophists (Mos. 1,92–94.277). Philo depended upon Plato for some of his
     criticisms. See B.W. Winter, Philo and Paul among the Sophists, Cambridge 1997, 91–
     92. For a sympathetic discussion of the Sophists, see J. de Romilly, The Great Sophists
     in Periclean Athens, Oxford 1992.

justice as its treasured effect in all human societies. That said, as far as Philo was concerned, Moses was the best teacher and paradigmatic world-citizen of such ideals.[67]

5. Conclusion

It is perhaps well-known, if only in general terms, that Philo modulated Moses into Classical and Hellenistic keys by portraying him as a philosopher-sage; and also that, with an extensive use of allegorical interpretation, Philo embellished the biblical texts while attempting to sound the same, basically pure tone. This was prompted by the need to defend Moses' reputation, and thereby that of the Jewish community, given the extent to which Moses had become a contested figure in Jewish and non-Jewish discourse. What has emerged in this study in stronger relief, however, is the deliberate attention that Philo gives to virtue as the defining feature of both Jewish wisdom and Greek philosophy, in their ideal forms, and as exemplified supremely in the ancient Jewish hero. Indeed, in the light of these insights, it is probably misplaced to speak in separatist terms, such are the ways in which Philo freely steps in and out of these cultural streams so as to imply that, in fact, they amount to one river of life. After all, according to Philo, their original human source was but one and the same person: Moses.

---

67 Prompted by Exod 2,2 LXX, Philo often applied to Moses the term 'refined, clever [ἀστεῖος]' (Mos. 1,9.15.18.48; cf. Acts 7,20; Heb 11,23) with the Stoic view that virtue defines world-citizenship (Conf. 106.109; Opif. 3; Mos. 1,155–162; Cong. 132; Her. 19; Somn. 2,227.230).

The Assumption of Moses and the Epistle of Jude

by John Muddiman

I

The text generally known as the Assumption of Moses[1] was discovered in 1861 in a palimpsest belonging to the Ambrosian Library in Milan. Both the beginning and end are missing and there are numerous indecipherable gaps in the surviving portion.[2] This 6th century Latin manuscript is derived from earlier witnesses, and the Latin itself is equally clearly a translation of a 1st or 2nd century Greek text. The 5th century Church History attributed to Gelasius Cyzicenus, recalling the Acts of the Council of Nicaea in 325 CE, quotes it and explicitly identifies the source as the Assumption of Moses.[3] Whether this Greek book was itself a translation of an earlier original written in Hebrew or Aramaic is disputed.[4] And that question depends to some extent on the equally disputed date of the writing.

The problem of dating the Assumption of Moses arises from the historical allusions and their sequence in the book. The references in chapter 6 to a "petulant king" (V.2) who will reign for 34 years (V.6) but whose sons will rule for shorter periods (V.7) have led most com-

---

1   Some prefer to use the term Testament of Moses (J. Priest, Old Testament Pseudepigrapha, ed. J.H. Charlesworth, London 1983, 925), as a more accurate description of the contents of the book, but it was known to the early Church fathers as the Assumption of Moses presumably because it originally ended with some sort of event that could be so described. The Testament of Moses was the alternative title of the Book of Jubilees. See next note.

2   Preceding it are fragments of the Book of Jubilees. – J. Tromp, The Assumption of Moses: a critical edition with commentary, Leiden 1993 explains that when both a testament and an assumption of Moses appear in some ancient lists of books, the former denotes Jubilees, see pp. 114f.

3   Gelasius, Hist. Eccl. 2,17,17. The match is precise: "And God foresaw me before the foundation of the world to be the mediator of his covenant" compare AssMos 1,14 "I who have been prepared from the beginning of the world to be the mediator of his covenant."

4   Tromp, Assumption of Moses, 81–85 contrast E.M. Laperrousaz, Le Testament de Moïse (généralement appelé 'Assomption de Moïse') Traduction avec introduction et notes, Semitica 19 (1970) 1–140.

mentators to identify him as Herod the Great (37–4 BCE). Although Archelaus ruled Judaea for only 10 years, the other sons Philip and Antipas reigned for almost as long or even longer.[5] From this the deduction is drawn that the book must have been composed shortly after the death of Herod in 4 BCE. But the logic of this deduction may be faulty. The author's chief concern is to show that Moses was a reliable prophet of Israel's future, not to describe in detail the present circumstances of his intended readership. This becomes clear when we move on to chapter 8, where allusions to opposition to circumcision and the promotion of idolatry point to the crisis under Antiochus Epiphanes IV, 150 years earlier. Furthermore, the enigmatic Taxo[6] of chapter 9, if it denotes an actual historical figure rather than a type, has been variously identified ranging from a contemporary of Judas Maccabeus in the mid second century BCE (so, Charles[7]) to the "rainbow" Rabbi Joshua who opposed the Bar Kochba revolt, in the mid-second century CE (so, Zeitlin[8]) or any number of candidates in between. From this evidence one could conclude either that chapter 6 and 7 have been displaced, and should follow chapters 8 and 9, or that a basically Hasmonean work has subsequently been updated in the Herodian period or later. Or indeed, that chronological sequence up to the time of writing is just not one of the author's concerns.[9]

The most tantalizing critical question concerns the lost ending in which Moses' assumption, which gave the book its title, would have been recounted. The question becomes important for New Testament exegesis because of the allusion to a dispute between the Archangel Michael and the Devil over the body of Moses in the Epistle of Jude 9.The Alexandrian Church fathers, Origen and Clement provide us with the only early evidence for the lost ending of the book they knew as the Assumption of Moses. Origen, in De Princip. 3,2,1, refers to the dispute and claims that it involved a charge against the Devil that he had engineered the fall of Adam and Eve. How that would fit into the envisaged

---

5   However, some later successors in Judea reigned for only short periods, like Herod Agrippa 1st (41–44 CE).

6   Tromp, Assumption of Moses, 124–128, surveys almost 30 different explanations of the name and possible identifications; he remains unconvinced by any of the suggestions yet made.

7   R.H. Charles, The Assumption of Moses, London 1897, 36.

8   S. Zeitlin, The Assumption of Moses and the Bar Kokhba Revolt, JQR 38 (1947/48) 1–45.

9   An early first century date for the Assumption is certainly possible, but that does not, of course, require or imply an early date for the Epistle of Jude.

scene is difficult to imagine and Origen may be mistaken.[10] Clement is more informative: in a passage in Strom. 6,15,2f, he describes the assumption itself. "It is therefore reasonable that Joshua the Son of Nun should have seen Moses being taken up in two forms, the one with angels, while the other was honoured with burial in the cleft of the mountains." And he goes on to explain why Joshua got a better view of this than his companion Caleb. These early patristic testimonies, however, throw no light on the substance of the dispute between Michael and the Devil.

Some slightly later texts[11] imply that the Devil's claim, made explicit in the scholia, was to be "the master of the material world". This claim is met by Michael's appeal to scripture to prove that God is the Creator of all matter.[12]

A late interpretation from Cremer's Catena[13], sees the issue as the Devil's accusation "that God lied in bringing Moses into the land which he swore he should not enter." For God apparently breaks his own word that Moses would never enter the promised land by allowing him to appear with Jesus on the Mount of the Transfiguration. This is self-evidently a wholly Christian preoccupation and cannot help us with the ending of a Jewish work like the Assumption of Moses.

More commonly in Christian commentary on Jude 9[14] the dispute turns on the Devil's accusation that Moses had killed the Egyptian (Exod 2,11–15) and therefore did not deserve the special privilege in death of being buried by God's angels in a tomb that would remain undiscovered. Although Christian authors, several of whom were Egyptian themselves (!), may have been troubled by the Devil's accusation, it is less likely that a Jewish work like The Assumption would have been so concerned by the charge. Jub 47,10–12 provides a précis of the incident without any apologetic commentary. Josephus simply ignores it (Ant. 2,254) and Philo (Vit. Mos. 1,44) fully justifies the action on the grounds that the overseer in question was a brutal murderer himself.[15] Given the number of Egyptian dead through the agency of Moses

---

10   Tromp, Assumption of Moses, 274f plausibly argues that Origen has confused the Assumption with the Apocalypse of Moses, otherwise known under its Latin title as the Life of Adam and Eve.
11   Gelasius, Hist. Eccl. 2,21,7.
12   With somewhat free citations of Ps 104,30 and Ps 33,6.
13   Quoted by R.Bauckham, Jude and the Relatives of Jesus, Edinburgh 1990, 258.
14   The texts are given in Bauckham, Relatives, 252.254f.261.
15   The same unembarrassed attitude, incidentally, is to be found in Stephen's speech (Acts 7,25) where any fault in the matter is laid firmly at the feet of the Israelites, with the comment: "He (Moses) thought his brothers realised that through him God would liberate them but they did not."

that the Exodus story involves this particular justifiable homicide is insignificant. Slightly more offensive maybe in Jewish eyes would be Moses' shame at what he had done, implied by his hiding the Egyptian's body in the sand and running away to Midian. A Jewish text like the Assumption would, if anything, have focussed on that sin of Moses and Aaron, the rebellion at Meribah (Num 20,2–13), which God punished by denying them entry into the promised land (Num 27,13–14 cf. Deut 32,51f). That more serious offence would also have been more immediately relevant to setting of the death of Moses.

In short, The Assumption of Moses in the Milan manuscript must have concluded with an account of Moses' death by the will of God.[16] Some kind of assumption would have followed, whether of his soul or also of his body. The biblical traditions of his burial by God in an unknown grave would not necessarily foreclose the issue; the grave could be unknown because the body had been taken up after its burial, and that would then correspond to the earlier ascent into heaven by Moses, while still in his earthly body, to receive Torah. The Devil must have appeared in this account playing his traditional role as prosecutor, accusing Moses of various sins and therefore of being unworthy of eternal life. Michael with due courtesy opposed him, with the words derived from Zech 3,2 ("May the Lord rebuke you"). More than this it is difficult to say with any certainty.

II

The Epistle of Jude purports to be the work of a certain Jude "servant of Jesus Christ and brother of James" (V.1). Although other candidates for this attribution are possible, like the Apostle "Jude of James" in Luke's list of the Twelve[17] (6,13; Acts 1,13), the generally held view is that Jude the Lord's brother (Mk 6,3) was intended. This so-called epistle is in reality an anti-heretical tract addressed to "all who are dear to God the Father and kept safe for Jesus Christ." – so presumably every good Christian is meant to read it. And consequently it is pointless to try to

---

16 Despite Deut 31,2, Moses appears to be in still vigorous health at Deut 34,7. He does not die of natural causes, then, but by an act of will in obedience to God. DeutRabba 11,10 recounts that the chief angels did not consider themselves worthy to take Moses' soul, that Satan was unable to, and that God had to do so himself. See further G. Coats, The Moses Tradition (JSOT.S 161), Sheffield 1993.

17 This may be a Lukan misunderstanding based on his knowledge of Johannine traditions, for the question posed by the Judas not Iskariot John 14,22 is so similar to the exhortations of Jesus' brothers at 7,2–5 that John may have intended to refer to one of these not to one of the Twelve.

construct a very precise "situation" with identifiable opponents.[18] As far as one can detect from Jude's generalised and lurid warnings, heretics are prone to advocate some kind of licentiousness (V.4) defiling the flesh (V.8) carousing together (V.12) as well as opposing authority and thinking of themselves as superior to angels. It could be second century incipient gnosticism of a morally lax kind that is in view (though most Gnostics, one should remember, were ethical rigorists) or it could just be the standard jibe of anti-heretical writings that bad doctrine is a mere cover for loose morals. It has several of the hall-marks of a post-apostolic pseudepigraphon; in particular, it appeals to its readers "to contend for the faith once for all delivered to the saints" (V.3) striking the same chord as references in the Pastoral Epistles to the unalterable deposit of sound teaching as the bulwark against heresy; and it reminds them of "the words spoken beforehand by the apostles of our Lord Jesus Christ" (V.17) about the coming of scoffers in the last days, which shares the same perspective as Eph 2,20, looking back to the apostolic foundations of the Church.

Its use of warning examples and metaphors, the death of rebellious Israelites in the Wilderness (V.5), the fall of the Watchers (V.6), the destruction of Sodom and Gomorrah (V.7), Cain, Balaam and Korah (V.11) and the list of abusive metaphors in Vv.12–13 point in the same direction, as stereotypical polemic. The only ray of light in this dark tirade, comes at the end and especially with the doxology, which is again a stereotype drawn from the Church's liturgy. Recent work on the rhetoric of Jude[19] has taken these considerations further. Light has been thrown on the conventional aspects of the composition. For instance, the epistolary clichés of 'compulsion' and 'salvation' in the opening *narratio* (V.3)[20], or the accusation of underhand infiltration (V.4), or the emphasis on slanderous speech, not only in the passage (Vv.8–10) that will concern us shortly, but also at Vv.15,16 and 19.[21]

Of special interest in the present context is the use of non-canonical Jewish literature in Jude. 1 Enoch is quoted at Vv.14a.15, and there is a possible allusion to the Assumption of Moses at V.9. The author may have seen a certain parallel between the figures of Enoch and Moses, i.e.

---

18 F. Wisse, The Epistle of Jude in the History of Heresiology, in: Essays on the Nag Hammadi Texts, ed M. Krause, Leiden 1972, 133–143.
19 D.F. Watson, Invention, Arrangement and Style: Rhetorical Criticism of Jude and 2 Peter, Atlanta 1988; T.R. Wolthuis, Jude and Rhetoricism, CTJ 24 (1989) 126–134; S.J. Joubert, Persuasion in the Letter of Jude, JSNT 59 (1995) 75–87.
20 See, Watson, Invention, 43–48.
21 See L. Thurén, Hey Jude. Asking for the Original Situation and Message of a Catholic Epistle, NTS 43 (1997) 451–465, here 463.

that both were assumed into heaven, but whether both in the body or only the former, it is less easy to decide.

The introduction to the example from the story of Moses (V.8) accuses heretics of "reviling or slandering (βλασφημοῦσιν) the glories". A plausible explanation of this peculiar phrase is that they refer contemptuously to the angels of glory who maintain the proper order of things, not least in matters of sexual conduct (see 1 Cor 11,10). The example is followed by a repeat of the former accusation that "they revile (βλασφημοῦσιν) what they do not know"(V.10). In between these two references to reviling or slander comes the reference to the dispute between Michael and the Devil over the body of Moses. The cause of the dispute is not mentioned, because it is not relevant to the author's argument. His point rather is Michael's demeanour. The Archangel did not dare to deliver a reviling judgement (κρίσιν βλασφημίας, adjectival genitive) but said "The Lord rebuke you." So Michael's reserve, even towards Satan, is being contrasted with the ignorant arrogance of heretics. This is the normal interpretation of the verse accepted by the majority of commentators. It receives immediate support from 2 Pet 2,11, where the adjectival genitive is correctly rendered with an adjective. Admittedly, if this is what was meant, it betrays a certain trivial mentality on the part of the author; there must surely be more intrinsic reasons why angels should not be treated disrespectfully than this! But the rest of the Epistle of Jude does nothing to challenge this as a reasonable estimate of the author's intelligence.

III

In the third and final part of this contribution I want to offer a critique of the very different interpretation of the lost ending of the precursor of the Milan text and of the Epistle of Jude advanced by Richard Bauckham.[22] Bauckham refuses to be "mesmerised by the authority of the Alexandrian Fathers in identifying Jude's source"[23] and reconstructs the ending using four other, very late texts, none of which refers to the book from which they are drawing their information: the 9th century Palaea Historica; the 15th century Slavonic Life of Moses; the 10th century Pseudo-Oecumenius' Commentary on Jude and one section of

---

22 First presented in an excursus to his Commentary on Jude and 2 Peter (WBC 50), Waco 1983, 65–76, and followed seven years later with an even more detailed exposition in chapter 5 of Bauckham, Relatives.

23 Bauckham, Relatives, 245.

Cremer's Catena[24]. I quote in full Bauckham's reconstruction, based on these four sources, of the ending of the Milan text, which he calls the Testament of Moses distinguishing it from the Assumption of Moses.

> "Joshua accompanied Moses up Mount Nebo, where God showed Moses the land of promise. Moses then sent Joshua back, saying, "Go down to the people and tell them that Moses is dead." When Joshua had gone down to the people, Moses died. God sent the archangel Michael to remove the body of Moses to another place and to bury it there, but Samma'el, the devil, opposed him, disputing Moses' right to honourable burial (The text may also have said that the devil wished to take the body down to the people so that they would make it an object of worship.) Michael and the devil engaged in a dispute over the body. The devil slandered Moses, charging him with murder, because he slew the Egyptian and hid his body in the sand [Exod 2,11–12]. But Michael, not tolerating the slander against Moses, said, "May the Lord rebuke you, Satan" At that the devil took flight, and Michael removed the body to the place commanded by God. Thus no-one saw the burial place of Moses".[25]

There are some minor flaws in this reconstruction and four major difficulties. The proper name for the devil, used only in the first source, is there actually rendered Samuel. Bauckham emends, reasonably enough, to Samma'el, a name for the devil which appears in some Jewish sources[26], hoping perhaps by this means to lend an air of antiquity to an otherwise obviously late text. The second motivation of the devil's action, placed in brackets in the above reconstruction, is again drawn exclusively from the Palaea Historica, and it creates a confusion in the portrayal of Satan, on the one hand as a stern defender of the cause of strict justice, or, on the other hand, as a tempter perverting true religion into idolatry. The motivation of the devil, to prevent an honourable burial, on the one hand, and to display the body in a suitably impressive manner for worship, on the other, is also quite confusing. So the bracketed element ought to be set aside. In this reconstruction Moses dies alone, but in the early part of the Assumption of Moses, at 1,15, after Moses has referred to his imminent death with the phrase "I will go to the resting place of my fathers" the Latin continues *et palam omnem plebem* followed by a lacuna; *moriar* has been suggested to fill it.[27] If this is correct, viz. "I will die in the sight of the whole people", it would explain why the body of Moses needed to be removed to a distant secret

---

24   This collection began in the 9th century but was added to continuously. Bauckham naturally discounts some of its evidence, such as the material from the Catena quoted above at note 13.
25   Bauckham, Relatives, 238f.
26   AscIs 1,8; 11,41 and DeutRabba 11,10.
27   See Tromp, Assumption of Moses, 144.

place before it was buried; otherwise that detail of the story is left un-explained.

But these are minor points compared to the following: Firstly, what Bauckham has achieved by this selection of late evidence is to elimi-nate from Jude's source any reference to an assumption, whether of soul or also of body, in the lost ending of the 'Testament' of Moses. He has to admit[28] that the topic of the fate of Moses' body became one of intense interest in later Jewish texts, and argues *e silentio* that the ab-sence of any such interest in his reconstructed lost ending proves that it is a very early version.

Secondly, while the Palaea Historica lacks the devil's slander against Moses for murder, it does have Michael's saying "May the Lord rebuke you". The Slavonic Life and Pseudo-Oecumenius, by contrast, have the slander but not the saying. Only the Catena has both. In Bauckham's estimate this is "an impressive indication of the comple-mentary value of the divergent accounts".[29] It is no such thing. It simply means that three out of the four sources have failed to see any essential relation between the slander and the saying, which according to Bauck-ham is the key to the proper interpretation of Jude 9. Again it is only the Catena that makes it clear that the slanderous accusation is by the Devil against Moses, and not that which Michael refrained from utter-ing against the Devil. The version in the Catena is perfectly under-standable as a deduction from a particular reading of Jude 9, with no other assistance.

Thirdly, at two key points in the reconstruction, the intention of the Devil to deprive Moses of an honourable burial, and the charge of mur-dering the Egyptian as the basis of that intention, Bauckham is unable to provide any parallel evidence in any non-Christian Jewish text. Given his extensive knowledge of the literature, one can only assume that such evidence does not exist.

Fourthly, Bauckham's reconstruction relegates all the much earlier evidence from Clement, Gelasius and others referred to above, to a quite different work, the Assumption of Moses properly so called, though he has to concede that it may have subsequently been appended to the Testament.[30] This originally separate work, he claims, is a second century refutation of Gnostic dualism. "The devil here is no longer the

---

28   Bauckham, Relatives, 240 with references at n. 16.
29   Bauckham, ibid., 253.
30   He is forced to make this concession by the clear quotation of Gelasius, Hist. Eccl. (see
      note 3 above) and because the Latin of the Milan text at 10,12 uses the word receptione
      to describe Moses' death; the most natural rendering of which would be a 'taking away'
      or assumption.

accuser of sinners, attempting to establish Moses' guilt. Rather he claims to be lord of the material world and to have a right to Moses' body for that reason. In other words, he is portrayed as a kind of Gnostic demiurge – or rather, as falsely claiming to be a demiurge".[31] But it plays into the hands of Gnostic dualism to have the Jewish God here claim the powers over the material world, allegedly possessed by the Devil: that is after all, what many Gnostics believed! Bauckham has exaggerated the anti-Gnostic import of the Assumption of Moses version known to the Alexandrian fathers, in order to differentiate it sharply from his own reconstruction. If the Assumption of Moses used by Jude as his source were indeed anti-Gnostic, it would of course be difficult if not impossible to make the case that Jude is an authentic letter penned by one of Jesus' own brothers and represents very primitive Palestinian Christianity. But the struggle between good and evil angels for possession of the soul of a departed person, and in Moses' case maybe also his body, does not need to be seen as anti-Gnostic; it is a simply a standard *topos* in Jewish and early Christian literature concerned with life after death.[32]

Turning from Bauckham's reconstruction of Jude's source to his exegesis of the Epistle itself, we find as many serious difficulties with his proposals.

Firstly, the crucial issue is how to take the phrase κρίσιν βλασφημίας at V.9, whether as a condemnation of the devil's slander against Moses (objective genitive), or as a reviling judgement which Michael refrains from uttering against the devil (adjectival genitive). Bauckham has to argue for the first of these options, but the context is against him. For most commentators on Jude the context provided by Vv.8 and 10 is determinative for the meaning of V.9. Mayor, in his commentary of 1907 – the standard English work on Jude for many years – observed: "The verse is introduced to show the guilt attached to speaking evil of dignities i.e. of angels. If Michael abstained from speaking evil even of a fallen angel, that is appropriate; not so, if he simply abstained from charging the devil with speaking evil of Moses".[33] The same point is made more succinctly by J.N.D. Kelly, – in the standard modern student commentary, until Bauckham wrote his own. He translates the phrase "a reviling judgment", and adds "this rendering fits the context

---

31   Bauckham, Relatives, 244.
32   See K. Berger, Der Streit des guten und des bösen Engels um die Seele. Beobachtungen zu 4QAmr[b] und Judas 9, JSJ 4 (1973) 1–18.
33   B. Mayor, The Epistle of St Jude and the Second Epistle of St Peter, London 1907, 36.

better than a judgment on his revilings".[34] So Bauckham has to argue against the context. He does this by appealing to "catchword connection" which "is primarily a literary technique ... It does not require too strict a conceptual parallel between the blasphemy of the false teachers Vv.8 & 10 and the blasphemy to which verse 9 refers".[35] In the previous chapter on Jude's exegetical techniques he had explained what he means by catchword connections.[36] Following Horgan's work on the Qumran pesharim[37], he argues that catchwords can be used to link a 'text' and the interpretation of that 'text'. The examples he gives are as follows: Lord V.5[38] (of the deliverance from Egypt) and Flesh V.8 (of the Sodomites), taken up in V.8 with the repeated words Flesh and Lordship; Error V.11 (of Balaam) taken up by Errant V.13. Much less convincing is they Spoke V.15 (from the quotation of 1 Enoch) taken up by the mouths that Speak boastful things in V.16. In each of these cases, text precedes and is picked up by interpretation. But at V.9 the opposite is the case: interpretation V.8 precedes the text V.9. And in no other example is there a radical shift in conceptuality from text to interpretation. This argument fails.

Secondly, against the normal contextually sensitive interpretation, Bauckham argues that "The idea that the devil should not be insulted seems a questionable principle, which it is not easy to imagine Jude[39] advocating. Moreover, it is unparalleled in Jewish and early Christian literature (with the exception of 2 Pet 2,11)".[40] The exception is important and we will return to it shortly. But the general point is doubtful. On Bauckham's own interpretation the devil is acting in his role as prosecutor, and the charge he brings against Moses is a reasonable one which deserves a respectful hearing. Even if, as we have argued above, the grounds for the devil's disputing possession of the body of Moses was a more general indictment of sinfulness, that also deserves to be taken seriously.

Thirdly, it is crucial to Bauckham's case that Jude's audience – a specific audience presumably – has recent and intimate knowledge of the way his source, the Testament of Moses, originally ended, or else

---

34 J.N.D. Kelly, A Commentary on the Epistles of Peter and of Jude (BNTC), London 1969, 264.
35 Bauckham, Relatives, 271.
36 Bauckham, ibid., 207.
37 M.P. Horgan, Pesharim. Qumran Interpretations of Biblical Books, Washington D.C. 1979.
38 The variant reading Jesus is more difficult and better attested.
39 It is unclear whether he is speaking of the historical Jude, or of the author the Epistle. If the latter, it is perfectly easy to imagine.
40 Bauckham, Relatives, 273.

the allusion would be lost. The circularity of the argument becomes only too clear at this point. The reconstructed source is needed to secure this interpretation of Jude 9, but Jude 9 may itself be the main source for the reconstruction, as we have argued above.

Fourthly, as just mentioned, the first known reader of Jude 9, the pseudonymous author of 2 Peter, took κρίσιν βλασφημίας naturally in context as βλάσφημον κρίσιν (2 Pet 2,11). Bauckham argues that his misunderstanding was due to his ignorance of the story on which Jude 9 is based. More plausibly, he rightly understood the intended meaning and omitted reference to the story because it fell outside what he accepted as authoritative canonical literature.[41]

Lastly, as Bauckham reconstructs the scene to which Jude is alluding, Michael does not dare to utter a condemnation of the devil's slander, because the prerogative of judgment belongs to God. "He could not on his own authority dismiss the devil's accusations, he could only appeal to the Lord's judgment".[42] Logically, then a further episode would be necessary, when God himself delivers that judgment. There is no indication of this. Michael's words, like those of the angel at Zech 3,2, which he is echoing, are a performative utterance, and enact a dignified divine rebuke, without unnecessary verbal abuse, which is the natural reading of Jude 9 in context.[43]

---

41 For the emerging "canon-consciousness" of 2 Peter, see 2 Pet 1,20, and the reference to "all the letters of Paul and the other scriptures" at 2 Pet 3,16.

42 Bauckham, Relatives, 274.

43 It may be of interest to observe the influence of Bauckham's proposals on recent more popular treatments of Jude. J. Knight, 2 Peter and Jude, Sheffield 1995, 46 following Bauckham says "The devil then brought a charge of murder against Moses but this was simply slander." But curiously, he then continues "Not even Michael felt able to curse the devil on his own authority." Is Knight taking κρίσιν βλασφημίας as a reference to the condemnation of the devil's slander or as a curse, i.e. a reviling judgment which Michael refrains from uttering against the devil? Even more curiously, he adds that "this wider background (viz v. 9) sets the slander reference in Jude 8 in perspective." Surely, it is, if anything, the other way round! Similarly, D. Horrell, The Epistles of Peter and Jude, Peterborough 1998, 122 writes: "Although there is some uncertainty about how to understand the phrase, it seems that what Jude recounts is that Michael did not presume to condemn the devil for his slanderous accusation" (and Bauckham is referenced here). But he concludes his comment on V.9 with a statement that reverses this interpretation: "There is perhaps some irony in the fact that Jude (unlike Michael!) surely slanders his opponents."

IV

Conclusion: In Section I, I examined some selected introductory issues relating to the Assumption of Moses and in particular testimony to its lost ending. In Section II, I briefly examined some introductory questions regarding the Epistle of Jude and especially the interpretation in context of verse 9. These formed the background to Section III, where I offered a more detailed critique of the very different and currently quite influential theories of Richard Bauckham. His reconstruction of the lost ending of the Milan text is based on evidence that is carefully selected to remove any reference to Moses' soul or body being assumed after death, despite the early testimony of the Church fathers that Jude was dependent on a book that went by the title of the Assumption of Moses. The evidence he uses is all very late and is incoherent until fitted together around a paragraph in the Catena which could have no other basis than one particular line of Christian interpretation of Jude 9. There is no evidence that Moses' murder of the Egyptian or the devil's contestation of honourable burial figured in any Jewish legend concerned with the death of Moses. To account for the contradictory evidence, a separate, anti-Gnostic Assumption document is hypothesised, but its apologetic intention and late date have been exaggerated.

Bauckham's exegesis of Jude 9 flies in the face of context, and his appeal to "catchword connection" to counteract this problem fails. Respect for the devil's legitimate role as prosecutor is not unimaginable as the point at issue, indeed it is implicit in Bauckham's own exegesis. Jude 9 could only be understood in the way Bauckham suggests, if the book's original audience had detailed knowledge of its source as Bauckham reconstructs it. This argument is circular. There is no reason to think that 2 Peter has misunderstood Jude, and the words of the Archangel bring the dispute with the devil to a satisfactory closure.

Religious Authority Re–Evaluated
The Character of Moses in the Fourth Gospel

by Stefan Schapdick

Regarding the subject of Moses in the Fourth Gospel, I would like to start with a somewhat broader observation. It has something to do with what you might call a gap. A gap between the interest of the New Testament writings in the person or character of Moses and an astonishing reluctance of New Testament scholars to deal with this subject. On the one hand, the NT interest in Moses can simply be demonstrated by its number of occurrences. 81 times the name Μωϋσῆς is mentioned, more than any other name referring to an Old Testament character. That is not surprising because he is undoubtedly the most prominent person in and for Jewish history and religion. Whenever the name Moses is mentioned Israel's history and religious identity is on the agenda. Since Israel's history and identity is quite a prominent subject of the Christian writings we call the New Testament, too, it does not come as a surprise that Moses is not a rare figure. On the other hand, New Testament scholarship does treat the subject 'Moses' more or less with reserve:[1] A few articles here and there, a monograph now and then, especially limiting itself to specific areas of exegetical problems that need to include the Moses figure or theological issues that are related to him, specifically the Torah, the νόμος, i.e. the Law, But in the last 25 years, now referring to German publications only, there is not one comprehensive study dealing with Moses in the New Testament.[2] It would be quite interesting if the New Testament consideration of Moses is characterised only by selective correspondence within the various NT writings or if there is something like a shared basic concept in view of the Moses

---

[1] This observation has already been made in 1996 by D. Sänger: „Von mir hat er geschrieben" (Joh 5, 46). Zur Funktion und Bedeutung Mose im Neuen Testament: KuD 41 (1995) 112–135, esp. 112–114. After another ten years of New Testament research his observation still holds.

[2] J. Kastner (Mose im Neuen Testament. Eine Untersuchung der Mosetraditionen in den neutestamentlichen Schriften, Diss. Theol., München 1967) and T. Saito (Die Mosevorstellungen im Neuen Testament [EHS.T 100], Frankfurt a.M. 1977) were the two scholars recently dealing with this subject on a monographic level.

character. Definitely, the role of Moses in the NT writings deserves
more attention. My paper that limits itself to the Moses' perspective
presented in the Gospel of John will serve as a little contribution to this
project.

I. The Starting Point:
The Johannine Soteriology

The Fourth Gospel as many other NT writings is debating the question
of Jewish religious identity in its relation to the new Christian identity.
The Gospel of John chooses to deal with this relation mostly by the
means of conflict (cf. John 5,1–10.42). Nevertheless, Christian convictions of belief are always presented in regard to what is considered or
recognised as Jewish religious thinking. The Johannine community as
addressee of the Gospel needs reassurance of their own religious identity. The question in dispute is whether their own Christian identity can
still be considered Jewish: Are Christian believers still part of the Jewish Community or not?[3] To give an answer to this question it is necessary to re-evaluate the role of the prime representative of Jewish religious thinking, Moses. That is exactly what the Gospel is doing
throughout its version of the Jesus' story.

But first of all it has to be noticed that John's fundamental perspective like most of the NT writings is predominantly soteriological. The
topic of salvation is presented almost permanently in a repetitive way,
especially by means of various speeches of Jesus.[4] Perhaps it is best
described in the dialogue of Jesus with Nicodemus in chap. 3, particularly in V. 14–16.[5] The salvation for the cosmos, i.e. for all mankind,

---

3   The Fourth Gospel puts the question at issue to extremes. Passages of strong anti–
     Jewish polemics (e.g. John 8,44: ὑμεῖς ἐκ τοῦ πατρὸς τοῦ διαβόλου ἐστέ) alternate with
     an endorsed Jewish salvation perspective (cf. John 4,22: ἡ σωτηρία ἐκ τῶν Ἰουδαίων
     ἐστίν); on the so–called 'Anti–Judaism' in the Gospel of John cf. e.g. R. Bieringer / D.
     Pollefeyt / F. Vandecasteele–Vanneuville (ed.), Anti–Judaism and the Fourth Gospel,
     London / Louisville, KT 2001.
4   Cf. John 3,1–21; 5,19–47; 6,26–59; 7,1–24; 8,12–59; 10,1–39; 13,31–17,26.
5   Cf. esp. J. Blank, Krisis. Untersuchungen zur johanneischen Christologie und Eschato-
     logie, Freiburg 1964, 75–88; J. Frey, Die johanneische Eschatologie III (WUNT 117),
     Tübingen 2000, 248–289; A. Hammes, Der Ruf ins Leben. Eine theologisch–hermeneu-
     tische Untersuchung zur Eschatologie des Johannesevangeliums mit einem Ausblick auf
     die Wirkungsgeschichte (BBB 112), Bodenheim 1997, 68–175; H. Kohler, Kreuz und
     Menschwerdung im Johannesevangelium. Ein exegetisch–hermeneutischer Versuch zur
     johanneischen Kreuzestheologie (AThANT 72), Zürich 1987, 248–270; T. Knöppler,
     Die theologia crucis des Johannesevangeliums. Das Verständnis des Todes Jesu im
     Rahmen der johanneischen Inkarnations- und Erhöhungschristologie (WMANT 69),

represented by the concept of ζωὴ αἰώνιος[6] (cf. John 3,15), is the first and perhaps the only real interest of the Gospel. It is solely based on the one event of God's love[7] (John 3,16a: οὕτως γὰρ ἠγάπησεν ὁ θεὸς τὸν κόσμον). Furthermore, John 3,14–16 relates this divine soteriological plan to the entire life of Jesus of Nazareth culminating in his passion, particularly his crucifixion, which is interpreted as the act of exaltation (cf. John 3,14). The one unreserved act of God's love, the gift of His son, overcomes even the one definite obstacle to life, i.e. death. The death of the one sent by God deprives death of all its life–destroying powers once and for all. The only thing to do for men to participate in God's absolute and final gift of salvation, the ζωὴ αἰώνιος, is to accept, i.e. to believe, that the crucified Jesus is the one sent by God, revealing God's unrestricted love to all mankind.[8] Thus, all salvation is bound to Jesus Christ. Perdition is possible only in the rejection of the overall life–saving or, more precisely, life–giving quality of his life and death (cf. John 3,17–21).[9] Therefore, the Johannine language of soteriology is shaped by statements referring to Jesus Christ. Consequently, it is mostly characterised as "christological". Moreover, it must be noted that the christological perspective of the Gospel is the only one that guarantees any true perception and recognition of God. As John 1,18 clearly states, Jesus is the exclusive, the only accepted, and authorised son. God's presence is to be found in him only because they are one (cf. John 10,30). Thus, Jesus Christ is the sole "exegete", the sole inter-

---

Neukirchen-Vluyn 1994, 154–160; H. Merklein, Gott und Welt. Eine exemplarische Interpretation von Joh 2,23–3,21; 12,20–36 zur theologischen Bestimmung des johanneischen Dualismus, in: idem, Studien zu Jesus und Paulus II (WUNT 105), Tübingen 1998, 263–281, esp. 268–273; H. Weder, Die Asymmetrie des Rettenden. Überlegungen zu Joh 3,14–21 im Rahmen johanneischer Theologie, in: idem, Einblicke ins Evangelium. Exegetische Beiträge zur neutestamentlichen Hermeneutik, Göttingen 1992, 435–465, esp. 439–463.

6   "Weil der irdische Jesus als Menschensohn den Tod erleidet und ihn damit zugleich überwindet, schafft er dem Menschen Zugang zu einem Leben, das dem Tod nicht mehr verfallen ist, die ζωὴ αἰώνιος" (S. Schapdick, Auf dem Weg in den Konflikt. Exegetische Studien zum theologischen Profil der Erzählung vom Aufenthalt Jesu in Samarien (Joh 4,1–42) im Kontext des Johannesevangeliums [BBB 126], Berlin 2000, 268); for origin and purpose of the concept of ζωὴ αἰώνιος cf. ibid., 155f; Frey, Eschatologie III, 261–270; F. Mußner, ΖΩΗ. Die Anschauung vom "Leben" im vierten Evangelium unter Berücksichtigung der Johannesbriefe (MThS.H 5), München 1952, 144–186; M. Stare, Durch Ihn Leben. Die Lebensthematik in Joh 6 (NTA NF 49), Münster 2004, 150–152.

7   Cf. Kohler, Kreuz, 255: "Ereignis der Liebe Gottes".

8   Cf. ibid., 260; Weder, Asymmetrie, 450.

9   Cf. Blank, Krisis, 88–108; Frey, Eschatologie III, 290–300; Hammes, Ruf, 136–157; Merklein, Welt, 273–275.

preter of God. Any idea of closeness to God is exclusively communicated by Jesus himself and no–one else (cf. John 1,1,18).

II. Μωϋσῆς in the Fourth Gospel

This leads us immediately to the character of Moses. The christologically shaped view of salvation must come into conflict with the traditional role or function of Moses in the OT and, respectively, in many texts of early Judaism. Without dwelling into detail, his traditional role may be described as him being the mediator and interpreter of the will of God JHWH (cf. Exod 3,14). A special, almost intimate closeness to God is attributed to him (cf. Exod 34,28–34).[10] His specific function is primarily realised by mediating the Torah which serves as the definite rule of life for Israel. It is the source of all salvation and life, thus it means life or death, salvation or judgement for Israel, depending on Israel's attitude towards the Torah: Do they keep or follow it or not (cf. Deut 28,1–68)?[11] Accordingly, Moses' function is normative and paradigmatic.[12] But how does the Fourth Gospel deal with Moses traditional role in correspondence to its all out christological perspective of salvation? Does it still show any interest in the character of Moses and, if yes, what relevance does he still have? Which religious authority may be attributed to him if the notion of divine revelation is solely mediated christologically?

In John's Gospel the name Μωϋσῆς can be found quite often, at least 12 times, with an additional occurrence in John 8,5 (cf. John 1,17.45; 3,14; 5,45f; 6,32; 7,19.22[2x].23; 9,28f).[13] All passages mentioning the name Moses occur in the first half of the Gospel containing the divine revelation of Jesus of Nazareth for the world (cf. John 1,19–12,50).

---

10 To some extent the OT texts show a tendency towards deification of Moses (cf. Exod 34,29–34); cf. e.g. Zenger, Art. Moses I: TRE 23 (1994) 330–341, esp. 335f.
11 For equivalent Jewish evidence cf. Bill. III, 129–131.237.277f.498.
12 Cf. Zenger, Art. Mose I, 336.
13 The passage John 7,53–8,11 referring to the woman caught in adultery is probably not part of the original Gospel (cf. inter alia C. Dietzfelbinger, Das Evangelium nach Johannes I [ZBK.NT 4,1], Zürich 2001, 231–237; K. Wengst, Das Johannesevangelium I [ThKNT 4,1], Stuttgart et al. ²2004, 301–308). For that reason I will not include it in my considerations here; for the view on Moses in John 7,53–8,11 cf. esp. A. Lindemann, Mose und Jesus Christus. Zum Verständnis des Gesetzes im Johannesevangelium, in: U. Mell / U.B. Müller (ed.), Das Urchristentum in seiner literarischen Geschichte. FS Jürgen Becker (BZNW 100), Berlin / New York 1999, 309–334, esp. 329f.

Nine of the twelve occurrences turn up in the chap. 5–7 and in chap. 9. The narrative frame there is primarily a conflict between Jesus – in chap. 9 it is the healed blind born who to a certain extent acts on Jesus' behalf – and various adversaries (οἱ 'Ιουδαῖοι [chap. 5], οἱ 'Ιουδαῖοι, οἱ Φαρισαῖοι [chap. 9], ὁ ὄχλος [chap. 6/7]) regarding God's final revelation of salvation. Jesus' call to faith, more precisely, to faith in him, is the integral part of that revelation. It is presented as God's ultimate offer to salvation by simply believing that Jesus himself in all what he says and does is this offer. This claim of Jesus, to present and represent God's unsurpassing revelation, is constantly questioned and challenged. In the narrative sequence of dialogues, speeches, and debates the conflict presents itself with ongoing and increasing aggravation. On the one side we have Jesus permanently making all efforts to convince his counterparts of his rightful claim to divine revelation, on the other side this claim is rejected over and over again. The threat to kill Jesus by his adversaries is repeated various times from John 5,18 onwards until the final decision is made in John 11,53.[14]

The other three occurrences turn up in the chap. 1 and 3. Chap. 1 is to be described as the Gospel's twofold exposition with the prologue in John 1,1–18 on the one hand and the narrative introduction in John 1,19–51 on the other.[15] The prologue sets the Gospel's hermeneutical frame outside the narrative course of events by referring to Jesus as the pre–existent divine logos, the mediator of creation (cf. John 1,1–3.10) who becomes flesh (cf. John 1,11.14) to offer God's ultimate gift of life to all mankind. The narrative introduction in John 1,19–51 summarises this soteriological goal by attributing various christological titles to Jesus. The passage culminates in the final sequence of John 1,50f in which Jesus is introduced as the ultimate place of God's presence on earth. In chap. 3 Moses is mentioned in the dialogue of Jesus with Nicodemus (cf. John 3,1–21). The chap. 2–4 present Jesus' claim to divine revelation without explicit resistance to his message of salvation.[16] But these chapters set the stage for the later conflict. Chap. 3 especially serves to explain the specific contents of Jesus' revelation of salvation (cf. John 3,13–21.31–36).'

---

14 Cf. John 7,1,19f.25.30.32; 8,37.40; 10,31–33.
15 The prologue serves as the prior characterisation of the narrative's main character while John 1,19–51 adds the narrative frame in which the logos incarnate is integrated (cf. Schapdick, Konflikt, 47). C.H. Dodd adequately refers to John chap. 1 as the "prooemium" of the Gospel (Interpretation of the Fourth Gospel, Cambridge 1955, 292).
16 Cf. esp. Schapdick, Konflikt, 383–419.

1. John 1,17

Of the 12 occurrences of Μωϋσῆς in the Gospel the first in John 1,17 is probably the most difficult one. The prologue as the "Leseanweisung"[17] to the Jesus story of the Gospel wants to make clear who Jesus is and what his intentions are before he himself is beginning to play an active role in the narrative sequence of events. V.17 is following V.16 which is closely connected to the statement regarding the incarnation of the logos in V.14. The interpretation of V.17, particularly of the parallelism ὁ νόμος διὰ Μωϋσῆς ἐδόθη, ἡ χάρις καὶ ἡ ἀλήθεια διὰ Ἰησοῦ Χριστοῦ ἐγένετο, has caused and is still causing a lot of debate.[18] V.17 is connected to V.16 by the causative ὅτι. Thus, V.17 should be understood as an explanatory statement for V.16. V.16 on the other hand contains the conclusion from the δόξα-statement in V.14.[19] While the words χάρις and ἀλήθεια and the verb ἐγένετο have been mentioned before (cf. V.14.16), referring to the incarnation of the pre–existent logos,[20] νόμος and Μωϋσῆς have no explicit reference to what has been said in the prologue so far. The syntax does not follow the semantics here. The problem has to be solved pragmatically.[21] A lot of the motives in V.14.16–18 seem to echo Exod 33–34, the renewal of the covenant. As an example, ἡ χάρις καὶ ἡ ἀλήθεια is possibly referring to JHWH's חֶסֶד וֶאֱמֶת (cf. Exod 34,6). So it might be concluded that we are dealing

---

17   H. Merklein, Geschöpf und Kind. Zur Theologie der hymnischen Vorlage des Johannesprologs, in: idem, Studien zu Jesus und Paulus II (WUNT 105), Tübingen 1998, 241–261, here 260.

18   The quality of the parallelism is particularly in dispute: Is it synonymous (cf. J. Jeremias, Art. Μωϋσῆς: ThWNT IV [1942] 852–878, here 877; A. Obermann, Die christologische Erfüllung der Schrift im Johannesevangelium [WUNT II 83], Tübingen 1996, 54; H. Thyen, Das Johannesevangelium [HNT 6], Tübingen 2005, 104; Wengst, Joh I, 71f) or antithetical (so the majority among scholars; cf. inter alia C.K. Barrett, Das Evangelium nach Johannes [KEK.S], Göttingen 1990, 195; J. Becker, Das Evangelium nach Johannes, 2 Vols. [ÖTK 4,1–2], Gütersloh/Würzburg, I ³1991, 101; R. Bultmann, Das Evangelium des Johannes [KEK 2], Göttingen ²¹1986, 53; Dietzfelbinger, Joh I, 32; Sänger, Von mir, 124; R. Schnackenburg, Das Johannesevangelium I [HThK 4,1], Freiburg et al. 1965, 252; U. Schnelle, Das Evangelium nach Johannes [ThHK 4], Leipzig ²2000, 42f; U. Wilckens, Das Evangelium nach Johannes [NTD 4], Göttingen ¹⁸2000, 35)? However, an adversative δέ referring to antithetical meaning is missing. But this does not exclude an antithetical interpretation of V.17. The strict parallelism is neutralised by the choice of verbs. Regarding the context an antithetical meaning should be favoured; cf. esp. S. Pancaro, The Law in the Fourth Gospel. The Torah and the Gospel, Moses and Jesus, Judaism and Christianity According to John (NT.S 42), Leiden 1975, 537.

19   Who beholds the glory of God in the Logos Jesus perceives God in his fullness and receives grace from grace (cf. Dietzfelbinger, Joh I, 32).

20   The pre-existent Logos is identified with Jesus Christ in V.17b.

21   In agreement with Merklein, Geschöpf, 167.

with another revelation of God's Doxa (כָּבוֹד) here (cf. Exod 33,18.22), perhaps now in an unsurpassing manner. Even V.17 would fit into this perspective by mentioning the Law handed over to the mediator Moses (cf. Exod 34,10–29).[22] But the construction of V.17 seems to militate against such an understanding. It is to be understood as a comment to V.14. Two acts of mediation are mentioned, seemingly equivalent: The Law has been given by Moses, grace and truth (as divine predicates) became / came into being by Jesus Christ. The verb ἐδόθη certainly is to be interpreted as a divine passive[23] and ἐγένετο resumes the language of creation of V.14a (ὁ λόγος σὰρξ ἐγένετο).[24] Accordingly, the coming into being of grace and truth has the same quality as the becoming of flesh of the logos.[25] Furthermore, it can be concluded that one and the same act is described here. The logos was made flesh and by that grace and truth came into being. Truth (ἀλήθεια) becomes a very important term in the sequence of the Gospel referring to the manifestation of the divine reality on earth (cf. John 4,23; 8,32; 16,13; 17,17).[26] This reality is identified with the whole life of Jesus of Nazareth, thus describing it entirely as revelation of God. God's ἀλήθεια exclusively reveals itself in the life of Jesus. The grace and truth of God JHWH became reality in Jesus only and nowhere else.[27] This view is definitely supported by

---

22 Cf. M. Theobald, Im Anfang war das Wort. Textlinguistische Studie zum Johannesprolog (SBS 106), Stuttgart 1983, 59.

23 Cf. inter alia Becker, Joh I, 101; Hammes, Ruf, 154 n. 278; O. Hofius, "Der in des Vaters Schoß ist" Joh 1,18, in: idem / H.–C. Kammler, Johannesstudien (WUNT 88), Tübingen 1996, 24–32, 30; Theobald, Anfang, 60–63.

24 Contra Wengst, Joh I, 72 with n. 70, who claims ἐγένετο has to be interpreted in accordance to V.6, where the appearance of John the Baptist is mentioned; but cf. John 1,3 which refers to the mediation of the creation by the Logos: πάντα δι᾽ αὐτοῦ ἐγένετο, καὶ χωρὶς αὐτοῦ ἐγένετο οὐδὲ ἓν ὃ γέγονεν; for this view cf. inter alia Lindemann, Mose, 332.

25 Cf. Theobald, Anfang, 62.

26 Cf. also Schapdick, Konflikt, 219–223; Pancaro, Law, 92–101; for the term ἀλήθεια cf. esp. Y. Ibuki, Die Wahrheit im Johannesevangelium (BBB 39), Bonn 1972; I. de la Potterie, La vérité dans Saint Jean, 2 Vols., (AnBib 73/74), Rome 1977. The Fourth Gospel utilises the noun χάρις in V.14.16f of the prologue only. Thus, ἀλήθεια is the more important term for the Gospel.

27 Cf. also Theobald, Anfang, 61f; idem, Die Fleischwerdung des Logos. Studien zum Verhältnis des Johannesprologs zum Corpus des Evangeliums und zu 1 Joh (NTA NF 20), Münster 1988, 257f. Therefore, both statements of V.17 are not quite balanced. Grace and truth as the decisive revelatory components are clearly not connected to the Nomos. But there is little use in overstating this issue, especially in regard to the following conflict between Jesus and his Jewish adversaries (cf. John 5 – 10). Hofius, Schoß, 30, speaks of the polemical tone of V.17 (cf. also J. Kügler, Der andere König. Religionsgeschichtliche Perspektiven auf die Christologie des Johannesevangeliums [SBS 178], Stuttgart 1999, 68). But the goal of V.17 is not to place blame in a potentially polemical design. The author of V.17 attempts to present the thought of revelation

V.18. Nobody, not even Moses, has ever seen God ($\theta\epsilon\grave{o}\nu$ $o\dot{\nu}\delta\epsilon\grave{\iota}\varsigma$ $\dot{\epsilon}\acute{\omega}\rho\alpha\kappa\epsilon\nu$ $\pi\acute{\omega}\pi\sigma\tau\epsilon$). It has to be added here: With the exception of the Logos.[28] He is the $\mu\sigma\nu\sigma\gamma\epsilon\nu\grave{\eta}\varsigma$ $\theta\epsilon\acute{o}\varsigma$. So he is the only one who has the authority and capability to reveal God, His grace and truth, and to interpret Him ($\dot{\epsilon}\xi\eta\gamma\acute{\eta}\sigma\alpha\tau\sigma$). Any thought of revelation, always conjoint with the idea of salvation for all mankind, apart from the revelation of Jesus Christ is no longer possible.[29] Now, revelation is by definition christological or it is not revelation. But why mentioning Moses at all if his traditional role as interpreter of God's revelation is rejected? Why referring to his mediation of the Law whose divine origin is clearly confirmed (V.17a)? Why all the allusions to the Sinai revelation here?

First, for the Gospel the terms Moses – Law – Revelation are naturally linked and certainly of major importance. This is possible only if a Jewish background for the Gospel is assumed. A clear historical context of the Gospel's contents is given by the reference to Moses and the Law. It is more than plausible that we are looking at an internal Jewish/Jewish–Christian debate about what revelation is and where salvation for Israel and for all mankind can be found.[30] It is nothing less but a conflict which applies to the very bases of Jewish religious identity. The boundaries and definitions of Judaism are in dispute here.[31] Who does still live within these boundaries and who is not? For the Johannine community their faith in the christologically shaped divine revelation is no contradiction to the Jewish religious tradition at all but the

---

in a distinct christological perspective, but not without relating it to its own Jewish religious tradition which still is acknowledged as his own. It is redefined but not discarded.
28 Cf. Kügler, König, 67.
29 Cf. ibid.
30 Cf. esp. K. Wengst, Bedrängte Gemeinde und verherrlichter Christus. Ein Versuch über das Johannesevangelium (KT 114), München ⁴1992, 75–127; cf. also Schapdick, Konflikt, 441–458.
31 Cf. J.D.G. Dunn, The Question of Anti–Semitism in the New Testament Writings of the Period, in: idem (ed.), Jews and Christians. The Parting of Ways A.D. 70 to 135 (WUNT 66), Tübingen 1992, 177–211, 203: "The Fourth Evangelist is ... operating within a context of intra–Jewish factional dispute, although the boundaries and definitions are themselves part of that dispute".

only way to keep it.[32] Any disregard to Jesus Christ is in the end a disregard to Jewish tradition and beliefs.[33]

Second, it is clear that a Gospel which solely connects the thought
of divine revelation to Jesus Christ and his ministry has to deal with the
traditional revelatory role of Moses. In a prologue which constantly
elaborates on the christological perspective of salvation the mentioning
of Moses may seem to emerge out of thin air (cf. the lexical inventory).
But it is undoubtedly necessary to clarify or redefine what revelation is
and what it is not. If it is by definition christological only, Moses, the
νομοθέτης, and the divine Law need to be integrated somehow into this
new christological perspective. For one thing V. 17 clearly stands
proof: Moses and the Law are not abrogated at all. The divine act of
mediation is not contested.[34] Moses' revelatory role has to be redefined
just as a new soteriological perspective regarding the Torah has to be
developed. Intriguingly, the prologue does not address this issue any
further. V.18 returns to the christological perspective of salvation. That
is the reason John 1,17 will always appear somewhat enigmatic within
the context of the prologue. Only by a look at the Gospel as a whole its
interpretation is getting more evident. But it should be emphasised that
the christologically centered concept of unsurpassing divine revelation
in the prologue does not absorb the relation to Israel or Judaism entirely. At least, this relation is stated. Despite all the dominance of
christological thinking the author of the Fourth Gospel stresses the Jewish origin of the divine revelation of Jesus. But he does it with the dis-

---

32 This may be proved by a look at John 4,1–42. In the dialogue with the Samaritan
    woman Jesus characterises his divine revelation as Jewish in origin (John 4,22: ἡ σω-
    τηρία ἐκ τῶν Ἰουδαίων ἐστίν). This passage most certainly uses the Jewish–Samaritan
    religious conflict to emphasise "die *jüdische* Identität der johanneischen Gemeinde"
    (Schapdick, Konflikt, 452). The goal is to make explicitly clear, "dass *das christliche
    Bekenntnis ein genuin jüdisches Bekenntnis* ist, oder besser *das einzige jüdische* Be-
    kenntnis, dem sich dann auch die außerhalb der jüdischen Offenbarungstradition ste-
    henden Samaritaner anschließen" (ibid., 453); cf. John 4,39–42.
33 Regarding the historical background, it is not be assumed that the Christians of the
    Johannine community distanced themselves from their Jewish religious heritage. Most
    likely, the situation was reversed: Non–Christian Jews started to separate themselves
    from Christian Jews, denying them their Jewish identity. That way the Non–Christian
    Jews set the "Trennungsstrich" (Lindemann, Mose, 333). The phrase ἀποσυνάγωγος
    γενέσθαι, used three times in the Fourth Gospel, is considered as proof for this by relat-
    ing it to the expulsion of the Johannine Jewish–Christians from the synagogue (cf. John
    9,22f; 12,42; 16,2). In response, the author of the Gospel interprets this act as the self–
    exclusion of synagogue–organised Jews from the eschatological salvation offered by
    the God of Israel through Jesus. Any true Jewish confession is by definition a Christian
    confession or it is not Jewish. Consequently, Jewish faith is accepted only if it is Chris-
    tian faith (cf. Schapdick, Konflikt, 453).
34 The focus is not on the originator of the Law but on its function (cf. Hofius, Schoß, 30).

tinct intention to lay claim to it totally. He postulates: The pre–existent
God of all creation, the God of Israel and of Moses, is the God of the
logos incarnate of John 1,14. A substantial justification for this conviction is given in the Gospel as the narrative sequence of events unfolds.
The christological perception of Moses (and the Law) should be discovered by having a further look at other occurrences of the term
Μωϋσῆς in John's Gospel.[35]

2. John 1,45–51

A re–evaluation of Moses' role can already be detected in the second
passage of the Gospel referring to Moses (cf. John 1,45). In the second
part of the Gospel's narrative introduction (cf. John 1,35–51) we are
being told about the gaining of disciples by Jesus. The call to discipleship of Nathanael (cf. John 1,45–51) is mediated by Philip who was
called to discipleship immediately before (cf. John 1,43f). During Philip's invitation to Nathanael,[36] he refers to Jesus as "the one about
whom Moses and the Prophets wrote" (V. 45: ὃν ἔγραψεν Μωϋσῆς ἐν
τῷ νόμῳ καὶ οἱ προφῆται). In this instance, Moses is directly characterised as the writer (author) of the Law, the Nomos.[37] What it contains is
prophetic information about a coming Messiah,[38] information that
Philip understands Jesus to fulfill. John 1,19–51 is filled with what may
be called a "litany of christological titles"[39], all of them referring to
Jesus. He is the Lamb of God (cf. John 1,29.36), the Messiah or the
Christ (cf. John 1,20.25.41.45), the King of Israel (cf. John 1,49), the
Son of Man (cf. John 1,51). The variety and the different origins of all

---

35   In advance, this perception may be described as follows: The Nomos is not the divine
     revelation itself but functions as the signpost to it. The Nomos has been given by Moses
     to bear witness to the divine revelation of salvation in Jesus Christ. Therefore, it is defi-
     nitely correct to state that the divine gift of the Torah is not revoked or abrogated by the
     divine truth related to Jesus Christ only (cf. Thyen, Joh, 329). However, its soteriologi-
     cal relevance is redefined. The Nomos' role is only to bear witness to the salvation in
     Jesus Christ. A not–christological reading of the Torah is soteriologically irrelevant (cf.
     John 5,39); cf. esp. Wilckens, Joh, 125.
36   The Fourth Gospel is the only Gospel to call on mediators in narratives of disciple–
     gaining by Jesus (cf. S. Harstine, Moses as a Character in the Fourth Gospel. A Study of
     Ancient Reading Techniques [JSNT.S 229], Sheffield 2002, 52).
37   Cf. esp. Obermann, Erfüllung, 60–63.
38   Either the statement refers back to the notion of the Messiah in John 1,41 (cf. e.g. Bar-
     rett, Joh, 208; Wilckens, Joh, 50) or it poses as a comprehensive statement about Jesus
     in reference to all OT expectations of salvation (cf. e.g. Wengst, Joh I, 92).
39   T. Okure, The Johannine Approach to Mission. A Contextual Study of John 4,1–42
     (WUNT II 31), Tübingen 1988, 49.

these titles are not of major importance. They are all compiled to serve as a single consistent statement about Jesus culminating in the image of the open heaven in V.51. In all his life, in his ministry, Jesus of Nazareth, the son of Josef, is the ultimate place of God's presence in the world. He is the true 'Bethel', the gate to heaven (cf. Gen 28,17).[40] Regarding V.45 Moses is introduced as witness to Jesus, now in alliance with the prophets, i.e. the prophetical writings of the scriptures.[41] He and the prophets, the representatives of Israel, bear knowledge of Jesus as is written in their texts. That Jesus is the Messiah is foretold in their writings. All expectations of salvation for Israel are related and should be related to him. The Gospel's focus on the biblical tradition of Israel is obvious here. It is further supported by Jesus calling Nathanael an ἀληθῶς 'Ισραηλίτης and Nathanael calling Jesus the βασιλεὺς τοῦ 'Ισραήλ (V.47.49).

3. John 3,13–15

The third reference to Moses occurs in the Nicodemus episode of John 3,1–21 containing the first longer discourse of Jesus in the Gospel (cf. John 3,10–21). The next occurrences of Μωϋσῆς in the Gospel are all to be found in speeches of Jesus (cf. chap. 3, 5, 6, and 7). Moses is introduced in V. 14 to explain the necessity of the Son of Man's exaltation. The title υἱὸς τοῦ ἀνθρώπου has already been mentioned in John 1,51, just as the categories of ascent and descent which are readapted in John 3,13 again.[42] A comparison is framed in which the act of ὑψοῦν plays an important role including its life–giving or life–saving consequences. The background is the OT episode of Num 21,4–9.[43] On their trek from Sinai to Jordan, Israel had rebelled against God (once again) and as a punishment he sent serpents killing a lot of Israelites. To save them from the serpents Moses made a copper serpent, following a divine order, lifted it up on a standard so that every Israelite looking at it

---

40 Cf. Hammes, Ruf, 48; for further analysis of John 1,50f cf. ibid., 46–49.
41 The phrase ὃν ἔγραψεν Μωϋσῆς ἐν τῷ νόμῳ καὶ οἱ προφῆται only occurs here in the Fourth Gospel and refers to the "als inspiriert anerkannten Teile des Schriftenkreises" (Obermann, Erfüllung, 52); cf. also Schnackenburg, Joh I, 314; Wengst, Joh I, 92; Wilckens, Joh, 50.
42 Cf. esp. Hammes, Ruf, 46–49; Merklein, Welt, 269f; Schapdick, Konflikt, 238f.
43 Cf. esp. J. Frey, "Wie Mose die Schlange in der Wüste erhöht hat ..." Zur frühjüdischen Deutung der ‚ehernen Schlange' und ihrer christologischen Rezeption in Johannes 3,14f., in: M. Hengel / H. Löhr (ed.), Schriftauslegung im antiken Judentum und im Urchristentum (WUNT 73), Tübingen 1994, 153–205; M. Theobald, Herrenworte im Johannesevangelium (HBS 34), Freiburg i. Br. 2002, 213–218.

was saved. In reference to this event, the soteriological relevance of Jesus' mission is clarified. The statement that the Son of Man must be lifted up (ὑψωθῆναι δεῖ) originally refers to the act of exaltation that is understood as Jesus' enthronement on the right hand side of God (cf. esp. Acts 2,30–36; 5,31; Eph 1,20; Col 3,1; Heb 1,3.13).[44] This act is identified with the crucifixion here.[45] Its final goal is the gift of ζωὴ αἰώνιος for the believer (cf. John 3,15), i.e. for everyone who accepts the crucifixion as this act of exaltation. Despite the comparative structure of John 3,13–15, its content should not be described as a Moses–Jesus–Typology.[46] The point of comparison refers to the serpent and to the Son of Man regarding their life–giving or life–saving powers.[47] Both are affixed to elevated places to be visible.[48] Num 21,4–9 focuses on God as the actual originator of a single life–saving act performed by Moses. God is clearly introduced as Lord over life and death.[49] He preserves the earthly life of the Israelites, a life which is still limited by death. The quality of life which is connected with the divine act of exaltation is entirely different. The salvific gift of God, the ζωὴ αἰώνιος, is no longer affected by death. It is given to all believers as the final and unsurpassing act of divine salvation.

The reference to Num 21,4–9 in John 3,13–15 serves a special purpose: It prefigures the final act of salvation. A single historical event of a divine act of life–saving presents Moses as its mediator. He has a kind of soteriological function, then. But from the point of view of the Fourth Gospel the life that was saved there is βίος, not ζωή, earthly life, not eternal life.[50] Jesus' divine mission alone brings eternal life for

---

44   Cf. also Acts 1,9–11; Rom 1,3f; Phil 2,6–11.
45   Cf. esp. inter alia Hammes, Ruf, 123–127; Frey, Eschatologie III, 277–282; Knöppler, theologia crucis, 155–160; Merklein, Welt, 270–272; Wilckens, Joh, 71f; cf. also Schapdick, Konflikt, 267–269.
46   "Christus wird in 3,14f ... nicht als ein zweiter Mose charakterisiert, zumal dies mit 3,13 kollidierte. Denn dort wird ... bestritten, außer dem Menschensohn sei jemals einer in den Himmel aufgestiegen" (Sänger, Von mir, 126); cf. also M. Gawlick, Mose im Johannesevangelium, BN 84 (1996) 29–35, here 32 n. 21; Lindemann, Mose, 314. Moses certainly is the mediator of divine revelation. But his ἀναβαίνειν on Mt. Sinai (cf. Exod 19,3.20; 24,9.15.18; 34,4) does not correspond to the ἀναβαίνειν of the Son of Man. Compared to the divine revelation of Jesus, Moses is attached to earth and not to heaven like the Son of Man.
47   " ... wie die in der Wüste ,erhöhte' Schlange nach Gottes Willen das leibliche Leben rettete, so schenkt der am Kreuz Erhöhte den Seinigen ewiges Leben" (Schnackenburg, Joh I, 411).
48   Crucial are the events related to the verb ὑψοῦν, particularly the difference between Moses' single act of ὕψωσεν and the theologically qualified ὑψωθῆναι δεῖ with regard to Jesus Christ (cf. Lindemann, Mose), 314); cf. also Knöppler, theologia crucis, 157.
49   Cf. Wengst, Joh I, 135.
50   Cf. Mußner, ΖΩΗ, 70–73.

every believer. It is given once and for all without any local or temporal limitations.[51] The ultimate plan of salvation, characterised by the divine 'must' ($\delta\epsilon\hat{\iota}$), exceeds the biblical tradition of Num 21, even, if both passages refer to God as the one who gives, preserves, and may also take life. In John 3,14 "Moses' personal limitations regarding salvation are brought centre stage here"[52]. But once again, this is verbalised from the christological perspective of the Fourth Gospel. John 3,13–15 and Num 21,4–9 agree on the perception of God as life–saviour. The difference is to be found in the soteriological gift, earthly or eternal life. With reference to the conflict about Jewish/Jewish–Christian religious identity in the Gospel the passage John 3,13–15 makes definitely clear that the crucifixion of Jesus with its overall soteriological quality can not be dismissed as violation of the Nomos of Moses (cf. Deut 21,22f) because in the same Nomos a prefiguration of this soteriological act can be found, with Moses as its mediator.[53]

4. John 5,45–47

In the next relevant passage referring to Moses in John 5,45–47 the conflict between Jesus and his Jewish adversaries has already erupted. It is presented as a series of dialogues in which Jesus' claim to divine revelation is questioned and challenged. Jesus himself presents Moses as part of his discussion with his various opponents. In chap. 5 it is the Jews who challenge his claim following Jesus' act of healing on the Sabbath (cf. John 5,1–18). V.45f belong to the Jesus–speech of John 5,19–47, more precisely, to its second part in John 5,31–47. Here Jesus calls upon various witnesses who have testified on his behalf, i.e. John the Baptist (V.33–36), God himself as the father (V.37f), and the scriptures (V.39: $\tau\grave{a}\varsigma\ \gamma\rho\alpha\phi\acute{a}\varsigma$). V.45–47 refer to the scriptures again. The name $M\omega\ddot{\upsilon}\sigma\tilde{\eta}\varsigma$ is mentioned twice (V.45f). As in John 1,45, he is introduced as their writer (V.46f: $\pi\epsilon\rho\grave{\iota}\ \gamma\grave{a}\rho\ \acute{\epsilon}\mu o\hat{\upsilon}\ \acute{\epsilon}\kappa\epsilon\hat{\iota}\nu o\varsigma\ \acute{\epsilon}\gamma\rho\alpha\psi\epsilon\nu$; $\tau o\hat{\iota}\varsigma$ $\acute{\epsilon}\kappa\epsilon\acute{\iota}\nu o\upsilon\ \gamma\rho\acute{a}\mu\mu\alpha\sigma\iota\nu$)[54] and characterised as witness for Jesus' divine revelation. In his speech Jesus accuses the Jews of misinterpreting their

---

51 Cf. Gawlick, Mose, 33.
52 Harstine, Moses, 56.
53 Cf. Dietzfelbinger, Joh I, 290. However, this pre–figuration cannot be interpreted in terms of ‚Verheißung' and ‚Erfüllung'. The exclusively christological mediation of any thought of revelation militates against this (cf. John 3,13). Nevertheless, it is emphasised here that the God of Jesus is no other than the God of Israel. He alone gives and preserves life, whether it is $\beta\acute{\iota}o\varsigma$ or $\zeta\omega\acute{\eta}$. The Fourth Gospel's interest obviously is on the $\zeta\omega\acute{\eta}\ (\alpha\grave{\iota}\acute{\omega}\nu\iota o\varsigma)$ alone.
54 The pronoun $\acute{\epsilon}\kappa\epsilon\hat{\iota}\nu o\varsigma$ refers to Moses in each case.

own biblical traditions. They study the scriptures believing that they contain eternal life (cf. John 5,39). From the point of view of the Gospel there is nothing wrong with that. But what the Jews refuse to understand is that the scriptures testify for Jesus and his divine revelation. Moses as the author of the scriptures wrote about Jesus (cf. John 5,46). If they really would believe Moses they would believe Jesus (cf. John 5,47). Their studies of the Torah and the Prophets fail without a christological interpretation standard.[55] By rejecting this standard they show that they do not have God's love in themselves and that they do not search for his Doxa[56] (cf. John 5,42.44). In the end they refuse to acknowledge God at all. As a consequence they cannot rely on Moses as their intercessor anymore. His classical role as intermediary between God and Israel who always intercedes for the Israelites (cf. e.g. Exod 32,11–13; Num 21,7; Deut 5,5)[57] is turned into its direct opposite. By defying God's revelation in Jesus, Moses, not Jesus, becomes the prosecutor of the Jews (cf. John 5,45).[58] In John 5,45 it is clearly stated that the Jews pin their hopes for Moses (Μωϋσῆς, εἰς ὃν ὑμεῖς ἠλπίκατε). But their interpretation of Moses' scriptures is a misreading proving their own disbelief in these scriptures.[59] Subsequently, all their hopes are in vain.[60]

John 5,45–47 explicitly shows the key role of Moses in the Fourth Gospel as a witness for the divine revelation of Jesus Christ. Moses is not Jesus' opponent as are the Jews, but his supporter, right from the beginning because he wrote in the scriptures about him. His role is to serve the divine revelation of Jesus Christ by testifying for it. This role as a witness is qualified specifically in reference to the interpretation of Israel's biblical tradition. The authority of Moses guarantees the only

---

55   Any interpretation of the scriptures without the adaptation of christological hermeneutics is declared a futile act because it misses their true meaning; cf. esp. Dietzfelbinger, Joh I, 209f; Gawlick, Mose, 34; Obermann, Erfüllung, 60; Schnelle, Joh, 113; Wilckens, Joh, 125.

56   Doxa means ‚honour' here and has the aspect of acknowledgement (cf. Dietzfelbinger, Joh I, 208).

57   On the intercessory function of Moses cf. esp. D. Crump, Jesus, the Intercessor. Prayer and Christology in Luke–Acts (WUNT II 49), Tübingen 1992, 210–212.214f.218–231; Pancaro, Law, 256f.

58   Cf. Pancaro, Law, 254–258.

59   Cf. also Lindemann, Mose, 316.

60   The reference of the verb ἐλπίζειν is not quite clear though an eschatological meaning cannot be excluded here. It is conceivable that Moses' intercessory role on the day of final judgment is in view here. But a non–eschatological interpretation is also possible so that the verb simply refers to Moses' Nomos as the guarantee for a true life of the Israelites before God (cf. Thyen, Joh, 329). Whether ἐλπίζειν is used here instead of πιστεύειν to avoid a term otherwise preferred for the faith in Jesus Christ (cf. so Pancaro, Law, 259) remains to be seen.

adequate, i.e. Christian exegesis of the scriptures. Going against this interpretation standard makes him the prosecutor to such a misguided reading.[61] Thus, he definitely acts as the most prominent warrantor for their Christian interpretation. It becomes obvious that the biblical tradition of Israel is the biblical tradition of the Johannine community. The debate focuses on its appropriate interpretation. Moses guarantees its correct reading in a christological perspective. This perspective is open for all Jews as has already been proven by the character of Philip in John 1,45. He poses as the counter–example to the Jews in John 5. Philip as a Jew shows the adequate comprehension of the scriptures by interpreting Jesus as the one Moses has written about.[62]

5. John 6,31–33

Moses is next mentioned in John 6,32. The reference is to him in his role as the provider of manna in the wilderness (cf. Exod 16,1–36). The Johannine interest in this specific tradition focuses on the idea of life–preservation by supplying the people of Israel with special nourishment, the manna. Thus, the soteriological concept of life–gaining is reactivated again (cf. John 3,14). Moses is introduced in the discourse section of chap. 6 (cf. John 6,26–59) following two of the so–called Johannine *semeia* (cf. John 6,1–15; 6,16–21). Partners in dialogue are Jesus and the crowd (ο' ο;χλος). The discussion in John 6,26–59 concentrates mainly on the topic of bread, giving the Gospel another opportunity to display its soteriological concept again. The starting–point of the discourse is the different perception of the bread miracle in John 6,1–15. Jesus begins the discourse by stating its wrong perception by the crowd (cf. John 6,26). Instead, he challenges them to do the ἔργον τοῦ θεοῦ (cf. John 6,27–29), i.e. to believe in the one God sent, Jesus. In response, the crowd demands a legitimisation from Jesus so that they may believe in him (cf. John 6,30). As norm for this legitimisation they refer to Moses, more precisely, to the events depicted in Exod 16. "The work of God is to believe in the one God sent. For the crowd, the identity of this one is clear. They believe Moses. They keep the Law. They choose to compare Jesus' action on the preceding day with the wonders done by Moses."[63] The crowd demands a sign comparable to Moses'

61   Cf. Obermann, Erfüllung, 61.
62   Cf. Merklein, Welt, 267; Schapdick, Konflikt, 337.
63   Harstine, Moses, 62.

greatest miracle, the provision of the manna (cf. John 6,31).[64] The question whether to believe (in Jesus) or not is connected with Moses and his miraculous activities. The manna fed an entire nation for 40 years. It was considered bread out of heaven (ἄρτον ἐκ τοῦ οὐρανοῦ). Now the crowd expects a legitimisation of the same kind from Jesus and they expect it on a physical, materialistic level.

In his reply, Jesus introduces Moses to demonstrate the insufficiency of this past provision in comparison to what is currently available, the bread of life given by God (cf. John 6,32). The goal here is to contrast the claim for a sign with the claim to believe (cf. John 6,35.40.47).[65] First a misunderstanding concerning the source of the provision is rectified. The quotation in V.31 refers to the giver of manna by use of the 3rd Person Singular (ἔδωκεν). This utterance is quite unspecific. Who is meant here, God or Moses? In view of the correction in V.32 it can be assumed that Moses should be introduced as the provider of the Manna[66] though the biblical tradition clearly proves God to be in the providing role (cf. Exod 16,4f.11f.29).[67] Nevertheless, V.32 makes perfectly clear that Jesus' father[68], i.e. God, is the true origin of the heavenly bread.[69] But the bread Jesus is referring to is

---

64 The OT quotation in V.31 is not literal but a combination of various text passages (cf. Exod 16,4; Ps 78,24; 104,40f; Neh 9,15); cf. Dietzfelbinger, Joh I, 156; M.J.J. Menken, Old Testament Quotations in the Fourth Gospel. Studies in Textual Form (Contributions to Biblical Exegesis and Theology 15), Kampen 1996, 47–65; Obermann, Erfüllung, 132–150; Schnackenburg, Joh I, 53f; Stare, Durch Ihn Leben, 142–145; Thyen, Joh, 351; Wengst, Joh I, 236; Wilckens, Joh, 101.

65 The specific meaning of Jesus' utterance in V.32 is a question of debate. Does it focus on the providing role of Moses which is rejected or does it concentrate on the quality of the bread by denying its heavenly origin; for various interpretations cf. esp. Barrett, Joh, 301f; Pancaro, Law, 462f.

66 Cf. inter alia Thyen, Joh, 351; Wengst, Joh I, 237.

67 It has been suggested by K. Wengst, that the author of the Fourth Gospel turns over the providing role to Moses because he does not intend to confront God with God (cf. Joh I, 237). In my opinion, this not the case here because the notion of life–sustenance or life–preservation has already been shaped by means of surpassing in John chap. 3 without obscuring the divine creatorship of both acts. The same concept is adapted here. The divine creatorship of the manna is explicitly stated by the biblical tradition (cf. as well Thyen, Joh, 353). It is more probable that subliminally a misunderstanding of their own biblical tradition is foisted upon the crowd as adversaries of Jesus. God gave the manna by the hands of Moses. In an inappropriate abridgement Moses is made the provider of the manna.

68 The use of the term πατήρ insinuates the exclusiveness of Jesus' relation to God (cf. Thyen, Joh, 353).

69 This is confirmed by OT tradition (cf. Neh 9,15; Ps 104,40; Wis 16,20). The contrast between manna and heavenly bread is overemphasised by entirely denying God's provisional role regarding the manna (cf. Wengst, Joh I, 237 n. 46; contra Becker, Joh I, 246).

not the manna as bread out of heaven but the true bread out of heaven (τὸν ἄρτον ἐκ τοῦ οὐρανοῦ τὸν ἀληθινόν) that is given now (Present: δίδωσιν).[70] This true bread never has been given by Moses (Perfect: οὐ δέδωκεν).[71] Whatever bread Moses did offer, it was not and is not the true bread.[72] This true bread descends from heaven and gives life, i.e. eternal life, to the cosmos (cf. John 6,33: ὁ ἄρτος τοῦ θεοῦ ἐστιν ὁ καταβαίνων ἐκ τοῦ οὐρανοῦ καὶ ζωὴν διδοὺς τῷ κόσμῳ). The crowd expects Jesus to replicate and surpass Moses' provision. They refer to their own religious tradition and expect it to recur once again. But the reference to the true bread of heaven makes clear that such a replication would be an earthly matter and in the end a misunderstanding of the scriptures. True bread, i.e. eternal life, can only be given by the one descending from heaven, i.e. the son of Man (cf. John 1,51; 3,13). All people that had been fed by Moses are dead now because the manna provided temporary sustenance only. It did not overcome death itself. But the bread God gives through Jesus does.

Regarding the life–saving or life–preserving gift Jesus surmounts Moses again. Moses could only offer daily sustenance for Israel by the will of God but not death–overcoming life (cf. John 6,49.51) which is provided by the will of God in and through Jesus alone.[73] John 6,31–33 in accord with John 3,14 deals with two divine acts: the act of manna–provision by Moses on the one hand (John 6,32) and the gift of eternal life in and through Jesus on the other (cf. John 3,14). The difference is to be found again in the quality of the soteriological gift, earthly manna that kept Israel alive in a specific situation, or the ζωὴ αἰώνιος given without any local or temporal limitations to all who believe in the one sent by God, Jesus of Nazareth. The divine gift of life preservation in the wilderness is again a pre–image of the final and unsurpassing reve-lation during the divine mission of Jesus.[74] The role of Moses is re-evaluated another time from the Christian perspective of the Johannine community. It is not contested that he was the divine mediator of Is-rael's survival in the desert. That was his role, nothing more, nothing

---

70   The entire discourse section John 6,26–59 essentially focuses on this true bread out of heaven (cf. John 6,33.35.48.51).
71   For the temporal contrast cf. esp. Pancaro, Law, 463; Wengst, Joh I, 237.
72   However, this does not mean at all to deny Moses' role as provider of the heavenly manna (cf. Thyen, Joh, 352).
73   To conclude God that did not *want* to give Israel the bread of life in the wilderness, then, is definitely overstating the contrast between those two gifts of life (contra Dietzfelbinger, Joh I, 157). The view is on the eternal gift of life alone which is solely given by the divine revelation of Jesus.
74   Cf. inter alia Sänger, Von mir, 126.

less.[75] But he never had the mission to give eternal life.[76] Subsequently, his actions written in the scriptures can never be adapted as a criterion to judge Jesus' mission. Therefore, an interpretation of the scriptures outside a christological horizon fails to acknowledge its only purpose, i.e. to accept Jesus' claim of unsurpassing divine revelation for the salvation of all people. Thus, the strategy of Jesus' adversaries to combine Mosaic authority with quotations from the scriptures in conjunction with their demand of a sign shows the inadequacy in the interpretation of their own biblical traditions.[77]

6. John 7,19–24

The next recurrence of Moses is in chap. 7 of the Fourth Gospel. Here the Gospel's plot of conflict between Jesus and his adversaries has further intensified. The narrative emphasises the forces of belief and unbelief now locked in aggravated dispute: "Official opposition to Jesus hardens through both misunderstanding and ignorance."[78] Chap. 7 gives account of a lot of attempts to finish this conflict by Jesus' opponents. They try to arrest or kill Jesus (cf. John 7,1,19.25.30.32.44). But all these efforts of such a conflict–resolution fail, at least for the time being. The scene is Jesus teaching in the Jerusalem temple at the festival of Sukkot (cf. John 7,14). In the passage of John 7,19–24 Moses is mentioned four times always in close connection to the νόμος (cf. John 7,19,22[2x].23). Moses is characterised as the one who gave the Law to the people (V.19: Μωϋσῆς δέδωκεν ὑμῖν τὸν νόμον). This statement is rephrased in V.22 with special reference to circumcision (Μωϋσῆς δέδωκεν ὑμῖν τὴν περιτομήν). Moreover, this act of Law-giving is commented on by clarifying that Moses did not originate the circumcision but the fathers did (οὐχ ὅτι ἐκ τοῦ Μωϋσέως ἐστὶν ἀλλ᾿ ἐκ τῶν πατέρων). Finally, V.23 determines the Law as ὁ νόμος Μωϋσέως, the Law of Moses.

Following a discussion over Jesus' own capability and authority to interpret the scriptures (V.14) – Jesus opponents are either the Jews (cf.

---

75 The characterisation of Moses as "*mere* mediator of the gift" (W.A. Meeks, The Prophet–King. Moses Traditions and the Johannine Christology [NT.S 14], Leiden 1967, 291; noted also by Gawlick, Mose, 35) is more or less a negative valuation of Moses and thus inappropriate because Moses should be nothing more but this mediator.

76 Compared to other references to the manna tradition in the NT (cf. 1Cor 10,3; Heb 9,4; Rev 2,17) John 6,31–33 certainly contains an unparalleled devaluation of this tradition (cf. Dietzfelbinger Joh I, 157).

77 Cf. Gawlick, Mose, 35; noted also by Dietzfelbinger, Joh I, 157.

78 Harstine, Moses, 65.

John 7,15) or the crowd (cf. John 7,20) – he introduces Moses in V.19 as the giver of the Law. This idea is presented in an interrogative form as a question to the Jews that expects affirmation (οὐ Μωϋσῆς δέδωκεν ὑμῖν τὸν νόμον;).[79] Jesus and the Jews share the idea of Moses being the giver of the Law. But the question is not stated here to ease the conflict. On the contrary, it is utilised to kindle the dispute again. Jesus accuses the Jews not to abide by the Law. He moves "the debate from an issue over his own authority to the issue of who actually keeps the Law given by Moses."[80] Thus, the real issue is not the question whether Jesus abides by the Law in his teachings but whether the people are doing God's will. Jesus' teachings are not his own but stem directly from God (cf. John 7,16). Anyone who recognises and accepts this is doing God's will (cf. John 7,17).[81] God is the sole and true originator of Jesus' teachings, as he is the sole and true originator of the Law (as His divine will) given by Moses. It is the same divine authority that stands behind Jesus' teachings and the Law given by Moses. The difference between Jesus and the Jews is that the Jews fail to grasp that. By challenging Jesus' claim to revelation in his teachings, they violate the Law because they do not recognise the only true authority behind the both of them.[82] Jesus' teachings are thus presented in alignment with the Law given by Moses because they have the same origin, i.e. God. "Jesus' teaching is thoroughly Jewish, even when it is not recognised as such by the Jews."[83] By questioning Jesus' teachings, they fail to understand the true meaning of the Law. As proof they seek to kill Jesus as he himself states it (V.19). Their intent to kill Jesus makes it obvious that they do not follow the Law.[84]

The discussion continues in V.20 with the direct reaction of the crowd to Jesus' accusation that they seek to kill him. They insinuate him to have some kind of persecution mania. For them, his charge is possible only if he is possessed by a supernatural negative power, a

---

79 The mediation role of Moses concerning the Law (cf. John 1,17) is taking a back seat here. The personal pronoun ὑμῖν should not be interpreted as deliberate alienation from the Law.
80 Harstine, Moses, 66.
81 God himself is referred to as ἀληθής (cf. John 7,18) which is supplemented by the phrase: ἀδικία ἐν αὐτῷ οὐκ ἔστιν. The latter alludes to the concept of δικαιοσύνη which definitely shapes the divine Law.
82 God's will is written down in the Nomos: You can keep the Law only by acknowledging Jesus. Who rejects Jesus does not keep the Law (cf. Wengst, Joh I, 280).
83 Harstine, Moses, 66.
84 Cf. Schnelle, Joh, 145; Wengst, Joh I, 280.

demon (δαιμόνιον ἔχεις).[85] Jesus' reply in V.21[86] does not respond to
the crowd's utterance but mentions the one ἔργον probably referring to
his act of healing on the Sabbath (cf. John 5,1–18).[87] The attempt to kill
Jesus is stated there for the first time in the Gospel (cf. John 5,18). By
looking back to this *semeion* a new debate is introduced regarding the
adequate interpretation of the Mosaic Law (cf. John 7,20–24). The
question is now whether anyone who rightfully claims to be sent by
God would violate the divine Law to keep the Sabbath as Jesus did in
his act of healing.[88] The premise here is a universal scope of the Law
without any exceptions. Jesus' counter–argument to such a perspective
refers to "a legal infringement"[89]. The Law of Moses assesses circumcision[90] as such an outstanding priority (cf. Gen 17,12; Lev 12,3) that it
even supersedes the Law to keep the Sabbath. Boys have to be circum-
cised on the eighth day after their birth whether it is a Sabbath or not
(cf. mShab 18,3; bShab 132a; jNed 3,9).[91] Consequently, circumcision
may involve a permitted violation of the (Sabbath) Law. Moreover,
such an exceptional case of (temporary) repeal is interpreted, as V.23
clearly states, as an act of preservation of the Mosaic Law (ἵνα μὴ λυθῇ
ὁ νόμος Μωϋσέως). By using a Qal–Wachomer–conclusion[92] it is then
stated: If the Law to keep the Sabbath may legally be violated by circumcision, concerning only a small part of the human body[93], how can
anyone possibly insist on detecting a violation of the Sabbath Law if a
'whole' man is healed.[94] If God's will preserved in the Law of Moses

---

85 People possessed by demons do not occur in the Fourth Gospel, but the idea of bedev-
    ilment is mentioned, always as an accusation of Jesus' adversaries (cf. as well John
    8,48.52; 10,20). It is rejected by Jesus in John 8,49.
86 The verb θαυμάζειν has to be interpreted as an act of taking offence connected to unbe-
    lief (cf. R. Schnackenburg, Das Johannesevangelium II [HThK 4,2], Freiburg u.a. 1971,
    187).
87 The close connection between John 5,1–18 and 7,15–24 caused a lot of interpreters to
    prefer a reordering of the Gospel's text by which John 7,15–24 is considered as the im-
    mediate continuation of John 5,1–18 (cf. e.g. Bultmann, Joh, 205–209; Dietzfelbinger,
    Joh I, 210; Schnackenburg, Joh II, 183f; Wilckens, Joh, 126f).
88 Cf. Schnelle, Joh, 145.
89 Harstine, Moses, 67.
90 The parenthesis in John 7,22 referring to the Fathers being the originators of the cir-
    cumcision appears a little enigmatic within the present context. It only defines Moses'
    role as being the one who integrated the circumcision into the Law as one of its most
    important regulations. But it does not contribute to the ongoing argumentation in any
    way (cf. Lindemann, Mose, 319, who suspects the parenthesis to be a gloss).
91 Cf. esp. Bill. II, 487f; Dietzfelbinger, Joh I, 213; Wengst, Joh I, 281.
92 Cf. Barrett, Joh, 328; Lindemann, Mose, 319; Schnackenburg, Joh II, 188; Wengst, Joh
    I, 281.
93 Cf. Dietzfelbinger, Joh I, 213; note also Bill. II, 488.
94 Cf. Lindemann, Mose, 319. A different view is introduced by K. Wengst who stresses
    the idea of quantity. He contrasts the frequent occurrences of Sabbath circumcisions

allows an exception to the rule on such a small account why should His will be disregarded by healing a man on the Sabbath?[95] Such an argumentation turns out to be an application of different interpretation standards to the Law as V.24 makes clear ($\tau\dot{\eta}\nu$ $\delta\iota\kappa\alpha\dot{\iota}\alpha\nu$ $\kappa\rho\dot{\iota}\sigma\iota\nu$ $\kappa\rho\dot{\iota}\nu\epsilon\tau\epsilon$). For the welfare of Israel the Law has been given and, as noted here, for the same welfare exceptions to the Law are permitted. Therefore, it is absurd to challenge Jesus on the basis of an act of healing taking place on a Sabbath because he is definitely committed to the welfare of Israel and all mankind.[96] The Sabbath miracle demonstrates God's salvific will which is present in the Law, too. Since Jesus represents God's ultimate will of salvation not a $\kappa\rho\dot{\iota}\nu\epsilon\iota\nu$ $\kappa\alpha\tau$' $\ddot{o}\psi\iota\nu$ is called for but faith in Jesus.[97]

Looking back at John 7,19–24, the first thing to be noticed is the positive perception of the Law. The Nomos with its regulations regarding the Sabbath and the circumcision is not abrogated at all. It is acknowledged in its fundamental obligatory character.[98] It forms the basis for the debate. In dispute, realising itself in a clearly Jewish context, is its correct interpretation.[99] Thus, secondly, the character of Moses is positively seen as the authority behind the religious code of the Law. His role here is to help illuminating that Jesus' adversaries prefer its ambiguous or better duplicitous interpretation. On the one hand, they approve its infringement regarding circumcision, on the other hand, they disapprove if Jesus infringes it by healing a man on the Sabbath. Therefore, the Gospel does by no means defy the Law as the religious code of Israel or Moses as its giver. The real problem from the Gospel's perspective is that this code "is not being followed by its confessed adherents"[100]. The divine Law of Moses is wrongfully utilised as a reason to reject Jesus. The assertion of allegiance to Moses and his Law by Jesus' various Jewish adversaries leads to the refutation of his revela-

---

with the one act of healing performed by Jesus on a Sabbath. Thus, Jesus' argumentation would be as follows: 'I committed only one violation of the Sabbath Law of which you have taken offence. But you are violating the Sabbath Law continuously with no-one ever taking offence' (cf. Joh I, 281).

95 Cf. Schnelle, Joh, 145.
96 Of course, Jewish scholarliness never would have approved of such an argumentation. Most certainly, they would have considered it as a 'prevarication of the Mosaic Law' (cf. Dietzfelbinger, Joh I, 213).
97 Cf. Pancaro, Law, 168; C. Welck, Erzählte Zeichen. Die Wundergeschichten des Johannesevangeliums literarisch untersucht. Mit einem Ausblick auf Joh 21 (WUNT II 69), Tübingen 1994, 202–204.
98 Cf. Thyen, Joh, 394.
99 Cf. Thyen, Joh, 394; Wengst, Joh I, 282.
100 Harstine, Moses, 67.

tion of God's ultimate will for salvation.[101] But the Mosaic Law – that is the perspective of the Johannine community – gives no reason at all to reject the divine revelation of Jesus. Faith in Jesus Christ and acknowledgment of the religious traditions of Israel are directly compatible with each other. They are one and the same if the correct interpretation standard is chosen.

7. John 9,24–34

The final occurrences of Μωϋσῆς are to be found in John 9,28f. After the healing of the blind born (cf. John 9,1–7), again taking place on a Sabbath (cf. John 9,14), an almost formal investigation of the event is conducted by the Pharisees and, respectively, the Jews.[102] However, instead of Jesus the healed blind born is interrogated (cf. John 9,13–17,24–34). He is questioned twice, only interrupted by an interrogation of his parents (cf. John 9,18–23). For the first time the name Μωϋσῆς is introduced by a group of Jesus' adversaries. The Jews/Pharisees present Moses as a justification for their negative attitude towards Jesus. As disciples of Moses (V.28) they know that God spoke to him (V.29).[103] This view is utilised to reject Jesus' actions and teachings. For them Jesus is a sinner (V.24: οὗτος ὁ ἄνθρωπος ἁμαρτωλός ἐστιν).[104] In regard to his revelation and its origin their comment is: οὐκ οἴδαμεν πόθεν ἐστίν (V.29).[105] But the most striking feature of John 9,1–41 is that the group identity of the Jews/Pharisees is described with reference to Moses. Thus, the dispute between Jesus and his adversaries takes shape of a proxy conflict between the disciples of Moses and the one disciple

---

101 Cf. ibid.
102 In John 9,13–17 the Pharisees are explicitly mentioned as interrogators of the healed blind born. The interrogation of the blind born's parents is conducted by the Jews (cf. John 9,18–23). The passage containing the second interrogation of the blind born in V.24–34 does not clarify who exactly the interrogators are. The text remains imprecise here.
103 The perfect λελάληκεν expresses the ongoing importance of the divine address to Moses. It is captured in the Law with the Pharisees/Jews as its only competent interpreters (cf. Thyen, Joh, 468).
104 The interrogators call upon the healed to give glory to God. It is meant either as a demand to tell the truth or as a calling for an public confession of being a sinner (cf. Jos 7,19; 1 Sam 6,5; Jer 13,16); cf. inter alia Dietzfelbinger, Joh I, 288; Wilckens, Joh, 159. However, the contents of this truth are already determined: Jesus is a sinner (cf. Dietzfelbinger, Joh I, 288).
105 As someone violating the Sabbath Law, Jesus' divine provenance is definitely in doubt (cf. John 9,16).

of Jesus, the healed blind born.[106] Both discipleships are presented in immediate confrontation (V.28: σὺ μαθητὴς εἶ ἐκείνου, ἡμεῖς δὲ τοῦ Μωϋσέως ἐσμὲν μαθηταί). They are declared incompatible to one another.[107] Who follows Jesus is *no longer* or simply *not* following Moses.[108] A sharp contrast between these two systems of teachings is emphasised,[109] especially by focusing on the topic of Moses' and Jesus' relation to God. Moses' relation to God is very well known to the Jews (cf. Exod 33,11; Num 12,8). The origin of Jesus, i.e. his divine provenance, is unknown to them.[110] Once again, the Law of Moses or, more precisely, its application serves as a criterion to judge Jesus (expressed by the verb οἴδαμεν). He performs a healing miracle on the Sabbath which is prohibited by the Law. Thus, Jesus is a sinner (cf. John 9,16.24).[111] Again, the Mosaic Law provides the interpretation standard to reject Jesus' mission. "Moses and the Law are set over against Jesus and his teaching; the authority of Moses is indisputable, the authority of Jesus is spurious."[112]

In John 9,30–34 follows the refutation of this view presented by the blind born. Again, the utterance is introduced by οἴδαμεν (V.31).[113] The blind born refers to the general conviction that a sinner would never be capable of performing such a miracle. Since Jesus does it is solid proof that he is παρὰ θεοῦ (V.33). Such an interpretation of the Moses' tradition is rejected by the Jews/Pharisees for reasons that are not rooted in the contents of this interpretation but in the authority of the interpreter,

---

106 In fact, the healed blind born is at that moment not a disciple of Jesus yet. But he is made a disciple during his second encounter with Jesus (cf. John 9,35–38).

107 To call the blind born a disciple of Jesus is meant as a revilement. It is not to be understood as a mere expression of opinion. Instead, the utterance serves as an expression of disparagement and contempt (cf. T. Kriener, "Glauben an Jesus" – ein Verstoß gegen das zweite Gebot? Die johanneische Christologie und der Vorwurf des Götzendienstes [Neukirchener theologische Dissertationen und Habilitationen 29], Neukirchen–Vluyn 2001, 148).

108 Cf. Lindemann, Mose, 320.

109 Cf. Harstine, Moses, 69.

110 The famous Johannine particle πόθεν is used here to allude the topic of Jesus' divine provenance again (cf. John 2,9; 3,8 etc.). Particularly with reference to John 8,14, it serves as the key to understand his mission (cf. Thyen, Joh, 469).

111 Since God spoke to Moses the interpretation of the Mosaic Law by the Jews/Pharisees is deduced from God himself (cf. Dietzfelbinger, Joh I, 288; noted as well by Welck, Zeichen, 177f).

112 G.R. Beasley–Murray, John (WBC 36), Waco, Texas 1987, 158.

113 The use of οἴδαμεν is quite remarkable here. The healed blind born reminds his interrogators of the commonly shared knowledge of all Jews that God does not answer to sinners but only to God–fearing people doing his will (cf. Thyen, Joh, 469).

the blind born.[114] According to their perspective on Moses' Law the blind born is born in sin.[115] Thus, he definitely is not authorised to be an acceptable and credible interpreter of the Law (V.34). In their view, the authority he assumes is arrogated.[116] John 9,34 underlines the resolute allegiance of the Jews/Pharisees to Moses as their prime religious authority. Their allegiance is associated with a special interpretation standard of the biblical traditions which has no expectation or place for the divine revelation of Jesus. The Jews/Pharisees refuse to accept Jesus' claim to divine revelation and condemn his followers, perfectly demonstrated by the ἐκβάλλειν (V.34) of the healed blind born.[117] Again, this is sharply criticised by the Fourth Gospel (cf. John 9,39–41). And again, it is not the Moses or the biblical tradition that are accused but a certain interpretation standard which helps to defy God's unsurpassing revelation of salvation in Jesus Christ.

John 9,1–41 presents this criticised interpretation standard as a genuine part of the Jews'/Pharisees' group consciousness. Essentially, this standard defines their identity. Their special knowledge of the Mosaic tradition, their insights gained from it, make them close their eyes to Jesus' divine mission. From the Gospel's perspective this is extremely condemnable because Jesus is played off against Moses and vice versa.[118] But John 9,1–41 clearly states that in the light of the Christian interpretation standard of the biblical tradition Jesus and Moses are in no real opposition to one another. On the contrary, the Mosaic tradition delivers the criteria that help to recognise and to accept who Jesus really is and what his divine revelation has to offer, i.e.

---

114 At this place, it is the intention of the Fourth Gospel to show the adversaries of Jesus running out of reasonable arguments (cf. Dietzfelbinger, Joh I, 289). They behave like intellectually inferior people who can only cope with their inferiority by turning to their physical superiority (cf. John 9,34: καὶ ἐξέβαλον αὐτὸν ἔξω). It is a symbol of their feeble theological competence (cf. ibid., 291).

115 Cf. Blank, Krisis, 261; Dietzfelbinger, Joh I, 289; Schnelle, Joh, 173; Wengst, Joh I, 369.

116 The rejection of this inconvenient witness to Jesus succeeds only by the use of official power (cf. Welck, Zeichen, 180f). The dispute is thereby resolved only by leaning on formal authority (Wengst, Joh I, 369).

117 Cf. Harstine, Moses, 71. On the one hand, the verb ἐκβάλλειν refers to the ejection of the blind born from the interrogation chamber, on the other hand, it hints at the expulsion of Christian believers from the synagogue (cf. John 9,22); cf. Pancaro, Law, 110f; Schnelle, Joh, 173 n. 107; Wengst, Joh I, 369.

118 Cf. Schnackenburg, Joh II, 319. It is the conviction of the Fourth Gospel that the antagonism of Jesus and Moses is construed by Jesus' adversaries only. The Gospel itself tries to integrate the traditional reverence for Moses in its own self–conception (similarly Gawlick, Mose, 35).

the eternal life.[119] But this demands an open mind to his revelatory actions and teachings.

III. Conclusions

1. The Fourth Gospel deals with the new and final revelation of God preached and represented by Jesus of Nazareth. From this it follows that the idea of divine revelation is definitely and exclusively shaped by christological thinking. Nevertheless, the Gospel clearly insists on this revelation taking place within a Jewish context. The God of the people of Israel is the God of all Christian believers. Thus, the God of Moses is the God of Jesus of Nazareth. This is the main reason why the Gospel develops a vivid interest for Moses. The Nomos, the divine Law, and its mediator or, respectively, writer, Moses, need to be integrated into the new christological perspective. Therefore, the Gospel of John is not concerned with challenging the religious authority of Moses and, furthermore, with abrogating the Nomos. The Johannine prologue explicitly states the divine origin of the Law and the mediating role of Moses without questioning it at all (cf. John 1,17). This observation is of paramount importance because otherwise the prologue's revelatory concern is invariably presented in reference to Jesus Christ, the pre–existent logos (cf. John 1,1–5.9–14.16.18). The final goal of this revelation is soteriological. The divine gift of the ζωὴ αἰώνιος stands for the definite salvation for all who believe in Jesus and his divine revelation (cf. John 3,16). However, the foremost soteriological concept of the Gospel is developed within the context of Israel's eschatological hopes. Jesus Christ is the fulfilment of everything Israel has hoped for and is still hoping for, respectively (cf. John 1,19–51). None the less, such a salvific concept demands a re–evaluation or, more precisely, a re-definition of Moses' traditional revelatory role. In addition, the function of the Mosaic Law has to be reconsidered if any idea of salvation is now based on God's unsurpassing revelation in Jesus Christ alone (cf. John 1,45f; 5,45f).

2. According to the Fourth Gospel the new and prevalent role of Moses and the Nomos is to serve as witness for Jesus' divine revelation. The eschatological hopes of salvation condensed in the scriptures become a definite reality in him (cf. John 1,45). Traditionally, the divine Law contains the way to life and salvation, and it still does, but

---

119 Cf. Lindemann, Mose, 321.

now only by pointing to Jesus' divine mission. Thus, the Nomos has been given by God with Moses as its mediator (cf. John 1,17). But its real and only purpose does not reveal itself until the revelation of Jesus Christ is initiated (cf. John 1,14.16–18). Its prior interpretation as the divine revelation itself can no longer be upheld.[120] Therefore, it cannot serve as an interpretation standard to judge Jesus' divine mission (cf. John 7,23; 9,16.24). The Law reveals the way to Jesus, nothing less, but also nothing more.[121] The same perspective is developed in reference to Moses, the 'writer' of the Law.[122] Likewise, his actions cannot function as criteria for Jesus' revelation (cf. John 6,31–33). Moses' new or better only true role is to bear witness to Jesus. For example, this is explicitly articulated in John 5,46: If the divine Law is read and interpreted adequately, i.e. in a christological perspective, it becomes obvious that Moses wrote about Jesus. The religious authority of Moses is entirely utilised for God's revelation in Jesus. Moses' role is to guarantee the only legitimate, i.e. christological interpretation of the scriptures. Any rejection of this interpretation standard is prosecuted by Moses himself. His traditional role as intercessor for Israel transforms into its direct opposite. He becomes the accuser of anyone who defies Jesus' divine revelation. The specific contents of the Mosaic Law are almost irrelevant to the Gospel. Concrete regulations are mentioned only if the legitimacy of Jesus' claim to divine revelation needs to be vindicated (cf. John 7,20–24: Sabbath; circumcision). All in all, this re–evaluation of Moses and his Law within the context of a christologically shaped theology of revelation definitely refers to an ongoing battle focusing on the interpretation of the biblical tradition of Israel. From the Gospel's perspective, Moses exclusively serves as witness for the divine revelation

---

120 Moses is not contested to have a divine revelation (cf. John 9,29: ἡμεῖς οἴδαμεν ὅτι Μωϋσεῖ λελάληκεν ὁ θεός). The criticism solely focuses on the denial to relate Moses' divine revelation to the unsurpassing divine revelation of Jesus. To conclude in view of Jesus: οὐκ οἴδαμεν πόθεν ἐστίν is from the Gospel's perspective the cardinal error (cf. John 9,29–34).

121 Cf. as well John 7,51; 8,17; 10,34; 12,34; 15,25; 18,31; 19,7; for further reference to the Nomos in the Fourth Gospel cf. esp. Lindemann, Mose, 321–329.

122 The Fourth Gospel develops different views on the relation of Moses and the Law without adjusting them to each other. On the one hand, the divine Law is mediated by Moses (cf. John 1,17), on the other hand, Moses appears directly as the giver of the Law or its specific regulations without explicitly mentioning its divine origin (cf. John 7,19.22). Thus, Moses can be referred to as the 'author' of the Law (cf. John 1,45; 5,46f. However, the efforts of the Gospel do not dwell on a consistent depiction of Moses and his relation to the divine Law but on integrating both the Law and Moses in its own christological perspective which inevitably leads to their subordination.

of Jesus. An appropriate interpretation of the Mosaic Law solely succeeds by applying the christological interpretation standard.[123]

3. The Fourth Gospel may predominantly relate the Moses character to the divine Law. Nevertheless, it also picks up certain events from
his life as they are described in the biblical traditions (cf. John 3,14;
6,31–33). The interest especially focuses on the life–saving or life–
preserving role of Moses. He saved Israel from the serpents sent by
God (cf. Num 21,4–9) and he preserved their lives by providing Israel
with the heavenly bread, the manna (cf. Exod 16,1–36). The Fourth
Gospel refers to these specific traditions by emphasising the true originator of all these life–preserving acts, God himself (cf. esp. John 6,32).
Both events present God as the Lord over life and death. Moses is depicted as the mediator of His divine will. Thus, the focus is primarily on
God as the one who gives and preserves life. This is tied in with God's
final and unsurpassing soteriological gift, the ζωή αἰώνιος. Its quality
lies in its death–overcoming power. The gift of eternal life is solely
related to the divine revelation of Jesus. As an inevitable consequence,
the importance of Moses' life–saving or life–preserving role for Israel
is diminished considerably. His mediating role is restricted to temporary life–preservation. He has no part in the provision of the sole gift of
salvation. All his efforts described in the biblical traditions which he
performed on behalf of God's will are nothing but a narrative 'foil' on
which the overall soteriological quality of Jesus' divine revelation can
be demonstrated. Moreover, none of Moses' actions can serve as a criterion to judge Jesus' mission. Nevertheless, his actions serve as a pre–
image of God's final soteriological gift, the ζωή αἰώνιος, referring to
the gift itself (chap. 6), or to Jesus' crucifixion with its overall soteriological quality (chap. 3). Thus, in these passages the Gospel definitely harks back on a clearly theologically centred perspective to show
God's sustained interest in salvation. He was and is always true to His
salvific will which is realised in the life of Jesus of Nazareth once and
for all.

4. John's Gospel essentially presents itself as a conflict between Jesus and various adversaries of Jewish provenance (cf. John 5,1–10,42).

---

123 In the course of the Gospel a non–christological exegesis of the scriptures typical for
Jesus' adversaries can also be referred to by speaking of 'their' or 'your' Law (cf. John
8,17; 10,34; 15,25; 18,31; 19,7). However, this expression is not meant as an alienation
from the Law itself (for this view cp esp. Becker, Joh, I, 344 [referring to John 8,17]; II,
589 [referring to John 15,25]) but from such interpreters who prefer to read it non–
christologically (cf. Lindemann, Mose, 326–329).

Predominantly, it mirrors an internal Jewish/Jewish–Christian debate
concerning the adequate and correct interpretation of the Mosaic Law.
The Nomos itself is mutually accepted as the basis for this dispute.
From the Johannine community's point of view there is no contradiction at all between faith in Jesus and adherence to Israel's biblical traditions. They are one, although of course, only in a christological perspective. Moses and the Law solely serve the divine revelation of Jesus.
It is the distinct intention of the Gospel to absorb the whole biblical
tradition of Israel christologically. Any preservation of these traditions
succeeds only by believing in Jesus and his revelation of salvation.
Thus, Jewish faith in God is realised only by faith in the divine revelation in Jesus. Any knowledge of God's prior actions for Israel and for
the world is in the end soteriologically irrelevant without acceptance of
Jesus' divine revelation.[124] Such a conviction leads to a charge against
'the Jews' who are not willing to believe in Jesus. From the Gospel's
perspective 'the Jews' reject Jesus by considering their own knowledge
of God as final and absolute. This absolute knowledge is contained in
the Law mediated or written by Moses (cf. John 9,28f). Subsequently, it
is soteriologically sufficient and God's final word of revelation.[125] That
is the point of view which is combated throughout the whole Gospel,
over and over again. The final and absolute word of God is not the
Law, not Moses, but Jesus of Nazareth.

5. The characterisation of Moses in the Fourth Gospel is altogether
developed by referring to his role as the supreme religious authority
within the boundaries of Jewish faith. His function as mediator, writer,
and giver of the divine Law is particularly in the Gospel's focus (cf.
John 1,17.45; 5,46f; 7,19). To lay claim on the (definitely divine) authority of Moses for one's own belief means to perceive oneself as part
of the religious tradition of Israel. It is the resolute intent of the Gospel
to confirm Christian faith (and this faith only) to be in complete continuity with God's salvific history with His people. Moses and the Law
are the prime witnesses for the divine revelation of Jesus (cf. John 1,45;
5,46f). As a result of the christological concentration of the idea of
revelation connected with its exclusive soteriological perspective, there
is hardly any real interest in specific topics of the Moses tradition, neither regarding his character nor in reference to the Law with its various
regulations. In addition, if the Gospel refers to the Moses tradition its
selection of the various topics is eclectic and solely defined by the de-

124 Cf. Schapdick, Konflikt, 367.
125 Cf. ibid.

gree of possible christological adaptation (cf. John 3,13–15; 6,31–33; 7,20–24). Thus, the characterisation of Moses in John's Gospel does not dwell on minutiae. Its original contents are basically negligible. Ultimately, the character of Moses is introduced to the Gospel as a simple cipher for religious authority within a Jewish/Jewish–Christian context of thinking. The whole emphasis is laid on this authority which is exclusively utilised for the Gospel's Christian point of view. But this (religious) authority lacks (its natural) contents which are entirely absorbed by the christologically shaped revelation of salvation.

Jannes and Jambres (2 Timothy 3,8–9)

by Johannes Tromp

In 2 Timothy 3,8–9 the following comparison occurs:

> As Jannes and Jambres were opposed to Moses, so are these people also opposed to the truth – people whose minds do not function and who are failures in the faith. But they will not prosper, because everyone will see how stupid they are. This is just what happened to Jannes and Jambres (trans. Good News Bible, slightly altered).

In this contribution, it will be discussed who Jannes and Jambres were and why they were introduced in this context.

1. Survey of some earlier research

Naturally, Jannes and Jambres have previously been the subject of scholarly attention.[1] In the early modern age, scholars at first drew their information from patristic authors. Erasmus (ca. 1467–1536) quoted John Chrysostom's Homilies on 2 Timothy for his own *Annotations*[2], and since then it has been commonly accepted that Jannes and Jambres are to be identified with the Egyptian magicians mentioned in Exod 7–8.

Exod 7–8 tells us that Moses performed miracles before Pharaoh, but that Pharaoh's sorcerers were able to perform the same wonders (Exod 7,11.22; 8,3), at least up to a point: from the plague of the gnats

---

1   For a complete survey of the history of research into 1 and 2 Timothy in particular, see L.T. Johnson, The First and Second Letters to Timothy (AncB 35a), New York 2001, 20–54.

2   Quoted from J. Pearson et alii (ed.), Critici sacri, Amsterdam/Utrecht ³1698, ad loc.; John Chrysostom, Homilies on the Second Epistle to Timothy, chap. 3, Hom. 8 (PG 62): Τίνες εἰσὶν οὗτοι οἱ μάγοι οἱ ἐπὶ Μωϋσέως; πῶς δὲ αὐτῶν τὰ ὀνόματα οὐδαμοῦ ἐμφέρεται ἀλλαχοῦ; Ἢ ἀγράφως παραδέδοται, ἢ ἀπὸ τοῦ Πνεύματος εἰκὸς ἦν εἰδέναι τὸν Παῦλον. A story and even a book of Jannes and Jambres were known in Christian circles long before Chrysostom (344–407), most notably to Origen (ca. 185–253/254), as was noted by Sixtus of Siena (1520–1569): Sixtus Senensis, Bibliotheca sancta, Venice 1566 (here quoted from the edition by John Hay, Cologne 1626), 87; see further A. Pietersma, The Apocryphon of Jannes and Jambres the Magicians (RGRW 119), Leiden 1994, 43.

onwards, the Egyptians were no longer able to imitate Moses' miracles (Exod 8,8; 9,11), and even came to acknowledge the divine origin of Moses' acts (Exod 8,15).

In the century after Erasmus, much more material about Jannes and Jambres was gathered. Eusebius' *Evangelical Preparation* cites a testimony from Numenius[3]; also, Jannes was mentioned by Pliny the Elder[4] and Apuleius[5]. Pliny, it may be noted, knew Jannes as a *Jewish* sorcerer, a point that will later prove to be of some interest[6], but it was mainly the rabbinical literature that provided a wealth of source material. "Tanquam aura inter stercora"[7], exclaimed Johannes Drusius (1550–1616), when he found references to stories about them in Nathan ben Yehiel's *Aruch*; Drusius became aware of information in, e.g., *Tanhuma Yelamdenu*; the *Targum* attributed to Jonathan; and the Babylonian *Talmud* (namely, *bMenahot* 85a).[8] Johannes Buxtorf's *Lexicon chaldaicum* contains a complete catalogue of early 17th-century knowledge about Jannes and Jambres according to rabbinical sources.[9]

---

3   I. Clarius (1495–1555), annotation on 2 Tim 3,8, in: Pearson (ed.), Critici sacri, ad loc.; Sixtus, Bibliotheca sancta, 87. The reference is to Numenius, apud Eusebius, Praep. Evang. IX, 8,1–2; for discussion, see J.G. Gager, Moses in Greco-Roman Paganism (SBLMS 16), Nashville/New York 1972, 139–140; M. Stern, Greek and Latin Authors on Jews and Judaism II, Jerusalem 1980, 212–213.

4   A. Scultetus (1566–1625), Annotation on 2 Tim 3,8, in: Pearson (ed.), Critici sacri, ad loc. The reference is to Pliny, Nat. Hist. XXX, 2,11; (A. Erusut [ed.], Pline l'Anaen. Histoire neburelle livre XXX, Paris 1963); for discussion, see Gager, Moses, 137–138; Stern, Greek and Latin Authors, I, 498–499.

5   J. Cappellus (1570–1624), in: Pearson (ed.), Critici sacri, ad loc. The reference is to Apuleius, Apology 90; for discussion, see Gager, Moses, 138–139; Stern, Greek and Latin Authors, II, 203–204.

6   Drusius, Annotation on 2 Tim 3,8, in: Pearson (ed.), Critici sacri, ad loc., observed that Jannes might be someone else than the Jamne mentioned by Pliny, (see above footnote 4) "Nam Jannes Aegyptius erat. Jamne autem, de quo Plinius, Judaeus erat" Drusius added: "Sed hic libenter ἐπέχω". For Drusius' reading Jamne, cf. S. Gero, The Enigma of the Magician Lotapes (Pliny, Naturalis Historia XXX, 11), JSJ 27 (1996) 304–323, esp. p. 308. Gero's insistence on the "disjunctive force of ac" in the quotation of Pliny (ibidem, pp. 311–314) is exaggerated.

7   The phrase is ascribed to Vergil by Cassiodorus, Inst. I, 1,18: "Vergilius, dum Ennium legeret, a quodam quid faceret inquisitus respondit: 'aurum in stercore quaero'."

8   Drusius, annotation on 2 Tim 3,8, in: Pearson (ed.), Critici sacri, ad loc.

9   J. Buxtorf II (ed.), Johannis Buxtorfii Lexicon chaldaicum, talmudicum et rabbinicum, Basel 1639. For a seventeenth century justification of the use of rabbinical sources for the interpretation of the Bible, see C. Cartwright (1603–1658), Praefatio to Electa thargumico-rabbinica sive Annotationes in Genesin, in: Pearson (ed.), Critici sacri, introductory matter to Genesis; note, however, that Cartwright appears unstable in his appreciation of rabbinic exegesis: he appreciates much of the material on Jannes and Jambres collected by Buxtorf as "nec injucunda, nec inutilia" in this Praefatio; but in his annotation on Exod. 1,16 he elaborately paraphrases the data extant in Targum Pseudo-Jonathan, and then flatly dismisses it: "Haec sunt somnia Rabbinorum".

The early critics were diligently searching for more and more source-material about Jannes and Jambres[10], but more far-reaching questions were rarely asked. Only one question was repeatedly posed: how did the apostle Paul know the magicians' names? Again, the answer had been anticipated by Chrysostom: through Jewish oral tradition, or simply through the Holy Spirit[11], though the possibility of a written apocryphal tradition was also soon acknowledged.[12]

The early critics did not ask *why* Paul would choose to mention Jannes and Jambres. Abraham Scultetus was exceptional in trying to pursue this question somewhat further. Scultetus is clearly aware that a simple identification of Jannes and Jambres with the Egyptian miracle-workers of Exodus does not explain why the apostle mentioned them; Scultetus sought an answer in the heresies of Paul's time, for which Jannes and Jambres could serve as an metaphor, and in the fact that the story of these two must have been widely known at that time.[13]

In the twentieth century, scholars have paid more attention to the question under discussion. The answer is often linked to a certain commentator's view on the opponents of the author of the Pastoral Epistles. 2 Tim 3,1–9 is commonly supposed to be directed against those opponents, identified with the "false teachers" who are believed to be the focal point of this group of writings.[14] Using this as his starting point, G. Wohlenberg explained the introduction of Jannes and

10 Buxtorf's Lexicon was succeeded and complemented by, e.g., J.A. Fabricius, Codex pseudepigraphus Veteris Testamenti I–II, Hamburg ²1722–1723 (on Jannes and Jambres: I, 813–825; II, 105–111); and, in our own age, by E. Schürer, The History of the Jewish People in the Age of Jesus Christ (175 B.C.–A.D. 135), translated and revised by G. Vermes et alii, Edinburgh 1979–1987 (on Jannes and Jambres: III, 781–783); A.-M. Denis / J.-C. Haelewyck, Introduction à la littérature religieuse judéo-hellénistique, Turnhout 2000 (on Jannes and Jambres: 491–505). All data concerning Jannes and Jambres known today is now collected in Pietersma, The Apocryphon.

11 See the quotation above.

12 See the annotations on 2 Tim 3,8 of Clarius and especially Cappellus in: Pearson (ed.), Critici sacri, ad loc.; Cappellus states: "Non est autem quod anxie disquiramus undenam Paulo, undenam Apulejo Jannes innotuerit, cum tot scriptores, non quidem Canonici, sed probae notae, et in historicis rebus fide digni pridem interciderunt. Quam multa Judaeorum Ἑβραϊζόντων scripta sub Apostolis exstabant quorum hodie neque vola neque vestigium superest! Quotusquisque jam praeter Canonicos eorumque Paraphrastas exstat liber Hebraice scriptus ante Pauli mortem? Omnes ad unum abolevit Vespasiani, dein Adriani persecutio."

13 Scultetus on 2 Tim 3,8, in: Pearson (ed.), Critici sacri, ad loc.: "Cum igitur in omnium ore fuerint hi Magi tempore etiam Apostolorum, mirum non est Apostolum haereticos sui temporis veritati resistentes et ipsos cum iis contendisse."

14 E.g., L. Oberlinner, Die Pastoralbriefe. II. Kommentar zum zweiten Timotheusbrief (HThK 11/2), Freiburg et alii 1995, 119, on 2 Tim 3,1–9: "Das alles prägende Anliegen und Thema der Past, die Auseinandersetzung mit Irrlehrern, bestimmt auch diesen Textabschnitt".

Jambres by assuming that the people who brought confusion into the Christian community also practiced witchcraft.[15] Alternatively, it was proposed by W. Lock that, since the author's opponents were themselves fond of Jewish myths and genealogies (cf. 1 Tim 1,4; 4,7; 2 Tim 4,4; Titus 1,14), he is treating them here to one of their own fables, thereby showing them how such people come to their end.[16]

Other commentators explicitly deny any connection with witchcraft or judaizing tendencies; they stress, for instance, that the issue at stake is not the practice of magic, but resistance to the truth.[17] In his commentary of 1936, E.F. Scott states that even the author himself had no real concept of the ideas of his opponents; instead, Scott draws attention to the way in which he ridicules them, "in the style of the modern orator who denounces communism or spiritualism or some other delusion of the day. He has never troubled to make a study of these subjects, and in this he may show wisdom."[18] Accordingly, Scott argues that the emphasis in the comparison is on notions such as foolishness and dullness.[19]

It appears from these examples that attempts to find a connection between the Egyptian sorcerers and the opponents of the Pastoral Epistles' community are laboured or result in flimsy generalisations. Moreover, there seems to be no thread that leads from the identification of Moses' opponents to the reason for their being mentioned in 2 Tim 3.

The next sections will examine two pieces of evidence about Jannes and Jambres that have become known in addition to the patristic, pagan and rabbinical material: the fifth page of the *Damascus Document*, and the *Apocryphon of Jannes and Jambres*, begining with the latter. These pieces of evidence were published in 1910 and 1994, respectively, but have so far had hardly any influence on the discussion about Jannes and Jambres in 2 Tim 3.

---

15 G. Wohlenberg, Die Pastoralbriefe (KNT 13), Leipzig/Erlangen ³1923, 317; cf. G. Holtz, Die Pastoralbriefe (ThHK 13), Berlin ²1971, 182; N. Brox, Die Pastoralbriefe (RNT 7/2), Regensburg ⁴1969, 256.
16 W. Lock, A Critical and Exegetical Commentary on the Pastoral Epistles, Edinburgh 1924, 107; cf. C. Spicq, Les épîtres pastorales, Paris ⁴1969, 778.
17 E.g., Brox, Die Pastoralbriefe, 255–256; Oberlinner, Die Pastoralbriefe, 131–132; J.D. Quinn / W.C. Wacker, The First and Second Letters to Timothy, Grand Rapids 2000, 727.
18 E.F. Scott, The Pastoral Epistles, London 1936, 30.
19 Scott, ibid., 121–122.

2. The Apocryphon of Jannes and Jambres

In 1994, a hundred fragments of a fourth-century Greek manuscript (Chester Beatty Papyrus XVI) were published by Albert Pietersma. This material could be added to several more fragments of Greek and Latin manuscripts that were already known. Together they provide some details of a story about Jannes and Jambres, magicians at Pharaoh's court in Memphis.[20] An important part of the story concerns the garden ($\pi\alpha\rho\acute{\alpha}\delta\epsilon\iota\sigma o\varsigma$) that they have in their possession. It seems that this garden is under threat from God, who has planned to destroy Egypt, as is revealed to Jannes' mother in a vision, interpreted by himself. A wall is built around this garden, apparently to protect it from damage. At a certain point in the story, Jannes is found in his garden under an apple tree, together with the wise men of Egypt who admire his plantation. Suddenly the garden is struck by an earthquake, with thunder and lightning, prompting Jannes to enter his library to fetch his $\delta\upsilon\nu\acute{\alpha}\mu\epsilon\iota\varsigma$, probably his magical tools or books. In his library he encounters men who tell him that they are about to lead him to Hades forever, but who also inform him of the decision to grant him respite for fourteen time-units, that is, days or possibly years. From the sequel it seems likely that he is smitten with ulcers that will finally kill him.

In a further fragment Jannes tells of a joyful wedding lasting seven days. Whether it was his own marriage which was celebrated, or someone else's, cannot be determined, but it is interesting to note that Jannes says that, after the wedding, he left the Hebrews. When Jannes has finished relating his story, messengers from Pharaoh enter, who demand Jannes' presence at the king's court, because Moses and Aaron are performing miracles, and it is necessary that someone resists them (the word $\alpha\nu\theta\iota\sigma\tau\acute{\alpha}\nu\alpha\iota$ is used, as in 2 Tim 3,8). Jannes obeys, but as soon as he opposes Moses, his ulcer becomes so bad as to bring him to the verge of death. He abandons his efforts and sends a message to the king that he is unable to resist the power of God.

In subsequent fragments, Jannes is described as saying goodbye to his mother and moving back to Memphis, probably to die. He hands his book over to his brother Jambres, and tells him to keep it secret. Moreover, he warns him not to follow Pharaoh in pursuit of the Hebrews.

---

20 In the following paragraphs, I attempt to paraphrase the contents of the fragments in the order as proposed in Pietersma's edition; this order differs from the one in which Pietersma and Lutz presented the fragments in Charlesworth's Old Testament Pseudepigrapha (A. Pietersma / R.T. Lutz, Jannes and Jambres, in: OTP II, London 1985, 427–442). I occasionally deviate in minor detail from Pietersma's understanding of the fragments, without, however, going into elaborate discussions about them.

Indeed, when Pharaoh and his army have perished in the Red Sea, Jambres appears to be still alive.

A final part of the *Apocryphon of Jannes and Jambres* seems to be a tale in which Jambres and his mother visit Jannes; the details are obscure, but it is possible that the story relates how they arrive just in time to witness Jannes being dragged into the fiery furnace of hell. The mother also dies, and is buried in Jannes' grave. Back in the garden, under the apple tree, Jambres takes Jannes' magical books and with them summons Jannes' spirit. Jannes tells Jambres that his death was justified, because he opposed Moses and Aaron; he also informs him of the harsh conditions in Hades for those who, like himself, can expect no forgiveness. One fragment that belongs in this context mentions idolatry, sorcery, false oaths and lending money, probably reflecting a list of highly reprehensible sins.

At present, nothing more is known about the rest of the *Apocryphon of Jannes and Jambres*. The surviving fragments, though yielding much information about these brothers, do not provide even tentative answers to the most elementary questions, especially about the *Apocryphon* as a literary work—its form, provenance and meaning. There is enough information, however, to nourish the suspicion that the *Apocryphon of Jannes and Jambres* does not contain the story with which the author of the Pastoral Epistles was familiar. That story was probably similar to the one also known to the author of the *Damascus Document*, to which we shall now turn.

3. Jannes and Jambres in the Damascus Document

CD 5,17–19 contains the earliest mention of Jannes and Jambres, or at least of Jannes "and his brother"[21]; it is commonly dated to the second century BCE. The passage under discussion forms part of the so-called *Admonition*.

The literary pre-history of this writing, as well as its associative way of arguing, make it extremely difficult to discern any structure in it. Various proposals attempting to distinguish between the separate

---

21 Editions and translations: S. Schechter, Fragments of a Zadokite Work, in: idem (ed.), Documents of Jewish Sectaries, Cambridge 1910 = New York 1970; E. Lohse, Die Texte aus Qumran, Darmstadt ²1971; F. García Martínez / E.J.C. Tigchelaar, The Dead Sea Scrolls: Study Edition, Leiden 1997–1998. The fragments from cave 4 (ed. J.M. Baumgarten, Qumran Cave 4. XIII. The Damascus Document [4Q266–273] [DJD 18, Oxford 1996), where they overlap with the Cairo codex, reveal small text-critical variations that need not detain us here.

links in its chain of thought have been made, but none has been generally accepted.[22] Lack of space precludes a discussion of them here. I shall just add my own proposal, and must postpone a more detailed discussion of this matter for another occasion.

I propose to assume that the mention of Jannes – or: יחנה, as he is called in the *Damascus Document* – and his brother in CD 5,17–19, forms part of a more or less coherent portion that begins in 4,10, and runs through to 6,11. The main reason for beginning in 4,10 is the prominent adjunct of time there: בשלום הקץ, "in the fulfilment of time". The sentences which follow are connected to each other by the repetition of words and motifs. In the sentence beginning with the adjunct of time just quoted, the word מצוד, "net", occurs (4,12)[23]; after it has been said that "in all these years Belial will be let loose against Israel" (4,12–13), this leads to a quotation of Isa 24,17, which is subsequently explained in a *pesher*-commentary as referring to the three nets of Belial: fornication, wealth and contamination of the sanctuary (4,15–18) – whoever escapes from one net, will be caught in the others (4,19–20). Next comes an intricate elaboration on the theme of fornication (4,20 – 5,11), followed by a list of invectives against the people of Israel in general (5,11–15). In the next lines (5,15–19) the situation of the end of time is compared with that in the time of the exodus:

> For since ancient times God saw their deeds, and his wrath flared up against their actions, for it is not an wise people; they are a folk bereft of advice, in that there is no wisdom in them. For in ancient times there arose Moses and Aaron, by the hand of the prince of lights, and Belial, with his cunning, raised up Jannes and his brother during the first deliverance of Israel.

The text then continues with references to the age of the land's destruction, when other evil people led Israel astray (5,20 – 6,1), and to descendants of Aaron who by the grace of God "dug the well" (6,2–3), that is, discovered the proper interpretation of the law; quotations and *pesharim* are added, expanding on the law and the converts of Israel; their interpretation will be valid until the end of time (6,4–11); this eschatological note concludes this unit by way of an *inclusio*.

Although there is no formal division, a new section is begun in 6,11, dealing with issues of the community's conception of the law. These matters need not detain us at this moment.

---

22 See the survey in P.R. Davies, The Damascus Document. An Interpretation of the "Damascus Document" (JSOT.S 25), Sheffield 1983, 3–47.

23 It is often assumed that מצוד in this context means "watchtower" or "fortress," as in Hab 2,1, to which reference is assumedly made; however, whatever the meaning of the word in Habakkuk, the direct context of the Damascus Document (see esp. 4,15) makes it likely that it should here be understood as "net" (so also Schechter's translation).

A paraphrase of the passage just isolated might run as follows: In the fulfilment of time Belial will be unleashed against Israel, as has been predicted by Isaiah: "Panic, pit and net against you, inhabitant of the land!" These three things, as a *pesher*-commentary explains, refer to the three nets of Belial: fornication, wealth, and defilement of the temple; from which nobody will escape. After having expatiated on fornication and defilement, the text continues to point out that there have always been people who lack comprehension and follow Belial, he who already raised up Jannes and his brother against Moses and Aaron when Israel was saved for the first time. Obviously, now that the end is approaching and Israel is being saved for the second time, it can hardly be expected that Belial's aggression will be less severe. Accordingly, many people calling themselves "Israel" actually do not deserve that name, because they are trapped in Belial's nets and succumb to sin. Only those who follow the correct interpretation of the law will be saved, all others will perish.

The author describes his and his audience's days in a traditional way as the penultimate stage of history. He refers to immoral behaviour in everyday life and seems particularly exasperated by the common occurrence of second marriages.[24] He finds that people are extremely lax in their dealings with God's laws, and concludes that he is living in the time immediately preceding God's intervention in history. This is the time before God's eventual deliverance of the pious among his people from the misery of a world increasingly dominated by immorality and evil. It is also the time in which the devil launches his final offensive, in an ultimate and unfortunately quite successful attempt to lead as many people as possible to perdition – also a time, therefore, in which the few who have remained pious need to be extremely vigilant and steadfast in their devotion to God and his commandments.

An important aspect of the author's frame of mind is that he sees moral corruption everywhere: there are three nets of Belial, and it is impossible to escape them. The author exposes this world as universally sinful, a dangerous and fatal place to be. This is a typical feature of the author's eschatological world-view, for which many parallels can be listed.[25]

---

24 For the numerous problems in the interpretation of CD 4,20 – 5,11, see, e.g., A. Schremer, Qumran Polemic on Marital Law: CD 4,20 – 5,11 and its Social Background, in: J.M. Baumgarten et alii (ed.), The Damascus Document. A Centennial of Discovery (StTDJ 34), Leiden 2000, 147–160.

25 P. Volz, Die Eschatologie der jüdischen Gemeinde im neutestamentlichen Zeitalter, Tübingen ²1934, 153–157. In the context of 2 Timothy: M. Wolter, Die Pastoralbriefe als Paulustradition (FRLANT 146), Göttingen 1988, 229.

Jannes and his brother are introduced as examples from a much earlier time, the time of Israel's first salvation. The earlier history of Israel's exodus from Egypt is constantly being cited in the *Admonition* as a whole as a model for the later, now impending, salvation of the few. The opposition of Jannes and his brother to Moses and Aaron is accordingly explained in terms of diabolical opposition to the Prince of Lights (presumably the archangel Michael[26]). The message seems to be that one should not be surprised by the great number of people who refuse to follow God's commandments, because Belial's resistance against God has always been active, and he has always set his traps.

The reference to the story of Jannes and Jambres is intended to explain the people's stubborn refusal to gain insight and find the true way of God. Jannes and his brother were sent by Belial to thwart God's designs and now once more, people are being misled by Belial, as stupid as that may seem to the few who have insight.

This explanation of why Jannes and Jambres are mentioned in the *Damascus Document*, calls into question the identification of these two as Egyptian sorcerers. As has cogently been argued by Pietersma, Jannes and his brother are unlikely to have been Egyptians in the story to which the *Damascus Document* refers. In the first place Jannes' name (Ἰάννης or יחנה) is Hebrew in origin, so that the element of his Egyptian extraction may in any case be secondary.[27] Secondly, the way in which he is mentioned in CD 5,17–19 gives the impression of Hebrew resistance against Moses and Aaron, rather than Egyptian resistance. Finally, it may be added that the *Apocryphon*, even in the fragmentary state in which it survives, seems to lack any sense of eschatological urgency or even of the brothers' fiendish inspiration.

Pietersma has suggested that in the *Damascus Document*, Jannes is presented as an opponent of Moses in order to provide an historical precedent for the opposition experienced by the author of the *Damascus Document* and his audience; this would mean that Jannes would actually have been the name of the author's contemporary opponent, and this name would have been projected upon a figure from the past. Pietersma has proposed Yannay as a candidate for this contemporary

---

26 D. Hannah, Michael and Christ: Michael Traditions and Angel Christology in Early Christianity (WUNT 2 109), Tübingen 1999, 64–67.

27 One unpublished fragment of the Apocryphon of Jannes and Jambres has been reported to contain Pentephres as the name of the brothers' father (Pietersma, The Apocryphon, 99); if this is true, this author no doubt considered them to be Egyptians. The published fragments are silent about their origin. Some late rabbinic traditions regard them as sons of Bileam.

opponent, that is, the Maccabean leader Jonathan, who in 1 Maccabees is often presented in tandem with his brother Simon.[28]

This suggestion by Pietersma is not convincing. It is unlikely that this is the way in which narrative traditions are born: one does not invent a story about a figure from the past in order to damage a contemporary opponent's reputation. It is necessary for a story to be well known to one's audience if it is to serve as a convincing example; newly invented stories cannot fulfill this function. That the author believed his audience to be familiar with the story is also clear from the fact that it is not being re-told here, but reference is made to it.

Pietersma is probably right, however, in his contention that the story of the *Apocryphon of Jannes and Jambres* is not the story that the author of the *Damascus Document* knew.[29] In the next section, it will be argued that it was not the story that the author of 2 Tim 3,1–9 knew, either.

4. 2 Timothy 3,1–9

First of all it is useful to pay attention to the structure of 2 Tim 3,1–9. In 2 Tim 3,1 (as compared to the preceding verse, 2,26) a new beginning is marked by the use of the future tense, and the adjunct of time ἐν ἐσχάταις ἡμέραις. There are two main parts, the first of which is both introduced and concluded by imperatives: τοῦτο δὲ γίνωσκε in V.1, and τούτους ἀποτρέπου in V.5. The second part begins with ἐκ τούτων γάρ εἰσιν in V.6 (resuming τούτους in V.5), and ends with a reference to the fate of these people in V.9. In 3,10 a new section begins with the marked use of the personal pronoun σύ, indicating a contrast with the preceding lines. So 2 Tim 3,1–9 is a distinct textual unit, neatly demarcated from both the preceding and the succeeding pericopes.

---

28 Pietersma, ibid., 19–22.
29 Pietersma's arguments have been embraced by G. Häfner, "Nützlich zur Belehrung" (2 Tim 3,16). Die Rolle der Schrift in den Pastoralbriefen im Rahmen der Paulusrezeption (HBSt 25), Freiburg et alibi 2000, 175–182, who concludes from them that the author of 2 Timothy did not quote from a book of Jannes and Jambres, but referred to Exod 7 – 8, albeit that the sorcerers mentioned there had received names in oral tradition. Häfner finds support for his conclusion in his observation that the Damascus Document, too, knew the tradition of Jannes and his brother in a form that was "noch nicht stark entwickelt" (cf. A.T. Hanson, Studies in the Pastoral Epistles, London 1968, 27). Häfner's conclusions, in turn, have been closely followed by A. Weiser, Der zweite Brief an Timotheus (EKK 16/1), Düsseldorf et alibi/Neukirchen-Vluyn 2003, 245. However, the authors of both 2 Timothy and the Damascus Document referred to stories they assumed their audiences knew; what form those stories had, and to which extent the traditions contained in them were developed, is far beyond our ability to establish.

It is also transparently structured. The introduction of this section contains a warning for the addressee: he should know that, in the final days, there will be difficult times (V.1). This is illustrated by a list of vices that are said to be characteristic of mankind as a whole[30] in the final days (Vv.2–5a). This list of the moral standards of a world in its final days is brought to an end with the advice to avoid people who accept those standards. It should be stressed that 3,1–5a describes humanity as a whole; efforts to read V.5a as a reference to false teachers in particular[31] fail in light of the form of this unit. It is not said that there will be some people who are selfish and greedy; or specifically designated groups that are conceited and ungrateful; or identifiable individuals who put on a big act of piety, but deny religion's real power – instead, it is said that all people are, and do, all of these things.[32]

In the second part, the description of mankind's moral decay is continued by the mention of a specific group, of whom it is said that they "enter homes and ensnare the silly little women" (V.6a); the lines which follow contain a brief excursus on the moral shortcomings of these females (V.6b–7). The author then returns to the men of the final age, comparing their opposition to the truth with Jannes and Jambres' opposition to Moses, and concluding the pericope with the prophetic announcement that their foolishness will be fully exposed, as was that of Jannes and Jambres (Vv.8–9).

In the scholarly discussion, much attention is paid to the meaning of 2 Tim 3,6a, about the men who enter homes to do something with women. Almost invariably, commentators see in them the author's concrete opponents, the "false teachers" against whom the Pastoral Epistles as a whole are presumed to be directed.

The most cogent argument for supposing that the men in 3,6a are false teachers, is the fact that in V.7 the women they are visiting are portrayed as unteachable: "they are ever learning, but will never be able to attain knowledge of the truth". So if these women are trying to learn something (however futile their efforts), the men who visit them are apparently trying to teach them something.

---

30 Spicq, Les épîtres pastorales, 772: "Il aura une corruption massive de l'humanité (οἱ ἄνθρωποι, premier article du chapître souligne l'universalité)"; contrast I.H. Marshall, A Critical and Exegetical Commentary on the Pastoral Epistles, Edinburgh 1999, 771–772, who notes that the phrase suggests that people in general are intended, "but it must refer to nominal Christians in view of the description in V.5. The list is basically descriptive of godlessness in general, but is applied to the heretics."
31 E.g., Lock, A Critical and Exegetical Commentary, 103–104; Spicq, Les épîtres pastorales, 776; Oberlinner, Die Pastoralbriefe, 124; Weiser, Der zweite Brief, 239.
32 Accordingly, V.5b does not refer to "Mitchristen" (Weiser, Der zweite Brief, 250–251), but to the low moral standards of society at large.

Underlying this argument is the idea that "learning something", and "to attain knowledge of the truth" are activities that require the active pursuit of mental (intellectual, religious) aims. However, the author of the Pastoral Epistles uses μανθάνειν in a wide spectrum of meanings: it sometimes means to "learn" something as in an intellectual or theological activity (μανθάνειν as opposed to διδάσκειν; so 1 Tim 2,11; 2 Tim 3,14), but it can easily have a much more general meaning, such as "to get used to something" (so 1 Tim 5,4, 13; Tit 3,14).

Furthermore, the concept of ἀλήθεια in the Pastoral Epistles comprises much more than just a set of philosophical or religious convictions about reality in the cognitive sense; it refers to everything that is "true", or "right" and "just", in any sense, relating, for instance, to decency and chastity.[33] In the Pastoral Epistles, ἀλήθεια is the embodiment of the entire range of the teachings of Paul as perceived by the author of these writings, regardless of whether those teachings concern creed, ethics, or etiquette (e.g., 1 Tim 2,4,7; 4,3; 6,5).[34] "To attain knowledge of the truth" is to escape from the devil's snare (ἐκ τοῦ διαβόλου παγίδος) and to stop doing his will (so 2 Tim 2,25–26; cf. 1 Tim 3,7; 5,15).

If this is accepted, it is evident that by his derogatory remarks about women who are unable to ever learn the truth, the author does not necessarily restrict himself to matters of theology. It may even be possible that the author was not thinking of Christian women in particular.[35] Taken in a more general sense, his words may mean that there are women who, even if they try continuously, are unable to learn anything that would bring them closer to a good, Christian life. They are mindless and evil women, as is also suggested by the terms used in V.6b: "they are heavily loaded with sins and driven by all kinds of lust."

By themselves, ἁμαρτία and ἐπιθυμία have no specific connotations of sexual licentiousness in the Pastoral Epistles. Indeed, the instances in which these words occur are strikingly vague, often meaning no more than "something wrong" (e.g., 1 Tim 5,20.22), and "desire" (e.g., 1 Tim 6,9; 2 Tim 2,22; Titus 2,12), respectively.[36] More importantly, however, the short excursus on the immoral character of these women should not make us forget that the main subjects of 2 Tim 3,1–9

33 Cf. F. Young, The Theology of the Pastoral Letters, Cambridge 1994, 95.
34 Weiser, Der zweite Brief, 258, correctly states that ἐπίγνωσις ἀληθείας in the Pastoral Epistles means "Christwerden bzw. Christsein", but incorrectly narrows that concept down to "Erkenntnis und Annahme der christlichen Glaubenswahrheit in ihrer traditionell geprägten Form".
35 Against Weiser, Der zweite Brief, 252.
36 Oberlinner, Die Pastoralbriefe, 127.

are the men of the final age, some of whom even enter people's homes to ensnare women.

I know of only one convincing parallel to 2 Tim 3,6a – PsSol 4,4–5:

> He has eyes for every woman, without distinction,
> his tongue is false when he enters into a sworn covenant.
> He commits his sins by night and in hidden places, believing he is seen by no one,
> with his eyes he invites any woman to meet, with evil intent;
> he is quick to enter any home with the cheerful air of someone innocent.[37]

Notwithstanding some uncertainties in the interpretation of this description, the intentions of this man who enters the homes of women (any woman will do) are manifest.[38] One commentator, discussing the question of whether 2 Tim 3,6 has sexual connotations, remarked that, had the author wanted to be more explicit about such matters, he would certainly have done so.[39] In the light of the parallel from PsSol 4, it can only be answered that things can hardly be more explicitly stated than in 2 Tim 3,6.[40]

Seen from a literary point of view, the exception of some ἐκ τούτων is not made to move from one category to another, from the people in general to a specifically identifiable group of opponents, but simply to achieve a climax in the expansion of evil in the final days. What we have in 2 Tim 3,1–9 is, as has been noted by many commentators, a portrayal of "the penultimate times ... as a time of moral upheaval".[41] As has been said above, such portrayals are not unusual in writings espousing an eschatological world-view.

Some interpreters have suggested that the use of eschatological language is no more than a literary device, whereas the author's real interest would have been certain theological positions within the Christian community, characterized by him as false teachings.[42] This view

---

37 See further Prov 5,8 and chap. 7; for the motif of shamelessness, see Prov 30,20; cf. perhaps also Job 24,16 LXX.

38 The Syriac version differs in some places (J.L. Trafton, The Syriac Version of the Psalms of Solomon: A Critical Evaluation [SCSt 11], Atlanta 1985, 59.62), but the point is the same.

39 Brox, Die Pastoralbriefe, p. 255: "Bei den Sünden und Gelüsten der Frauen dürfte kaum speziell an Unzucht gedacht sein, weil der Autor das im Stil der hier betriebenen Polemik sicherlich ohne Umschweif gesagt hätte", quoted approvingly by Häfner, "Nützlich zur Belehrung", 179.

40 See also Pietersma, The Apocryphon, 133–134.

41 R.F. Collins, 1 & 2 Timothy and Titus. A Commentary, Louisville/London 2002, 244.

42 Brox, Die Pastoralbriefe, 253: "Wie in 1 Tim 4,1ff., so wird auch hier ein ganzer Abschnitt über die Irrlehrer in die Form einer endzeitlichen Weissagung gekleidet"; Oberlinner, Die Pastoralbriefe, 119–120; Weiser, Der zweite Brief, 239–241.246–247.260.

does not do justice to the eschatology of these writings as something lucid, concrete, and appearing at crucial moments.[43]

It is important to note how eschatology, such as that which surfaces in 2 Tim 3,1–9, functions in its literary context.

The reader of the Pastoral Epistles is invited to sympathize with the apostle Paul, his friends Timothy and Titus, and a few other companions. They are living in a world under constant threat of the devil, and even their own small community of true Christians is continuously falling apart. Some who have abandoned Paul are mentioned by name (2 Tim 1,15; 4,10), so that the apostle's fatigue and loneliness are vividly evoked. But many more anonymous people are cited who had not the strength or the courage to remain steadfast—it has to be this way, the Holy Spirit has predicted it, as the author makes Paul say in 1 Tim 4,1–2.

The author of the Pastoral Epistles attempts to explain to his audience the phenomenon of people who had been standing close to them leaving their Christian community. If considerable numbers of people are renouncing their membership of a community, it gives rise to questions and doubts for those left behind (cf. 1 Tim 1,19).

It may not be too speculative to conjecture that at the time when the Pastoral Epistles were written, the expectation of Christ's imminent *parousia* had come under heavy pressure. The author answers existing doubts and insecurities by repeating time and again that the Christian faith is an eschatological faith. He does not employ eschatological language to describe false teachers, but uses the fact that there are people who "teach differently" as an unmistakable sign that the end is approaching. However, that is only one sign. A depiction of the atrocious immorality which the readers can see around them, should also convince them that they are living in the final stage of history. All this is part of the devil's ultimate assault, a test for the faithful.[44]

Jannes and Jambres are singled out because of their stupidity. In the Pastoral Epistles "stupidity" and related concepts are usually used to designate people who were once good Christians, but are no longer. For

---

43 See now especially D.J. Downs, 'Early Catholicism' and Apocalypticism in the Pastoral Epistles, CBQ 67 (2005) 641–661.

44 This is also the understanding of 2 Tim 3,1–9 by Cyprianus, who quoted that passage as a prophecy by Paul about his own time, and added: "Adimplentur quaecumque praedicta sunt et, adpropinquante iam saeculi fine, hominum pariter ac temporum probatione uenerunt. Magis ac magis aduersario saeuiente, error fallit, extollit stupor, liuor incendit, cupiditas excaecat, deprauat impietas, superbia inflat, discordia exasperat, ira praecipitat" (De ecclesiae catholicae unitate 16; ed. M. Bévenot, in: R. Weber / M. Bévenot [ed.], Sancti Cypriani episcopi opera [CChr.SL 3], Turnhout 1972, 243–268, here 261).

instance, it is said of false teachers that they are talking like idiots (ἐξ-ετράπησαν εἰς ματαιολογίαν) and do not understand what they are reading or stating themselves (1 Tim 1,6; cf. Titus 1,10); they understand nothing (1 Tim 6,4) and have lost their minds (1 Tim 6,5, the same words in 2 Tim 3,8); compare further 1 Tim 4,7. Also, the former state of converts to the true faith can be referred to as a state of "not-knowing", as in 1 Tim 1,13; see esp. Titus 3,3, and cf. 1 Tim 4,3; 2 Tim 2,25. The concept of knowledge, then, is used to define those within the Christian community, as well as those who are so stupid as to leave it.

If this is the message of 2 Timothy, and of 2 Tim 3,1–9 in particular, then the reference to Jannes and Jambres as earlier examples of the phenomenon that the author observes in his own time, would make the most sense if Jannes and Jambres were known, not as Egyptian magicians, but as Hebrew apostates in Belial's service who were working on the destruction of God's people from within, not unlike, for instance, Dathan and Abiram. No doubt, that would be quite unlike the story told in the *Apocryphon of Jannes and Jambres*, but it would probably resemble the one to which reference is made in the *Damascus Document*.

5. Summary

A brief summary of our findings is in order.

(1) In 2 Tim 3,8–9 Jannes and Jambres are presented as examples of the great stupidity of leaving the path of truth. In the Pastoral Epistles, "truth" defines everything that is conducive to eschatological salvation, including a decent, Christian life. To gain knowledge of the truth, is to cease being worldly and thus be liberated from the devil's net. To succumb to sin and leave the road to salvation, is patent idiocy. That it nonetheless occurs, as the members of the author's community doubtless observe, is an unmistakable indication that the end of this world is near, so that the devil is intensifying his aggression, in order to prevent as many people as possible from being delivered.

(2) The exemplary function of Jannes and Jambres is brought out most clearly, if the author of 2 Timothy in 3,8–9 refers to a narrative tradition that considered both as apostates: people who left the Hebrew community and resisted Moses in his mission to liberate Israel. The possibly apostate character of Jannes and his brother is supported by the *Damascus Document*; in that text they also seem to be presented as opponents of Moses and Aaron from within the people. The parallel

between the CD 5,17–19 and 2 Tim 3,8–9 is very much strengthened by the eschatological context of both passages, by the notion that the devil is behind the activities of Jannes and Jambres, and by the sociological situation of the readers and hearers, who in both cases form part of groups with strong convictions not shared by society at large.

(3) The story in the *Apocryphon of Jannes and Jambres* is most unlikely to be the one to which the *Damascus Document* and 2 Timothy refer. It appears that the question of who Jannes and Jambres were has obscured the much more important question of why they are mentioned. Indeed, only if one lets the latter question precede the former, can one reveal that all previously collected material about Jannes and Jambres probably has no bearing on 2 Tim 3,8–9.

Let me conclude with a suggestion regarding the origin of the story of Jannes and Jambres as Egyptian magicians. It may have originated with early readers of 2 Tim 3,8–9, who were unfamiliar with the story of Jannes and Jambres and looked into their Old Testament for opponents of Moses who might fit the description. The Egyptian miracle-workers of Exod 7–8 are anonymous, opposed Moses, and were ultimately unsuccessful. If the name of Jannes was in some way associated with sorcery, as is suggested by Pliny's testimony, this would only have promoted the Egyptian magicians' candidacy. This suggestion accounts for the existence of one story about Jannes and Jambres known to the authors of the *Damascus Document* and the Pastoral Epistles, and another about two opponents of Moses that seems to have no relationship to the former.

Moses in Gnostic Writings

by Christopher M. Tuckett

This essay clearly takes the risk of arousing scholarly derision or ridi-
cule from a number of points of view. In the eyes of some, its very title
may implicitly make a number of unjustified assumptions in referring
to writings as 'Gnostic' at all. Further, the main argument of this essay
is to argue for a fundamentally negative result, viz. that Moses plays
little or no significant role in many Gnostic writings; this runs the risk
of all claims to establish a negative result, viz. that the non-appearance
of an element in one set of texts might be shown to be totally misguided
if one or two extra Gnostic texts were discovered where Moses played a
more important role. (Alternatively, and worse for any author's self-
esteem or scholarly reputation, would be the possibility that existing
references in extant texts have been overlooked and illegitimately ignored!) Nevertheless, despite these dangers of proceeding at all, it does
seem to be a striking phenomenon that the figure of Moses is something
of an 'absent friend' in so many Gnostic texts.[1] And even if some more
texts were to be discovered in the future giving a rather different picture, the picture emerging from our existing texts is still quite striking
(if the corpus can never, almost by definition, be 'complete' in terms of
the totality of Gnostic writings that may have existed in the past).

First, however, a few preliminary remarks on the term 'Gnostic'
and the associated noun 'Gnosticism'. As is well known, there have
been vigorous debates over the years about what, if anything,
can/should be labelled 'Gnostic' or 'Gnosticism'. And in recent discussions, there has been a move by some to argue that the terms 'Gnostic'
and 'Gnosticism' should be abandoned altogether as meaningful in contemporary discussions of the ancient texts which have been labelled

---

1 The term 'absent friend' was evoked in part by the famous study of C.K. Barrett, From
First Adam to Last. A Study in Pauline Theology, London 1962, 22–26: Barrett discusses key OT figures in Paul, and notes that e.g. Enoch and Noah are striking by their
absence and hence 'absent friends'. It will be argued here that Moses is quite striking by
his relative absence in the texts considered here; whether he is a 'friend' is debatable.
Cf. n. 41 below.

'Gnostic' in the past.[2] In part this arises from the great variety of ideas, concepts etc. which have been included under the umbrella term 'Gnosticism'.[3] Yet even those such as Williams and King (who have been in the vanguard of arguing for abandoning the term Gnostic as a meaningful category) have agreed that some texts (often regarded by others as stemming from 'Sethian Gnosticism') do constitute a subset of text with sufficient common elements to make it meaningful and useful to consider them together.[4] Some have insisted that to qualify for the label 'Gnostic', one must have a reference to an ignorant and/or evil Demiurge figure who is different from the supreme God. Others have however argued that, while this is certainly a significant feature in many texts usually labelled 'Gnostic', such a feature should be seen as part of a broader spectrum of ideas, including the notion of a divine spark in (some) human beings, of 'salvation' as involving the escape of the soul from the present world and its return to its place of origin, in part as a result of the 'knowledge' brought by a redeemer figure.[5] Certainly too many would argue that, however many differences there may be between so-called 'Valentinian Gnosticism' and 'Sethian Gnosticism', there is still sufficient commonality between them to make it meaningful and sensible to use a single noun ('Gnosticism') to refer to both.[6]

In what follows, therefore, I shall look at the references to the figure in Moses in some of the texts often assumed to be 'Gnostic' in some shape or form, without making too many further assumptions about the precise category. Most are from the Nag Hammadi library and certainly in relation to the figure of Moses they do present a striking and distinctive picture which distinguishes them from many other

---

2   See M.A. Williams, Rethinking "Gnosticism". An Argument for Dismantling a Dubious Category, Princeton 1996; also K. King, What is Gnosticism?, Cambridge, MA / London 2003; also the essays in A. Marjanen (ed.), Was there a Gnostic Religion?, Helsinki/Göttingen 2005.

3   And in turn leading then to claims about the existence of different branches of Gnosticism, e.g. Valentinian Gnosticism, Sethian Gnosticism etc.

4   Cf. e.g. Williams, Rethinking Gnosticism, 51–52, on what he calls 'biblical demiurgical traditions'.

5   See e.g. B.A. Pearson, Gnosticism as a Religion, in: idem, Gnosticism and Christianity in Roman and Coptic Egypt, New York / London 2003, 201–223, esp. 202–207, 212; also C. Markschies, Art. Gnosis/Gnostizismus, RGG[4] 3 (2000) 1045–1053; idem, Gnosis: An Introduction, London 2003, 16–17.

6   Cf. e.g. B. Layton, Prolegomena to the Study of Ancient Gnosticism, in: L.M. White / O.L. Yarbrough (ed.), The Social World of the First Christians. Essays in Honor of Wayne Meeks, Minneapolis 1995, 334–350, on p. 343. For further discussion of this whole issue of the definition of 'Gnosticism', see my forthcoming The Gospel of Mary, Oxford 2007 and the section in the Introduction on 'How Gnostic is the *Gospel of Mary*?'.

writings of the period, in both Judaism and Christianity, so that it seems
sensible to treat them as a distinct, separate set of texts.

*

An a priori assumption of someone with just a little knowledge about
Judaism in the early years of the Christian era on the one hand, and
about Gnosticism on the other, might be that the figure of Moses and
debates about his significance would feature prominently in Gnostic
texts.

In relation to Judaism, it has become almost universally accepted
scholarly orthodoxy to note the cardinal importance of the Mosaic Law
(and the establishment of the covenant associated with it) for Jewish
writers and thinkers of the time. James Dunn asserts that the idea of
'covenant focussed in Torah' was one of the 'four pillars of Second
Temple Judaism'.[7] Claims about the importance of 'covenantal
nomism' as the fundamental 'pattern of religion' underlying Judaism at
this time are well known from the work of E.P. Sanders on 'Palestinian
Judaism', and underlies too the 'new perspective' on study of Paul
which has been so dominant in Pauline studies in recent years.[8] Sanders' theory about the prevalence of 'covenantal nomism', in particular
his claims that Judaism had no idea of 'earning' one's salvation by legalistic obedience but was just as much dominated by ideas of divine
grace as Christianity, has been questioned by some on the grounds that
a more 'legalistic' attitude to the Law may not be so easy to eradicate
and/or ignore in some strands of Judaism at this period. Nevertheless,
the centrality of the Mosaic Law for Judaism has never been seriously
questioned: within this debate, the issue is about attitudes *to* the Law
(does one 'earn' salvation but obeying the Law? Or is the Law God's
gracious gift, given by his initiative, to his covenant people whom he
first freely chose by an act of pure grace?). It is not about whether the

---

7   See J.D.G. Dunn, The Partings of the Ways between Christianity and Judaism, London
     1991, 23–31. The other three are monotheism, election, and Law focussed in Temple.
     (Clearly the latter would have been redundant after the events of 70 CE.) For a similar
     view of the importance of the Law for Judaism, see M. Casey, From Jewish Prophet to
     Gentile God. The Origins and Development of New Testament Christology, Cambridge
     1991, 12, who lists eight 'identity factors' of Second Temple Judaism, viz., 'ethnicity,
     scripture, monotheism, circumcision, Sabbath observance, dietary laws, purity laws and
     major festivals'. Apart perhaps from the first, all of these relate in one way or another to
     parts (or the whole) of the Mosaic Law.

8   E.P. Sanders, Paul and Palestinian Judaism, London 1977.

Law was central for Jews at this time – that is taken as read as almost self-evident.

On the side of Gnosticism, it has been a widely held view (though not as universally held as the theory of the centrality of the Mosaic Law for Judaism) that Gnosticism may have emerged from some kind of Jewish roots.[9] It is well known that many Gnostic texts provide a detailed engagement with the creation accounts in the first chapters of the book of Genesis. This engagement involves of course a highly distinctive and 'unusual' presentation of the creation story, offering a mythological scheme that seems in many ways alien to any 'original' and/or 'normal' interpretation of these stories as they appear in Genesis. Nevertheless, the prevalence of attempts to provide (what is at one level) an 'alternative' interpretation of the Genesis creation stories has led may to suggest that the roots of Gnosticism lie in some kind of 'heterodox' Judaism and that the Jewish basis for Gnostic ideas and Gnostic mythology is very deep-seated – certainly perhaps more deep-seated that any possible Christian basis since, as often as not, Christian elements often seem to be marginal and/or tangential to the main thrust of many Gnostic texts.[10] So too others have sought to show that many other details (about words and word plays, or about longer arguments) depend critically on Jewish traditions and/or Hebrew words and names.[11] Others have sought to find the background of what is evidently a central feature of at least some Gnostic writings, viz. the story about the fate of Sophia, in Jewish language and talk about the figure of 'wisdom'.[12]

---

9   See e.g. surveys in A.H.B. Logan, Gnostic Truth and Christian Heresy, Edinburgh 1996, xvi; King, What is Gnosticism?, 175ff. For an older (at the time somewhat unfashionable) presentation of such a view, see M. Friedländer, Der vorchristliche jüdische Gnosticismus, Göttingen 1898 and the discussion in B.A. Pearson, Friedländer Revisited: Alexandrian Judaism and Gnostic Origins, in: idem, Gnosticism, Judaism and Egyptian Christianity, Minneapolis 1990, 10–28. For others advocating a Jewish origin for Gnosticism, cf. J.M. Robinson, Trajectories through Early Christianity, Minneapolis 1971, 66–67; K. Rudolph, Gnosis, Edinburgh 1984, 276–282; G. Quispel, Der gnostische Anthropos und die jüdische Tradition, ErJb 22 (1954) 195–234; idem, Gnosticism and the New Testament, in: J.P. Hyatt (ed.), The Bible in Modern Scholarship, Nashville 1965, 252–271; G. MacRae, The Jewish Background of the Gnostic Sophia Myth, NT 12 (1970) 86–101; P. Perkins, Gnosticism and the New Testament, Minneapolis 1993, 39–42; also a number of essays by B.A. Pearson, including his Jewish Elements in Gnosticism and the Development of Gnostic Self-Definition, in: idem, Gnosticism, Judaism and Egyptian Christianity, 126–130.
10   This last claim is of course something of a sweeping generalisation! Cf. S. Pétrement, A Separate God. The Christian Origins of Gnosticism, London 1991; Logan, Gnostic Truth and Christian Heresy, both arguing that Gnosticism is an offshoot of Christianity.
11   See Perkins, Gnosticism, and Pearson, Friedländer Revisited.
12   See MacRae, The Jewish Background.

Clearly the development of Gnostic myths which involve a recasting and/or retelling of the Genesis story suggest that the 'authors' of such myths were engaged in some kind of process of identity formation *vis à vis* other Jews and their appeals to, and interpretations of, the same stories from Genesis. In one way, one could argue that the amount of trouble, time and effort which have evidently gone into the production of these literary texts reflects a desire both to lay claim to Jewish scripture and Jewish heritage, and also to distinguish the claims being made here from competing claims in the contemporary context in which Gnostic texts arose.

Given this general background, one might expect that the figure of Moses, and issues about the Mosaic Law, would feature equally prominently in Gnostic texts as part of the same process of identity formation and/or self-definition by Gnostics in relation to other Jewish groups. What is perhaps surprising (and is sometimes noted but rarely commented on in detail) is the surprising *absence* of references to Moses – and also to discussions about the Mosaic Law – in so many Gnostic texts.

The figure of Moses himself is rarely mentioned in Gnostic texts. On the few occasions that he is, it is not in relation to his role as the person who received, and passed on, the Torah. Rather, he is the one who is presumed to be the (literary) author of the Genesis creation accounts which, for whatever reason, occupy so much space and attention in Gnostic mythology. Thus the *Apocryphon of John* has four references to 'Moses', but each time is in an almost stereotyped phrase with the writer asserting that it is 'not as Moses said/wrote'; and in each case what is in view is some detail of the stories in the early chapters of Genesis.[13]

> 13,19–21 (BG 45,8–10): Do not think it is, as Moses said, 'above the waters' (cf. Gen 1,2)
>
> 22,22–24 (BG 58,16–18): It is not the way Moses wrote (and) you heard, For he said in his first book 'He put him to sleep' (Gen 2,21)
>
> 23,1–4 (BG 69,17–19): And he brought the part which he had taken from the power of the man into the female creature, and not the way Moses said, 'his rib–bone' (cf. Gen 2,21–22)
>
> 29,6–7 (BG 73,4–6): It is not as Moses said, 'they hid themselves in an ark' (Gen 7,7).

---

13 References given are to the version of the text of *ApocJohn* in Codex II of the Nag Hammadi library with references to the version in the Berlin codex (BG 8502) in brackets.

'Moses' is thus above all the author of the creation accounts; he is not seen in his capacity as a legislator or mediator of the Torah.[14]

Similarly, *On the Origin of the World* 102,9 refers to the 'Archangelic (Book) of the Prophet Moses'; but again this is in the context of a discussion of the names of the seven archontic powers, the claim being made here that information about these names are to be found in this writing of Moses. Once again 'Moses' (even here designated a 'prophet') is above all the author of literary texts about the creation of the world and the universe. He is not related to the Jewish Law in any way.

Further, the thrust of all the four references in the *Apocryphon of John* is to substantiate the claim that the account of the creation story in the text here is *not* as Moses said or wrote. The references thus serve not to reinterpret the Genesis story but to *deny its validity*. It is true that, at one level, the terms of reference (and much of the detail) is taken from the Genesis account: this *is* the story of the creation of Adam and Eve by the God of the Hebrew Bible. But the references to Moses here seem to be designed to show that the Hebrew Bible's version of the story is *in*correct. This is then, at one level, not a matter of different *interpretations* of a shared common story, providing as it were an alternative exegesis of a widely accepted authoritative text. Rather, the Gnostic author's account seeks to deny the authority of the OT text itself. Rather then than sharing very much in common with Judaism, this branch of Gnostic thought seems diametrically opposed to Jewish thinking, Jewish self-understanding and Jewish presuppositions about the status of the Torah. 'Moses' here then is not (just) reinterpreted: rather it is a case apparently of a wholesale *rejection* of 'Moses'. 'Moses' and the 'Law' (i.e. the Pentateuch, including Genesis) only come into the picture as opponents to be distanced from.

Elsewhere in the Nag Hammadi texts, Moses is striking by his relative absence. References to Adam abound; so too stories about figures such as Eve, Seth, Norea etc. are highly developed. References to Moses are thus notable by their relative paucity. And when such references do occur, they again appear to be as negative about Moses as those in the *Apocryphon of John*.

---

14 Though the reference in 22,23 to the 'first' book of Moses suggests that the author was aware of the existence of other books attributed to Moses (presumably the other books of the Pentateuch are at least included, and these would of course include Exodus). Hence the author of *ApocJohn* may have known of the existence of the traditions associating Moses with the Law; but that is not what he chooses to allude to here in his references to Moses.

In the *Second Treatise of the Great Seth* (NHC VII,2) 63,26ff., Moses is mentioned and called a 'laughing stock' (along with a whole range of figures from the Hebrew Bible, including Adam, Abraham, Isaac, Jacob, David, Solomon, the prophets, and the creator god):

> 'Moses was a laughing stock, a faithful servant, being named 'the Friend'; they bore witness concerning him in iniquity, since he never knew me. Neither he nor those before him, from Adam to Moses and John the Baptist, none of them knew me nor my brethren'.[15]

Riley in his edition of the text summarises this whole section (62,27 – 65,1) aptly as a 'Litany of laughingstocks: Rejection of the Hebrew tradition'.[16] 'Moses' is thus referred to as a figure who, along with virtually all other significant figures of the Hebrew Bible, is given a wholly negative evaluation (cf. 'he never knew me').

It is also perhaps noteworthy that the prime epithets associated with Moses here – Moses as 'faithful servant' and 'friend' – may be taken from the Biblical tradition[17], but they do not directly relate to Moses qua law-giver. It is true that the text does go on, immediately after the section quoted above on Moses, to speak about the Law:

> 'For a doctrine of angels is what arose through them, to keep dietary rules and bitter slavery. They never knew truth, nor will they know it' (64,1–4).

For 'doctrine of angels', Riley notes the parallels in Gal 3,19 (also Acts 7,3) and Heb 2,2, noting that 'the angels in Gnosticism in general ... are inimical spirits, and their Law is a means to enslave humanity';[18] he also notes the references in Irenaeus (Adv.Haer. 1,30,11) where the Law is said to be given by Ialdabaoth to Moses. But that is not said here: there is no connection drawn explicitly between Moses and the Law. 'Moses' is thus imply yet another figure of the OT era whose value is rejected almost in toto.

In the *Testimony of Truth* (NHC IX,3), there is a set of references to 'Moses' in a somewhat fragmentary part of the text focusing on the 'serpent':

> 'And in one place Moses writes "He made the devil a serpent (for) those home he has in his generation". Also in the book which is called "Exodus", it is written thus: "He contended against the magicians, when the place was full of serpents according to their wickedness; and the rod which was in the hand of

---

15 English translation from G. Riley, in: B.A. Pearson (ed.), Nag Hammadi Codex VII (NHMS 30), Leiden 1996, 183–185.

16 Riley, ibid., 141.

17 Though, intriguingly, they closer to descriptions found in the New Testament rather than the Old Testament: thus Riley, ibid., 183, notes the parallel in Heb 3,5 to Moses as a 'faithful servant', and to Jas 2,23 for 'friend of God' (though of Abraham here, not Moses).

18 Riley, ibid., 184–185.

Moses became a serpent, and it swallowed the serpent of the magicians".
Again it is written, "He made a serpent of bronze and hung it on a pole"
(48,16–28).[19]

At one level, Moses thus appears as the literary author of texts from the
Hebrew Bible; and also in actions in battling with the Egyptian magicians is mentioned. In one way it could be argued that 'Moses' is presented a little more positively here: this section of the text seems to be
some kind of 'midrash' on the OT texts[20]; and insofar as any 'midrash'
regards its base text positively (however 'richly' it may find hidden
meaning in the text), it may be that the implied attitude to Moses (as
protagonist in the story being recounted, and as the author of the account itself) is thus positive. On the other hand, Pearson suggests that
'the expression "Moses writes" (48,16) is a signal that the truth is to be
sought elsewhere than in the bare words of Moses'.[21]

A little later, in another (unfortunately very fragmentary) part of the
text, it is said:

'You do not understand Christ spiritually when you say "we believe in
Christ". For this is the way Moses writes in every book. The book of the gen-
eration of Adam is written for those who are in the generation of the Law.
They follow the Law and they obey it...' (50,1–8).[22]

Again Moses seems to be aligned clearly with the opponents of the author as lacking any genuine insight at all. And again, the reference to
the 'books' of Moses indicates that Moses is seen primarily as the author of literary texts, not as the lawgiver as such, nor necessarily as any
kind of personal mediator of divine revelation.[23] But in any case, any
lack of explicit reference to Moses in his capacity as a lawgiver does
not suggest any more positive attitude to the Law than to Moses (as
author of books written); both are associated clearly and definitively
with the opponents of the author of the text here.

The section on p. 48 of the text (and perhaps also p. 50, though the
present manuscript is too fragmentary to be certain) may be part of a

---

19 English translation from B.A. Pearson (ed.), Nag Hammadi Codices IX and X (NHS
    15), Leiden 1981, 167. I have omitted the (many) square brackets indicating where the
    text here is fragmentary and the translation given represents a reconstructed part of the
    text. For more details, with the full Coptic text, see Pearson's critical edition.
20 Cf. B.A. Pearson, Jewish Haggadic Traditions in *The Testimony of Truth* from Nag
    Hammadi (CG IX,3), in: idem, Gnosticism, Judaism and Egyptian Christianity, 39–51.
21 Pearson, ibid., 43, referring to the passages in *ApocJohn* noted earlier here in this essay.
22 Pearson, Nag Hammadi Codices IX and X, 169: again I have omitted all the square
    brackets showing where the text has had to be restored (and hence its precise wording is
    uncertain).
23 Pearson, ibid., again compares the references to Moses in *ApocJohn* as all of a piece
    with the general attitude to Moses shown.

separable section of the text.[24] Earlier, at the start of the present text, there is a polemical passage (29,6 – 31,22) attacking those who are under the Law. However, when it comes to what precisely in 'the Law' is being opposed, it is clear that it is primarily the command (or exhortation) to marry and produce children: 'The Law commands one to take a husband (or) to take a wife, and to beget, to multiply like the sand of the sea' (30,2–5, which then becomes the prime focus for the subsequent debate and disagreement by the author here). But here the primary reference is to passages in the narrative sections of the book of Genesis (cf. 1,18; 2,24; 8,17; 9,1 etc.) rather than the legal rulings mediated through Moses (and appearing in Exodus, Leviticus, Deuteronomy etc). The 'Law' that is attacked here is once again associated with the creation accounts in Genesis, rather than the detailed provisions of the Mosaic Law as such. The latter simply does not come into view here at all.

One other brief reference to Moses may be noted in the *Treatise on Resurrection* (NHC I,4) 48,9: 'if you remember reading in the Gospel that Elijah appeared and Moses with him...' But this is simply a reference to the story in the NT synoptic gospel tradition of the transfiguration of Jesus, told in order to establish the reality of the claims about the resurrection. It is true that Moses is presented more positively (as an example of someone whose 'resurrection' is affirmed). But this really adds nothing to our discussion here: there is no reference to Moses as an independent figure in his own right; if he is 'rescued' here as a figure who can appear positively, it is by virtue of his appearance in the gospel stories, not as an independent figure in his own right.

If one extends the scope of the discussion to include issues about the validity or otherwise of Jewish legal observances, the picture is again notable by the lack of concrete evidence which can be adduced in this context. One may note that the question does seem to arise in the *Gospel of Thomas* (though whether it is appropriate to include the *Gospel of Thomas* among 'Gnostic' texts is of course a matter heated debate!). At some points, sayings of Jesus in *Thomas* do seem to address aspects of the broad question of whether observance of the Jewish Law is demanded or not. Some parts of the evidence are notoriously difficult to interpret.[25] However, Antti Marjanen has argued persuasively that a reasonably consistent picture may emerge from *Thomas*: either the Jesus of *Thomas* implies that the Jewish law is not to be obeyed (cf. the entirely negative references to prayer, fasting and almsgiving in Saying

---

24 See Pearson, Jewish Haggadic Tradition, who calls it 'the Serpent Midrash'.
25 E.g. the reference to 'sabbatizing the sabbath' in saying 27.

14); or the Law's commands are no radically redefined and reinterpreted that the resulting commands seem to bear no relation to anything
that would be recognisable as obeying the Jewish Law.[26]

In line with this might be Saying 52 in *Thomas* which appears (according to one interpretation at least) to imply that, contrary to the perception represented by the disciples, the '24 prophets' of Israel are all
'dead' by contrast with Jesus who is the 'living one'. The '24 prophets'
may well represent the sum of the books of Jewish scripture. As such,
the saying may then be claiming that Jewish scripture as a whole has no
positive significance for the (Gnostic?) reader of *Thomas*.[27] In relation
to the creation stories of Genesis, this might suggest that any rewriting
of these stories (*if* such rewriting is presupposed in *Thomas*) would be
seen as 'reinterpreting' them in such a way as effectively to *reject*
them: i.e. it would not really be reinterpretation of the stories at all but
rather a radically alternative account of what 'really' happened to
Adam, Eve et al – *un*like what is said in Genesis.[28] And in relation to
the Jewish Law, this would then fit with the otherwise negative attitudes to particular parts of the Jewish Law reflected elsewhere in *Thomas*. 'Moses' and the Law seem then to be regarded uniformly nega-
tively here.

One other possible reference to the Jewish Law (and possibly to
Moses) occurs in the *Gospel of Mary* 9,1ff: 'Do not lay down any rules
beyond what I appointed for you, and do not give a law *like the lawgiver* lest you be constrained by it'.[29]

Who exactly is in mind in this reference to the 'lawgiver' (νομοθέτης), or indeed what is in mind in the broader instruction here not

---

26   E.g. the reference to 'fasting to the world' in saying 27, which now may refer to a gen-
     erally ascetic life-style; also the reference to circumcision of the spirit in saying 53
     clearly removes the discussion from anything to do with physical circumcision (as in-
     deed does Paul!). And the reference to 'sabbatizing the sabbath' in context, like the fast-
     ing saying with which it is placed in parallel, may also refer to a more general 'absti-
     nence from the wolrd and worldly values'. See the full discussion in A. Marjanen,
     '*Thomas* and Jewish Religious Practices', in: R. Uro (ed.), Thomas at the Crossroads.
     Essays on the Gospel of Thomas, Edinburgh 1998, 163–182, esp. 179.

27   See Marjanen, ibid., 180; also M. Moreland, The Twenty-Four Prophets of Israel are
     Dead: *Gospel of Thomas* 52 as a Critique of Early Christian Hermeneutics, in: Jon M.
     Asgeirsson / A. DeConick and R. Uro (ed.), Thomasine Traditions in Antiquity. The
     Social and Cultural World of the *Gospel of Thomas* (NHMS 59), Leiden 2006, 74–91.

28   This too would fit with what is said consistently in the *Apocryphon of John*: it is '*not*'
     as Moses said/wrote. Moses is thus a character whose literary output is *not* regarded as
     authoritative.

29   For the issue of whether the *Gospel of Mary* should be regarded as a Gnostic text, see
     my Gospel of Mary, 'How Gnostic is the *Gospel of Mary*?'(n. 6 above) with further de-
     tailed discussion, arguing that it is appropriate to regard the text as in some way 'Gnos-
     tic'.

to lay down any rules or laws (beyond what the Saviour has said), is not certain.[30] Most agree that probably the reference to the 'lawgiver', or at least the implied 'law' concerned, relates to the Jewish Law, though whether the lawgiver himself is Moses or the Demiurge/God of the Hebrew Bible is not so clear.

This could then be part of a broader polemic apparently employed by some Gnostics against the 'orthodox' that the latter are too dependent on the Jewish Law and attach too much importance to it (perhaps in comparison with the teaching of Jesus seen as all-important). Thus Irenaeus reports the charge (by some, i.e. the 'Gnostics' or 'heretics' he is opposing) that the 'orthodox' 'intermingle the things of the Law with the words of the Saviour';[31] And we may also note the polemic implied in *ApocPet* (NHC 7,3) 77,22–28: 'others who are numerous and who oppose the truth, who are the messengers of error, will concoct their error *and their law* against these pure thoughts of mine' (stress added).[32] Similarly Origen's argument about Celsus in C. Cels. 6,29 seems to reflect a situation where some[33] refer to 'contradictions' between 'laws' laid down by Moses and by Jesus to justify the claim that this shows the existence of different gods. Thus in part the dualism inherent in Gnostic cosmogonies and/or 'theo'-logies, whereby the OT creator god is sharply distinguished from the one supreme God, is connected in some way with differences, or tensions, between the Mosaic Law and the traditions about the teaching of Jesus.

The one text where the issue of the status of the Jewish Law, and of Moses as the Jewish lawgiver, does arise explicitly is the *Letter of Ptolemy to Flora*, though how representative that is of other Gnostics we do not know for sure. Certainly though here, the somewhat ambiguous attitude to Jewish scripture by Gnostic thinkers and myth-makers led to an (at best) ambivalent attitude to the Mosaic legislation. Thus in Ptolemy's *Letter to Flora* some Old Testament laws are rejected; some are affirmed but only if they accord with the teaching of the true God. Once again, any acceptance of Moses and/or the Law is fairly heavily qualified.

---

30 For discussion of suggestions that perhaps Paul and/or other Christians might be in mind here (e.g. laying down 'laws' restricting the role of women), see my Gospel of Mary, ad loc.

31 Adv.Haer. 3,2,2; See A. Pasquier, L'Évangile selon Marie, Québec 1983, 25; A. Marjanen, The Woman Jesus Loved. Mary Magdalene in the Nag Hammadi Library and Related Documents (NHMS 40), Leiden 1996, 121. Cf. too Adv.Haer. 3.12,12: 'the apostles preached the Gospel still somewhat under the influence of Jewish opinions'.

32 Translation from M. Desjardins, in Pearson (ed.), Nag Hammadi Codex VII, 233–235.

33 Christians according to Celsus; Ophites according to Origen.

*

This brief survey of references and/or attitudes to Moses in Gnostic writings suggests that any Jewish influence on Gnosticism may have been at most rather superficial. Given the centrality of Moses and/or the Jewish Law for Jewish self-identity in the period when Gnosticism must have been flourishing[34], the absence of many significant references to Moses as Lawgiver in Gnostic texts is surely a striking silence.[35] In forging their own self-identity, Gnostics do not appear to have felt any need to relate positively to that aspect of Jewish self-identity which focused on the Mosaic Law.[36] Such references as we do have in Gnostic texts suggest that, if anything, Gnostics were very negative about the Law and, derivatively, about Moses as Lawgiver.

Further, as we have seen, the few references to 'Moses' are mostly also couched in negative terms. The prime idea associated with the person of Moses appears to be that he was the author of the literary texts in the Hebrew Bible. His role as the mediator of the Law is mostly ignored. (And even when there are negative things said about the Law, it is for the most part independent of the figure of Moses himself). He is not primarily a lawgiver, or a mediator, but an author. Further, as we saw in relation to the references in the *Apocryphon of John* (and possibly elsewhere as well), the books in Jewish scripture which 'Moses' is presumed to have written are generally presumed to be in error.[37] With the 'alternative' accounts of the creation of the world offered in Gnostic texts, it is generally not a case of a 'reinterpretation' of an existing literary account with the base story being accepted as valid and simply a different interpretation of the text being offered; rather, the text itself is assumed to be erroneous. Some basic elements of the story remain the same: figures like Adam, Eve, the creator God, the serpent etc. all reap-

---

34 Gnosticism was clearly flourishing in the second century CE, when, in the post-70 era, the centrality of the Law was unquestioned. Equally, if Gnosticism is to be traced back to an earlier period, prior to 70 CE, the same would apply: the movement which led to the central importance being ascribed to he Law spans the whole period when Gnosticism may have been flourishing.

35 And this despite the dangers of any argument from silence.

36 Similarly Markschies, Gnosis, 70: 'they [Gnostics] are interested in the Old Testament only to the degree that it contains a history of creation up to the story of the flood, which is interpreted... But no independent interest in other biblical books, for example the legal texts, which might expect from pious Jews, can be demonstrated either in the Nag Hammadi writings or in those of Medinet Madi.'

37 Equally though, one should recall that 'Moses' can also be appealed to as the claimed author of other texts which may be regarded most positively: cf. the reference to 'Moses' as the author of a book giving information about the names of the archontic powers in OrigWorld 102.9, noted above.

pear in Gnostic retellings of the creation story, but in such a way that what is offered is not just a different interpretation of the biblical account, but a radical rejection of that account.[38]

All this may suggest that any links between Gnosticism and Judaism are at best somewhat superficial, secondary and non-essential. Judaism appears as an entity which Gnostic writers seem intent on opposing at almost every step.[39] There is little sign of any underlying *continuity* between Gnosticism and Judaism.[40]

In terms of any possible social history of Gnosticism, this may suggest that any contact with Judaism only took place as Judaism was encountered as a threat from *out*side that was later opposed (for whatever reason). At what may have been a later stage, Gnosticism and Christianity encountered each other, and Gnosticism met with considerable opposition and hostility from non-Gnostic Christians. In this process, Gnosticism often took over a number of features from Christianity, above all often identifying in some way the redeemer/revealer figure of Gnosticism with the person of Jesus. In relation to Judaism, such positive links seem to be much rarer. In particular, Moses qua lawgiver is

---

38 I would thus agree with Pearson's comment (Development of Gnostic Self-Definition, 129) in saying that 'the Gnostics proclaim their sovereignty over the Old Testament scriptures' and that 'they can baldly "correct" the text of the Torah' (with reference to the passages from *ApocJohn* noted earlier). But I am not quite so convinced by the phrase he uses just prior to the latter comment, when he refers to the Gnostics as 'utilizing the scriptures *as a canonical authority* for their own doctrines' (my stress; cf. too Rudolph, Gnosis, 277: 'Many of the writings .. can be understood as interpretations or paraphrases of Old Testament texts ...The Old Testament tradition is appealed to even when its official interpretation is rejected and this shows that Gnosis is also *dependent on the authorisation by "Holy Writ"'* [my stress]). Jewish scripture does not seem to be any authoritative basis for Gnostic writings – rather it seems to be more a text whose authority is rejected rather than acknowledged.

39 The exception may be the *Letter of Ptolemy to Flora*.

40 Hence the view of scholars such as Pearson, who whilst proposing that Gnosticism may have originated in Judaism, maintain that by the time one reaches the stage of Gnosticism itself, Gnostics have moved so far away from anything that could be reasonably said to be 'Jewish' that they are effectively no longer Jewish in any meaningful sense. For stronger statements about the radically *un*-Jewish nature of Gnosticism, see e.g. H. Jonas, Response to G. Quispel's "Gnosticism and the New Testament", in: Hyatt (ed.). Bible in Modern Scholarship, 279–93; G.P. Luttikhuizen, The Jewish Factor in the Development of the Gnostic Myth of Origins. Some Observations, in: T. Baarda et al. (ed.), Text and Testimony. Essays on New Testament and Apocryphal Literature in Honour of A.F.J. Klijn, Kampen 1988, 152–161; ibid., 'The Thought Pattern of Gnostic Mythologizers and their Use of Biblical Traditions', in: J. D. Turner / A. McGuire (ed.), *The Nag Hammadi Library after Fifty Years* (NHMS 44), Leiden 1997, 89–101.

mostly ignored; and Moses is mentioned at times as the presumed author of the Genesis, but only to reject what he has allegedly written.[41]

It may be that the encounter between Gnosticism and Judaism reaches back further in time than the encounter between Gnosticism and Christianity. So too the encounter with Judaism was evidently serious enough for Gnostics to seek to distance themselves from Jewish claims by providing an alternative reading of the creation stories. But this alternative reading did not apparently involve shared presuppositions about the validity of the Biblical account. Rather, at one level, the Biblical account is rejected by favour of the alternative offered (even if the terms of reference are the same so that the same characters appear).

This may then give some further small support to those who argue that, rather than looking to Judaism (heterodox or otherwise) for the roots of Gnosticism, we should look elsewhere, perhaps to some kind of radicalised Platonism[42], with Judaism only coming into the picture at a logically secondary stage as an entity from which Gnostics sought to differentiate themselves, and not as one with which they sought to identify in any way. Perhaps the encounter was serious enough for Gnostics to feel the need to provide their alternative readings of the Jewish creation stories. If so, it is striking that this encounter has left little mark in other literature apart from the Gnostic texts themselves. For some, this may show the inherent weakness and unconvincing nature of the case suggested here. On the other hand, such silence in other texts may simply be a further example showing how little we know of the various currents of life and thought in Judaism, Gnosticism and early Christianity at this period.

---

41 At the start of this essay, I referred to the possibility of Moses as an 'absent friend'. I have tried to show how much he is absent; but even when he is not absent, he scarcely appears to be a 'friend'.

42 The debt of Gnosticism to Platonism is widely recognised: see Pearson, Gnosticism as Platonism, in: idem, Gnosticism, Judaism, and Egyptian Christianity, 148–164; R. Roukema, Gnosis and Faith in Early Christianity, London 1999; J.D. Turner / R. Majercik (ed.), Gnosticism and Later Platonism: Themes, Figures and Texts, Atlanta 2000; J.D. Turner, Sethian Gnosticism and the Platonic Tradition, Quebec/Leuven 2001; Markschies, Gnosis, among relatively recent literature (as well as many older treatments). The claim is also made by several 'orthodox' ancient writers opposing Gnosticism: cf. Irenaeus, Adv.Haer. 2,14,1–6; Hippolytus, Ref. 1,11; 6,21–29.

Eusebius's appropriation of Moses in an Apologetic Context

by Sabrina Inowlocki

Eusebius appears at the outset as a crucial figure in early Christianity and late antiquity. He witnessed not only the transformation of the Roman Empire into a Christian Empire, but also the transformation of the status of Christianity from *religio illicita* into a political phenomenon. To a large extent, he contributed to offer new representations of Christianity and power in this age of transition.

As G. Dagron has shown[1], the relation between secular and religious powers in the Byzantine age is a very complex phenomenon. As the panegyrist of Constantine, Eusebius had to deal with the difficult question as to how to offer a new, adequate representation of the first Christian political leader in a manner suitable to the Christian faith. Dagron has pointed out that the past pagan representations of the emperor were not at once rejected but that they were rather gradually 'corrected'[2]. He has also emphasized that despite his enthusiasm, Eusebius somehow proved to be reluctant to present the emperor as a bishop *à part entière*[3]. In such a context, it is worth asking why, in the *Vita Constantini*, Eusebius decided to compare Constantine to Moses[4].

1　G. Dragon, Empereur et prêtre: étude sur le "césaropapisme" byzantin, Paris 1996.
2　Ibid. 143.
3　Ibid. 142–148.
4　On Eusebius and Constantine, see the classical work of T.D. Barnes, Constantine and Eusebius, Cambridge (Mass.) 1981. See also the introduction, notes and translation of the *Vita Constantini* by A. Cameron and S.G. Hall: Eusebius. Life of Constantine, Translated with Introduction and Commentary by A. Cameron and S.G. Hall, Oxford 1999. On the comparison made by Eusebius between Constantine and Moses, see e.g. M. Hollerich, Myth and history in Eusebius' De Vita Constantini: *Vit. Const.* I. 12 in Its Contemporary Setting, HThR 82 (1989) 421–445; Cl. Rapp, Imperial Ideology in the Making: Eusebius of Caesarea on Constantine as 'Bishop', JThS 49 (1998) 685–695; idem, Comparison, Paradigm, and the Case of Moses in Panegyric and Hagiography, in: M. Whitby (ed.), The Propaganda of Power (Mnem.S 183), Leiden 1998; idem, Holy Bishops in Late Antiquity. The Nature of Christian Leadership in an Age of Transition, Berkeley 2005.

A. Cameron has convincingly argued that the *Vita Constantini* is above all an apologetic work[5]. In this narrative, Constantine appears as a new Moses, liberating his people from pagan tyrants, implementing the divine Godly polity in the Roman world[6]. Moses is used by Eusebius as an *exemplum*, in the technical sense, in order to construct the Christian image of Constantine. By doing so, he was ushering in a long tradition. Indeed, as Dagron has pointed out, the byzantine emperors looked at themselves in the mirror of the Old Testament, whereas the New Testament was the *chasse gardée* of the clergy[7]. The parallel between Moses and Constantine has been analyzed in detail by Cameron and others and I will not return to this.

However, Eusebius' choice continues to baffle the students of late antiquity. Indeed, there were many other potential *exempla* that could have been used in order to represent Constantine. Eusebius himself explored some other possibilities. For instance, in the *Vita Constantini*, Constantine is also briefly compared to Alexander and Cyrus[8].

Eusebius' decision to draw a parallel between Constantine and Moses, however explained, points to the importance of Moses in the Christian discourse at the turn of the constantinian revolution. In this paper, I wish to investigate further the manner in which Moses was represented by the bishop of Caesarea in his grand apology, the *Praeparatio evangelica* and the *Demonstratio evangelica*. This may help us to shed some light on both the evolution of the Mosaic figure in Christianity and on Eusebius' decision to portray Constantine as a new Moses.

Eusebius inherited from his predecessors (including Philo of Alexandria and Clement of Alexandria, for instance), the concept that Moses was an ideal political leader, prophet, legislator and priest. As many other Christians, he saw him as a prominent figure, if not the most prominent figure, among the Christians' ancestors. Therefore, he was always careful to use laudatory adjectives when dealing with Moses. In Eusebius' eyes, he is, like Paul, a "Hebrew of the Hebrews", a prophet, a great theologian, all-wise ($\pi\alpha\nu\sigma\sigma\phi\delta\varsigma$); he is the amazing Moses ($\theta\alpha\nu\mu\alpha\sigma\tau\delta\varsigma$), the legislator, the great philosopher and, perhaps more surprisingly, the great historian of the Hebrews. Indeed, it seems

---

5 A. Cameron, Eusebius' *Vita Constantini* and the Construction of Constantine, in: M.J. Edwards and S.C.R. Swain (ed.), Portraits: Biographical Representation in the Greek and Latin Literature of the Roman Empire, Oxford 1997, 145–174, esp. 163–169.172–173.

6 Cf. for the parallels, VC I, 12.20.45.46; II, 21; 5,27; III, 48.54–55; IV, 23 etc.

7 Dagron, Empereur et prêtre, 68–70.

8 VC I, 7–8, see Hollerich, Myth and history, 421.

that Moses came to be considered by late antique Christian historians, as an important predecessor in historiography[9]. This may be explained by the fact that he had told the story of his people from the beginnings and had offered portrayals of sages who were to be imitated.

In the *Praeparatio* and the *Demonstratio*, Eusebius confers on Moses a crucial apologetic role. This was a strategic move because Moses' role was not only central in both Judaism and Christianity, but also, to a certain extent, in paganism[10]. Indeed, in some pagan milieus, he was revered as a νομοθέτης, a philosopher, and a figure of great antiquity. For instance, he was perceived and used by some middle- and neo-platonists as a major philosophical figure. Consequently, he was included into their philosophical project, which aimed to appropriate eastern wisdom by associating it to Platonic philosophy. To cite only one example, one may think of Numenius of Apamea's famous claim "what is Plato but Moses atticizing?", a claim that was quoted twice by Eusebius in the *Praeparatio*[11].

In the Christian world, Moses was seen as an important ancestor[12]. If some so-called heretics rejected the Jewish Scriptures and Moses' authority, the 'orthodox' Church held on to Moses and his books, even though it rejected the literal interpretation of its legal prescriptions. From the beginnings onwards, the apologists called onto Moses in order to confer philosophical legitimacy on Christianity. In order to do so, they especially focused on the antiquity of Moses and took pain to demonstrate times and times again that he antedated the Trojan war, Homer and Plato[13].

Nevertheless, in both the pagan and the Christian worlds, Moses remained a deeply ambiguous figure. Among the pagans, some Graeco-Egyptian narratives denigrated him by portraying him as a sorcerer and

9   Cf. Theodoret, History of the Monks I. 1, where Moses is invoked almost as a patron of the Christian historians. On this topic, see the illuminating study of D. Krueger, Writing and Holiness: The Practice of Authorship in the Early Christian East, Pennsylvania 2004.
10 See J. G. Gager, Moses in Graeco-Roman Paganism (SBLMS 16), Nashville 1972.
11 PE IX, 6; XI, 10.
12 On Christian perceptions and presentations of Moses, from the origins of Christianity on, the amount of bibliography is enormous. See e.g.: T. Francis Glasson, Moses in the Fourth Gospel, London 1963; M.R. D'Angelo, Moses in the Letter to the Hebrews (SBLDS 42), Missoula 1979; D.C. Allison, Jr., The New Moses, a Matthean Typology, Minneapolis 1993; J. Daniélou, Moïse l'homme de l'alliance, Cahiers sioniens 8 (1954), which includes several articles on the subject (Christian latinity, Syrian Christianity, iconography etc.).
13 See A. J. Droge, Homer or Moses? Early Christian Interpretations of the History of Culture (HUTh 26), Tübingen 1989.

an Egyptian fugitive[14]. These claims were taken over by pagan enne-
mies of Christianity such as Celsus[15].

Eusebius' portrayal of Moses also testifies to the ambiguity of the
legislator in Christianity. Yet I would argue that, more than other
Christian writers, Eusebius is well-aware of this ambivalence, and he
skilfully exploits it in order to achieve apologetic purposes. Indeed, the
way he uses and presents Moses is subjected to two contrary
movements: On the one hand, in the Pagan-Christian debate as
represented in the *Praeparatio*, the figure of Moses is continuously
glorified. On the other hand, in the Jewish-Christian debate as
represented in the *Demonstratio*, Eusebius' description of Moses is by
far less enthusiastic, even though the bishop is careful not to deny him a
role in his Christian salvation history. In other words, Moses appears as
an ambivalent character whose different facets are exploited according
to the context. Nevertheless, in all cases, Eusebius uses him as a highly
efficient apologetic weapon in both the *Praeparatio* and the
Demonstratio. I will now attempt to argue along these lines that Moses
is used by the bishop of Caesarea as a pivotal figure around which
Christianity, Judaism and Hellenism are articulated. I will also
endeavour to show that in his grand apology, Eusebius' ambiguous
Moses becomes, as it were, a *figure de l'entre deux*.

I. Eusebius' Moses in the *Praeparatio*

Around the 2nd and 3rd centuries CE, important criticism had been
addressed to Christians both by Celsus and Porphyry[16]. As is well-
known, the latter was Eusebius' archennemy; The *Praeparatio* and
Demonstratio may have been redacted, if only in part, as an answer to
Porphyry's *Against the Christians*[17].

---

14 Cf. the authors quoted in Flavius Josephus, *Contra Apionem* in: Flavius Josèphe. *Contre
    Apion*. Texte établi, traduit et annoté par Th. Reinach et traduit par L. Blum, Paris 1930.
15 Cf., e.g., Origen, C. Cels. I, 23 in M. Borret, Origène. Contre Celse (SC
    132.136.147.150.227), Paris 1967–1976.
16 On which see, e.g., A. Meredith, Porphyry and Julian Against the Christians, ANRW II,
    23,2 (1980) 1119–1149, and S. Benko, Pagan Criticism of Christianity During the Two
    First Centuries A. D., ANRW II, 23,2 (1980) 1055–1118.
17 J. Sirinelli, Les vues historiques d'Eusèbe de Césarée durant la période prénicéenne
    (Publications de la section de langues et littératures de la faculté des lettres et sciences
    humaines de l'université de Dakar 10), Dakar 1961, 56–57.165–166; J. Sirinelli and É.
    des Places, Eusèbe de Césarée. La Préparation évangélique. Introduction générale. Li-
    vre I (SC 206), Paris 2002, 28–32; A. Kofsky, Eusebius Against Paganism (Jewish and
    Christian Perspectives series 3), Leiden/Boston 2000, 250.

According to both philosophers, the Christians were apostates of their fathers' piety and philosophy. They had unrightfully appropriated the Jewish scriptures and yet rejected the Jewish prescriptions of the Law. Even worse, they had innovated in religious matters. Eusebius repeats this criticism several times in the *Praeparatio*[18].

Following Christian predecessors as Clement of Alexandria or Origen, Eusebius found in the figure of Moses the answer to such criticism. Therefore, appropriating Moses was a crucial apologetic endeavour. It also constituted a serious challenge.

As Eusebius' best enemy, Porphyry's view of Moses is important in order to understand Eusebius' strategy. Unfortunately little of his opinions on Moses has been preserved. We know that he attacked the Christian allegorization of the books of Moses[19]. He also argued that nothing of Moses' writings was preserved after the burning of the Temple and that "everything written thereafter in the name of Moses was actually written 1180 years later by Ezra and his colleagues"[20] (reference to 4 Ezra 14,21ff). Furthermore, he seems to have made calculations on the chronology of Moses. Eusebius ascribes to him the claim that Moses was 850 years earlier than the Trojan War[21]. These various fragments seem to indicate not only that Moses was at the center of polemical debates with the Christians, but also (provided that Eusebius accurately reports Porphyry's scholarship) that Moses was respected by Porphyry due to his antiquity.

Eusebius, whose *Praeparatio* and *Demonstratio* may at least in part aim to answer Porphyry, abundantly referred to Moses in order to defend Christianity. Moses could be used as an ideal apologetic weapon thanks to his antiquity. Developing the so-called "dependency theme"[22], Eusebius, as others before him, could claim not only that Christianity was the heir of the most ancient religious tradition, but also that the Greeks had borrowed from it, and therefore, somehow depended upon Christianity. Yet in order for such claims to be valid, Eusebius had to explain in which way exactly the Christians were related to Moses.

This was made through the identification of Moses as a "Hebrew". For one of the first times, the role of Moses in Christianity was carefully and thoughtfully explicitated. The bishop of Caesarea was

---

18 E.g., PE I, 2 ; DE I, 2.
19 Adv. Christ., Frgm. 39 = Eusebius, HE VI, 19,4.
20 Adv. Christ., Frgm. 68 = Macarius Magnes, Apocriticus III, 3.
21 Yet R. Goulet, Porphyre et la datation de Moïse, RHR 192 (1977) 137–164 = Études sur les vies des philosophes de l'antiquité tardive, Paris 2001, 245–266, suspects that this is an invention on Eusebius' part.
22 On which see D. Ridings, The Attic Moses: the Dependency Theme in Some Early Christian Writers (SGLG 59), Gothenburg 1995.

not only content with including Moses in the mythical Christian prehistory he had constructed in addition, but he also gave him a role which at once clarified the link between him and the Christians, and amplified the ambivalence of the Mosaic figure.

Indeed, in the *Praeparatio* and the *Demonstratio*, Eusebius draws a well-known distinction between the "Hebrews" and the "Jews"[23]. In book VII of the *Praeparatio evangelica*, he claims that the "Hebrews" are the Christians' ancestors, and reached the summit of piety through a natural religion without needing the Law in order to gain the true knowledge of God[24]. They antedated Moses. In contrast, the "Jews" are those who lived from the time of Moses on, strayed from the path of the Hebrews, and were contaminated by Egyptian idolatry. The law of Moses was sent in order to cure them from their illness[25]. Unlike them, Moses is not a Jew[26]. Although he gave them the Law, for Eusebius, he is both one of the most prominent figure of the Hebrews and the last Hebrew before the Christian era. Judaism is just an intermediate period during which the covenant was, as it were, asleep[27]. With the coming of Christ, the pious life of the Hebrews is, so to speak, re-activated. The apostles, the evangelists and some others qualify as Hebrews[28].

This reconstruction of Christian prehistory does not stand out as particularly original. Similar concepts may be found, for instance, in Origen. Yet as De Lange and Gallagher have emphasized[29], the mythical prehistory of Christianity proposed by Eusebius constitutes the first systematic attempt to describe the origins of Christianity. In this historical scheme, Moses is given a pivotal role which enables the bishop to articulate Hebraism, Judaism, and Christianity.

In the passages examined above, Moses' role in Eusebius' system appears fairly clear. Labelling Moses a "Hebrew" constitutes a strategy

---

23   See A. Arazy, The Appellations of the Jews (Ioudaios, Hebraios, Israel) in the Literature from Alexander to Justinian, Diss. New York, II 1977, 30–31; M. Simonetti, Eusebio tra ebrei e giudei, ASE 14 (1997) 121–134, n. 53; J. Ulrich, Euseb von Caesarea und die Juden. Studien zur Rolle der Juden in der Theologie des Eusebius von Caesarea (PTS 49), Berlin / New York 1999; S. Inowlocki, Eusebius and the Jewish Authors. His Quotation Technique in an Apologetic Context (Ancient Judaism and Early Christianity Series 64), Leiden/Boston 2006.

24   See PE VII, 3,2–3; 6,2–4.

25   PE VII, 8,37–40 and DE I, 6,17 a–19d.

26   PE VII, 6,4.

27   DE I, 6,16d. The lethargy motif will persist as late as the nineteenth century, e.g., in Adolphe Pictet's (1799–1875), Origines indo-européennes, ou Les Aryas primitifs: Essai de paléontologie linguistique, Paris 1863.

28   See e.g. DE II, 3,63.80d.

29   E.V. Gallagher, Eusebius the Apologist: the Evidence of the *Praeparatio* and the *Proof*, StPatr 26 (1991) 251–260 and N. De Lange, Origen and the Jews: Studies in Jewish-Christian Relations in Third-Century Palestine, Cambridge 1976.

in order to christianize him. Being a Hebrew, the latter becomes the emblematic figure of the Christian prehistory constructed by Eusebius. This was a crucial move because the philosophical legitimacy of Christianity largely depended upon Moses. This was notably due to his antiquity, which, as we have seen, was widely acknowledged in the pagan world.

Nevertheless, Eusebius feels the need to insist once more on the antiquity of the Hebrew religion. In book X of the *Praeparatio evangelica*, he deals at length with the antiquity of the Hebrews and the theft of the Greeks. He quotes Tatian, Clement of Alexandria, and Julius Africanus in order to support his claims[30].
This enables him to argue against the Greeks that even the great Plato derived his best doctrines from Moses the Hebrew.

This idea is extensively developed in books XI–XIII, in which he compares "Hebrew" and Greek philosophy/theology. This contest soon turns out to be a textual *synkrisis* opposing Plato and Moses. Moses is constantly presented as Plato's teacher, and as having anticipated on him[31]. According to Eusebius, Plato transposed Moses' theological doctrines or even translated them into Greek[32].

Both the similarities between Plato and Moses and Moses' anteriority constituted powerful answers to Porphyry. Indeed, these arguments suggest that the Christians did not desert Greek philosophy for useless barbarian writings. In Eusebius' reasoning, Mosaic philosophy proves to be a superior form of Platonism. If Plato was an atticizing Moses, thanks to the adjustments made by Eusebius, Moses was also in part a "Hebrew" Plato (that is a Christian Plato).

In the theological rivalry opposing the great legislator and the great philosopher, "Moses the theologian"[33] is used by the apologist as the spokesman of Christianity. Likewise, the Old Testament is not presented as the Jewish scriptures but as the receptacle of Christian truth. This reconstruction of the Christian prehistory occasionnally leads to surprising claims. For instance, Eusebius, as others, went as far as to say that Plato had drawn his trinitarian doctrine from Moses[34].

Eusebius' representation of Moses as a "Hebrew", that is as a Christian *avant la lettre,* takes different forms. In the *Praeparatio evangelica,* in which the bishop only deals indirectly with Christianity but

---

30   PE X, 10–12.
31   E.g., PE XI, 6.23.
32   E. g., PE XIII, preface.
33   E.g., PE XI, 18.
34   PE XI, 20, 2, Cf. Justin, 1.Apol. 60,6–7; Clemens of Alexandria, Strom. V, 103,1 cf. VII, 9,3; Athenagoras, Leg. 23,4.

focuses on Paganism, 'Hebraeism', and Judaism, Moses undeliberately becomes a first-choice apologetic weapon. He is used in order to answer Greek criticisms against Christianity. As we have seen earlier, Moses' role and relation to Christianity are clarified thanks to the construction of a dichotomy between "Hebrews" and "Jews". However, in the same work, Moses is not only presented as a Hebrew, but, in a surprising way, he is not denied his role as the Jews' ancestors.

As we have seen, in PE VII, Eusebius clearly defines him as the last Hebrew, providing the Jews with a law aiming to cure them from idolatry. This law is presented as necessary to the Jews, but as useless to their pious Hebrew ancestors. Consequently, it is also useless to the Christians, who are the righful heirs of the Hebrews.

However, in books VIII and IX, Eusebius deals at length with that which he labels "the life according to Moses". However, this lifestyle should not be confused with 'Judaism'. In contrast to Ἰουδαϊσμός, the "life according to Moses" represents in Eusebius' eyes what is best and worthy of appropriation in the Jewish godly polity and law. These books include almost no Old Testament citation. Instead, Eusebius cites at length Jewish Greek authors whose writings were cherished in the patristic tradition[35]. This appears as an important point. Indeed, Eusebius' Moses is not only the biblical Moses, but also, and perhaps foremost, the Moses described by Greek-speaking Jewish authors.

In book IX of the *Praeparatio*, quotations of Pseudo-Eupolemus, Artapanos, Ezekiel the tragedian, and others are given. Pseudo-Eupolemus claimed that Moses invented the letters and that they only reached the Greeks through the Phoenicians[36]. Artapanos goes as far as to say that Moses created various technical inventions, as well as philosophy; surprisingly, he ascribes to him the creation of the Egyptian cult[37]. Ezekiel proved to be more faithful to the bible, except in a passage where he describes Moses' throne vision[38]. Yet Eusebius does not appear to be interested in these testimonies for their own sake. He cites them through Alexander Polyhistor, a polygraph of the 1st century BCE, in order to show that the most famous Greeks knew the Hebrews and biblical history[39]. In contrast, Philo, Josephus, Pseudo-Aristeas and Aristobulus are quoted at length in their own name.

---

35   On this topic, see my Eusebius and the Jewish Authors (see n. 23).
36   PE IX, 26.
37   PE IX, 27.
38   PE IX, 28. On Moses' throne vision, see, e.g., P. W. van der Horst, Moses' Throne Vision in Ezekiel the Dramatist, in: idem, Essays on the Jewish World of Early Christianity (NTOA 14), Göttingen/Fribourg 1990, 63–71.
39   See my Eusebius and the Jewish Authors (see n. 23)

Thanks to them, Moses is given an idealized description. It is no co-incidence if Eusebius draws their citations from their apologetic works rather than from their more historical works. Indeed, neither Philo's *De Vita Mosis* nor Josephus' *Antiquities* are cited. Eusebius rather chose the *Hypothetica* and *Contra Apionem*. All these works are useful in describing Moses not only as the first and best legislator and philoso-pher, but also as the liberator of his people. They enhance Moses' care for Greek virtues such as justice, δίκη, love of humankind, and φιλανθρωπία. Pseudo-Aristeas helps him to demonstrate the moral values of the Mosaic prescriptions through allegory.

This accumulation of quotations on Moses and his Law enable Eu-sebius to reinforce the authority of Moses as a legislator and a philoso-pher outshining his Greek counterparts. Needless to say, Eusebius was not interested in glorifying Moses for the sake of the Jews. Although this remains implicit, at this stage of the apology, Moses already pre-figures Jesus. As a liberator of his kinsmen and a legislator who had set up the first theocracy, Moses anticipated on Christ. Consequently, it was necessary to confirm the political and philosophical legitimacy of Moses and of his legislation, in which Jesus and the Gospel were rooted.

For the same reason, Eusebius selected Jewish passages which an-swered the accusation that Moses was a sorcerer. Indeed, Jesus was also accused of being a sorcerer, an attack which Eusebius attempts to deny in the *Demonstratio*[40]. Therefore, the defense and glorification of Moses constitutes a first step in the defense of Jesus, as developed in the *Demonstratio*.

The idealization of Moses is achieved through citations of Jewish propagandistic testimonies such as those of Josephus. One of the most important citations of the latter includes the claim that Moses the legis-lator innovated in creating a "theocracy", a term coined by the Jewish historian, as he himself admits, which was to have a long afterlife[41]. According to Josephus, theocracy meant giving the ultimate authority and power (ἀρχὴ καὶ κράτος) to the one God.

He also added that Moses' legislation was superior to any other be-cause of its utility (χρήσιμον). Moses did not make piety part of virtue, but turned virtue into a part of piety. After him, the Jews did not inno-

40 DE III, 3–6.
41 PE VIII, 8, for this claim and the others below. On this term, see, e.g., See Y. Amir, θεοκρατία as a Concept of Political Philosophy: Josephus' Presentation of Moses' *Politeia*, SCI 8–9 (1985–1989) 83–105; idem, Josephus' and the Mosaic Constitution, in: H. Reventlow, Y. Hoffmann, B. Uffenheimer (ed.), Politics and Theopolitics in the Bible and Postbiblical Literature (JSOT.S 171), Sheffield 1994, 13–27.

vate: the legislation was kept unchanged because of its excellence. Thanks to the Law, concord (ὁμόνοια) prevailed among the Jews. Moses created a hierarchy in which God is the leader of the universe (ἡγεμὼν τῶν ὅλων); he gave the priests the responsibility to take care of the important affairs in common (κοινόν) while the high priest is their ἡγεμών. Josephus argues that in everything Moses "taught us civility and philanthropy" (ἡμερότητα καὶ φιλανθρωπίαν ἡμᾶς ἐξεπαίδευ-σεν)[42]. Like the word φιλανθρωπία, in the passage from the *Contra Apionem* selected by Eusebius, the term ἐπιείκεια (reasonableness, equity) and its cognates appear several times. According to Josephus, Mosaic legislation can only trigger an astonishment full of admiration (θαυμασίαι); Moses has best arranged the laws and reached "the most just faith to God" (τῆς δικαιοτάτης περὶ τοῦ θεοῦ πίστεως)[43].

This instance examplifies that, although Eusebius occasionally dissociates the Law and the Jews from Moses, in this case, he accepts the Jewish authors' identification of Moses as The Jewish leader as well as the glorified image they built.

How are we supposed to understand this apparent contradiction? First, one should bear in mind that these 'propagandistic' Jewish texts are quoted for apologetic purposes. In the *Praeparatio evangelica*, Eusebius has to justify the Christians' decision both to adopt the Jewish scriptures and to reject the Jewish way of life. These texts, which offer philosophical and allegorical interpretations of the Law, enable Eusebius to answer these Greek criticisms. Secondly, even though, according to the Christians, with the coming of Christ the Law lost its binding force, the Mosaic way of life continued to be perceived by them as a model.

Hardwick has rightly pointed out that, by appropriating Josephus' representation of Moses in the *Contra Apionem*, Eusebius, more than Clement of Alexandria or Pseudo-Justin, introduced into Christian literature the strongly Hellenized representation of Moses as "ultimate philosopher"[44]. Yet I would add that thanks to both Josephus and Philo, he also introduced into the Christian imagination the Jewish Greek representation of Moses as ultimate legislator.

---

42 C.Ap. II, 213. On philanthropy in Josephus and ancient Judaism, see K. Berthelot, Philanthrôpia Judaica, le débat autour de la "misanthropie" des lois juives dans l'Antiquité (JSJ.S 76), Leiden/Boston 2003.

43 C. Ap. II, 163.

44 M.E. Hardwick, Josephus as an Historical Source in Patristic Literature through Eusebius, Atlanta 1989, 119–120.

His legislation is presented as a first step towards holiness and as the second degree in piety, after Christianity[45]. This tradition goes back to Clement of Alexandria. According to him, Moses "furnished a good polity, which is the right discipline of men in social life"[46]. He also claimed that "the Greek polity is brass, that of the Jew is silver, and that of the Christian is gold"[47]. Eusebius agreed with this. In the *Praeparatio evangelica*, in which he does not deal with Christianity in a direct way, he used the Jewish texts in order to demonstrate to the Greeks the superiority of the Jewish polity in which Christianity was rooted. In contrast, in the *Demonstratio*, he seeks to show the superiority of Christianity vis-à-vis Judaism, and the supersession of the latter by the former. I will go back to this shortly.

Significantly, Philo's portrayal of Moses as a prophetic figure is absent from book VIII of the *Praeparatio*. The fact that, despite its popularity in Christian circles, Eusebius did not cite Philo's *De vita Mosis*, must be of some significance. This, I would argue, is due to the fact that in this book, it was necessary to his purpose that Moses the prophet remain a "Hebrew" figure predicting the coming of Christ. This side of the Mosaic coin is exploited in the *Demonstratio,* in which the debt to Philo is not acknowledged[48]. Consequently, when he deals with the way of life Moses gave the Jews, Eusebius prefers to describe him as a lawgiver and philosopher outshining his Greek counterparts.

II. Eusebius' Moses in the *Demonstratio*

Moses' role dramatically changes in the *Demonstratio*, in which Eusebius focuses on Christianity. In the second part of his apology, Moses' legislation is no longer glorified due to the importance of Christ in this work. Moses himself now looses some of his authority in contrast to Christ.

Whereas in the *Praeparatio* Moses was portrayed not only as a legislator but also as a great theologian, in the *Demonstratio*, he is mainly represented as a legislator, whose relation to Christ must be clarified. Although Eusebius continuously emphasizes Jesus' superiority to Moses, he also stresses the continuity between these two figures.

---

45 PE VIII, 1.
46 Strom. I, 26.
47 Strom. V, 14.
48 In my opinion, this is because in this case the Philonic interpretation has been completely appropriated by Christianity, at least in Eusebius' eyes. As a result, he does not feel the need to include Philo in his account.

This is best exemplified in the σύγκρισις drawn by Eusebius between Jesus and Moses[49]. The σύγκρισις takes place in an exegetical context. Eusebius wishes to demonstrate that the "prophet like unto Moses" (Deut 18,18) can only be Jesus

Eusebius' argument is based on the fact that only Jesus can be the prophet like Moses because only Jesus was a legislator after Moses[50]. Unlike Ezekiel, Isaiah, Daniel or the twelves, he did not only proclaim a new legislation, but also fulfilled Moses' Law.

The continuity between Jesus and Moses is a crucial point in the *Demonstratio*. According to Eusebius, both figures mirror each other. Yet Christ did everything in a way superior to Moses. For instance, Moses is said to be the first to have turned the Jews away from idolatry, to have published the theology of the One God, and to have built a pious godly polity for the Jews. Jesus did the same things. However, Moses' innovations were geographically restricted to Judaea, whereas those of Jesus applied to the whole world.

Along the same line, Moses and Jesus are said to have promoted the same pious doctrines about God, the immortality of the soul and "other doctrines". But Jesus, again, did it in a more divine way and on a grander stage (πολὺ κρειττόνως, θεοπρεπέστερον). Eusebius then goes on to compare both figures' deeds to show their similarity. Again, in each case, Jesus' superiority is emphasized.

In addition, Eusebius provides a detailed comparison of both figures' deeds and stories[51], which can be summarized as follows:

---

49 DE III, 2.
50 Cf. DE III, 2,4–5: ἆρ' οὖν οἱ μετὰ Μωσέα προφῆται, Ἡσαΐας, φέρε, ἢ Ἰερεμίας ἢ Ἰεζεκιὴλ ἢ Δανιὴλ ἤ τις ἕτερος τῶν δώδεκα Μωσεῖ κατέστη παραπλήσιος νομοθέτης; οὐδαμῶς. ἀλλὰ τὰ ὅμοιά τις ἐκείνων Μωσεῖ διαπέπρακται; οὐκ ἔστιν εἰπεῖν. ἕκαστος γοῦν αὐτῶν ἀπὸ [τοῦ] πρώτου καὶ εἰς τὸν τελευταῖον ἐπὶ Μωσέα τοὺς ἀκροωμένους ἀνέπεμπον, καὶ τόν γε κατὰ τοῦ λαοῦ ἔλεγχον διὰ τὰς παραβάσεις τοῦ Μωσέως ἐποιοῦντο νόμου, προὔτρεπόν τε οὐδὲν ἄλλο ἢ τῶν παρὰ Μωσεῖ νενομοθετημένων ἐξέχεσθαι. οὐδένα γοῦν ... τούτων ὅμοιον· Μωσῆς δὲ περὶ ἑνὸς ὡρισμένως ἀναφωνεῖ. τίνα τοίνυν ὁ χρησμὸς θεσπίζει Μωσεῖ παραπλήσιον ἔσεσθαι προφήτην ἢ μόνον τὸν σωτῆρα καὶ κύριον ἡμῶν Ἰησοῦν τὸν χριστόν;
51 Such comparisons can be found in Syriac literature such as Aphraat, Expositio 21 and Archelaus, Disputatio with Manes 44.

Eusebius, *DE* III, 2

Moses	Jesus
• First to turn the Jews away from idolatry	• First to turn the nations away from idolatry
• First to teach them the belief in one God	• First to teach them to venerate the supreme God
• First legislator to show them the pious life	• First legislator and teacher of a godly life
• Freed the Jews from Egyptian slavery	• Freed the world from idolatry
• Promises the Land to those who respect the law	• Announces that 'the meek will inherit the earth', a heavenly land
• 40 days fast	• 40 days fast
• Manna	• Multiplication of bread loaves
• Crossing of the red sea	• Malk on the sea
• Transfiguration at Sinai	• Transfiguration on Mount Thabor
• Name change of Nave	• Name change of Simon Peter
• 70 elders	• 70 disciples
• 12 spies	• 12 apostles

We have seen earlier that in the *Praeparatio* the figure of Moses is exploited by Eusebius in order to articulate Hellenism and Christianity. In this case, Moses serves to define the relation between the Jewish godly polity and the Christian polity which has now replaced it.

As Bruns has noted, a rabbinic quotation ascribed to a rabbi contemporaneous to Eusebius provides a σύγκρισις similar to that presented by Eusebius, except that Moses is compared to a redeemer yet to come[52]. This seems to indicate that the Jesus-Moses comparison is used by Eusebius as an argument in a polemic conversation with the Jews. Furthermore, the continuity between Moses and Jesus as illustarted by the σύγκρισις may also serve to oppose the heretic rejection of the Old Testament. At the beginning of the *DE*, the bishop refers to such heretics, stressing that his work will demonstrate the continuity between the Old and the New Testament[53]. Along the same line, such a comparison may also have been an answer to pagan attacks. We know that Celsus, for example, asserted that Jesus' teaching was a corruption of Moses' teaching and that both figures contradicted each other. Emphasizing both the continuity between the two figures and the superiority of Christ may have been an efficient strategy in order to silence such attacks.

---

52 J.E. Bruns, The 'Agreement of Moses and Jesus' in the Demonstratio evangelica of Eusebius, VigChr 31 (1977) 117–125.

53 DE I, 1.

Yet Moses is not only presented as foreshadowing Christ. Like many other Christian authors, Eusebius stresses that Moses predicted his coming. Nevertheless, it seems to me that he goes further than his predecessors by ascribing to Moses a more active role in the *praeparatio evangelica*. He is not content with the common typology according to which Moses was said to prefigure Jesus. Instead, he goes for a more historical interpretation. According to him, Moses did not restrict his legal prescriptions to Jerusalem and Judaea by chance. In fact, he did so on purpose, so that when the city would be destroyed, the Jews would be forced to turn to the Gospel. If not, they would be subjected to Moses' curse against the Jews who break the Law[54]. In this scenario, Moses played, as it were, the role of a double agent: he apparently worked for the Jews but in fact he actively worked for the Christians.

III. Conclusion

In his double apologetic work, Eusebius takes advantage of the ambivalence and multifaceted character of Moses. The bishop provides him with a pivotal role which contributes to support his apologetic and polemical arguments. The importance of the Mosaic figure in the Jewish, pagan and Christian milieus had crucial apologetic advantages because Moses stood at the center of the triangle formed by the three communities. Eusebius seems to have been fully aware of this situation and he drew the best from it. As a result, his representation of the Jewish legislator fluctuates according to the context in which he is used.

In the *Praeparatio*, he clearly distinguishes between Moses and those labelled as "Jews", and labels him a "Hebrew", implicitly defining him as the spokesman of Christianity. As a consequence, Christianity can be represented as a superior form of Platonism, stemming from an illustrious and ancient tradition.

Yet as we have seen, in the same work, Moses is also closely associated with the pre-Christian Jews, thanks to Jewish Greek quotations. In this context, Moses is acknowledged as being the legislator of the Jews and as a most prominent philosopher whose philosophical and political achievements outshone those of his Greek counterparts.

In contrast, in the *Demonstratio evangelica*, he looses some of his aura because of the presence of Christ. In this work, the representation of Moses as an ambivalent figure reaches a peak. As we have seen, in the *Demonstratio*, Eusebius ascribes to him, so to speak, the role of a

---

54   DE I, 8,18a.

double agent, apparently working for the Jews but actually preparing the rise of Christianity.

Whatever the orientation taken by Eusebius in his portrayal of Moses, it seems to me that in both the *Praeparatio* and *Demonstratio*, we find the most careful attempt to clarify Moses' place in Christianity. One may also add that Eusebius' undertaking to Christianize Moses is one of the most radical in ancient Christianity.

In the light of this analysis, it comes as no surprise that Eusebius chose Moses as an *exemplum* for Constantine. As Dagron has shown, despite his enthusiasm concerning Constantine, Eusebius was not prepared to grant him the status of bishop and he was uncomfortable with the emperor's wish to be remembered as an apostle. One may therefore suggest that, by comparing him to Moses, Eusebius was implicitly identifying the emperor as a *figure de l'entre deux*.

Mitarbeiter

Dr. Hywel Clifford, Lecturer in Old Testament, Ripon College Cuddesdon, Oxford

Heinz-Josef Fabry, Professor für Einleitung in das Alte Testament und Geschichte Israels an der Katholisch-Theologischen Fakultät der Universität Bonn

Sebastian Grätz, Privatdozent für Altes Testament an der Evangelisch-Theologischen Fakultät der Universität Bonn

Axel Graupner, Privatdozent für Altes Testament an der Evangelisch-Theologischen Fakultät der Universität Bonn und Lehrbeauftragter für Altes Testament am Fachbereich Evangelische Theologie der Philosophischen Fakultät I der Universität des Saarlandes; Regionallehrer für Hebräisch am Wilhelm-Dörpfeld-Gymnasium Wuppertal

Privatdozent für Altes Testament an der Evangelisch-Theologischen Fakultät der Universität Bonn

Mark Harris, Chaplain and Lecturer in Theology, Oriel College, Oxford

Sabrina Inowlocki, Chargée de Recherches du Fonds National de la Recherche Scientifique, Université Libre de Bruxelles, Belgium.

Pierluigi Lanfranchi holds a PhD in Early Jewish Studies from the University of Leiden and is at present a post-doc researcher in the field of Judaism in Late Antiquity at the Research Institute for History and Culture (OGC), Utrecht University

Phoebe Makiello, The Queen's College, University of Oxford

John Muddiman, George Caird Fellow in New Testament Studies, Mansfield College, Oxford.

Stefan Schapdick, Dr. theol., Dozent am Institut für Katholische Theologie der Universität Paderborn

Johannes Schnocks, wissenschaftlicher Assistent am Alttestamentlichen Seminar der Katholisch-Theologischen Fakultät der Universität Bonn.

Arie van der Kooij, Professor for Old Testament Studies at Leiden University.

Wido van Peursen, Research Fellow at the Peshitta Institute Leiden and director of the Turgama Project, Leiden University.

Udo Rüterswörden, Professor für Altes Testament an der Evangelisch-Theologischen Fakultät der Universität Bonn

Christopher M. Tuckett, Professor of New Testament Studies and Fellow of Pembroke College, Oxford

Michael Wolter, Professor für Neues Testament an der Evangelisch-Theologischen Fakultät der Universität Bonn

Autorenregister

Steudel, A.	140	Watson, D.F.	173
Steymans, H.U.	52	Waltke, B.K.	34, 35, 36, 38
Stipp, H.J.	61, 62, 72, 76	Weber, B.	80
Strack, H.L.	35	Weder, H.	183
Strugnell, J.	119, 132, 133	Wehrman, C.	92
Sullivan, K.P.	115, 116, 127	Weimar, P.	46, 65, 67, 71
		Weiser, A.	220, 221, 222, 223
Talstra, E.	106, 112	Welck, C.	201, 204
Tate, M.E.	79	Wells, J.B.	38
Theobald, M.	187, 191	Wengst, K.	186, 187, 188, 190, 192
Thurén, L.	173		196, 197, 199, 200, 201, 204
Thyen, H.	186, 190, 194, 196, 197	Wevers, J.W.	35, 92, 95, 146
	201, 202, 203	Wiener, M.H.	20
Tiede, D.L.	157, 161, 165	Wilcke, C.	45
Tigchelaar, E.J.C.	99, 104, 111, 131, 216	Wilckens, U.	186, 190, 192, 194
Trafton, J.L.	223		196, 202
Trevisanato, S.I.	21	Wildberger, H.	37, 44
Tromp, J.	111, 169, 170, 171, 175	Willi, T.	77
Turner, J.D.	240	Williams, M.A.	159, 228
		Wilson, I.	21
Ulrich, J.	246	Winston, D.	158, 159
		Winter, B.W.	167
Van de Walle, R.	38	Wise, M.	99, 104, 107, 111
Van den Hoek, A.	156	Wisse, F.	173
Van der Horst, P.W.	248	Wohlenberg, G.	214
Van der Kooij, A.	37, 38, 43, 48, 90, 97	Wolff, H.W.	42
Van der Woude, A.S.	139	Wolter, M.	218
Van Peursen, W.	106, 112, 129, 134	Wolthuis, T.R.	173
Van Seters, J.	44		
VanderKam, J.C.	99, 100, 101, 104, 105	Xeravits, G.	99, 100, 110, 111, 140
	110, 111, 117, 134		
Vanoni, G.	37	Young, F.	222
Veijola, T.	56, 59		
Velikovsky, I.	22	Zeitlin, S.	170
Vermes, G.	99, 104, 107, 110, 111	Zenger, E.	44, 79, 184
Vitaliano, C.J.	19	Zimmerli, W.	45
Volz, P.	218	Zimmermann, J.	99, 100, 101, 103, 104
			105, 107, 110, 111, 139
Wacker, W.C.	214	Zwickel, W.	65

Stellenregister

1. Altes Testament

1.1. Hebräischer Kanon

Genesis		3,3	146	14,19	7
1,2	231	3,4	67	14,20	10
1,18	235	3,6	67, 154	14,21–22,29	7
2,21–22	231	3,7–9	67–69	14,21	5, 7, 8, 9, 14
2,21	231	3,8f	71	14,22	5
2,24	235	3,9–12	65, 66, 68, 69	14,23	9
7,7	231	3,9	70	14,24	7, 11
8,17	235	3,10	70	14,25	13
9,1	235	3,12	71, 72	14,26–28	7
10,10	42	3,14	184	4,28	149
15	155	3,16f	69	14,31	15
17,9aα	46	3,16	97	15	14, 150
17,9aβb	48	3,20f	69	15,1–4	9
17,10a	46,47	3,20	71	15,4	9
17,12	200	4,2–4	67	15,22	9
18,17–19	84	4,3	146	16	195
18,19	83	4,4	146	16,1–36	195, 207
20,9	42	4,10–16	72	16,4f	196
28,17	191	4,10	146	16,4	196
32,31	104	4,12	72	16,11f	196
37,3	125	4,19ff	68	16,29	196
		5	68	17,6	105
Exodus		5,6	67	19–23	85
1,15–20	68	5,10	67	19–20	110
1,15–21	147	5,13f	67	19	33, 40
1,16	212	6,12	146	19,2–11	44
1,20b	67	7–8	211, 220, 226	19,2b	46
2,1–22	67	7	81	19,3b–9	39
2,2	167	7,1	118, 160	19,3b–8	36, 39, 40, 44
2,3	144, 147	7,10	146		46, 47, 48
2,4	148	7,11	212	19,3	44, 192
2,6	145	7,22	212	19,3a	44, 46
2,10–11	152	8,1	162	19,3b	42
2,11–12	175	8,3	212	19,4–20	46
2,11–15	171	8,15	212	19,4	37, 42, 45, 47
2,11–20	68	8,18	212	19,5f	39, 41,48
2,16	145	9,8	147	19,5	37, 41, 47, 48, 49
2,23f	67, 68, 70	9,11	212	19,5a	37, 42, 46, 47, 49
3f	68, 71, 72	9,35	80	19,6	34, 37, 40, 41, 43, 97
3	67–72, 76	13,17	20	19,6a	35, 37, 38, 39
3,1–4,18	66, 68	13,18	9		40, 42, 46, 48
3,1–6	67	13,21–22	7	19,7	49
3,1–8(aα–γ)	69	14	5, 6, 12, 23, 30	19,8	41, 47, 49, 110
3,1ff	69	14,2	9, 11	19,8aα	42
3,1b	67	14,9	9	19,8b	43
3,2	145	14,16	9	19,9	39, 44

1.2. Apokryphen

2. Pseudepigraphen

Äthiop. Henoch-Apokalypse		8–9	170	1,9–14	131
89	134	8	170	1,9	131
93	134	9	170	1,14	131
		11,16–17	111, 142	31,14	111, 124
Assumptio Mosis	169–180	11,17	111	33,20	36
1,15	175			47,10–12	171
6–7	170	*4. Esra*		47,7	148
6	169	14,21ff	245		
6,2	169			*Psalmen Salomos*	
6,6	169	*Jubiläenbuch*		4	223
6,7	169	1,1	92	4,4–5	223

3. Qumran

CD		*1QS*	130	*4Q216*	130
2,12	123, 138, 141	1,2–3	127	1,6	92
4,10	217	1,3	130	2	131
4,12–13	217	5,8	130		
4,12	217	6,6	142	*4Q255*	
4,15–18	217	8,15	130	1,3	130
4,15	217	8,22	130		
4,19–20	217	9	130	*4Q258*	
4,20–5,11	217, 218	9,11	141	6,7	130
5,8	130				
5,11–15	217	*1Q22*	130, 131	*4Q266*	
5,15–19	217	1,7–10	131	1a–b,16	130
5,17–19	216, 217, 219			11,2	130
	226	*1QSa*			
5,18	130	2,13–14	97	*4Q270*	
5,20–6,1	217			2,II	135
5,21–6,1	136	*1Q29*	132	7,I,17	130
6,1	123, 138				
6,2–11	142	*2Q21*	132	*4Q287*	
6,2–3	217			10,13	141
6,4–11	217	*2Q25*			
6,11	217	1,3	130	*4Q364*	
8,14	130			14,4	92
15,2	130	*4Q158*	131		
15,9	130	6,4	130	*4Q368*	99, 121
15,12	130	7–8,5	130		
16,2	130	7–8,3	130	*4Q374*	115–127, 132f
16,5	130				
19,26	130	*4Q174*	140–142	*4Q375*	132
		1–3,III,3	130		
1QM				*4Q376*	132
10,6	130	*4Q175*	130, 140f		
11,7–8	123			*4Q377*	99ff, 115ff, 134ff
11,7	141	*4Q180–181*	134	2,II	130

4. Jüdisch–hellenistische Literatur

5. Neues Testament

6. Neutestamentliche Apokryphen und Nag–Hammadi–Texte

7. Altkirchliche Schriften und Autoren

8. Rabbinische Literatur

9. Pagane antike Autoren und Texte